Content Area Mathematics for Secondary Teachers

The Problem Solver

Allen Cook and Natalia Romalis

D1509712

Christopher-Gordon Publishers, Inc.
Norwood, MA

Credits

Christopher~Gordon Publishers, Inc.
Bridging Theory and Practice

1502 Providence Highway, Suite 12
Norwood, MA 02062
800-934-8322
781-762-5577
www.Christopher-Gordon.com

Printed in Canada

10 9 8 7 6 5 4 3 2 1   09 08 07 06

ISBN: 1-929024-95-9

Library of Congress Catalogue Number: 2006921718

Contents

Preface

Individuals with very different backgrounds want to be math teachers. While traditional math majors frequently become teachers, the job also appeals to people trained in fields as diverse as engineering, economics, and natural sciences, and even law, religion and philosophy. This variety of background interests ensures that students have mathematics teachers with many different personal stories. It also raises a number of potential problems for teacher educators. How can we ensure that teachers from many different backgrounds all have an excellent understanding of content material in mathematics?

The assumption is often made that mathematics teachers " basically know" the mathematics they need to teach. As one principal once exclaimed to us, "I don't need people who know mathematics, I have that already. I need people who can teach it!" Her emphasis was on the importance of colleges and universities training teachers who can unpack content knowledge in order to help students construct meaningful mathematical understandings. While this book recognizes that teachers must be proficient in pedagogy, it also emphasizes the importance of teachers having a thorough understanding of mathematical content. Teachers do not "basically know" mathematics. They do not need simply to take some undergraduate or graduate courses in analysis, algebra, or other areas of mathematics. To be a good math teacher you need to be constantly learning and re-learning math, and not just be proficient in reproducing mathematical factoids. It is the constant examination and re-examination of mathematics that provides the cornerstone for teaching it.

The book provides hundreds of content problems across the entire spectrum of content materials needed for middle and secondary school teachers. It does not replace the traditional methods course literature, which concentrates on how to teach the subject. It supplements such a course. *Content Area Mathematics for Secondary School Teachers: The Problem Solver* looks at traditional mathematical content as a "whole," from an analytically rigorous perspective: arithmetic, geometry, analysis, and linear and abstract algebra "under one roof."

A PROFESSIONAL BRIDGE BETWEEN THEORY AND PRACTICE

We have found this book to be useful to teachers who have many different agendas. In general, it serves as a useful bridge between materials math majors learn at the university and materials math teachers find suitable for teaching secondary mathematics. Candidates for teaching licensing frequently must pass content exams; two of the most common of these exams is Praxis II in Secondary and Middle School Mathematics. For these individuals *Content Area Mathematics for Secondary School Teachers: The Problem Solver* serves as an excellent source of problems for exam preparation.

For new teachers already in the classroom, states often mandate exams for permanent licensing, which address teachers' content knowledge and their ability to teach this content in context of actual classroom environments. These teachers express their need to have a rich source of content materials from which they can draw ideas for their lesson plans.

This book serves as an excellent source of materials for experienced classroom teachers who are eager to see traditional topics, which they may have taught for years, in a new light. Experienced teachers repeatedly express the need to "be rejuvenated mathematically." They want new challenges and insight into mathematics. Teachers do not only want to discuss just how to teach mathematics. They want to discuss mathematics, which they can use as the basis for creating new lessons. (A follow-up to the book is planned that will contain a selection of such lesson plans, based on selected topics in the book.)

The book may be used in conjunction with other texts. For example, suppose individuals read Chapter 6 (Probability and Statistics). They may find some material particularly challenging. They might then reference this text with a standard text in statistics, and need not necessarily plow through an entire statistics text. Other areas for intensive review might require a more deliberate process. Suppose someone is unclear about trigonometry, for example. The topic is found in a number of sections in different chapters (4, 5, 8, and 10).

Instructors interested in creating content courses for secondary mathematics teachers may use this material as a basis in a number of ways. A course in analysis for teachers could consist of Chapters 1, 2, 4, 7, and 8. A similar course in finite mathematics for teachers could be based on Chapters 1, 2, 7, and 9. A course in geometry and linear algebra for teachers might include material from Chapters 2, 3, 7, and 10. In general, to cover all the material in the text requires two three-credit courses: one in analysis and related topics (Chapters 1, 2, 4, 5, 7, and 8); the other in geometry, statistics, finite math and elementary linear algebra (Chapters 2, 3, 6, 7, 9, and 10).

WHAT BACKGROUND IS EXPECTED?

At the University of Bridgeport we use the material as part of a sequence of four content courses in an M.A. program in secondary/middle school mathematics education. These courses are taught as a cooperative venture between the School of Education and the Department of Mathematics. They include not only materials from the book but numerical analysis and mathematical modeling. In our program we have licensed teachers, graduate students (in education), and advanced undergraduates (in mathematics). They usually all have a good operating knowledge of a graphing calculator, and have studied at least three semesters of calculus and a semester of modern algebra. For prospective teachers a mandatory methods course in secondary/middle school mathematics education parallels the content courses. The methods course explores some of the problems in designing lessons that may incorporate content materials in the teacher's own classroom activities. Clearly, the problems in the book may be viewed from many different perspectives, although most of the solutions follow a strictly analytical format. In fact, it would take a professional lifetime to "unpack" all of these problems from the many possible perspectives that teachers can take in their own classrooms. We are constantly impressed by the creativity of teachers in exploring such possibilities in their lesson plans.

Teaching is a creative process than requires a great deal of subject matter knowledge. *Content Area Mathematics for Secondary School Teachers: The Problem Solver* gives teachers a content basis for this creativity. Whether novice or pro, any individual who masters these content materials surely has taken a big step toward being an excellent math teacher.

Acknowledgments

A number of people have been involved in the preparation of this manuscript whose support we would like to acknowledge. Our respective spouses, Joyce Cook and Zinovy Reytblatt, for their proofreading. We would also like to thank Satish Illya, Swathi Birudavolu, Khurram Rajput, Yogesh Kodmelwar, David Valla, and Jessica Conic for all their work in preparing the text, diagrams, and tables. A special thanks to Nial Neger for his many suggestions about the content and format of the book and to James Tucci for his technical assistance. Finally, we would like to thank Sue Canavan, Jennifer Bengston, and Kate Liston at Christopher-Gordon for their help. It was a real pleasure to work with such professionals.

We would like to take this opportunity to acknowledge the helping hands of all these individuals with the recognition that the authors take full responsibility for the accuracy of the text.

CHAPTER ONE

Arithmetic and Basic Algebra

To most mathematics students the term number *refers to real numbers—those numbers represented by points on a line. Nevertheless, this deceptively simple model has evolved from sophisticated concepts developed over thousands of years: whole or counting numbers, positive integers, integers, rationals, and irrationals. Two dimensional, or complex, numbers then result from general solutions for equations of real numbers. Complex numbers generalize to tertiary numbers, quaternions and general vector spaces. From a somewhat different perspective (the solutions to polynomial equations) numbers can be viewed as either algebraic or transcendental numbers.*

Such a picture consists of layer on layer of mathematics. Much like paintings, which Renaissance artists created by juxtaposing layers of paints on top each other for a dazzling effect, Chapters 1 and 2 reflect these intricacies. They explore basic properties of real numbers from the theoretical perspective of groups and fields, and weave into this discussion a wide variety of topics that may appear only loosely connected: fractions, equations, linear functions, and the metric system. These materials can be found in most texts on arithmetic, algebra, pre-calculus, calculus, and abstract algebra.

OF TERMS

Whole Numbers	0, 1, 2, 3, 4, …
Natural Numbers	1, 2, 3, 4, …
Integers	…, −2, −1, 0, 1, 2, …
Rationals	Fractions; $\dfrac{a}{b}$ where a, b are integers
Irrationals	Nonrepeating decimals; all real numbers that cannot be expressed as fractions, e.g., $\sqrt{2}$
Real numbers	All numbers on the number line
Complex number	$a + bi$ where $i = \sqrt{-1}$ and a, b are real; all numbers in the coordinate plane
$\overline{a + bi}$	$a - bi$ (conjugate of $a + bi$)

SECTION 1.1

BASIC PROPERTIES OF REAL AND COMPLEX NUMBERS

Arithmetic and Basic Algebra

This section explores some of the most basic concepts of real and complex numbers. It starts with a basic schema for real numbers. It then examines the salient characteristics of this schema in the context of rationals, irrationals, continued fractions, and countable sets.

TYPES OF REAL NUMBERS

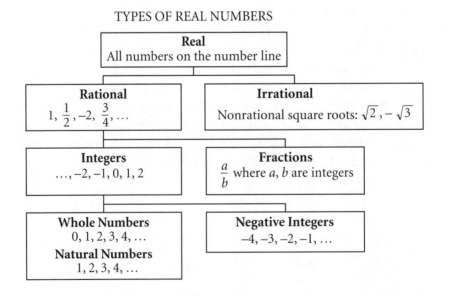

Some very common misunderstandings occur concerning this schema. For example, decimal representations for rationals differ from fractional representations in their uniqueness. Fractional representations in lowest terms for rationals are unique. In contrast, though rationals may be represented as terminating or repeating decimals, such decimal representations are *not* unique. In particular, consider the two-decimal representations of 1:

$$1 = .999\ldots = .\overline{9} \quad [\text{Let } x = .\overline{9} \text{ then } 10x = 9.\overline{9} \text{ which means } 9x = 9 \text{ or } x = 1]$$

Complex Numbers

Carl Friedrich Gauss introduced the term *complex number*. By definition, a complex number z is an ordered pair (x, y) of real numbers x and y, written as $z = (x, y)$ or $z = x + iy$, where $i = \sqrt{-1}$. The variable x is called the real part and y is the imaginary part of z.

Operations with complex numbers

Addition and subtraction of complex numbers:

$(x_1 \pm iy_1) \pm (x_2 \pm iy_2) = (x_1 \pm x_2) \pm i(y_1 \pm y_2)$

Example: $(3 + i) + (6 - 2i) = (3 + 6) + (1 - 2)i = 9 - i$

Multiplication:

$(x_1 + iy_1)(x_2 + iy_2) = x_1 x_2 + i(x_1 y_2 + x_2 y_1) - y_1 y_2 = x_1 x_2 - y_1 y_2 + i(x_1 y_2 + x_2 y_1)$

Example: $(3 + 2i)(6 - i) = 18 + 12i - 3i + 2 = 20 + 9i$

Quotient of complex numbers:

$$\frac{z_1}{z_2} = \frac{x_1 + iy_1}{x_2 + iy_2} = \frac{(x_1 + iy_1)(x_2 - iy_2)}{x_2^2 + y_2^2} = \frac{x_1 x_2 + y_1 y_2 + i(x_2 y_1 - x_1 y_2)}{x_2^2 + y_2^2}$$

$$= \frac{x_1 x_2 + y_1 y_2}{x_2^2 + y_2^2} + i\frac{x_2 y_1 - x_1 y_2}{x_2^2 + y_2^2}$$

Example: $\dfrac{3 + i}{4 + 2i} = \dfrac{(3 + i)(4 - 2i)}{16 + 4} = \dfrac{12 + 4i - 6i + 2}{20} = \dfrac{14 - 2i}{20} = \dfrac{7 - i}{10} = \dfrac{7}{10} - i\dfrac{1}{10}$

Geometric representation of the complex plane

How can one intuitively see that the complex number i represents a number one unit above the origin, on the y-axis? Let $\overline{CP}$ in right triangle ABC be a perpendicular with length y dropped from vertex C to side $\overline{BA}$. By similar triangles, $\triangle ABC \sim \triangle ACP \sim \triangle CBP$, so $y^2 = BP \cdot PA$.

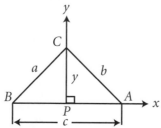

Consider a similar diagram in the Cartesian Coordinate System,

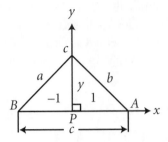

By a corresponding argument $y^2 = -1 \cdot 1 = -1$ or $y = \sqrt{-1} = i$. Of course the two arguments are slightly different, since one deals with lengths of line segments, while our "intuitive" argument deals with directed line segments. Nevertheless, this simple geometric model provides a hands-on insight into what may be a rather bewildering assertion: Complex numbers can be represented as points in the Cartesian coordinate system. We consider the x-axis to be the real axis and y axis to be the imaginary axis.

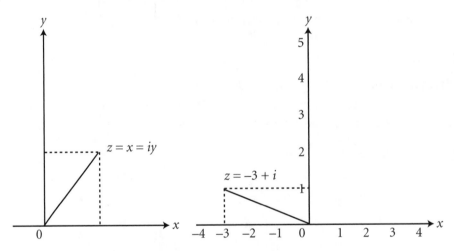

Complex conjugate numbers

The **complex conjugate** of $z = x + iy$ is $\bar{z} = x - iy$. It can be obtained geometrically by reflecting the point z in the real axis. Conjugates are useful since $z \cdot \bar{z} = x^2 + y^2$.

The following rules apply for operations on complex conjugates:

1. $\overline{(z_1 + z_2)} = \bar{z_1} + \bar{z_2}$

2. $\overline{(z_1 - z_2)} = \bar{z_1} - \bar{z_2}$

3. $\overline{(z_1 \cdot z_2)} = \bar{z_1} \cdot \bar{z_2}$

4. $\overline{\left(\dfrac{z_1}{z_2}\right)} = \dfrac{\bar{z_1}}{\bar{z_2}}$

We illustrate the third rule by an example. We want to show $\overline{z_1 \cdot z_2} = -7 - 26i = (\overline{z_1} \cdot \overline{z_2})$ when $z_1 = 4 + 3i$ and $z_2 = 2 + 5i$.

Example:

$$\overline{(z_1 \cdot z_2)} = \overline{((4+3i)(2+5i))} = \overline{((8+6i+20i+15i^2))} = \overline{(8-15+6i+20i)} = \overline{((-7+26i)}$$
$$= -7 - 26i.$$

Similarly,

$$\overline{(z_1 \cdot z_2)} = \overline{(4+3i)}\,\overline{(2+5i)} = (4-3i)(2-5i) = (8-6i-20i+15i^2) = (8-15-6i-20i)$$
$$= -7 - 26i$$

1.1 SOLVED PROBLEMS

1. Divide the area of hexagon *ABCDEF* into seven equal parts.

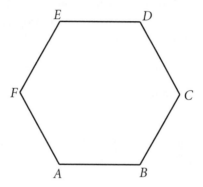

Solution: Divide each side of the hexagon into seven equal parts; giving 42 parts for all 6 sides. Take 6 of the first 42 parts; this represents one seventh of the hexagon. Continue this process until you have seven sevenths.

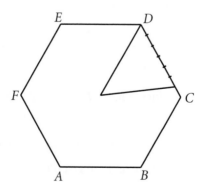

2. a) Calculate: $\left(9\dfrac{8}{45}-7\dfrac{22}{45}+6\dfrac{17}{30}-1\dfrac{13}{18}\right)\cdot\left(6\dfrac{1}{7}-4\dfrac{1}{2}+1\dfrac{1}{3}\right)$

   b) Suggest an alternate method to calculate the answer of (a) by approximation.

   Solution:

   a) $\left(9\dfrac{8}{45}-7\dfrac{22}{45}+6\dfrac{17}{30}-1\dfrac{13}{18}\right)\cdot\left(6\dfrac{1}{7}-4\dfrac{1}{2}+1\dfrac{1}{3}\right)$

   $=\left[\left(9\dfrac{16}{90}+6\dfrac{51}{90}\right)-\left(7\dfrac{44}{90}+1\dfrac{65}{90}\right)\right]\cdot\left[\left(6\dfrac{3}{21}+1\dfrac{7}{21}-4\dfrac{1}{2}\right)\right]$

   $=\left[15\dfrac{67}{90}-9\dfrac{19}{90}\right]\cdot\left[7\dfrac{20}{42}-4\dfrac{1}{2}\right]=\left[6\dfrac{8}{15}\right]\cdot\left[7\dfrac{20}{42}-4\dfrac{1}{2}\right]=\left[6\dfrac{8}{15}\right]\cdot\left[2\dfrac{41}{42}\right]$

   $=\dfrac{98}{15}\cdot\dfrac{125}{42}=\dfrac{175}{9}=19\dfrac{4}{9}$

   b) Unless one either specifies how to estimate, or the degree of accuracy required of the estimation, different answers are possible. The best interpretation remains the one with which the reader feels most appropriate. For example, if one decides to roundoff fractions: $(15-8)(7-4)=(7)(3)=21$.

3. Let $\overline{AB}$ be a given line segment of length r. (a) Construct a length equal to $\dfrac{1}{5}r$. (b) Construct a length equal to $\dfrac{6}{5}r$.

   Solution:

   a) Construct any angle ABC using the original line $\overline{AB}$ as a side. Divide $\overline{BC}$ into five equal parts, using A_1, A_2, A_3, A_4, C.

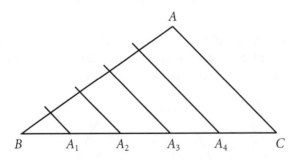

   Connect A to C. Reproduce angle ABC using A_1, A_2, A_3, A_4 as corresponding vertices.

   b) To get a length equal to $\dfrac{6}{5}$ consider one of the 5 equal parts of $\overline{AB}$ found in part (a) and extend $\overline{AB}$ by that length, to give $\overline{BB_2}$.

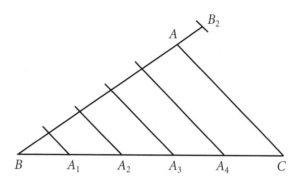

4. Illustrate the following using geometric models: $\dfrac{3}{5} \cdot \dfrac{3}{4} = \dfrac{9}{20}$.

Solution: Divide a rectangle into five equal vertical parts and shade three of those five parts. Divide the same rectangle into four equal horizontal parts and shade three of those four parts. The area that satisfies both of these conditions illustrates the fractional product $\dfrac{3}{5} \cdot \dfrac{3}{4} = \dfrac{9}{20}$.

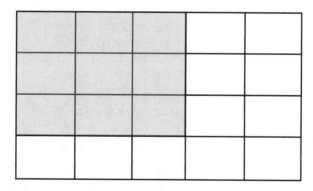

5. Calculate $\dfrac{2^2}{1+1+2}, \dfrac{(33)^2}{1+1+2+2+3}, \dfrac{(444)^2}{1+1+2+2+3+3+4}$.

Discuss any patterns you see resulting from these calculations.

Solution: $\dfrac{4}{4}, \dfrac{(33)(33)}{3 \cdot 3}, \dfrac{(444)(444)}{4 \cdot 4}, \ldots = 1, 121, 12321, \ldots$ For the nth term $(0 < n \le 9)$ the pattern will be $123\ldots n\ldots 321$.

6. Express $1\dfrac{1}{2}$ in two different decimal representations.

Solution:

Notice $x = 1.49\overline{9}$, so $10x = 14.9\overline{9}$ and $9x = 13.5; x = 1.5$. Two representations for $1\dfrac{1}{2}$ are 1.5 and $1.49\overline{9}$.

7. Suppose $\dfrac{x}{y} = \sqrt{2}$, so that $\dfrac{x}{y}$ is a fraction reduced to lowest terms.

Why does this supposition result in a contradiction? (The Greeks used this argument to show that $\sqrt{2}$ is not rational.)

Solution: Suppose $\dfrac{x}{y} = \sqrt{2}$ where $\dfrac{x}{y}$ is a fraction in lowest terms; $\dfrac{x^2}{y^2} = 2$, then x^2 must be an even number $(x^2 = 2y^2) \Rightarrow x$ must be an even number, since the square of any odd number is odd: $(2n+1)^2 = 4n^2 + 4n + 1$. If x^2 is even, then y^2 must also also be even, since $y^2 = \dfrac{x^2}{2} = \dfrac{(2m)^2}{2} = \dfrac{4m^2}{2} = 2m^2$. But if y^2 is even then y is even.

This is impossible since $\dfrac{x}{y}$ cannot be in lowest terms if both x and y are even.

8. Let $x = 1 + \dfrac{1}{2 + \dfrac{1}{2 + \dfrac{1}{2 + \ldots}}}$. Show that $x = \sqrt{2}$.

Solution:

Let $x = 1 + \dfrac{1}{2 + \dfrac{1}{2 + \dfrac{1}{2 + \ldots}}}$. Then $x = 1 + \dfrac{1}{1 + 1 + \dfrac{1}{2 + \dfrac{1}{2 + \dfrac{1}{\ldots}}}}$ or $x = 1 + \dfrac{1}{1 + x}$.

Thus, $x(x+1) = 1 + x + 1$; $x + x^2 = 2 + x$; or $x^2 = 2$ and $x = \sqrt{2}$ (notice that $-\sqrt{2} < 0$).

9. The positive integers give one way to determine the size of an infinite set. If a one-to-one correspondence exists between a set and the positive integers we call the set **countable**. Notice that the set of even integers is *countable* $(2n \to n)$. The following problem gives a very well-known argument, which shows that the set of rational numbers is also countable.

Solution: Consider the array of rational numbers:

$$\frac{1}{1}, \frac{1}{2}, \frac{1}{3}, \frac{1}{4}, \frac{1}{5}, \ldots$$

$$\frac{2}{1}, \frac{2}{2}, \frac{2}{3}, \frac{2}{4}, \frac{2}{5}, \ldots$$

$$\frac{3}{1}, \frac{3}{2}, \frac{3}{3}, \frac{3}{4}, \frac{3}{5}, \ldots$$

Count them as the arrows indicate. Clearly, these terms have a one-to-one corre-spondence with the integers. For example, the number $\dfrac{4}{1}$ is the 10th term.

10. a) Solve $x^2 + 1 = 0$ in terms of i. Define $i = \sqrt{-1}$.

   b) Find values of i^2, i^3, i^4, i^5, i^n.

   Solution: a) $x^2 = -1$ or $x = \sqrt{-1} = i$; b) $i^2 = -1$; $i^3 = i^2 \cdot i = -i$;
   $$i^4 = i^2 \cdot i^2 = (-1)(-1) = 1; \ i^5 = i^4 \cdot i = i. \text{ Clearly,}$$

   $$\begin{aligned}
   i^n &= i && \text{when } n = 4k+1; \\
   i^n &= -1 && \text{when } n = 4k+2; \\
   i^n &= -i && \text{when } n = 4k+3; \\
   i^n &= 1 && \text{when } n = 4k.
   \end{aligned}$$

11. Let $(x, y) = x + iy$. Let the product $(a, b)(c, d)$ be represented in the form $x + yi$. Let $(a, b)^{-1}$ be the multiplicative inverse of (a, b) $[(a, b)(a, b)^{-1} = (1,0)]$. Represent $(a, b)^{-1}$ in the form $x + iy$.

   Solution: $(a,b)^{-1} = \dfrac{1}{a+bi} = \dfrac{1}{a+bi} \cdot \dfrac{a-bi}{a-bi} = \dfrac{a-bi}{a^2+b^2} = \dfrac{a}{a^2+b^2} + i \dfrac{-b}{a^2+b^2}$

1.1 UNSOLVED PROBLEMS

1. Illustrate the following using the geometric models: $\dfrac{3}{8} \div 3 = \dfrac{1}{8}$.

2. Evaluate: $\dfrac{\left(1\frac{1}{3} + 1\frac{3}{13}\right)}{\left(1\frac{1}{7} + 2\frac{2}{3}\right) \cdot \left(1\frac{1}{2} - \frac{2}{13}\right)}$

3. Take an educated guess:

   a. Which number (if any) does the sum $\dfrac{1}{2} + \dfrac{1}{4} + \dfrac{1}{8} + \dfrac{1}{16} + \ldots$ approximate?

   b. Which number (if any) does the sum $\dfrac{1}{2} + \dfrac{1}{3} + \dfrac{1}{4} + \dfrac{1}{5} + \ldots$ approximate?

   c. What conjecture can you make from these two examples?

4. Graph the denominator as y values, and the numerator as the x values for a set of equal fractions (for example $\dfrac{1}{2} = \dfrac{2}{4} = \ldots$). What figure do you get? Compare two distinct graphs (e.g., $\dfrac{1}{2}$ and $\dfrac{3}{4}$). What can you say about the value of the fraction and the slope of the graph?

5. Simplify: $\dfrac{1}{3 + \dfrac{1}{3 + \dfrac{1}{3+1}}}$

6. i) $\frac{2}{9} = .\bar{2}$; ii) $\frac{7}{9} = .\bar{7}$; iii) $\frac{2}{9} + \frac{7}{9} = .\bar{9}$; iv) $1 = .\bar{9}$

Which of the following is true?

A) i) is not correct;

B) ii) is not correct;

C) iii) is not correct;

D) iv) is not correct;

E) all answers are correct.

7. Find the difference between the mean of the positive square roots of 16 and 9 and the positive square root of their mean, correct to 2 decimal places.

8. The following x_1, x_2, and x_3 are approximations for $\sqrt{29}$:

$$x_1 = 5$$

$$x_2 = x_1 - \left[\frac{x_1^2 - 29}{2x_1} \right]$$

$$x_3 = x_2 - \left[\frac{x_2^2 - 29}{2x_2} \right]$$

Using this algorithm compute x_3 correct to 2 decimal places.

9. Rationalize the denominator: $\left[\dfrac{5 - 2\sqrt{3}}{8 + \sqrt{5}} \right]$

10. Express $\dfrac{1}{3 + 2i}$ in the form $a + bi$.

OF TERMS

Cartesian cross-product $S \times S$	All elements (a, b) such that $a \in S$ and $b \in S$
* is closed on S	For any $a, b \in S, a * b \in S$
* is commutative on S	For any $a, b \in S, a * b = b * a \in S$
e is the identity for * on S	For any $a \in S, a * e = e * a = a$
a^{-1} is the inverse for any element $a \in S$ under *	For any $a \in S$ there exists an $a^{-1} \in S$ such that $a^{-1} * a = a * a^{-1} = e$ (where e is the identity for * on set S)
Commutative group	A set S with an operation * such that S is closed under *; S is commutative under *; S is associative under *; an identity exists in S under *, and every element in S has an inverse under *
Commutative field	A field is a set with two operations $(+, \cdot)$, such that $(S, +)$ and $(S - \{0\}, \cdot)$ are commutative groups; furthermore, $a \cdot (b + c) = a \cdot b + a \cdot c = (b + c) \cdot a$ (A commutative field is frequently just called a *field*)

SECTION 1.2

PROPERTIES OF REAL NUMBERS

The concept of a group grows out of the extraordinary work of Galois in the nineteenth century. Galois investigated why certain polynomial equations do not have a general formula for their roots. The concept of a group (in particular solvable groups) is essential to the proof that no such formula exists for equations of degree five or more. To this day, Galois' work remains one of the intellectual mountain peaks of mathematics. The idea of a group is fundamental for an axiomatic development of the real numbers. This section explores the basic concepts of groups and gives concrete models for groups.

A Model for a Group

Consider the following four statements: $9 + 9 = 18$; $9 + 4 = 1$; $6 + 7 = 1$; $4 + 4 = 3$. Are these statements sometimes, always, or never true? Most people probably agree that the first statement is always true (if you have 9 apples and add 9 more apples you will have 18 apples). They probably also conclude that the remaining three statements are never true.

In fact, all four statements are only sometimes true. An everyday item explains statements two and three: the clock. If it is nine o'clock, in four hours it will be one o'clock. If it is six o'clock now, in seven hours it will be one o'clock. Statement four is a bit trickier: it holds if you have a clock with only five "hours." Such models produce finite or Gaussian arithmetics, which provide models for a group.

If the number of elements in this arithmetic is prime, the model serves as a model for real number arithmetic. Consider the following addition table for Gaussian arithmetic (clock arithmetic) with seven elements (hours) in it: 0, 1, 2, 3, 4, 5, 6. This arithmetic is called **Gaussian Arithmetic (Z_7,+).**

$(Z_7,+)$	0	1	2	3	4	5	6
0	0	1	2	3	4	5	6
1	1	2	3	4	5	6	0
2	2	3	4	5	6	0	1
3	3	4	5	6	0	1	2
4	4	5	6	0	1	2	3
5	5	6	0	1	2	3	4
6	6	0	1	2	3	4	5

Properties of Finite Arithmetics
(only some clock arithmetics have all these properties)

i) Notice that for any $x, y \in (Z_7,+)$, $x + y \in (Z_7,+)$: Z_7 is **closed** under the operation of addition. In other words, the "answers" you get from adding any two "numbers" in this arithmetic gives an "answer" which is also a number in this arithmetic.

ii) For any $x, y, z \in (Z_7,+)$, $(x + y) + z = x + (y + z)$: the operation $+$ is **associative**. The associative property usually can be found to hold true by trial and error. If it holds for a few examples, then it is likely (but *only likely!*) to hold for all other possible examples. In this situation, $2 + (3 + 4) = 2$ and $(2 + 3) + 4 = 5 + 4 = 2$.

iii) There exists an element $0 \in (Z_7,+)$ such that $0 + x = x + 0 = x$ for all $x \in (Z_7,+)$: $(Z_7,+)$ has an **identity**. An identity under addition does not change the original listing of elements in either the addition row or column. The row and column value in our system associated with addition by 0 repeat the original listings.

iv) Finally, for any $x \in (Z_7,+)$, there exists an element which we call $-x$ such that $x + (-x) = (-x) + x = 0$: every element in $(Z_7,+)$ has an **inverse**. When an element is added to its inverse you get the identity.

One final property, not necessary for all groups but one which holds for most of the groups we use, is the **commutative** property: for all $a, b \in (Z_7,+)$, $a + b = b + a$.

Another model for a group

The operation of multiplication in our clock arithmetic follows the same idea of repeated addition as usual multiplication for real numbers. To multiply three by four you either add the number three four times, or add the number four three times. The same principle holds in $(Z_7,\cdot)$ or Z_7 under multiplication. In other words, $5 \cdot 6 = 6 + 6 + 6 + 6 + 6$. More readily, we write $5 \cdot 6 = 30 \equiv 2(\mathrm{mod}\ 7)$ to mean "if you go around" 30 digits in the clock, you eventually "end up" at 2 (if you divide 30 by 7 the remainder is 2).

$(Z_7,\cdot)$	0	1	2	3	4	5	6
0	0	0	0	0	0	0	0
1	0	1	2	3	4	5	6
2	0	2	4	6	1	3	5
3	0	3	6	2	5	1	4
4	0	4	1	5	2	6	3
5	0	5	3	1	6	4	2
6	0	6	5	4	7	2	1

If you remove the element 0, $(Z_7,\cdot)$ has the same properties as $(Z_7,+)$ (0 has no inverse).

A Field

If we combine the two operational systems $(Z_7,+)$, $(Z_7 - \{0\},\cdot)$ and connect the two systems by the ring or distributive property $a \cdot (b + c) = a \cdot b + a \cdot c$, we define a mathematical field. This finite field gives a good model for the real numbers. In fact, we perform most of our numerical reasoning in either one of two fields, the first being embedded in the second: the real and complex numbers.

The Real Numbers as a Commutative Group

Under the operations of addition and multiplication the real numbers have the following fundamental properties: closure, commutativity, associativity, there exists an identity, and every element has an inverse. (Notice that the operations of subtraction and division are the inverses for addition and multiplication.) These properties are fundamental to a communtative group. Let S be a set. Consider $S \times S$, the **Cartesian cross-product** of S: $S \times S = \{(a, b)\,|a, b \in S\}$. Consider the following properties for the system $(S,*)$:

1. The operation $*$ is closed on S, if for any $a, b \in S$, $a * b \in S$
2. The operation $*$ is commutative if for any $a, b \in S$, $a * b = b * a$
3. The operation $*$ is associative if for any $a, b, c \in S$, $a * (b * c) = (a * b) * c$
4. The identity e exists for $*$ if for any $a \in S$, $a * e = e * a = a$
5. Given any $a \in S$ there exists $a^{-1} \in S$ (inverse element for a) such that $a * a^{-1} = a^{-1} * a = e$

In general, the system $(G,*)$ is called a **group** if $*$ is an operation on G such that: G is closed under $*$; G is associative under $*$; an identity $e \in G$ exists for $*$; every element in G has an inverse. A system $(G,*)$ is called a **commutative group** if it is a group and commutative under $*$.

The Real Numbers as a Commutative Field: Definition of a Field

A set R together with two operations called addition and multiplication defines a commutative field $(R, +, \cdot)$ provided that for $a, b, c \ldots \in R$:

1. $a + b$ is a unique element of R
2. $a + b = b + a$
3. $a + (b + c) = (a + b) + c$
4. For each element a in R there exists an element 0 in R such that $a + 0 = 0 + a = a$
5. For each element a in R there exists a unique element $-a$ in R such that $a + (-a) = 0$
6. $a \cdot b$ is a unique element of R
7. $a \cdot b = b \cdot a$
8. $a \cdot (b \cdot c) = (a \cdot b) \cdot c$
9. For each element a in R there exists an element $1 \neq 0$ such that $1 \cdot a = a \cdot 1 = a$
10. For each element $a \neq 0$ there exists a unique element a^{-1} in R such that $a \cdot a^{-1} = a^{-1} \cdot a = 1$
11. Under $+$ and $\cdot$, the operations are connected by a distributive law: $a \cdot (b + c) = (b + c) \cdot a = a \cdot b + a \cdot c$

1.2 SOLVED PROBLEMS

1. Consider the permutation table for five elements $S = \{A, B, C, D, E\}$ under the operation $*$:

$*$	A	B	C	D	E
A	A	B	C	D	E
B	B	C	D	E	A
C	C	D	E	A	B
D	D	E	A	B	C
E	E	A	B	C	D

For example: $A * B = B$. Does $(S, *)$ form a group?

Solution:

i) Notice every possible product $x * y \in S$ for $x, y \in S$. Hence, the system is closed.

ii) Consider one or two examples that suggest the system is associative:

$$A * (B * C) = A * D = D \text{ while } (A * B) * C = B * C = D$$
$$B * (C * D) = B * A = B \text{ while } (B * C) * D = D * D = B$$

iii) The operation by element A keeps the original row and column listing unchanged: $X * A = A * X = A$ for all $x \cdot S$. Hence, the identity is A.

iv) Notice $A * A = A \Rightarrow A^{-1} = A$; $B * E = E * B = A \Rightarrow B^{-1} = E$. Similarly, $C^{-1} = D$. The same equations imply $D^{-1} = C$ and $E^{-1} = B$. Hence, S forms a group under $*$.

2. Define $\circ$ on the natural numbers by the table:

$\circ$	1	2	3
1	6	8	10
2	7	10	13
3	8	12	16

Define a general rule for $a \circ b$ (a is in the column, b in the row).

Solution:

This is a function of two variables. By trial and error you can find: $a \circ b = 2 \circ 3 = 3 + 6 + 4$, or $a \circ b = b + ab + 4$

3. Find a set that is closed under the usual subtraction operation. Find a set that is not closed under subtraction.

Solution: Let $Z = \{\text{integers}\} = \{\ldots -2, -1, 0, 1, 2, \ldots\}$. Notice that if $x, y \in Z$ then $x - y \in Z$ (set of integers contains positive and negative whole numbers). This set is closed under subtraction. Let $W = \{\text{whole numbers}\} = \{1, 2, 3, 4, 5, \ldots\}$. Notice that $4 - 5$ is not a whole number. This set is not closed under subtraction.

4. Given any identity under $*$ on set S, show it must be unique.

Solution: Consider any set S with e as the identity under $*$: $x * e = e * x = x$ for all $x \in S$. Suppose two identities e and e_1 exist under $*$: $e_1 = e * e_1 = e_1 * e = e$.

5. Which sets are closed under the corresponding operation?

$\{0, 1\}$ under $+$; $\{-1, 0, 1\}$ under $-$; $\{-1, 0, 1\}$ under $\cdot$; $\{0, 1\}$ under $\div$

Solution: Consider the following operational tables:

a)

+	0	1
0	0	1
1	1	2

b)

$-$	-1	0	1
-1	0	-1	-2
0	1	0	-1
1	2	1	0

c)

$\cdot$	-1	0	1
-1	1	0	-1
0	0	0	0
1	-1	0	1

d)

÷	0	1
0	1	0
1		1

Clearly, $\{-1, 0, 1\}$ under $\cdot$ is the only closed operational table.

6. Consider the following solution $4x + 3 = 7$ to indicate the properties of real numbers used to solve the equation. Assume the axiom: equals added to equals are equals.

Solution:

A. $4x + 3 + (-3) = 7 + (-3)$ A. The additive inverse exists

B. $4x + 0 = 7 + (-3)$ B. Additive property of the inverse

C. $4x = 7 + (-3)$ C. Property of the additive identity

D. $4x = 4$ D. Simplification; closure

E. $4x(4^{-1}) = 4(4^{-1})$ E. The multiplicative inverse exists

F. $44^{-1}x = 4(4^{-1})$ F. Commutative property of multiplication

G. $1x = 1$ G. Property of multiplicative inverses

H. $x = 1$ H. Property of multiplicative identity

7. In a group, the order of an element is the least multiple (power) of the element, which gives the identity element. Find the order of 1, 2, 3, 4 in the following group. Can you conjecture a theorem from these results?

$(Z_5, +)$	0	1	2	3	4
0	0	1	2	3	4
1	1	2	3	4	0
2	2	3	4	0	1
3	3	4	0	1	2
4	4	0	1	2	3

Solution: Notice that 0 is the identity. Define $5a$ as $a + a + a + a + a$. Notice: $5(1) = 5(2) = 5(3) = 5(4) = 0$. Conjecture: $o(S) \cdot a$ (or $a^{o(S)}$) $= e$, where a is any element in $(S, *)$, e is the identity for $(S, *)$, and $o(S)$ is the number of elements in the set S.

8. Define ordered pair (a, b) on the set S of $a, b \in R$ $a \neq 0, b \neq 0$: $(a, b)(c, d) = (ac, bd)$. Determine whether the system is closed, associative, commutative, has an identity, and if every element has an inverse.

Solution:

a) If a, b, c, d are real numbers, their products are real. Hence, $ac \in R$ and $bd \in R$. This implies $(ac, bd) \in S$. S is closed under this operation.

b) $[a(ce), b(df)] = [(ac)e, (db)f]$, so $(a, b)[(c, d)(e, f)] = [(a, b)(c, d)](e, f)$. Hence, the operation is associative.

c) $(a, b)(c, d) = (ac, bd) = (ca, df) = (c, d)(a, b)$. Hence, the operation is commutative.

d) Consider $(1,1) \in S$: $(a, b)(1, 1) = (1, 1)(a, b) = (1a, 1b) = (a, b)$. Hence, $(1, 1)$ is the identity.

e) For every $a, b \in R, \dfrac{1}{a}, \dfrac{1}{b} \in R$ and $\left(\dfrac{1}{a}, \dfrac{1}{b}\right) \in S$. But

$$(a,b)\left(\dfrac{1}{a}, \dfrac{1}{b}\right) = \left(\dfrac{1}{a}, \dfrac{1}{b}\right)(a,b) = \left(a \cdot \dfrac{1}{a}, b \cdot \dfrac{1}{b}\right) = (1,1). \text{ Hence, } \left(\dfrac{1}{a}, \dfrac{1}{b}\right) \text{ is the inverse}$$

of any element $(a,b) \in S$. Every element has an inverse.

9. Define operation $*$ on the set of all (a, b), where a and b are whole numbers, and $a * b = a^2 + b^2$. Show that $*$ is commutative but not associative.

Solution: $a * b = a^2 + b^2 = b^2 + a^2 = b * a$. Hence, the operation $*$ is commutative.

$(a * b) * c = (a * b)2 + c^2 = (a^2 + b^2)^2 + c^2 = a^4 + 2a^2b^2 + b^4 + c^2$

$a * (b * c) = a * (b^2 + c^2) = a^2 + (b^2 + c^2)^2 = a^2 + b^4 + 2b^2c^2 + c^2$.

Hence, $(a * b) * c \neq a * (b * c)$, which means the operation $*$ is not associative.

10. Define $\circ$ so that for all (a,b), where a and b are whole numbers, and $a \circ b = a$. Show that $a \circ b$ is associative but not commutative.

Solution: $a \circ (b \circ c) = a \circ b = a$ and $(a \circ b) \circ c = a \circ c = a$. Hence, $a \circ (b \circ c) = (a \circ b) \circ c$. The operation is associative. $a \circ b = a$ and $b \circ a = b$. Hence, the operation is not commutative.

11. Find the identity for the following operation $*$ on the set $\{a, b, c\}$, if

$*$	a	b	c
a	c	a	a
b	a	b	c
c	a	c	a

Show the system is commutative.

Solution: Note $b * x = x * b = x$ for all x (i.e., the b column and b row repeat the regional listing). It follows that b is the identity. Geometrically, one sees that the system is commutative, since it has reflective symmetry around the diagonal.

12. Give an example of one operation under which the real number system is not closed.

Solution: $\sqrt{-1}$ can never be negative, positive or 0, since the square of 0 is 0; the square of any other real number is positive. Hence, the real number system is not closed over square roots.

13. In fraction $\dfrac{a}{b}$, a and b are integers such that $a < b$ and $\dfrac{a}{b}$ is reduced to lowest terms.

Define an operation $\circ$ by $\dfrac{a}{b} \circ \dfrac{c}{d} = \dfrac{a+c}{b+d}$ where $\dfrac{a+c}{b+d}$ is reduced to lowest terms.

Find $\left(\dfrac{3}{5} \circ \dfrac{1}{2}\right) \circ \dfrac{2}{3}$. Is the operation associative?

Solution: $\left(\dfrac{3}{5} \circ \dfrac{1}{2}\right) \circ \dfrac{2}{3} = \left(\dfrac{4}{7} \circ \dfrac{2}{3}\right) = \dfrac{6}{10} = \dfrac{3}{5}$. Consider: $\left[\dfrac{2}{5} \circ \left(\dfrac{2}{3} \circ \dfrac{1}{4}\right)\right] = \left[\dfrac{2}{5} \circ \dfrac{3}{7}\right] = \dfrac{5}{12}$

but $\left[\left(\dfrac{2}{5} \circ \dfrac{2}{3}\right) \circ \dfrac{1}{4}\right] = \left[\dfrac{1}{2} \circ \dfrac{1}{4}\right] = \dfrac{1}{3}$. The operation $\circ$ is not associative.

1.2 UNSOLVED PROBLEMS

1. Define $a * b = a + 2b$ for all whole numbers a and b. Is the set closed under $*$?

2. Define the operation $*$ on whole numbers as multiplication of any whole number by 3. On what subset of whole numbers is this operation closed?

3. Consider $a * b = ab$ on the set $S = \{0, 1\}$ and usual multiplication. Is the set S closed under $*$?

4. Define $x \sim y$ to mean $= |x - y|$ for all x, y integers. Show the integers that do not form a group under this operation.

5. Consider the following set S under $*$. Why isn't $(S, *)$ a group?

*	a	b	c
a	a	b	c
b	b	c	a
c	c	c	b

6. Suppose $(S = \{a, b, c\}, *)$ is a commutative group. Create its operational table.

7. Which illustrates a distributive law?

   a) $a \Delta (b \Diamond c) = (a \Delta b) \Diamond c$

   b) $a \cap (b \cup c) = (a \cup b) \cap (a \cup c)$

   c) $(a \Delta b) \Diamond c = (c \Diamond a) \Delta (c \Diamond b)$

   d) $a \Delta (b \Diamond c) = (a \Delta b) \Diamond (a \Delta c)$

   e) $a \div (b \pm c) = (a \div b) \pm (a \div c)$

8. Which of the following systems is commutative?

   a)
*	A	B	C	D	E
A	A	B	C	D	E
B	B	C	D	E	A
C	C	D	E	A	B
D	D	E	A	B	C
E	E	A	B	C	D

b)

$*$	1	a	a^2
1	1	a	a^2
a	a	a^2	1
a^2	a^2	1	a^3

c)

$+$	v	x	w
x	x	w	v
w	w	v	x
y	x	w	v

9. Show that if an inverse exists for an element $a \in (S, *)$, then it must be unique.

10. Let $f(a, b) = av(a, b) = \dfrac{a+b}{2}$ where a, b are real numbers under usual addition and division. Show that av is commutative but not associative.

GLOSSARY	OF TERMS
Counting numbers	{1, 2, 3, 4, …}
Whole numbers	{0, 1, 2, 3, 4, …}
Prime number	A number that only has factors of 1 and itself (Note: 1 is not a prime)
Composite number	A number that is not a prime
Least common multiple of two numbers	The smallest number that both numbers divide
Greatest common divisor of two numbers	The largest number that divides into both numbers
Even number	Any multiple of two
Odd number	Any number that is not even
Order of operations	Parentheses, powers, multiplication, division, addition, and subtraction performed from left to right

SECTION 1.3

COUNTING NUMBERS AND ORDER OF OPERATIONS

Number theory gives many insights into the properties of positive integers. This section explores some basic ideas (divisibility, prime, factor, algorithm, order of operations) in number theory. One of the most fundamental concepts in arithmetic is that of divisibility. Some "rules" help determine if a number is divisible by: 2, 3, 4, 5, 6, 8, 9, or 10 (see Solved and Unsolved Problems):

Some Basic Divisibility Rules

TABLE 1.3	
A number is divisible by 2.	It is an even number.
A number is divisible by 3.	The sum of its digits is divisible by 3.
A number is divisible by 4.	Its last two digits give a number that is divisible by 4.
A number is divisible by 5.	The number ends in a 0 or 5.
A number is divisible by 6.	The number is divisible by both 2 and 3.
A number is divisible by 8.	Its last three digits give a number that is divisible by 8.
A number is divisible by 9.	The sum of its digits is divisible by 9.

Definition of a Prime

If a number is only divisible by 1 and itself, then it is called a prime (1 is not a prime). Any number that is not a prime is called a composite number.

Fundamental Theorem of Arithmetic

Any number n can be uniquely decomposed into primes $n = p_1^{\alpha_1} p_2^{\alpha_2} \ldots p_n^{\alpha_n}$ where p_i is called a prime factor of n, with α_i as a multiplicity of the prime p_i.

Greatest Common Divisor (GCD) and Least Common Multiple (LCM)

Let $n = p_1^{\alpha_1} p_2^{\alpha_2} \ldots p_x^{\alpha_x}$ and $m = q_1^{\beta_1} q_2^{\beta_2} \ldots q_y^{\beta_y}$ decomposed into their prime factors.

Define (n, m), **the greatest common divisor (GCD)** of m and n: $(m, n) = r_1^{\gamma_1} r_2^{\gamma_2} \ldots r_z^{\gamma_z}$ where r_i is a prime factor that m and n have in common, and γ_i is the smallest power of this factor.

Define $[n, m]$, **the least common multiple (LCM)** of m and n: $[m,n] = n = s_1^{\delta_1} s_2^{\delta_2} \ldots s_w^{\delta_w}$ where s_i is any prime factor in either m or n and δ_i is the greatest power of the s_i factor.

Odd and Even Numbers

An odd number is any number of the form $(2n + 1)$, where n is a whole number. An even number is any number of the form $2n$, where n is a whole number.

Order of Operations

The following order of operations is used to evaluate any numerical expression (from left to right): evaluate the operations within the parentheses, brackets or other grouping symbols; take powers; multiply and divide; add and subtract.

Arithmetic Strategies

Individuals usually think that the commonly used algorithms are the only way to perform arithmetic operations. While clever ideas, common algorithms are only shortcuts. Many other strategies for these computations are possible. For example, assume that you can count between 1 and 20 and can perform basic arithmetic operations with numbers of this magnitude. You then can perform a two-digit subtraction problem $(65 - 47)$ in a number of different ways. If you rewrite 65 as $67 - 2$, you have $65 - 47 = 67 - 47 - 2 = 20 - 2 = 18$. Alternatively, you can rewrite the original problem as $68 - 50 = 18$.

Another strategy would be to count by tens and see how many units of 10 you need to get from 47 (47, 57, 67)—until you get close to 65, and then compensate by subtracting 2: $20 - 2 = 18$. The following rule gives an algorithmic procedure for finding the greatest common divisor. Clearly, it is not the only way.

Euclidean Algorithm

This example illustrates the Euclidean algorithm for finding the greatest common divisor of two numbers. (For a statement and proof of the algorithm see the Unsolved Problems.)

Find the greatest common divisor of 650 and 440:

$$650 = 440(1) + 210$$
$$440 = 210(2) + 20$$
$$210 = 20(5) + 10$$
$$20 = 10(2)$$

Since 10 is the last nonzero remainder, it is the greatest common divisor.

1.3 SOLVED PROBLEMS

1. Calculate: $5 \cdot 10 \div 2 \cdot 3$ and $(2 \cdot 5 + 3)^2 \cdot 2$.

   Solution: $5 \cdot 10 \div 2 \cdot 3 = 50 \div 2 \cdot 3 = 25 \cdot 3 = 75$; $(10 + 3)^2 \cdot 2 = (13)^2 \cdot 2 = 169 \cdot 2 = 338$

2. Consider $a^b = 121$; for whole numbers a and b find b^a.

   Solution: Notice that $11^2 = 121$, so that $2^{11} = 2048$.

3. Both 5 and 29 are prime numbers that can be written as sums of squares: $5 = 1^2 + 2^2$ and $29 = 2^2 + 5^2$. Which of the following numbers has the same properties: 137, 71, 153, 23, 169?

   Solution: Notice that 137 is prime. We must only look at values that are less than $\sqrt{137}$. By trial and error we find that $137 = 121 + 16 = 11^2 + 4^2$.

4. Find 5 values of n such that $2^{n-1} - 1$ is a multiple of n.

   Solution: (This problem hints at Fermat's Theorem: $2^{n-1} - 1$ is a multiple of n where n is a prime greater than 2.) Define the symbol $a|b$ to mean "a divides b" with no remainder. Pick $n = 2, 3, 5, 7, 11$. If $n = 3$, $3|(2^2 - 1)$; if $n = 5$, $5|(2^4 - 1)$; if $n = 7$, $7|(2^6 - 1)$; if $n = 11$, $11|(2^{10} - 1)$.

5. Show: If the sum of a number's digits is divisible by 3, the number is divisible by 3.

   Solution: This result is perhaps easiest to see using an example (the argument will be the same for a general proof). Let n_1, n_2, n_3, n_4 be the digits of n.

   $$n = n_4(10{,}000) + n_3(1000) + n_2(100) + n_1(10) + n_0(1)$$
   $$= n_4(9999 + 1) + n_3(999 + 1) + n_2(99 + 1) + n_1(9 + 1) + n_0$$
   $$= n_4(9999) + n_3(999) + n_2(99) + n_1(9) + n_4 + n_3 + n_2 + n_1 + n_0.$$

Notice that 3 divides all the terms in the parentheses; so if 3 divides $n_4 + n_3 + n_2 + n_1 + n_0$, then 3 divides the original number.

6. Find the prime decomposition for 16940.

   Solution: $16940 = 2^2 \cdot 5 \cdot 7 \cdot 11^2$.

7. For any number N define the set $S = \{$all proper factors of $N\}$, (1 and N are not in S). Find the number of elements in S when $N = 32$.

   Solution: $32 = 2^5$ the factors of 32 are 2, 4, 8, 16. There are 4 elements in S.

8. Find $[16940, 1540]$ and $(16940, 1540)$.

   Solution:

   $16940 = 2^2 \cdot 5 \cdot 7 \cdot 11^2$; $1540 = 2^2 \cdot 5 \cdot 7 \cdot 11$; $(16940, 1540) = 2^2 \cdot 5 \cdot 7 \cdot 11$
   and $[16940, 1540] = 2^2 \cdot 5 \cdot 7 \cdot 11^2$.

9. Let $a - b = 4$; $a - c = 2$; $d = 3$. Find $[(a - b) - (a - c)][a - (c - d)]$.

   Solution:

   $[(a - b) - (a - c)][a - (c - d)] = [(a - b) - (a - c)] \, [(a - c) + d] = (4 - 2)(2 + 3) = 10$.

1.3 UNSOLVED PROBLEMS

1. What is the greatest number in the intersection of the set of factors of 1089 and the set of factors of 198? Find $(315, 294)$.

2. Prove that a number is divisible by 8, if its last three digits create a number that is divisible by 8.

3. Suppose a set S has n elements in it; how many elements are there in the set of all its subsets?

4. Consider the Sieve of Eratosthenese for all the numbers between 1 and 100. Cross out 2, and all the multiples of 2 greater than 2. Continue the process for all the numbers you have not crossed out up to 100. What numbers are not crossed out?

5. Show that the product of two odd integers must always be odd.

6. Prove the Euclidean algorithm for finding the $gcd(a, b)$, a and b integers:

   Let a and b be positive integers with $a \geq b$, let

   $$a_0 = bq_1 + r_2 \qquad\qquad 0 \leq r_2 < b;$$
   $$b = r_2 q_2 + r_3 \qquad\qquad 0 \leq r_3 < r_2$$

   $$\cdots$$

   $$r_{n-2} = r_{n-1} q_{n-1} + r_n \qquad b = r_2 q_2 + r_3$$
   $$r_{n-1} = r_n q_n \qquad\qquad 0 \leq r_n < r_{n-1}$$

   Show $gcd(a, b) = r_n$.

Ratio	Two quantities compared by division
$\dfrac{a}{b}$, $a : b$, $a \div b$	The ratio of a to b
***x*% (*x* percent)**	x divided by 100; the ratio of x to 100
Density	The ratio of mass to volume

SECTION 1.4

RATIO, PROPORTION, AND PERCENT

Concepts of Ratio, Proportion, and Percent

Ratios compare quantities by division. The ratio of a to b, when both quantities are expressed in the same unit, is $\dfrac{a}{b}$ or $a \div b$. Ratios can be expressed in a number of alternate ways $a : b$, $\dfrac{a}{b}$, $a \div b$, as a decimal or as a percent. For example, the ratio $1 : 4 = \dfrac{1}{4} = 1 \div 4 = 0.25 = 25\%$.

Size Transformations as Ratios

One visual way to represent ratios involves the concept of a *size transformation*. In light of the Cartesian coordinate system, for any $k \neq 0$ the transformation that maps the point (x, y), the pre-image, onto the point (kx, ky), the image, is a size transformation with the origin as the center of the transformation. The two images are similar, with the ratio of similarity equal to k. Alternatively, one transforms a polygon by a ratio k with a given point as center, by connecting each vertex of the polygon to the fixed point (one transforms the vertices). The ratio determines the distance between the center and the vertex of the transformed polygon. Intuitively, size transformations operate much the same way as the relationship between a projector and a screen. If you want the sizes of an image on the screen to double, you move the projector twice the distance from the screen; if you want it half as big you move it in one-half the distance.

Size transformations also help to visualize the ratios between length, area, and volumes. If the ratio of the sides of two similar two-dimensional figures is $a : b$, the ratios of the areas of these figures is $a^2 : b^2$. If the ratio of the sides of two similar three-dimensional figures is $a : b$ the ratio of the volumes of these figures is $a^3 : b^3$. To illustrate the property, consider the size transformation of the following figure:

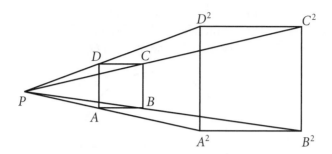

If figure $ABCD$ is transformed so that $2AB = A'B'$, then four areas of $ABCD$ are equal to the area of $A'B'C'D'$. One computes the area from the product of the two linear quantities. When both of these quantities are multiplied by n, the area is multiplied by n^2. In particular, if the area of square X is a^2, then the area of the square Y is $(2a)(2a) = 4a^2$. A similar result holds for three-dimensional figures.

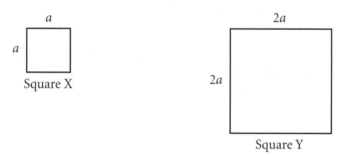

1.4 SOLVED PROBLEMS

1. If a is 95% of b, what percent of b is a?

   Solution: $\dfrac{a}{b} = \dfrac{95}{100}$ then $\dfrac{b}{a} = \dfrac{100}{95} = 1\dfrac{5}{95} \approx 1.06$ or 106%.

2. If the price of the gasoline goes up by 5% per gallon and then goes down 5%, what is the ratio of the old price of gasoline per gallon to the new price of gasoline per gallon?

   Solution: Gas costs \$1 per gal, goes up 5% to \$1.05, then down 5% to \$.9975. The ratio is $\dfrac{1.00}{0.9975} = \dfrac{10000}{9975}$.

3. A wheel rotates once a second. Object two (O) is twice the distance from the center of the wheel as object one (O_1). How fast is O moving in comparison to O_1?

Solution: Let x be the distance from the center of the wheel O_1. In one second O_1 goes a distance $2\pi x$. The distance O goes in the same second is $2\pi(2x)$ or twice the distance O_1 goes. Hence, O goes twice the speed of O_1.

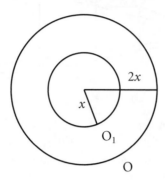

4. A new map is to be derived from a given map so that areas in the new map are three times the areas in the given map. The scale of the given map is 1cm = 100m. What will be the scale of the new map as a ratio?

Solution: The scale is 1cm = 100 m but 100 cm = 1m. Hence, the scale of the map is $1 : (100 \cdot 100)$ or $1 : 10000$. If the new map must have its area tripled, its linear measures must be multiplied by $\sqrt{3}$.

1) Old ratio is 1 : 10000.

2) New ratio is $\sqrt{3} : 10000$ or $\dfrac{\sqrt{3}}{10000} = \dfrac{1}{\dfrac{1}{\sqrt{3}} \cdot 10000} = \dfrac{1}{\dfrac{10000\sqrt{3}}{3}} = \dfrac{1}{5773}$.

5. If $\dfrac{a}{b} = .11\bar{1}$ find $\dfrac{b}{a}$.

Solution: If $x = .111\bar{1}$, $10x = 1.1\bar{1}$ or $9x = 1$ and $x = \dfrac{1}{9}$. Hence, $\dfrac{a}{b} = \dfrac{1}{9} \Rightarrow \dfrac{b}{a} = \dfrac{9}{1} = 9$.

6. If $\dfrac{b}{a} = \dfrac{2}{3}$ and $\dfrac{d}{c} = \dfrac{4}{5}$, find $\dfrac{bc - ad}{ac}$.

Solution: $\dfrac{b}{a} - \dfrac{d}{c} = \dfrac{bc - ad}{ac}$ which means $\dfrac{3(4) - 2(5)}{2(3)} = \dfrac{12 - 10}{6} = \dfrac{2}{6} = \dfrac{1}{3}$.

7. Show that the period of repetition for any fraction cannot be larger than 9 digits in length.

Solution: You cannot have more than 9 different remainders in such a division, since only 9 distinct digits occur. This means that repetition of the division process will have to occur in 9 or less digits.

8. a) Show that $.\overline{2} + .\overline{2} = \dfrac{4}{9} = .\overline{4}$ b) Find $.\overline{20} - .\overline{02}$ c) Is $.\overline{8} + .\overline{1} = .\overline{9} = 1?$

   Solution:

   a) $.\overline{2222} + .\overline{2222} = .\overline{4444}$ b) $.\overline{202020} - .\overline{020202} = .\overline{181818}$ c) Yes

9. Compare the density (density = mass/volume) of birch and oak, if the mass of birch is 36g for a volume of 60cm^3 and the mass of oak is 56g for a volume of 80 cm^3. Give one practical application.

   Solution: For birch: density = mass/volume = $\dfrac{36g}{60cm^3} = .6g/cm^3$

   For oak: density = mass/volume = $\dfrac{56g}{80cm^3} = .7g/cm^3$

   Oak is a denser wood than birch. This result implies that oak might be a better wood to use for flooring than birch (but oak may be more expensive!).

1.4 UNSOLVED PROBLEMS

1. The volumes of two cubes have the ratio of 1 : 27. Give the ratio of the area of the face of one of the cubes to that of the face of the other cube.

2. Given the ratio of surface areas of two cubes are 1 : 2, find the ratio of their volumes.

3. In a video game the volume (v) of a cubic box is represented by 100,000 small cubes v_1. What will be the surface area of each of these small cubes (v_1) in terms of v?

4. Suppose the size of a circumference of the circle is doubled to 8π. How much will the difference be between the area of the new square, which is circumscribed around the circle, and the area of the original circumscribed square?

5. Suppose the ratio of two weights is $\dfrac{w_1}{w_2} = \dfrac{2}{3}$. Assume w_1 increases its weight by 20% and w_2 increases by 10%. If $w_1 = 50$ kilos, find the difference between the two increased weights.

6. Draw a square with a side of one decimeter. Show geometrically that $(.1)(.1) = .01$ and $(.5)(.15) = .075$.

CHAPTER TWO

Arithmetic and Algebraic Structures II

This chapter continues to look at basic relationships between real numbers. It introduces the concepts of counting, linear and quadratic functions, and some fundamental relationships involving distance. Much like letters of the alphabet, these ideas are essential in developing the language of mathematics. They are the building blocks for mathematical communication. The topics are simultaneously theoretical and general (how to solve problems), yet mechanical and specific (how to operate with polynomials). The ideas introduced here are developed in more detail in later chapters.

OF TERMS

Real variable	A symbol that represents any real number
Monomial	A constant, a variable or a product of a constant and one or more variables often also called a term (e.g., $5x$)
Binomial	An expression consisting of two terms separated by $+$ or $-$ signs (e.g., $5x - 1$)
Polynomial	An expression consisting of one or more terms separated by $+$ or $-$ signs (e.g., $5x^3 - 2x^2 - x + 1$)
Degree of a monomial	The sum of the powers of the variables in the monomial
Degree of a polynomial	The greatest degree of the monomials in the polynomial (e.g., $5xy^2 + 3x$ has degree 3, $5xyz^3 + 3x^4 - 2x + 1$ has degree 5)
Rational expression	The ratio of a polynomial to another polynomial
Algebraic factoring	A polynomial expressed as a product of irreducible algebraic factors

SECTION 2.1

ALGEBRA, PROBLEM SOLVING, LINEAR FUNCTIONS, AND ABSOLUTE VALUES

This section explores results in classical algebra: operations with polynomials, factoring, and elementary equation solving. The material frequently appears in standard courses in first- and second-year algebra.

■ If $x = 5$, $y = -2$, evaluate $x - xy + x^2 + y^2$.

Replace x and y in the algebraic expression and perform indicated operations:

$$5 - 5(-2) + 5^2 + (-2)^2 = 5 - (-10) + 25 + 4 = 44$$

■ Add $5x - 2y + 3$ and $-3x + y - 7$.

Add the coefficients of terms with the same variable, and simplify:

$$
\begin{array}{l}
5x - 2y + 3 \\
-3x + y - 7 \\
\hline
2x - y - 4
\end{array}
\quad \text{or} \quad
\begin{aligned}
5x - 2y + 3 + (-3x + y - 7) &= 5x - 3x - 2y + 3 - 7 \\
&= 2x - y - 4
\end{aligned}
$$

■ Subtract $5x - 2y + 3$ from $-3x + y - 7$.

Subtract (change signs and add) the coefficients of terms with same variable, and simplify:

$$
\begin{array}{ll}
-3x + y - 7 & \text{or} \quad -3x + y - 7 - (5x - 2y + 3) = -3x + y - 7 - 5x + 2y - 3 \\
\underline{-5x + 2y - 3} & \phantom{\text{or} \quad -3x + y - 7 - (5x - 2y + 3)} = -8x + 3y - 10 \\
-8x + 3y - 10 &
\end{array}
$$

■ To multiply monomials you add exponents of like variables and multiply coefficients:

$$(-5xyz)(-3x^2y^3) = (15x^3y^4z)$$

■ To multiply polynomials you use the distributive law and apply the rules of multiplication for monomials:

$$(-2x + y)(-3x - y) = (-3x)(-2x + y) + (-y)(-2x + y) = 6x^2 - 1xy - y^2$$

■ Factoring reduces a polynomial into its factors:

$$x^2 - 25y^2 = (x + 5y)(x - 5y)$$

$$x^3 - a^3 = (x - a)(x^2 + ax + a^2)$$

$$x^2 - 3xy + 2y^2 = (x - 2y)(x - y)$$

$$x^2 - 10x + 1 = \left(x - \frac{10 + \sqrt{100 - 4}}{2}\right)\left(x - \frac{10 - \sqrt{100 - 4}}{2}\right)$$

$$= \left(x - \frac{10 + \sqrt{16 \cdot 6}}{2}\right)\left(x - \frac{10 - \sqrt{16 \cdot 6}}{2}\right) = \left(x - \left(5 + 2\sqrt{6}\right)\right)\left(x - \left(5 - 2\sqrt{6}\right)\right)$$

$$\left(\text{i.e., } ax^2 + bx + c = \left(x - \frac{-b + \sqrt{b^2 - 4ac}}{2a}\right)\left(x - \frac{-b - \sqrt{b^2 - 4ac}}{2a}\right)\right)$$

■ To divide a polynomial you either factor and cancel common factors, or perform the process of long division:

a) $\dfrac{x^3 + a^3}{x + a} = \dfrac{(x + a)(x^2 - ax + a^2)}{x + a} = x^2 - ax + a^3$

b) $\dfrac{x^2 + x + 1}{x - 1}$

$$
\require{enclose}
\begin{array}{r}
x + 2 \\
x - 1 \enclose{longdiv}{x^2 + x + 1} \\
\underline{x^2 - x} \\
+2x + 1 \\
\underline{2x - 2} \\
+3
\end{array}
$$

Hence, $\dfrac{x^2+x+1}{x-1}=x+2+\dfrac{3}{x-1}$

■ To combine algebraic fractions you find the LCM of the algebraic expression in the denominator, convert each fraction into an equivalent fraction having the LCM as its denominator, and combine as usual when adding fractions.

$$\frac{1}{x^2-1}+\frac{2x}{x+1}+\frac{3x}{x-1}=\frac{1}{(x+1)(x-1)}+\frac{2x(x-1)}{(x+1)(x-1)}+\frac{3x(x-1)}{(x+1)(x-1)}=\frac{5x^2+x+1}{(x+1)(x-1)}$$

2.1 SOLVED PROBLEMS

1. Consider a rectangle with one side 20 units longer than the other. Within the rectangle there is another rectangle with length of one-half the width of the larger rectangle. If the width of this smaller rectangle is one-half its length, find the area between the two rectangles.

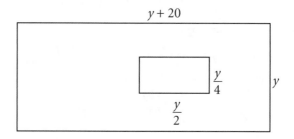

Solution: Let A represent the required area:

$$A=y(y+20)-\frac{y}{2}\left(\frac{y}{4}\right)=y^2+20y-\frac{y^2}{8}=\frac{7y^2}{8}+20y$$

2. How many of the first positive integers must be added together to get the sum 5050?

Solution: This problem is a variation on a famous (but probably legendary) story about Gauss. Young Gauss had a teacher who wanted to give him busy work. The teacher told him to add up the numbers between 1 and 100. Within a minute or so, Gauss had the answer: 5050. Instead of adding the first to the second term, Gauss added the first and the last term (101), the second and next to the last term (101), to get 50 groups of 101, or 5050. In general, to get the sum of an arithmetic sequence, add the first term to the last term, and multiply this sum by the number of terms divided by two: $1+2+\ldots+n=\dfrac{n}{2}(1+n);\dfrac{n}{2}(1+n)=5050$

$$n(1+n)=5050\cdot 2; n^2+n=10100; n^2+n-10100=0$$
$$n^2+101n-100n-10100=0; (n+101)(n-100)=0; n=-101 \text{ or } n=100$$

Reject $n = -101$. The answer is 100.

3. Find an infinite sum for $\dfrac{x^2}{x^2 - 1}$. Find one value for x that makes this sum meaningless.

Solution: By long division:

$$
\begin{array}{r}
1 + x^{-2} + x^{-4} + \ldots \\
x^2 - 1 \overline{\smash{\big)}\ x^2 } \\
\underline{x^2 - 1 } \\
1 \\
\underline{1 - x^{-2} } \\
x^{-2}
\end{array}
$$

Clearly, if $x = 1$ the fraction is undefined. (In general, the Remainder Theorem states that if $f(x)$ is divided by $(x - a)$ so that $f(x) = (x - a)\,g(x) + R$, then $f(a) = R$.)

4. Simplify: $\dfrac{3a - 5m}{a^2 - 5am + 6m^2} + \dfrac{1}{a - 2m} - \dfrac{2}{a - 3m}$.

Solution:

$$\dfrac{3a - 5m}{a^2 - 5am + 6m^2} + \dfrac{1}{a - 2m} - \dfrac{2}{a - 3m} = \dfrac{3a - 5m}{(a - 2m)(a - 3m)} + \dfrac{1}{a - 2m} - \dfrac{2}{a - 3m}$$

$$= \dfrac{3a - 5m + a - 3m - 2(a - 2m)}{(a - 2m)(a - 3m)} = \dfrac{3a - 5m + a - 3m - 2a + 4m}{(a - 2m)(a - 3m)}$$

$$= \dfrac{2a - 4m}{(a - 2m)(a - 3m)} = \dfrac{2(a - 2m)}{(a - 2m)(a - 3m)} = \dfrac{2}{a - 3m}$$

5. Given the equation $x^3 + x^2 - x + 2 = 0$ with roots x_1, x_2, x_3. Find an equation with roots $x_1 + 1$, $x_2 + 1$ and $x_3 + 1$.

Solution: Let the roots for the required equation be t_1, t_2, t_3 so that $t_1 = x_1 + 1$, $t_2 = x_2 + 1$, $t_3 = x_3 + 1$. In other words, $t_1 - 1 = x_1$, $t_2 - 1 = x_2$, $t_3 - 1 = x_3$. The following equation has the required roots: $(t - 1)^3 + (t - 1)^2 - (t - 1) + 2 = 0$.

6. Find the expression for the sum and product of the roots x_1, x_2 for the equation $x^2 + bx + c = 0$ in terms of b and c.

Solution: Since x_1, x_2 are roots of the equation $(x - x_1)(x - x_2) = 0$, the equation is $x^2 - (x_1 + x_2)x + x_1 x_2 = 0$. In other words, $(x_1 + x_2) = -b$ and $x_1 x_2 = c$.

7. Given the equation $3x^2 - 7x + 6 = 0$ with roots α, β. Find $\dfrac{1}{\alpha} + \dfrac{1}{\beta}$.

Solution:

Rewrite $3x^2 - 7x + 6 = 0$ so that $x^2 - \dfrac{7}{3}x + 2 = 0$. In this form $\alpha + \beta = \dfrac{7}{3}$, $\alpha \cdot \beta = 2$.

Notice that $\dfrac{\alpha + \beta}{\alpha\beta} = \dfrac{1}{\alpha} + \dfrac{1}{\beta}$. Hence, $\dfrac{1}{\alpha} + \dfrac{1}{\beta} = \dfrac{\dfrac{7}{3}}{2} = \dfrac{7}{6}$.

2.1 UNSOLVED PROBLEMS

1. If $a * b = a + b + ab$, find an expression for $(a * a) * (b * b)$.

2. If a rectangle is $(x + 1)$ cm wide and its area is $(x^3 + 1)$ cm, what is its length?

3. How much must you add to $\dfrac{1}{x^2}$ to get x^2?

4. What is the remainder when $x^3 + x^2 + x + 1$ is divided by $x - 1$?

5. Find the factors of $x^2 - 4ax + 4a^2$.

6. Factor: $x^2 - 10x + 2$.

7. Factor: $(x - 4)^2 - 3(x - 4)(x + 1) - 10(x + 1)^2$.

8. Consider $(a + b)^4$. Find the sum of the coefficients of this expression.

9. Simplify: $(10002)^2 - (10001)^2$ using an algebraic identity for $x^2 - y^2$.

10. Simplify: $\dfrac{x^4 + 4x^3 y + 6x^2 y^2 + 4xy^3 + y^4}{x + y}$.

11. Given $a^2 + b^2 = \dfrac{13}{36}$, $ab = \dfrac{1}{6}$. Find $a + b$.

12. Let $x = \dfrac{2a + 3}{3a - 2}$. Express $\dfrac{x - 1}{2x + 1}$ in terms of a.

13. Simplify: $\dfrac{m^2 - 4mn + 3n^2}{m^2 - mn - 2n^2} \div \left(\dfrac{m^2 + mn - 2n^2}{m^2 + 3mn + 2n^2} \cdot \dfrac{m^2 - 2mn}{m^2 + mn} \right)$.

14. Given the equation $x^3 + ax^2 + bx + c = 0$. Express a, b, c in terms of the roots of this equation α, β, γ.

15. If $x^3 + x^2 + ax + b$ is divided by $x + 1$ the remainder is 5. If it is divided by $x - 1$ the remainder is 4. Find a and b.

Kilo	Thousand (kilometer means one thousand meters)
Hecto	Hundred (hectometer means one hundred meters)
Deka	Ten (decameter means ten meters)
Deci	One tenth (decimeter means one tenth of a meter)
Centi	One hundredth (centimeter means one hundredth of a meter)
Milli	One thousandth (millimeter means one thousandth of a meter)
Average of a population	The number obtained if the entire amount of a quantity is dispersed equally to each individual in a population
Weighted average	The average of a population when individual members have the amount of a quantity in different ratios

SECTION 2.2

METRICS AND PROBLEM SOLVING

Measurement

Problems frequently involve units of measure in the English as well as the metric system of mass and capacity. Increasingly, students are also familiar with the metric system of length. Some intuitive insights provide students with a "rough feel" for the metric system in terms of the English system. For example:

- A mile is approximately 1.6 km; 100 miles, it is around 160 km.
- A comfortable day is 70°–75°F (20°–25°C); a very hot day is 95°F (35°C).
- A kilogram is around 2.2 lb; a person who is 100 kilos is large (220 lbs), while a person who is 50 kilos is quite small (about 110 lbs).

The following tables give the most common metric measures and their equivalents:

TABLE 2.1						
Prefix	kilo	hecto	deka	deci	centi	milli
Value	1000	100	10	.1	.01	.001

Length:

TABLE 2.2	
Kilometer (km)	1000 m
Hectometer (hecto)	100 m
Decameter (deka)	10 m
Meter	1 m
Decimeter	.1 m
Centimeter	.01 m
Millimeter	.001 m

Mass:

TABLE 2.3	
Kilogram	1000 g
Gram	1 g
Ton	1t (1000 kg)

Volume:

TABLE 2.4	
Milliliters	.001 L
Liters	1 L

The following table gives the most common **English measures:**

TABLE 2.5	
12 in (inches)	1 ft (foot)
3 ft (feet)	1 yd (yard)
1760 yd (yard)	1 mi (mile)
5280 ft (feet)	1 mi (mile)
16 oz (ounces)	1 lb (pound)
2000 lb	1 t (ton)
2 pt (pints)	1 qt (quart)
4 qts (quarts)	1 gl (gallon)

Some conversions between English measures and metric measures:

TABLE 2.6	
1 in = 2.5cm	4 in = 10cm
1 yd = .9m	1.1 yd = 1m
1 mile = 1.6 km	.6 miles = 1km
1 oz = 28g	.035 oz = 1g
Centigrade $C° = \dfrac{5}{9}(F - 32)$	Farenheit $F° = \dfrac{9}{5}C° + 32$

Average and Weighted Average

Average and weighted average are two other important concepts of measurement.
Definition: Let $\{X_1, X_2, ..., X_n\}$ be any set of real numbers. Define the **average** as

$$\frac{X_1 + X_2 + ... + X_2}{n} = \sum_{i=1}^{n} \frac{X_i}{n} = \frac{\sum_{i=1}^{n} X_i}{n}.$$

The average of elements $\{X_1, X_2, ..., X_n\}$ is that number which multiplied by n, results in the sum $X_1 + X_2 + ... + X_n$. For example, suppose five people collectively had $120. If $120 is distributed evenly to all of them (the mean), each person receives $24.
Definition: Let $\{X_1, X_2, ..., X_n\}$ be any set of real numbers, with weights $W_1, W_2, ..., W_n$.

The **weighted average** is defined by: $\dfrac{X_1 W_1 + X_2 W_2 + ... + X_n W_n}{W_1 + W_2 + ... + W_n} = \dfrac{\sum_{i=1}^{n} X_i W_i}{\sum_{i=1}^{n} W_i}.$

Problem Solving

A general discussion of problem solving can be found in a small book entitled *How to Solve It* by George Polya (1888–1985), who gave a four-part overview of how to solve any problem.

Four-Part Plan

• Understand the problem.
• Devise a plan.
• Carry out the plan.
• Check the completed solution.

This list may appear at first to be too general to be of help in actual situations. But on closer examination, it provides practical ideas about problem solving.

Understand the Problem What do we know and what does the problem exactly ask us to find out? Perhaps you might restate the problem in a number of different ways, or draw a diagram or table that might help you get an overall image of the problem.

Devise a Plan There is no single way to "attack" a problem. Go back to the problem over and over, try to solve one part of it, not all of it. See if you can reason backwards from the conclusions. One of the most discouraging attitudes people have about problem solving is that only those blessed with a "mathematical gift" can solve mathematical problems—the implication being that only extremely intelligent people can solve problems. On the contrary, people interested in mathematics know that the great majority of mathematical problem solving simply involves work, coupled with a genuine desire to solve a problem.

Carry Out the Plan To carry out a plan requires that a person check each step of the plan. This process may yield results that connect with other problems; it may create new insights into how to solve other problems. Even if you fail to carry out the plan because of some unforeseen problem with it, new ideas may arise.

Check the Completed Solution Look at the completed solution. Make sure you address the questions asked. Be extremely critical of the work done, and accept the potential criticism of others. The solution may enable a person to extend and generalize results. The process may create a stronger solution than one had initially designed.

2.2 SOLVED PROBLEMS

1. If the temperature measures 15°C, find its equivalent in Fahrenheit.

   Solution: $F = \dfrac{9}{5}C + 32$. If $C = 15$, $F = \dfrac{9}{5} \cdot 15 + 32 = 27 + 32 = 59$. Hence, $15°C = 59°F$.

2. The average weight of 8 people in a class is 140 lbs. One more person joins the class. If the average weight of this group is 150 lbs, what is the weight of the new person?

   Solution: The original average weight of the eight people in the class was 140. We have $\dfrac{P_1 + P_2 + P_3 + \ldots + P_8}{8} = 140$ or $P_1 + P_2 + \ldots + P_8 = 8 \cdot 140$. Similarly, since the average weight of the 9 people in class is 150, we have $\dfrac{P_1 + P_2 + P_3 + \ldots + P_8 + P_9}{9} = 150$ or $\dfrac{8 \cdot 140 + P_9}{9} = 150$. It follows that $p_9 = 9 \cdot 150 - 8 \cdot 140 = 230$ lbs.

3. Compute the average weekly (40-hour week) wage of 10 units of labor, if three units receive $10 an hour, four units receive $20 an hour, and three units receive $30 an hour.

Solution: $W = \left(\dfrac{3 \cdot 10 + 4 \cdot 20 + 3 \cdot 30}{10}\right) 40 = 800.$

4. Closely related to the idea of weighted average is the concept of a "balance point" or centroid. Through experimentation you can find that if two weights are attached to the ends of a light rod AB, 2 kg at A and 3 kg at B, the balance point P is such that $2AP = 3PB$. Let AB with length 5 be located on the x-axis with the origin at A. Find P.

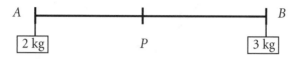

Solution: Let $P = (x, 0)$. Hence, $2x = 3(5 - x)$; $2x = 15 - 3x$; $5x = 15$; $x = 3$. P is the point $(3, 0)$.

5. Given the balance point of a line segment is the point that divides the line segment into the ratio of $1 : 1$, what can one conjecture about the balance point of a triangular plate? (If you were to balance a triangular plate on your fingertip, where would you place your fingertip?)

Solution: For simplicity, consider the area of a triangle to consist of thin strips, each of which has a balance point at its center. These midpoints are all collinear (the median). The balance point of the triangle should probably then lie on the median from C to side AB. The same argument holds for CB or AC. The intersection of the three medians is called the centroid—the balance point for the triangle.

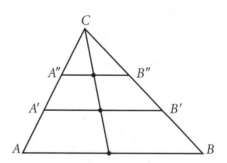

6. Consider a robot designed to take the place of one worker in a factory. It costs $100,000, but operates at an average weekly rate of $1. Consider a factory worker who receives an average of $1,000 a week. How long is it before the robot pays for itself?

Solution: Let w = weeks it takes for robot to pay for itself. Then $100,000 + 1w = 1000w$; $100,000 = 999w$; $100 \approx w$ (about two years).

7. The following figure is a trapezoid connected with a half-circle.

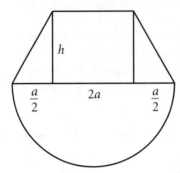

Find the area of the figure. If the diameter of the circle and the top of trapezoid are doubled, find the perimeter of the resulting figure.

Solution: In this problem you see a number of different shapes: two triangles, a rectangle, a half-circle, a trapezoid. The trapezoid and the half-circle dominate the figure. The area of a half-circle with a radius $\frac{3}{2}a$ is $\frac{\pi}{8}9a^2$. The area of a trapezoid is $\frac{1}{2}h(b_1 + b_2)$ where h is its height and b_1 and b_2 are its bases. In this case, the area is $\frac{1}{2}h(2a + 3a) = \frac{5}{2}ha$. Adding the quantities we get $\frac{a}{2}(5h + \frac{9}{4}a\pi)$. If the diameter of the circle is doubled, the (half) circumference of the circle is also doubled. In addition, the top base of the trapezoid is doubled. But the legs of the trapezoid are NOT doubled. Each must be calculated as the hypotenuse of a right triangle with legs a and height h. The perimeter of a half-circle is $\frac{1}{2}(6\pi a) = 3\pi a$. The hypotenuses of two right triangles are $2\left(\sqrt{a^2 + h^2}\right)$. The top of trapezoid is $4a$. The perimeter of the resulting figure is $3a\pi + 2\sqrt{a^2 + h^2} + 4a$.

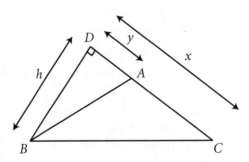

8. Find the area of the $\triangle ABC$.

Solution: The key to this problem involves seeing in $\triangle BDC$ the two right triangles $\triangle BDC$ and $\triangle BAD$. This means that the area of $\triangle ABC$ = area of $\triangle ABC$ = $\triangle$area of of $\triangle BDC$ − area of $\triangle BAD = \frac{h}{2}x - \frac{h}{2}y = \frac{h}{2}(x - y)$.

9. A man makes a trip of 10 km at x km/hr followed by a trip of 20 km at a rate of 5 km/hr faster. What is the total time taken? On average how long did each part of the trip take?

Solution: The total time taken equals the time taken for the first part plus the time taken for the second part. Let x = rate on initial leg of trip. The total time equals the sum of the two times for each part of the trip (t_1 and t_2) where $t_1 = \dfrac{10}{x}$ and $t_2 = \dfrac{20}{x+5}$. This means $t_1 + t_2 = \dfrac{10}{x} + \dfrac{20}{x+5}$. The average of these two times is $\dfrac{1}{2}(t_1 + t_2) = \dfrac{5}{x} + \dfrac{10}{x+5}$.

10. Suppose a train travels on the plains of Spain at 50 m/sec and rain on the plane falls vertically at a speed of 10 m/sec. Find the direction of the streaks of rain on the train's side windows.

Solution: The problem is best done by vector addition (see Chapter 9), but it can also be solved by common sense. After 1 second the rain travels 10 m (vertically) and the train travels 50 m (horizontally).

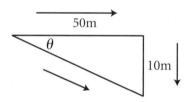

Notice that the direction of the streaks on the train window is given by θ where $\tan \theta = \dfrac{10}{50} = 0.2$. This means $\theta = \tan^{-1}0.2 \approx 11°$ ($11°$ below the horizontal).

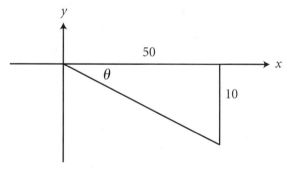

11. In a town of 150 people 70 have TVs, 90 have cars, 55 have pets, 65 have TVs and cars, 20 have TVs and pets and 25 have cars and pets. If 15 have all three, how many people have neither TV, car, nor a pet?

Solution: This solution follows from the observation that to find the number of elements in $A \cup B$, given the number of elements in A and B, you add the number of elements in A and B and then subtract the number of elements in their intersection. With this observation you can start your calculations where the three sets in question all intersect:

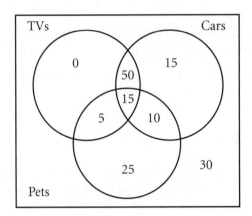

Fifteen have cars, pets, and TVs. If 65 have TVs and cars, then 50 have cars and TVs but not pets; hence, 30 have neither.

2.2 UNSOLVED PROBLEMS

1. A person spends on the average $200 for food whenever she goes to the store; $\frac{1}{3}$ of the time she spends around $180, $\frac{1}{2}$ of the time she spends $210. What is the aver-average amount she spends the rest of the time?

2.

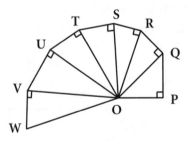

If OP = PQ = QR = ... = VW and OP is 1 with QP, RQ, SR, TS, UT, UV, WV correspondingly perpendicular to OP, OQ, OR, OS, OT, OU, OV, OW. Find the lengths of OP, OQ, OR, OS, OT, OU, OV, OW. How many have integral length?

3. Some artists have a special interest in the golden ratio where $\frac{AB}{BC} = \frac{BC}{AC}$. Calculate this ratio (see accompanying figure)

$$A \quad B \qquad C$$

4. Suppose $1 is deposited in the bank at 5% interest rate compounded annually. Find the amount in the bank after n years.

5. The earth is moving around the sun in an orbit, which is approximately a circle with a radius of 1.50×10^8 km. What is its speed?

6. Consider the regular tetrahedron $ABCD$ with equilateral triangular faces. Let E be the midpoint of $\overline{CD}$. Find AE (the length of the line from vertex A to the midpoint of the side on the opposite triangular face). What is the altitude of the tetrahedron?

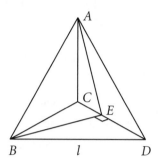

7. Suppose one person takes twice as long as another to do a job. If it takes them $5\frac{1}{2}$ hrs to do the job together, how long will it take each of them to do the job on her own?

8. The wheels shown are in contact and turn together without slipping. The gear ratio of S to T is 8 to 3. The gear ratio of R to S is 3 to 2. What is the rotation of T when R turns a full circle?

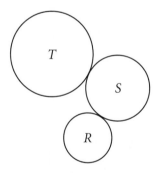

OF TERMS

Slope-intercept form of the line	$y = mx + b$; m is slope of line, b is y-intercept
Two-point form of a line	$y - y_1 = \dfrac{y_1 - y_2}{x_1 - x_2}(x - x_1)$; the line passes through (x_1, y_1) and (x_2, y_2)
Point-slope form of a line	$y - y_1 = m(x - x_1)$; the line has a slope of m and passes through (x_1, y_1)
Intercept form of the line	$\dfrac{x}{a} + \dfrac{y}{b} = 1$; a is the x-intercept of the line, while b is the y-intercept of the line
Standard form of the line	$Ax + By = C$, where coefficients of x and y are not both zero.

SECTION 2.3

LINEAR AND QUADRATIC EQUATIONS AND INEQUALITIES

The Equation of a Line

The line defines one of the most basic functions from the real numbers (x-axis) onto the real numbers (y-axis). Given two points (x_1, y_1), (x_2, y_2), determine the equation of the line passing through these two points.

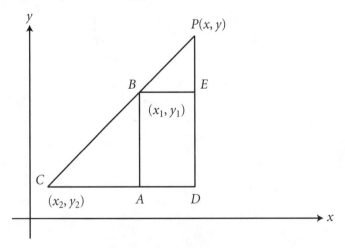

Let (x, y) be a point on the requisite line (see figure). If l is a straight line, then $\triangle BCA \sim \triangle PBE$ (similar): both are right triangles with $\angle C \cong \angle B$. Hence, the sides of the triangles are in proportion, or on simplification we have **two-point form of the equation of a line:**

$$(1) \quad y - y_2 = \left(\frac{y_1 - y_2}{x_1 - x_2}\right)(x - x_2)$$

Let $\dfrac{y_2 - y_1}{x_2 - x_1} = \dfrac{\Delta y}{\Delta x} = m$. We call this quantity the slope of the line. Equation (1), then, can be written as **point-slope form of equation of a line:**

$$(2) \quad y - y_2 = m(x - x_2)$$

Simplify equation (2) and we get the **slope-intercept form of the line:**

$$(3) \quad y = m(x - x_2) + y_2 \text{ or } y = mx + b$$

where m is the slope of the line and the point $(0, b)$ is on the line (b is the y intercept). Rewrite (3) by transposing and dividing through by $-b$ and get: $1 = \dfrac{x}{-b} + \dfrac{y}{b}$, or letting $a = \dfrac{-b}{m}$ we have the **intercept form of the line:**

$$(4) \quad 1 = \frac{x}{a} + \frac{y}{b}$$

Notice that this last equation can be written in the **standard form** as:

$$(5) \quad Ax + By = C$$

Systems of Equations

Given two lines $ax + by = c$, $dx + ey = f$. If the lines have a common point (the intersection point), it can be found by linear elimination: $ax + by = c \Rightarrow adx + bdy = cd$ and $dx + ey = f \Rightarrow adx + aey = af$, or, on subtraction, $y = \dfrac{af - cd}{ae - bd}$ and $x = \dfrac{ce - bf}{ae - bd}$.

Linear Inequalities

Consider the inequality $x + y < 3$. Graph the equation of the line $x + y = 3$ (see accompanying figure).

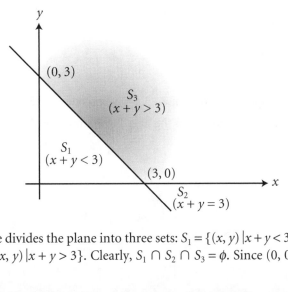

Notice that this line divides the plane into three sets: $S_1 = \{(x, y) \,|\, x + y < 3\}$; $S_2 = \{(x, y) \,|\, x + y = 3\}$; $S_3 = \{(x, y) \,|\, x + y > 3\}$. Clearly, $S_1 \cap S_2 \cap S_3 = \phi$. Since $(0, 0)$ satisfies the inequality, $x + y < 3$, S_1 defines the region of all points $\{(x, y) \mid x + y < 3\}$. To find out which of these regions corresponds to the given inequality, take a point in one of the regions and see if it satisfies the inequality. If one point in the region satisfies the inequality, all the points in the regions satisfy it. Similarly, if one point in a region does not satisfy the inequality, none of the points in the region satisfy the inequality.

Quadratic Functions

A second basic relationship between the real numbers is the *quadratic function*: $y = ax^2 + bx + c$. For the quadratic expression $y = ax^2 + bx + c$, solve for $x = \dfrac{-b \pm \sqrt{b^2 - 4ac}}{2a}$.

Determine whether the resulting curve is a curve upward (if y and a have the same sign) downward (if y and a have opposite sign). In general, if $b^2 - 4ac < 0$ the graph $y = ax^2 + bx + c$ never intersects the x-axis (no real roots for the equation); if $b^2 - 4ac = 0$, the graph $y = ax^2 + bx + c$ intersects the x-axis at one point (both roots of equation are equal); if $b^2 - 4ac > 0$, the graph $y = ax^2 + bx + c$ intersects the x-axis at two distinct points (both roots of the equation are real but not equal).

Polynomial Inequalities

Assume $f(x) = y$ is a polynomial function. The inequalities $f(x) < 0$ or $f(x) > 0$, $f(x) \leq 0$ or $f(x) \geq 0$ can be found by graphing $y = f(x)$, and determining for which values of x will the graph be above, below, or on the x-axis.

2.3 SOLVED PROBLEMS

1. Prove: Two lines $y = m_1 x + b_1$ and $y = m_2 x + b_2$ are parallel if $m_1 = m_2$, and $b_1 \neq b_2$.

   Solution: What we need to show that under these conditions $y = m_1 x + b_1$ and $y = m_2 x + b_2$ do not have a common solution. Solving this system by subtraction you find: $m_1 x + b_1 = m_2 x + b_2$ or $(m_1 - m_2)x = b_2 - b_1$. A solution does not exist if $m_1 = m_2$ and $b_1 \neq b_2$.

2. Sketch the line $y = 3x - 5$.

   Solution:

   Method 1: Slope of the line equals 3 and y-intercept is -5.

   Method 2: Find two points on the line. Two points are $(2, 1)$ and $(1, -2)$.

Both methods give the following graph:

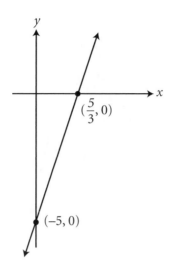

3. Show $p(ax + by + c) + q(a_1x + b_1y + c_1) = 0$ represents all lines passing through the intersection (x_0, y_0) of $ax + by + c = 0$ and $a_1x + b_1y + c_1 = 0$.

Solution: Notice $p(ax + by + c) + q(a_1x + b_1y + c_1) = 0$ is a linear equation in x and y. Hence, it represents a line. Also, notice that (x_0, y_0) lies on this line for any p and q, since $p \cdot 0 + q \cdot 0 = 0$.

4. Consider the following system of inequalities: (1) $y \le 2x + 4$; (2) $y \ge -x - 2$; (3) $y \le 4 - 4x$. Find the maximum and minimum of the expression $2x + 3y$ under these conditions.

Solution: Graph of the solution set for the three equations 1, 2, 3. **The Theorem of Linear Programming** asserts that the maximum and minimum of the linear expression $2x + 3y$ will occur at the vertices of the convex polygon formed by the three inequalities. In particular, the accompanying table indicates that the maximum occurs when $x = 0$ and $y = 4$; while the minimum occurs when $x = 2$ and $y = -4$:

Vertex	$2x + 3y$
$A(2, -4)$	-8
$B(-2, 0)$	-4
$C(0, 4)$	12

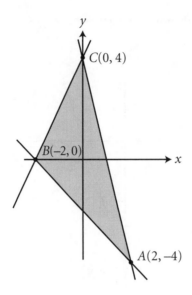

5. Determine the solution set for $-2(x^2 + 1) \geq x - 1$.

   Solution: $-2(x^2 + 1) \geq x - 1$ implies $2x^2 + x + 1 \leq 0$, which gives $x = \dfrac{-1 \pm \sqrt{1 - 4(2)}}{2(2)}$

   or $b^2 - 4ac < 0$. The graph $y = 2x^2 + x + 1$ never intersects the x-axis. Hence, no values for x satisfy the original inequality.

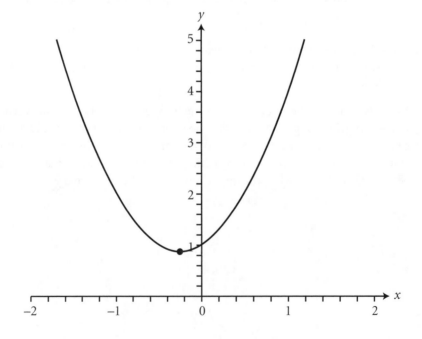

2.3 UNSOLVED PROBLEMS

1. For what values of k is the point $(2, -1)$ a solution for these two equations:

$$3x - y = 7?$$
$$2x + ky = 3?$$

2. For what value of k are there no solutions (inconsistent solutions) to the two equations in problem 1?

3. Solve the following systems for x and y in terms of a, b, and c:

$$\frac{x}{a+b+c} = \frac{2y(c-a)}{c^2 + cb - a^2 - ab} = 4$$

$$\frac{x(c-a)}{c^2 + cb - a^2 - ab} - \frac{y}{a+b+c} = -1$$

4. Find a solution to the system $ax + y - 2z = a$; $x + ay + 2z = 1$, $x + y = 1$.

5. Solve the following system of equations:

$$x + y + z = 2(a + b + c)$$

$$x + y - z = 2b$$

$$\frac{x}{a+b} + \frac{y}{b+c} + \frac{z}{a+c} = 3.$$

6. a) Factor the following radical expression: $a\sqrt{a} - ab - \sqrt{ab} + b\sqrt{b}$.
   b) Solve for x: $x^2 + \left(b + \sqrt{b} - a - \sqrt{a}\right)x + a\sqrt{a} - ab - \sqrt{ab} + b\sqrt{b} = 0$.

7. Solve:

$$\frac{x-a}{x+a} - \frac{x+a}{x-a} = \frac{x^2 - 12a^2}{x^2 - a^2} \quad \text{where } x^2 \neq a.$$

8. Solve: $x^2 + 2x - 3 > 0$.

9. Solve: $x^2 + 2x - 3 > 0$, and $2x - 3 > 0$.

10. Consider: $y = ax^2 + bx + c$ with $b^2 - 4ac > 0$. Suppose $a > 0$, $b < 0$ and $c > 0$.

   Determine the general shape of the parabola and the number of solutions of the equation when $y = 0$.

11. If x and y are whole numbers such that $x + y < 18$; $y > 2x$; $3y + x > 33$; $x \geq 0$.

   What is the solution to this system if $3x + y$ is to have a maximum value?

12. Find the equation of the line with slope of 1, passing through the origin, but having no values at $x = 1$ or $x = 2$.

13. Show that two lines $l_1 : y = m_1x + b_1$ and $l_2 : y = m_2x + b_2$ are perpendicular if and only if (iff) $m_1m_2 = -1$.

$\|x\|$	Distance of point x from the origin
$\|x+y\| \le \|x\| + \|y\|$	Triangle inequality
$\|x - a\| < \varepsilon$	All x at most ε units away from a; in other words, the distance between x and a is less than ε

SECTION 2.4

EQUATIONS AND INEQUALITIES INVOLVING ABSOLUTE VALUES, AND THE TRIANGLE INEQUALITY

Definition of Absolute Value

$$\text{Let } x \in R; \ |x| = x, x \ge 0; \ |x| = -x, x < 0$$

This definition is frequently misunderstood. It appears that $|x|$ has a negative value. In fact, the definition asserts that the absolute value of a number is always positive. The absolute value of a number is the number itself, when the number is nonnegative; it is the opposite of the number (i.e., it is positive) when the number is negative. From a geometric point of view, the absolute value of a number x on the number line is the number of units between x and the origin. Thus $|2| = 2$, $|-3| = 3$. The absolute value of a number gives only its distance from the origin, not its direction. Notice $|a - b| = |-(a - b)| = |b - a|$. The distance between two points on a number line is obtained by subtracting the coordinates of one of the numbers from the other, and taking the absolute value of this difference.

The Triangle Inequality

Notice that for any value of x, $-|x| \le x \le |x|$. Similarly, if $-|x| \le a \le |x|$ then $|a| \le |x|$. In general, for any x, y : $-|x| \le x \le |x|$ and $-|y| \le y \le |y|$. Adding these inequalities we find that: $-|x|-|y| \le x+y \le |x| + |y|$ or $(|x| + |y|) \le x+y \le |x| + |y|$.

We thus conclude: $|x + y| \le |x| + |y|$ (**Triangle Inequality**).

The triangle inequality has a two dimensional interpretation in light of vectors. If $\overrightarrow{v_1} = (a, b)$ defines the vector that starts at the origin and ends at point (a, b), while $\overrightarrow{v_2} = (c, d)$ defines the vector that starts at the origin and ends at (c, d), then $\left|\overrightarrow{v_1}\right|$ is the distance of (a, b) from the origin, and $\left|\overrightarrow{v_2}\right|$ is the distance of (c, d) from the origin.

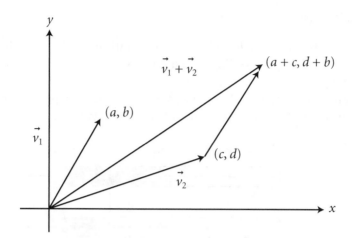

Under this interpretation the triangle inequality means $\left|\vec{v}_1 + \vec{v}_1\right| \le \left|\vec{v}_1\right| + \left|\vec{v}_2\right|$. Geometrically, the inequality implies that the length of the resultant vector $\vec{v}_1 + \vec{v}_2$ is less than the sum of the lengths of $\vec{v}_1$ and $\vec{v}_2$. Alternatively, it means that in a triangle formed by $\vec{v}_1, \vec{v}_2$ and $\vec{v}_1 + \vec{v}_2$, the sum of the lengths of the two sides of the triangle is greater than the length of the third side.

2.4 SOLVED PROBLEMS

1. Find the set determined by $|x - 2| \le 1$.

    Solution: $|x - 2| \le 1$ means $-1 \le x - 2 \le 1$ or $1 \le x \le 3$.

2. Solve $|3x - 7| = 8$.

    Solution: By definition of absolute value we have that $|3x - 7| = 8$ means $3x - 7 = 8$, or $3x - 7 = -8$. Hence, $x = 5$ or $-\dfrac{1}{3}$.

3. Solve $\left|\dfrac{3}{x} - 2\right| < 4$.

    Solution: The inequality is equivalent to $-4 < \dfrac{3}{x} - 2 < 4$. We have two cases.

    Suppose $x > 0$. We then conclude: $-4x < 3 - 2x < 4x$ or $-2x < 3 < 6x$, which means that $x > -\dfrac{3}{2}$ and $x > \dfrac{1}{2}$; equivalently, $x > \dfrac{1}{2}$.

    Suppose $x < 0$. Multiplying by $x > 0$ changes the sense of the inequalities. We then conclude: $-4x > 3 - 2x > 4x$ or $-2x > 3 > 6x$, which means that $x < -\dfrac{3}{2}$ and $x < \dfrac{3}{2}$; equivalently $x < -\dfrac{3}{2}$. Thus the solution sets are the union of $\left(-\infty, -\dfrac{3}{2}\right)$ and $\left(\dfrac{1}{2}, \infty\right)$.

4. Solve $x^2 < 8x - 15$.

Solution: The technique for solving this quadratic inequality resembles a solution of two linear inequalities (in this sense it is similar to solving an absolute value equation). Notice that $x^2 < 8x - 15$ means that $x^2 - 8x + 15 < 0$ or $(x - 3)(x - 5) < 0$. The following graph of each of the separate linear factors represent where each factor is 0 (a point), greater than 0 (black), less than 0 (white):

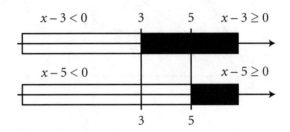

Notice that the value of the equality will be less than zero for $3 < x < 5$, when one factor is positive and the other factor is negative.

5. Solve for x, if $|x - 1| = 1 - x$.

Solution: By definition of the absolute value $|a| = -a$ when $a < 0$. Hence, $x - 1 < 0$ or $x < 1$.

6. What can you say about x, if $|x - 1| \le 1 - x$?

Solution: If $|x| \le a$ for $a > 0$, it means that $-a \le x \le a$. Hence, $-(1 - x) \le (x - 1) \le (1 - x)$ or $-1 + x \le x - 1 \le 1 - x$. In particular, $-1 + x \le x - 1$ (always true) and $x - 1 \le 1 - x$ or $2x \le 2$, which means $x \le 1$. The inequality is true when $x \le 1$.

7. Explain why the statement $|x| = \sqrt{x^2}$ is true.

Solution: $\sqrt{a}$ is defined as the principle or positive square root of a; $\sqrt{x^2}$ is the positive square root of x^2 or $|x|$.

8. Describe the solution set $|x - a| \le 2$.

Solution: By definition of absolute value, $|x - a| \le 2$ means $-2 \le x - a \le 2$ or $-2 + a \le x \le 2 + a$. Hence, all x two units or less away from a.

9. Prove for the real numbers a, b and c: $|a - b| \le |a - c| + |b - c|$.

Solution: It follows by the triangle inequality that $|x + y| \le |x| + |y|$. Let $x = a - c$ and $y = c - b$, then $x + y = a - b$. It follows that $|a - b| \le |a - c| + |c - b|$ or $|a - b| \le |a - c| + |b - c|$.

2.4 UNSOLVED PROBLEMS

1. What can you say about the number x, if $|2x| \geq 2x$?

2. Suppose $a < b$. Which follows?

   a) $\dfrac{a}{3} < \dfrac{b}{3}$

   c) $a + 5 \leq b + 4$

   b) $\sqrt{|a|} < \sqrt{|b|}$

   d) $a^{-1} > b^{-1}$

3. Solve for x:

$$\left|\frac{1}{x}\right| < 2$$

4. Solve for x:

$$\left|\frac{1}{x} - 2\right| < 2$$

5. Show that $||a| - |b|| \leq |a - b|$.

6. Describe the interval $|x - a| < \varepsilon$.

7. Describe the interval $|x - a| \leq \varepsilon$.

8. Describe the interval $0 < |x - a| < \varepsilon$.

9. Solve $x^2 < 3x + 40$.

10. Solve $|x - r_1|(x - r_2)(x - r_3) \leq 0$.

CHAPTER THREE

Geometry

Most individuals study Euclidean geometry in secondary school and then never take a formal class in the subject again. Although a formal mathematics course in geometry in the university is not usually offered, geometry remains one of the cornerstones of mathematics. Geometric relations give clarity to a great variety of subjects in both classical and modern mathematics. In fact, there is hardly an area of mathematics in which you cannot find geometry.

This chapter looks at geometry from classical Euclidean and from transformational perspectives. It explores problems useful to teachers both in terms of mathematics they might use in their classrooms, and more advanced problems that they may find interesting in their own right. Much of the Euclidean geometry in this chapter may be found in secondary texts; the transformational geometry may also be found in secondary, as well as college algebra, discrete mathematics, or even standard calculus texts.

$\overleftrightarrow{AB}$	A line passing through points A and point B
$\overline{AB}$	A line segment starting at A and ending at B
AB	The length of line segment $\overline{AB}$
$\overrightarrow{AC}$	Ray AC consists of $\overline{AC}$ and all other points P such that C is between A and P
$\angle ABC$	Angle ABC or $\overrightarrow{BA} \cup \overrightarrow{BC}$
$m\angle ABC$	The measure of the number of degrees in $\angle ABC$
A and B are Complementary angles	$m\angle A + m\angle B = 90°$
A and B are supplementary angles	$m\angle A + m\angle B = 180°$
A is an acute angle	$m\angle A < 90°$
A is a right angle	$m\angle A = 90°$
A is an obtuse angle	$90° < m\angle A < 180°$
A is a straight angle	$m\angle A = 180°$
Three points A, B, C are collinear	A, B, C line on a straight line
Lines l_1, l_2 and l_3 are concurrent	l_1, l_2 and l_3 pass through the same point
Lines l_1 and l_2 are parallel ($l_1 \parallel l_2$)	l_1 and l_2 are in the same plane and never intersect (segments of $\parallel$ lines are $\parallel$)
Lines l_1 and l_2 are perpendicular ($l_1 \perp l_2$)	l_1 and l_2 intersect at right angles
Alternate interior angles	If two parallel lines are cut by a transversal the angles that occur between the two parallel lines on either side of the transversal
Corresponding angles	If two parallel lines are cut by a transversal the angles that occur in the same positions on the same side of the transversal
Isosceles triangle	A triangle with two equal sides
Equilateral triangle	A triangle with three equal sides
Median of a triangle	The line that connects a vertex of the triangle to the midpoint of the opposite side
Inscribed circle for a triangle	A circle drawn inside a triangle, tangent to (one point in common with) each side of the triangle
Circumscribed circle around a triangle	A circle drawn around a triangle with the vertices of the triangle on the circle

SECTION 3.1

PARALLEL AND PERPENDICULAR LINES, SPECIAL TRIANGLES AND PARTS OF TRIANGLES

Any discussion of parallelism deserves at least a remark on one of the most famous postulates in mathematics. One of the key Euclidian assumptions is the Parallel Postulate, which is crucial to all the material in this section. Euclid assumes that through a point not on a given line, one and only one line can be drawn parallel to the given line. Intuitively, this postulate sounds more like a theorem than a simple statement of fact (e.g., two points determine a line). In fact, for over a thousand years this postulate remained "suspect," until in the nineteenth century when alternative geometries were created that do not assume the truth of this postulate. In fact, non-Euclidean geometries may better describe the actual nature of space than Euclidean geometry! (Unfortunately, non-Euclidean geometries remain beyond scope of this book.)

The following table gives some basic information about angles in classical Euclidean space.

TABLE 3.1	
Two complementary angles	Angles whose measures have a sum of 90°
Two supplementary angles	Angles whose measures have the sum of 180°
An acute angle	An angle θ such that $0° < m\angle\theta < 90°$
An obtuse angle	An angle θ such that $0° < m\angle\theta < 180°$
A reflex angle	An angle θ such that $180° < m\angle\theta < 360°$
A right angle	An angle θ such that $m\angle\theta = 90°$
A straight angle	An angle θ such that $m\angle\theta = 180°$
Three points are collinear	Three points A, B, C are such that $m\angle ABC = 180°$
Lines are concurrent	Three or more lines pass through the same point

Parallel Lines

Parallel lines are lines that lie in the same plane but never meet. Three types of angles occur when two parallel lines are cut by a third line, which is called a transversal.

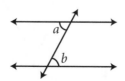

Alternate interior angles $\angle a \cong \angle b$

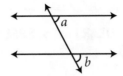

Corresponding angles $\angle a \cong \angle b$

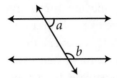

Interior angles $m\angle a + m\angle b = 180°$

If two parallel lines are cut by a transversal, we postulate that alternate interior angles and corresponding angles are equal (we also assume that if these quantities are equal then the lines are parallel). For example, to find the number of degrees in $\angle A$ subtract the sum of 20° and 40° from 360°.

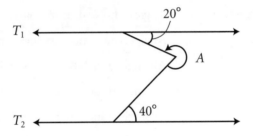

Triangles

Consider $\triangle ABC$ where $\overline{BC}$ is extended to D and $\overleftrightarrow{CE}$ is parallel to $\overleftrightarrow{BA}$.

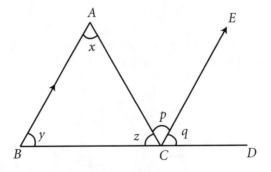

Notice $m\angle x = m\angle p$ (alternate interior angles) and $m\angle y = m\angle q$ (corresponding angles). Hence, $m\angle z + m\angle p + m\angle q = 180°$ and $m\angle x + m\angle y + m\angle z = 180°$. In other words, the sum of the angles of a triangle is 180°.

Special Triangles

- ▧ A triangle with all sides equal is an *equilateral triangle*.
- ▧ A triangle with two sides equal is an *isosceles triangle*.
- ▧ In an isosceles triangle, the angles opposite equal sides (base angles) are equal (see Solved Problems). All angles in an equilateral triangle are equal (see Solved Problems).

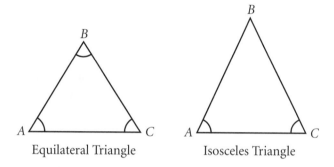

Equilateral Triangle   Isosceles Triangle

3.1 SOLVED PROBLEMS

1. Calculate the angle turned by the minute hand of a 12-hour clock in 100 minutes.

   Solution: 100 minutes $= 60$ minutes $+ 40$ minutes $= 360° + \frac{2}{3}(360°) = 360° + 240° = 600°$.

2. If $\overline{CE}$ is parallel to $\overline{BA}$ find $m\angle BCE$ and $m\angle ACD$.

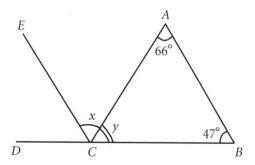

Solution: $m\angle BCE = m\angle x + m\angle y$; $m\angle x = 66°$ (since $\overline{EC} \parallel \overline{AB}$); $m\angle y = 180° - (47° + 66°) = 67°$. Hence, $m\angle BCE = 66° + 67° = 133°$.

Notice that $\angle ACD$ is supplementary to $\angle y$, which means it is 113°.

3. Given $\angle AEC$ with EB and EC drawn as indicated.

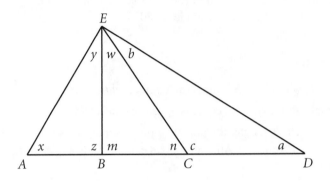

Show:

   i) $m\angle x + m\angle a + m\angle y + m\angle w + m\angle b$

$$= \frac{1}{2}(m\angle z + m\angle m + m\angle n + m\angle c).$$

   ii) $m\angle x + m\angle y + m\angle n = m\angle a + m\angle b + m\angle m$

Solution:

   i) Notice: $(m\angle z + m\angle m) + (m\angle n + m\angle c) = 180° + 180°$
             $m\angle x + (m\angle y + m\angle w + m\angle b) + m\angle a = 180°$

Hence, $m\angle x + m\angle a + m\angle y + m\angle w + m\angle b$

$$= \frac{1}{2}(m\angle z + m\angle m + m\angle n + m\angle c).$$

   ii) Notice: $m\angle x + (m\angle y + m\angle w) + m\angle n = 180°$ and $m\angle a + m\angle b + m\angle w + m\angle m = 180°$. Hence, $m\angle x + m\angle y + m\angle n = m\angle a + m\angle b + m\angle m$.

4. Prove: Base angles of an isosceles triangle are congruent.

Solution: Let $AB = AC$ in $\triangle ABC$. Draw $\overline{BD}$ bisecting $\overline{AC}$, notice $\triangle ADB$ and $\triangle BDC$ have three pairs of equal sides. Hence, they are congruent. It follows that $\angle A \cong \angle C$.

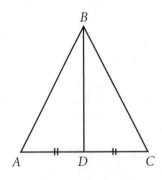

5. Show that all angles of an equilateral triangle are equal. Hence, each angle is 60°.

   Solution: Since an equilateral triangle is an isosceles triangle with all sides equal, it follows that any angle of an equilateral triangle may be considered as a base angle. Hence, all angles are equal since base angles must be equal. For any angle A in an equilateral triangle $3(m\angle A) = 180°$ or $m\angle A = 60°$.

3.1 UNSOLVED PROBLEMS

1. The hour hand and minute hand of a 12-hour clock exactly overlap at noon. Find, in minutes, the time before they overlap exactly again.

2. Given isosceles triangle $\triangle ABC$ (with $\overline{AB} \cong \overline{BC}$) with inscribed equilateral triangle $\triangle DEF$. Find a relationship between a, b, c.

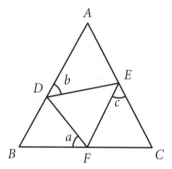

3. If an exterior angle of $\triangle ABC$ is 110° and $m\angle A = m\angle B - 5°$, find the angles in $\triangle ABC$.

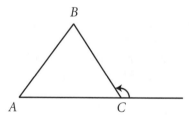

4. In $\triangle ABC$, $\overline{AC} \cong \overline{CD}$ and $m\angle CAB - m\angle ABC = 80°$. Find $m\angle BAD$.

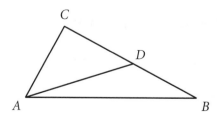

ΔABC ~ ΔA′B′C′	Two triangles are similar if their sides are in proportion
Law of Pythagoras	In a right triangle the square of the hypotenuse equals the sum of the squares of the two legs

SECTION 3.2

SIMILAR TRIANGLES AND THE LAW OF PYTHAGORAS

Similar Triangles

Definition: Two triangles are similar if the lengths of their corresponding sides are in proportion; alternatively, two triangles are similar if two angles of one triangle are congruent to two angles of the other triangle.

 Theorem 1: In a right triangle, the perpendicular from the right angle to the hypotenuse divides the triangle into two triangles that are similar to each other and to the original triangle.

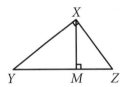

Given: $\triangle XYZ$ is a right triangle, $\angle YXZ$ is a right angle, with $\overline{XM}$ perpendicular from X to $\overline{YZ}$. Prove: $\triangle XYZ \sim \triangle MYX \sim \triangle MXZ$.

 Notice that $\angle YXZ \cong \angle YMX$, and $\angle Y$ is common. Therefore, $\triangle XYZ$, and $\triangle MYX$ are similar. By the same argument $\triangle MXZ \cong \triangle XYZ$. Hence, triangles $\triangle XYZ$, $\triangle MYX$, and $\triangle MXZ$ are similar.

 Corollary 1: The square of either of the sides that contain the right angle is equal to the product of the hypotenuse and the segment of the hypotenuse adjacent to the side.

Since $\triangle XYZ \sim \triangle MYX$; $\dfrac{XY}{MY} = \dfrac{YZ}{YX}$ $\therefore XY^2 = YZ \cdot YM$. Similarly, $XZ^2 = YZ \cdot MZ$. This corollary leads to a proof of the **Law of Pythagoras:**

$$XY^2 = XZ^2 = YZ \cdot YM + YZ \cdot MZ = YZ(YM + MZ) = YZ^2$$

3.2 SOLVED PROBLEMS

1. Show the square of the perpendicular from the right angle to the hypotenuse is equal to the product of the segments into which it divides the hypotenuse.

   Solution: Since $\triangle MYX \sim \triangle MXZ$, it follows that $\dfrac{MX}{MZ} = \dfrac{MY}{MX}$, or $MX^2 = MY \cdot MZ$.

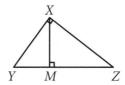

2. Given that an angle inserted in a semicircle is a right angle. Let $ABCD$ be a rectangle; let $\overline{BH}$ be an extension of $\overline{AB}$ so that $BH \cong BC$. Show that the square with side PB has an area equal to the area of $ABCD$, where $\overline{PB}$ is the extension of BC that meets the semicircle with diameter $\overline{AH}$. (Assume that a triangle inscribed in a semi circle is a right triangle. See Section 3.4)

   Solution: Since P is a point on the semicircle with diameter $\overline{AH}$, it follows that $\angle APH$ is a right angle. Hence, $PB^2 = AB \cdot BH$. But $\overline{BH} \cong \overline{BC}$. This means that $PB^2 = AB \cdot BC$.

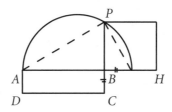

3. Assume that $\triangle ABC$ is such that $m\angle BAC = 90°$, $AB = 255$, $AC = 136$ and $\overline{AD}$ is an altitude. Calculate AD, BD and CD.

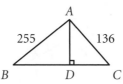

   Solution:

   Notice $AD \times BC = AB \times AC$; $BC = \sqrt{(255)^2 + (136)^2} = 289$; $AD \times 289 = 255 \times 136$

   $$\therefore AD = \frac{255 \times 136}{289} = \frac{17 \cdot 15 \times 17 \cdot 8}{17^2} = 120.$$

   $$BA = BD \times BC; (255)^2 = BD \times (17)^2 \therefore BD = \frac{17^2 \cdot 15^2}{17^2} = 225. \text{ Finally,}$$

   $$CA^2 = CD \times CB; (136)^2 = CD \times 17^2 \therefore CD = \frac{8^2 \cdot 17^2}{17^2} = 64.$$

4. Suppose $\triangle ABC$ is a right triangle $AB = \sqrt{7}$, and $BC = \dfrac{1}{2}\sqrt{7}$, with altitude BM. Show that $5BM = 2AC$.

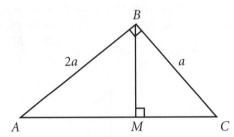

Solution: Let $AB = 2a$ and $BC = a$. By the Law of Pythagoras $AC^2 = 4a^2 + a^2 = 5a^2$. In other words the sides in $\triangle ABC$ are in the ratio of $1 : 2 : \sqrt{5}$. We have three similar triangles $\triangle AMB \sim \triangle ABC \sim \triangle BMC$ with $BM = \dfrac{2a\sqrt{5}}{5}$ and $AC = a\sqrt{5}$. Notice that $5BM = 2AC$.

5. The ratio of the legs of a right triangle is $1 : 3$. Find the ratio of the segments of the hypotenuse made by a perpendicular drawn to it from the vertex.

Solution: Let the height be h, one of the segments be x and the other $c - x$, where a and b are the legs of the right triangle and c is its hypotenuse. We have $a^2 = xc$ and

$$b^2 = (c - x)c, \text{ or } \frac{x}{c - x} = \frac{xc}{(c - x)c} = \frac{a^2}{b^2}. \text{ But } \frac{a}{b} = \frac{1}{3}. \text{ Hence, } \frac{a^2}{b^2} = \frac{1}{9} \text{ and } \frac{x}{c - x} = \frac{1}{9}.$$

3.2 UNSOLVED PROBLEMS

1. Show that the 45°, 45°, 90° right triangle has sides in proportion of $1 : 1 : \sqrt{2}$. Show the 30°, 60°, 90° right triangle has sides in proportion of $1 : \sqrt{3} : 2$.

2. Given $\angle C = 90°$, $AD = DB$, $\overline{DE} \perp \overline{AB}$, $AB = 20$ and $AC = 12$. Find DE.

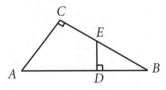

3. Let $ABCD$ be a square, P, Q, R, S are the midpoints of sides $\overline{AB}, \overline{BC}, \overline{CD}$, and $\overline{DA}$. Show: $SP^2 + PQ^2 = SQ^2$.

4. A right triangle $\triangle XYZ$ with right angle $\angle X$, and $XY = 5$, $YZ = 13$. Drop a perpendicular to YZ from X, which intersects YZ at D. Find the lengths of the two parts into which $\overline{YZ}$ is divided by $\overline{XD}$.

5. In $\triangle XYZ$, with right $\angle X$, and altitude $\overline{XM} : YZ = 4MZ$. Find $m\angle MZX$; $m\angle MXZ$.

6. A regular octagon is to be formed by cutting congruent isosceles right triangles from the corners of a square. If the square has the side of 10, find the length of the hypotenuse of each isosceles triangle.

GLOSSARY	**OF TERMS**
≅	Figures are congruent if they have the same size and shape
Δ***ABC*** ≅ Δ***DEF***	Two triangles are congruent
SSS ≅ **SSS**	Three sides of one triangle are congruent to the three sides of another triangle (the triangles are congruent)
SAS ≅ **SAS**	Two sides and an included angle of one triangle are congruent to two sides and included angle of another triangle (the triangles are congruent)
ASA ≅ **ASA**	Two angles and an included side of one triangle are congruent to two angles and an included side of another triangle (the triangles are congruent)
hy.leg ≅ **hy.leg**	The hypotenuse and leg of one right triangle are congruent to the hypotenuse and leg of another triangle (the triangles are congruent)
AAS ≅ **AAS**	Two angles and a nonincluded side of one triangle are congruent to two angles and a nonincluded side of another triangle (the triangles are congruent)

SECTION 3.3

TRIANGLES, QUADRILATERALS, AND POLYGONS

This section deals with lengths of sides, measures of angles, congruent triangles, quadrilaterals and polygons.

Triangles

Triangles are congruent according to SSS (three sides congruent), SAS (two sides and an angle included congruent), ASA (two angles and a side included congruent) or in the case of right triangles, hy.leg (the hypotenuse and one leg congruent). The method of AAS (two angles and a side) is actually ASA (see Solved Problems).

Parallelograms

A parallelogram is a quadrilateral with opposite sides parallel. It follows that opposite sides are congruent; opposite angles are congruent; each set of opposite sides are congruent and parallel; diagonals bisect each other (see Solved Problems).

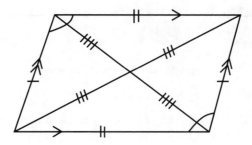

Rhombus

A rhombus is a parallelogram with equal sides and perpendicular diagonals (see Solved Problems).

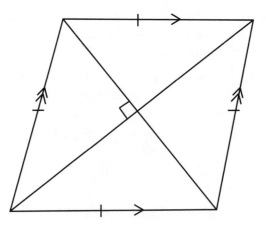

Trapezoid/Isosceles Trapezoid

A trapezoid is a quadrilateral that has two parallel sides and two nonparallel sides. In an isosceles trapezoid the two nonparallel sides are equal in length. In an isosceles trapezoid the diagonals are congruent (see Solved Problems).

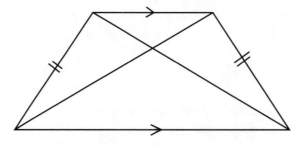

Polygons

A convex figure is a figure such that any line segment, which connects any two points on the figure, lies totally within the figure. A polygon is a convex plane figure with a specific number of sides consecutively connected to each other (some books allow polygons also to be concave). The sum of the measures of the angles in a regular polygon of n sides (all sides are equal) is: $(n-2)180°$. In a regular polygon of n sides, the measurement of one interior angle in degrees is given by $\dfrac{(n-2)180°}{n}$; the measurement of an exterior angle of a regular polygon of n sides is $\dfrac{360°}{n}$ (see Solved Problems).

3.3 SOLVED PROBLEMS

1. Prove that AAS is a method for showing that two triangles are congruent.

   Solution: The sum of the angles of a triangle is 180°. If two angles of two triangles are equal, then the third angles are also equal. The two triangles are congruent by ASA ≅ ASA.

2. If a quadrilateral has opposite sides parallel, show:

   (a) opposite sides are equal.

   Solution: Consider parallelogram $ABCD$ with $\overline{AB} \,\|\, \overline{DC}$ and $\overline{AD} \,\|\, \overline{BC}$. Draw $\overline{AC}$. Notice $\angle 1 \cong \angle 2$, $\angle 3 \cong \angle 4$ (two pairs of alternate interior angles). Hence, $\triangle ADC \cong \triangle ABC$ (ASA ≅ ASA); $\overline{AB} \cong \overline{DC}$ and $\overline{AD} \cong \overline{BC}$ (corresponding parts of ≅ triangles).

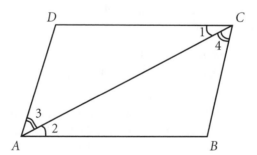

   (b) Opposite sides are ≅. The same argument as in 2(a).

   (c) Each pair of opposite sides are ≅ and ‖. This result follows immediately from 2(a).

   (d) Diagonals bisect each other. Consider parallelogram $ABCD$ with $\overline{AB} \,\|\, \overline{DC}$. In the following figures draw diagonals $\overline{AC}$ and $\overline{DB}$ which intersect at P. Notice $\angle 1 \cong \angle 2$ and $\angle 3 \cong \angle 4$ (two pairs of alternate interior angles); $\overline{AB} \cong \overline{DC}$ (see 2a). Hence, $\triangle APB \cong \triangle CPD$ (ASA ≅ ASA); it follows that $\overline{PB} \cong \overline{PD}$ and $\overline{AP} \cong \overline{PC}$ (corresponding parts of ≅ triangles).

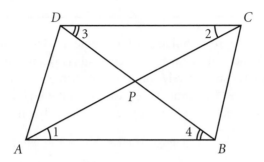

3. Given rhombus *ABCD*, show its diagonals are perpendicular.

Solution: Since *ABCD* is a parallelogram $\overline{AP} \cong \overline{PC}$ (see 2d); $\overline{AB} \cong \overline{BC}$ (definition of rhombus) and $\overline{PB} \cong \overline{PB}$ (identity). Hence, (SSS ≅ SSS); so ∠1 ≅ ∠2 (corresponding parts of congruent triangles). But ∠1 and ∠2 are supplementary, since their non-adjacent sides form a straight line, so $m\angle 1 = m\angle 2 = 90°$. Diagonal $\overline{AC} \perp \overline{BD}$

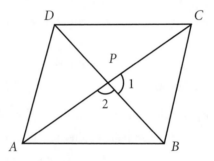

4. Given quadrilateral *ABCD* with one set of sides $\overline{AB} \| \overline{CD}$ and $\overline{AB} \cong \overline{CD}$. Prove *ABCD* is a parallelogram.

Solution: Draw diagonal $\overline{AC}$. Notice ∠1 ≅ ∠2 since angles are alternate interior angles; $\overline{AC} \cong \overline{AC}$, (identity) and $\overline{AB} \cong \overline{CD}$ (given). Hence, △*ABC* ≅ △*CAD* (SAS ≅ SAS). It follows that ∠3 ≅ ∠4 (corresponding parts of ≅ triangles). Notice $\overline{AD} \| \overline{CB}$, (if two lines are cut by a transversal so that alternate interior angles are equal, then the lines are parallel). Thus, quadrilateral *ABCD* is a parallelogram (opposite sides are parallel).

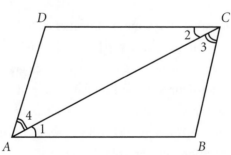

5. Given trapezoid $ABCD$ with $\overline{AB} \parallel \overline{CD}$ and $\overline{AC} \cong \overline{BD}$. Assume parallel lines are equidistant everywhere, prove that $\overline{AD} \cong \overline{CB}$.

   Solution: Drop perpendiculars $\overline{CE}$ and $\overline{DF}$ perpendicular to $\overline{AB}$.

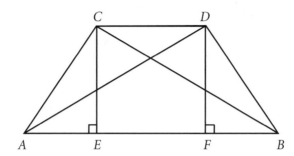

   Notice $\overline{CE} \cong \overline{DF}$ (parallel lines are equidistant everywhere); $\triangle ACE \cong \triangle BDF$ (hy.leg $\cong$ hy.leg). Hence, $\angle CAE \cong \angle DBF$. Notice $\overline{AB} \cong \overline{AB}$ (identity) and $\overline{AC} \cong \overline{DB}$ (given). It follows that $\triangle ACB \cong \triangle BDA$ (SAS $\cong$ SAS). This means $\overline{AD} \cong \overline{CB}$ (corresponding parts of $\cong$ triangles).

6. Show the number of degrees in a hexagon is $(6-2)180°$.

   Solution: Divide the hexagon into four different triangles. Let one vertex of the hexagon serve as a vertex for each of the triangles. Since the number of degrees in each triangle is $180°$, the number of degrees in the hexagon is $(6-2)180°$.

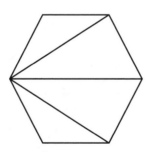

7. Prove that the number of degrees in an interior angle of a regular polygon with n sides is $\dfrac{(n-2)180°}{n}$.

   Solution: The number of degrees in a polygon with n sides is $(n-2)180°$ (Problem 6). Thus, the number of degrees in an interior angle of a regular polygon of n sides is $\dfrac{(n-2)180°}{n}$.

9. Show that the number of degrees in an exterior angle of a regular polygon with n sides is $\dfrac{360°}{n}$.

Solution: Extend one of the sides of the polygon. By problem 8, the number of degrees in one interior $\angle A$ is $\dfrac{(n-2)180°}{n}$. Hence, the number of degrees in exterior $\angle 1$ is $180° - \dfrac{(n-2)180°}{n} = \dfrac{180°n - 180°n + 360°}{n} = \dfrac{360°}{n}$.

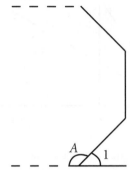

10. Prove that the angle bisector of the two intersecting lines defines the locus (path) of points equidistant from these lines.

    Solution: Consider t_1 and t_2 intersecting at point P; let t be the unique angle bisector of the resultant angle formed by t_1 and t_2. Take any point X on the angle bisector. Drop a $\perp$ from X to t_1 and t_2 that intersects at P_1 and P_2. Notice that

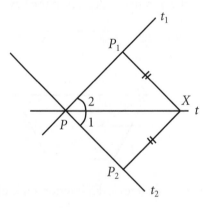

    $m\angle XP_1P = m\angle XP_2P = 90°$; $\overline{PX} \cong \overline{PX}$ by identity; $\angle 1 \cong \angle 2$ since t is the angle bisector. It follows that $\triangle PXP_1 \cong \triangle PXP_2$ by AAS $\cong$ AAS. This means $P_1X = P_2X$ (a similar argument holds for the line that bisects the angle supplementary to $\angle P_1PP_2$).

11. Show that the intersection point of the angle bisectors of a triangle is the center of the inscribed circle for that triangle. (Assume: The locus of points equidistant from two intersecting lines is the pair of angle bisectors, which bisect the angles formed at the intersection of these line; see Table 3.2.)

Solution: Suppose the internal angle bisectors of ∠B and ∠C meet at *I*. Let $\overline{IX}$, $\overline{IY}$, $\overline{IZ}$ be perpendicular to the sides of the triangle. Hence,

$$IX = IZ \ (I \text{ is on bisector of } B)$$
$$IX = IY \ (I \text{ is on bisector of } C).$$

Therefore, $IZ = IY$ and consequently *I* is on the bisector of the angle *A*. This implies that a circle can be drawn with center *I* and radius *IX* touches the sides of the triangle. In other words, the three angle bisectors of a triangle are concurrent and meet at the center of the inscribed circle.

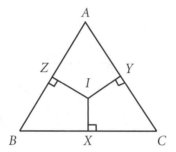

3.3 UNSOLVED PROBLEMS

1. Given regular pentagon *ABCDE*. Find $m\angle 1$.

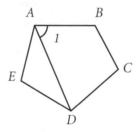

2. If 5, 12, 13 are legs of a right triangle, find the length of the radius of the inscribed circle. Given right triangle with legs *x*, *y*, find the radius of the inscribed circle.

3. Find: $m\angle x$

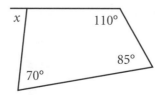

4. $\triangle XYZ$ and $\triangle PQR$ are $\cong$ and isosceles $QR \parallel YZ$ ($XY = XZ$); $m\angle X = 30°$. Find $m\angle A$.

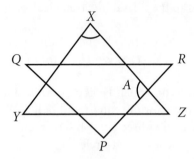

5. Given rhombus $ABCD$ with diagonals 10 and 24. Find the length of one of its sides.

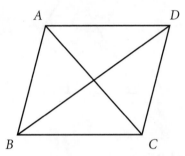

6. Prove that if a point is equidistant from two intersecting lines, it lies on an angle bisector of these lines.

7. Prove: The perpendicular bisectors of the sides of the triangle meet at one point, which is the center of its circumscribed circle.

Circle	The locus of points at a fixed distance (radius) from a fixed point
Chord	A line segment joining two points on the circle
Diameter	A chord passing through the center of the circle
Radius	One-half the diameter (alternately the line segment that connects the center of the circle to a point on the circle)
Secant	A line intersecting a circle at two points
Tangent	A line intersecting a circle at one point
Central angle	An angle with its vertex at the center of a circle
Inscribed angle	An angle with a vertex on the circle, whose sides contain chords of the circle
Inscribed polygon (circumscribed circle)	A polygon with all its vertices on a circle
Circumscribed polygon (inscribed circle)	A polygon that is drawn around a circle so that all sides of the polygon are tangent to the circle
Circumference	The perimeter of a circle

SECTION 3.4

CIRCLES

The locus of the points equidistant from a fixed point defines a circle; the fixed point is the center of the circle, the fixed distance is the radius of the circle. A chord is a line segment connecting two points on the circle. The diameter is a line through the center of the circle. A secant is a line that contains a chord, which intersects a circle at two points. A tangent is a line, which has one point in common with the circle.

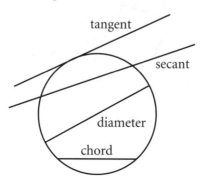

Angles and Circles

A central angle is an angle with its vertex at the center of the circle. The measure of a central angle is equal to the measure of its intercepted arc. An inscribed angle is an angle with its vertex on the circle, whose sides are chords of the circle.

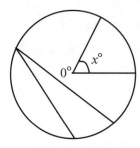

Theorem 1: The measure of an inscribed angle is one half of the intercepted arc.

To show this result we examine three cases. Case I: One side of the inscribed angle passes through the center of the circle. Notice that $\triangle AOC$ is isosceles. But $\angle COB$ equals $\angle A + \angle C$ ($\angle COB$ and $\angle A + \angle C$ are supplementary to $\angle AOC$). Hence, $m\angle COB = 2m\angle A$ or $m\angle A = \frac{1}{2}m\angle COB = \frac{1}{2}arc\,CB$.

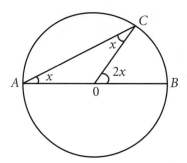

Case II: When the diameter of the circle lies inside the angle. The result follows from the distributive law.

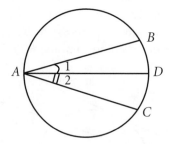

$$m\angle CAB = m\angle 1 + \angle 2;\; m\angle CAB = \frac{1}{2}arc\,DB + \frac{1}{2}arc\,CD = \frac{1}{2}arc\,CB.$$

Case III: When the diameter of the circle lies outside the angle. This result follows from the distributive law.

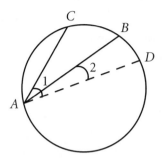

$$m\angle CAB = m\angle 1 - m\angle 2;\ m\angle CAB = \frac{1}{2}(arc\,CD - arc\,BD) = \frac{1}{2}arc\,CB.$$

Theorem 2: An angle formed by the two chords is measured by the average of the arcs formed by the chords.

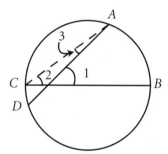

Draw $\overline{CA}$ and notice $m\angle 1 = m\angle 2 + m\angle 3$. But $m\angle 2 = \frac{1}{2}arc\,AB$, while $m\angle 3 = \frac{1}{2}arc\,CD$; Hence, $m\angle 1 = \frac{1}{2}arc\,AB + \frac{1}{2}arc\,CD$ or $m\angle 1 = \frac{1}{2}(arc\,AB + arc\,CD)$.

Theorem 3: An angle formed by two secants is measured by one-half the difference of their corresponding arcs.

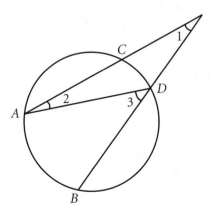

To prove this result draw $\overline{AD}$. Notice that $m\angle 1 + m\angle 2 = m\angle 3$ or $m\angle 1 = m\angle 3 - m\angle 2$. But $m\angle 2 = \frac{1}{2} arc\, CD$ and $\angle 3 = \frac{1}{2} arc\, AB$. Hence, $m\angle 1 = \frac{1}{2} arc\, AB - \frac{1}{2} arc\, CD = \frac{1}{2}(arc\, AB - arc\, CD)$. We can also show that the angle formed by a tangent and a secant, or two tangents will be measured by one-half the difference of the intercepted arcs (see Solved Problems).

Circles and Line Segments

Two secants are drawn to a circle from an external point. The product of one secant with length a and its external segment with length s equals the product of the length of the other secant with length b and its external segment with length t: $as = bt$.

Draw $\overline{AD}$ and $\overline{BC}$. Notice that $\angle P \cong \angle P, m\angle A = \frac{1}{2} arc\, BD$ and $m\angle C = \frac{1}{2} arc\, BD$. Hence, $\triangle ADP \sim \triangle CBP$, which means the sides of these triangles are in proportion: $\frac{a}{b} = \frac{b}{s}$ or $as = bt$.

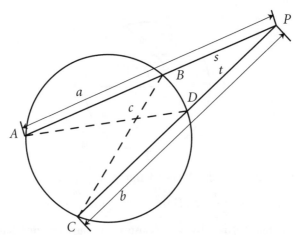

In a similar way we can show that the square of a tangent drawn to a circle from point P, equals the product of the secant drawn from point P and its external segment.

3.4 SOLVED PROBLEMS

1. If the angles of a triangle inscribed in a circle are X, Y, Z, find the ratio of the minor arcs cut off by the sides of the triangle on the circle.

   Solution: Since the ratio of the measures of the angles is $m\angle X : m\angle Y : m\angle Z$, the ratio of the measures of the minor arcs is $m\angle X : m\angle Y : m\angle Z$.

2. A cyclic quadrilateral is a quadrilateral whose vertices lie on the circumference of a circle. Show that opposite angles in a cyclic quadrilateral are supplementary.

Solution: Consider $m\angle B = \frac{1}{2} arc\,ADC$ and $m\angle D = \frac{1}{2} arc\,ABC$. But $arc\,ADC + arc\,ABC = 360°$. Hence, $m\angle B + m\angle D = \frac{1}{2}(360°) = 180°$.

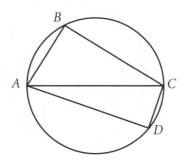

3. Find $m\angle A$ in the following figure.

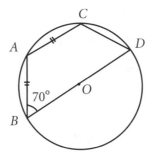

Solution: Notice that $arc\,ACD = 140°$ and $arc\,BAD = 180°$. Hence, $arc\,AB = 40°$. This implies that $arc\,AC = 40°$; $arc\,CD = 180° - (40° + 40°) = 100°$, or $\angle A = \frac{1}{2}(100° + 180°) = 140°$.

4. Find $m\angle 1$ in the following figure:

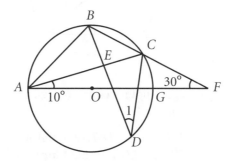

Solution: $30° = \frac{1}{2}(arc\,AB - arc\,CG)$, where $arc\,CG = 2(10°) = 20°$. It follows that $arc\,AB = 2(30°) + 10° = 70°$ or $arc\,BC = 180° - (arc\,CG + arc\,AB) = 180° - (20° + 70°) = 90°$ which means $m\angle 1 = \frac{1}{2}(90°) = 45°$.

5. In the following figure $\triangle ABC$ is an equilateral triangle with tangent $\overline{PC}$ and angle $m\angle P = 90°$. Find the number of degrees in $\angle BEC$.

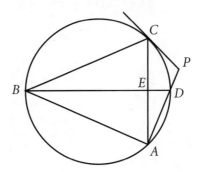

Solution: $arc\,BC = arc\,AB = arc\,CA = 120°$ so that $m\angle BDA = 60°$. Since $\angle P = 90°$, we have $90° = \dfrac{1}{2}(arc\,ABC - arc\,CD)$ or $180° = (240° - arc\,CD)$, which means $arc\,CD = 60°$. Hence, $m\angle CAD = \dfrac{1}{2}(60°) = 30°$. But vertical angles are equal, so $m\angle AED = 180° - (30° + 60°) = 90° = m\angle BEC$.

6. A chord is a distance of 3 units from the center of a circle of radius 5. Find the length of the chord.

Solution: Notice that $\triangle OCA \cong \triangle OCB$ by hy.leg = hy.leg. Hence, $BC = CA = 4$. By the Law of Pythagoras: $BC = \sqrt{5^2 - 3^2} = 4$, or $BA = 8$.

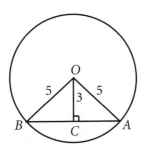

7. Let $ABCDEF$ be any hexagon (not necessary a regular hexagon) inscribed in a circle. Find $m\angle A + m\angle C + m\angle E$.

Solution: Notice that $arc\,FEDCB + arc\,CDEFA + arc\,FABCD = arc\,AB + arc\,AB + arc\,BC + arc\,BC + arc\,CD + arc\,CD + arc\,ED + arc\,ED + arc\,EF + arc\,EF + arc\,FA + arc\,FA = 720°$.

Hence, $m\angle A + m\angle C + m\angle E = \dfrac{1}{2}(720°) = 360°$.

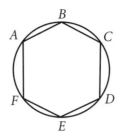

8. An equilateral triangle of area $3\sqrt{3}$ is inscribed in a circle. Find the area of the equilateral triangle circumscribed around the same circle. Find the ratio of the area of the inscribed triangle, to the area of the circle, to the area of the circumscribed triangle.

Solution: The area of the inscribed triangle is $3\sqrt{3}$, let X equal the side of this triangle:

$$3\sqrt{3} = \frac{1}{2}(X)\left(\frac{X}{2}\sqrt{3}\right); 3\sqrt{3} = \frac{X^2}{4}\sqrt{3}; 12 = X^2; 2\sqrt{3} = X$$

If the side of the inscribed triangle is $2\sqrt{3}$, then one half of the side is $\sqrt{3}$, which means the radius of the circle is 2. If the radius of the circle inscribed in the triangle is 2, then one half the side of the equilateral triangle circumscribed around the circle is $2\sqrt{3}$. The side of the equilateral triangle is $4\sqrt{3}$. Hence, the area of the triangle is $\frac{6 \cdot 4\sqrt{3}}{2}$ or $12\sqrt{3}$. The ratios of the areas are $3\sqrt{3} : 4\pi : 12\sqrt{3}$ or $9 : 4\pi\sqrt{3} : 36$.

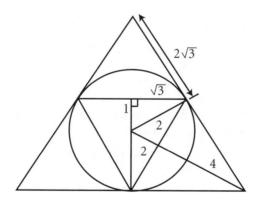

3.4 UNSOLVED PROBLEMS

1. Prove: An angle formed by a chord and tangent is measured by half the intercepted arc.

2. Show that the angle formed by a secant and a tangent is measured by one-half the difference of the intercepted arcs.

3. How many tangents can two circles in a plane have in common?

4. Let $APQRB$ be a pentagon inscribed in a semicircle with diameter AB. If $m\angle APQ = 120°$, find $m\angle QRB$.

5. Given AOB with center O. Chord AB is extended so that BC equals the radius of the circle. Find arc AD, if $y = 20°$.

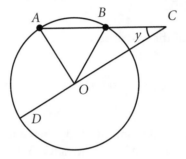

6. Find x:

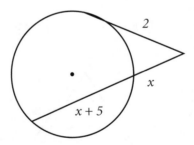

7. Given that $\overline{AB}$, $\overline{BC}$, $\overline{CA}$ are three equal chords of a circle, and tangents at B and C meet at T. Given $BC = 5$, find CT and BT.

8. Given A, B, C are three points on a circle with center O. If $m\angle ABC = 52°$, find $m\angle OCA$.

$A = bh$	Area of rectangle with base b and height h
$A = bh$	Area of parallelogram with base b and height h
$A = bh/2$	Area of triangle with base b and height h
$A = h(b_1 + b_2)/2$	Area of trapezoid with base b_1 and b_2 and height h
$A = ap/2$ $(p = b_1 + \dots$ $+ b_n$ **is the perimeter of the polygon)**	Area of the regular polygon with side b_i and apothem a (the radius of the circle inscribed in the polygon)
$A = \pi r^2$	Area of circle with unit radius r

SECTION 3.5

AREAS OF TRIANGLES, QUADRILATERALS, AND CIRCLES

We use the rectangle as the basic figure from which we derive the area of the other plane figures. The concept of the area relates directly to the idea of multiplication: the area of a rectangle of dimensions a, b is the product ab. Clearly, if two sides of a rectangle are equal ($a = b = s$), the resulting square has an area equal to s^2.

Parallelograms

A parallelogram with base b and with altitude a can be transformed into a rectangle by placing ΔI with altitude a, drawn to base b, into position II. The area of the resulting rectangle is ba. Hence, the area of the original parallelogram is ba.

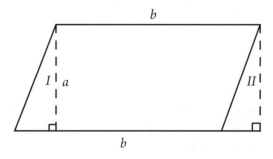

Triangles

In $\triangle ABC$, draw line $\bar{l}_1$, through B parallel to $\overline{AC}$. Draw line $\bar{l}_2$, through C parallel to $\overline{AB}$. Let $\bar{l}_1$ and $\bar{l}_2$ meet at D. Notice $\triangle ABC \cong \triangle CBD$ (ASA $\cong$ ASA). Hence, the area of $\triangle ABC = \dfrac{1}{2}$ area of the parallelogram $ABCD = \dfrac{1}{2}ab$.

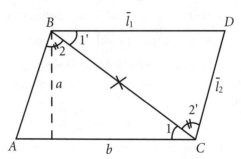

Trapezoids

Segment AD, divides trapezoid $ABCD$ into two triangles $\triangle ACD$ and $\triangle ABD$. Notice that the area of $\triangle ABD = \dfrac{1}{2}ab_1$, while the area of $\triangle ACB = \dfrac{1}{2}ab_2$. The area of the trapezoid $ABCD$ equals to the sum of these two areas: $\dfrac{1}{2}ab_1 + \dfrac{1}{2}ab_2 = \dfrac{1}{2}a(b_1 + b_2)$.

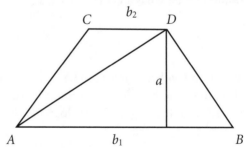

Regular Polygon

The center of a regular polygon is the center of its circumscribed circle. Define the apothem of a regular polygon to be the perpendicular distance a from the center of the polygon. The area of the polygon is the sum of the area of triangles each with bases $(b_1, b_2, b_3, \ldots)$ equal to the sides of the polygon, with altitudes (a) equal to the length of the apothem, and with a common vertex at the center of the polygon. The area of each of these triangles is $\dfrac{1}{2}ab_i$ Hence, $A(\text{polygon}) = \dfrac{1}{2}ab_1 + \dfrac{1}{2}ab_2 + \ldots = \dfrac{1}{2}a(b_1 + b_2 + b_3 + \ldots)$. But the perimeter of the polygon is $b_1 + b_2 + b_3 + \ldots = p$. Thus, the area is $A = \dfrac{1}{2}ap$.

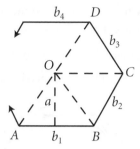

Circles

The circle can be seen as a limiting case of a polygon. In an intuitive sense, consider a polygon as the number of its sides increases without bound. In this limiting case a (apothem) $\rightarrow r$ (radius of circle O). Similarly, the sum of the sides of the polygon approaches the circumference of the circle $= 2\pi r$. It is the area of this "limit," which we call the

area of circle $O \rightarrow \dfrac{1}{2}$ (circumference of circle)(radius of the circle) $\rightarrow \dfrac{1}{2}(2\pi r)(r) = \pi r^2$.

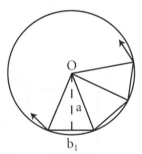

3.5 SOLVED PROBLEMS

1. Find the area of a regular octagon with side 20 and apothem 10.

   Solution: In this case the perimeter of the octagon is 160. The area of the octagon is

   $$A = \frac{1}{2}ap = \frac{1}{2} \cdot 160 \cdot 10 = 800.$$

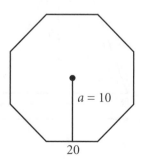

2. Given a regular hexagon with a side of 6, find the difference between the areas of its circumscribed and inscribed circles.

   Solution: The side of the hexagon is the radius of the circumscribed circle. The inscribed circle has a radius $3\sqrt{3}$. The difference in their areas is $36\pi - 27\pi = 9\pi$.

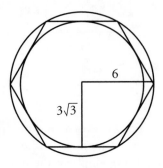

3. A square is inscribed in the triangle with sides 12, 10, 10, as indicated. Find its area.

   Solution: From the figure the area of the square is $4x^2$ where $\dfrac{2x}{6-x} = \dfrac{8}{6} = \dfrac{4}{3}$. In other words, $x = 2.4$, which means the area is $4(2.4)^2 = 23.04$.

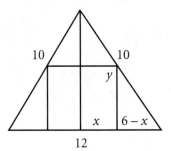

4. Find the area of the accompanying trapezoid if $EA = 1$, $DE = 5$, $AC = 7$, $DC = 7$. Assume the area of $\triangle ABC = \sqrt{s(s-a)(s-b)(s-c)}$ where $s = \dfrac{1}{2}(a+b+c)$.

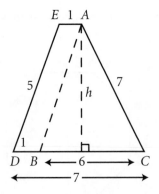

Solution: Draw $AB \parallel ED$; notice $DB = 1$ and $AB = 5$. The area of $\triangle ABC$ is

$A = \sqrt{s(s-a)(s-b)(s-c)} = \sqrt{9(2)(3)(4)} = 6\sqrt{6}$. This means the area is $\frac{1}{2} \cdot 6h = 6\sqrt{6}$

or $h = 2\sqrt{6}$. The area of the parallelogram $BAED$ is given by $h \cdot DB = 2\sqrt{6}$. The sum of the areas of the parallelogram and the triangle gives the area of the trapezoid $= 6\sqrt{6} + 2\sqrt{6} = 8\sqrt{6}$.

7. Find the area of a circle inscribed in a equilateral triangle with sides s.

Solution: Notice $\triangle AOB$ is a 60°, 30° right triangle, which means $OB = \frac{AD}{2\sqrt{3}}$ or

$OB = \frac{s\sqrt{3}}{6}$. Hence, area of circle $= \pi(OB)^2 = \pi\left(\frac{s\sqrt{3}}{6}\right)^2 = \frac{3s^2\pi}{36} = \frac{s^2\pi}{12}$.

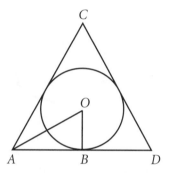

8. Given that circle C_1 with center O_1 is inscribed in a 60° sector of a circle C_2 with center O_2 where D, E and B are tangent points; $\overline{O_2B}$ passes through O_1, so that B is the midpoint of arc AC. Given that the area of circle C_1 is 4π. Find the area of circle C_2.

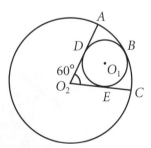

Solution: Notice $\triangle DO_2O_1$ is a right triangle. Since B is the midpoint of arc AC, $m\angle AO_2B = 30°$. It follows that if $DO_1 = 1$, then $O_2O_1 = 2$, or $O_2B = O_2O_1 + O_1B = 3$. The two radii are in the ratio of $1 : 3$. Hence, the areas of the circles are in the ratio $1 : 9$, which means the area of $C_2 = 36\pi$.

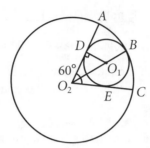

9. A square is inscribed in a circle. Find the ratio of the area of the square to the area of the circle.

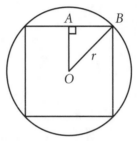

Solution: Let r be the radius of the circle. Notice $\triangle OAB$ is a 45°, 45° right triangle. Hence, one leg is $r\dfrac{\sqrt{2}}{2}$, which means the length of the side of the square is $r\sqrt{2}$. The area of the square is $2r^2$. The area of the circle is πr^2. The ratio of the areas is $2 : \pi$.

3.5 UNSOLVED PROBLEMS

1. Find the black and white areas of a ying-yang with a diameter of 10.

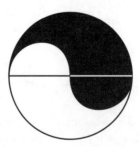

2. A hexagon of side 6 is inscribed in a circle. Find the area between it and the circle.

3. Suppose a trapezoid is reflected around the longest of its two parallel sides, with lengths of 8 and 12. If the distance between the corresponding vertices of reflection is 6, find the area of the hexagon produced by the reflection.

4. Given the square *ABCD* with side 5. Find the area of the rectangle *ADEF*.

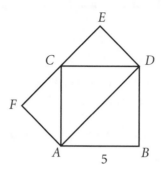

5. The ratio of the height of a step to its width is 2 : 3. Find the area of a cross-section of a staircase consisting of 10 steps, if the height of each step is 10 inches.

6. Given any two parallel lines l_1 and l_2

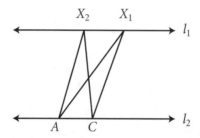

   Point X_1 on l_1. Draw $\triangle AX_1C$. Find point X_2 on l_1 so Area $\triangle AX_2C$ = Area $\triangle AX_1C$.

7. Given a square with side 10. On each of its sides draw a semicircle. The square and the semicircles form area *A*. A second square is drawn each of whose sides is tangent to one of the semicircles. Find the difference between the area of the large square and area *A*.

Lateral area of a right prism	$L.A = ap$, where p is the perimeter of the base of the prism and a is the altitude of the prism
Volume of a right prism	$V = Bh$, where B is the area of the base of the prism and h is the altitude of the prism to this base
Lateral area of a regular pyramid	$L.A = \dfrac{pl}{2}$, where p is its perimeter of the base and l is the slant height
Lateral area of a right cone	$L.A = \pi rl$, where r is the radius and l the slant height
Volume of a regular pyramid	$V = \dfrac{Bh}{3}$, where B is area of the base and h is the height
Volume of a right cone	$V = \dfrac{\pi r^2 h}{3}$, where r is radius and h is the height of the cone
Lateral area of a right cylinder	$L.A = 2\pi rh$, where r is the radius of the cylinder and h is height of the cylinder
Volume of a sphere	$v = 4\pi r^3/3$, where r is the radius of the sphere
Surface area of a sphere	$S.A = 4\pi r^2$, where r is the radius of the sphere

SECTION 3.6

SURFACE AREA AND VOLUME

Surface Area and Volume

Many formulas in solid geometry are derived in calculus and linear algebra. This section assumes such formulas for volumes of pyramids, cones, cylinders, and spheres. It then examines common geometric solids from a strictly geometric perspective.

Right Prisms

A right prism has lateral faces that are rectangles. The total surface area of a right prism is given by the sum of the areas of its faces. In the case of a right prism, with sides 2, 3 and 4, the total area equals $T.A. = 2(2 \cdot 3 + 3 \cdot 4 + 2 \cdot 4)$.

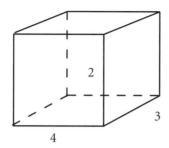

In a similar way, the volume of a right prism with sides 4, 2, 3 consists of the total volumes of the cubes contained in the prism. The volume has three layers of 4 · 2 cubes so $V =$ (area of base)(height) $= (4 \cdot 2) \cdot 3 = 24$ cubes. The same holds for all rectangular prisms.

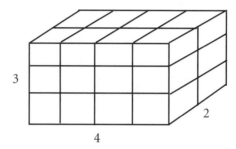

Regular Pyramids and Right Cones

A regular pyramid has a base that is a regular polygon, congruent lateral edges, and lateral faces, which are isosceles triangles, and an altitude that meets the base at its center. In a right cone the line that joins the vertex to the center of the circular base is an altitude. The volume formula (calculus) for both the pyramids and cones follows a general pattern: the volume of a cone or *pyramid-like figure* with base of area A and height h is $V = \frac{1}{3} Ah$.

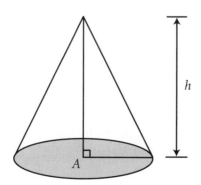

Notice that the lateral area of a regular pyramid is the sum of the area of its faces. Consider the lateral surface area of a regular pyramid with a square base:

$$L.A = \frac{1}{2}b_1l + \frac{1}{2}b_2l + \frac{1}{2}b_3l + \frac{1}{2}b_4l = \frac{1}{2}l(b_1 + b_2 + b_3 + b_4)$$

where l is the slant height. A similar formula follows for all pyramids. In the case of the cone, the same formula holds (see Solved Problems): $L.A = \frac{1}{2}pl$ (where l is the slant height). For a cone, $p = 2\pi r$ = (circumference of base of cone). Hence, $L.A = \frac{1}{2}(2\pi r)l = \pi rl$.

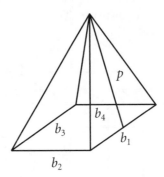

Right Cylinders

In a right cylinder the line segment that joins the centers of the circular bases is an altitude. The volume of cylinder follows the general form for the volume of a prism (calculus): $V = $ (area of base)$h = Bh$. In this situation, $B = \pi r^2$. Hence, $V = \pi r^2 h$. The lateral area of a right circular cylinder is the area of the rectangle formed when you cut the side of the cylinder by a plane perpendicular to its base:

$$L.A = a.p = (\text{height})(\text{perimeter}): L.A = h \cdot 2\pi r = 2\pi rh.$$

The total area of a cylinder (unwrap it) includes top and bottom of the cylinder: $T.A = 2\pi rh + 2\pi r^2$.

Spheres

The volume of a sphere can be found by calculating the volume of a circle with radius rotated around one of its diameters: $V = \frac{4}{3}\pi r^3$ (calculus). The surface area of a sphere can be found by considering the volume of a thin spherical shell, and letting the thickness of the shell approach zero. In particular:

$$\text{Volume} = \frac{4}{3}\pi(r+t)^3 - \frac{4}{3}\pi r^3 = \frac{4}{3}\pi(r^3 + 3r^2t + 3rt^2 + t^3) - \frac{4}{3}\pi r^3 = 4\pi r^2 t + 4\pi rt^2 + \frac{4}{3}\pi t^3.$$

But this volume can also be expressed as $V = (\text{Surface area})(\text{thickness}) = At$ (calculus).

Hence, $A \cdot t = 4\pi r^2 t + 4\pi rt^2 + \dfrac{4}{3}\pi t^3$ or $A = 4\pi r^2 + 4\pi rt + \dfrac{4}{3}\pi t^2$. Take the "limit" as $t \to 0$.

We then have the surface area of the sphere with radius: $A = 4\pi r^2$.

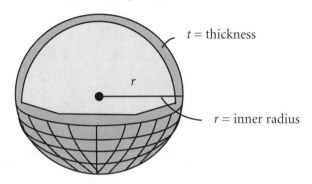

$t = \text{thickness}$

$r = \text{inner radius}$

Principle of Cavalieri

If two solids lying between two parallel planes have equal heights, and all cross-sections at equal distances from their bases have equal areas, then the solids have equal volumes. According to this principle, the formulas for the volume of cylinders in general, and cones in general, are the same as for the volumes of right cylinders and right cones.

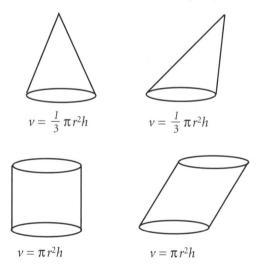

$$v = \frac{1}{3}\pi r^2 h \qquad\qquad v = \frac{1}{3}\pi r^2 h$$

$$v = \pi r^2 h \qquad\qquad v = \pi r^2 h$$

Similar Solids

If the sides of two similar solids are in the ratio of $a : b$, then their areas are in the ratio of $a^2 : b^2$ and their volumes are in the ratio $a^3 : b^3$. To illustrate this idea, consider a right regular rectangular prism with sides a_1, a_2 and a_3, and a similar prism with sides $b_1 = xa_1$,

$b_2 = xa_2$, $b_3 = xa_3$. The total surface area for the first prism is $A = 2(a_1a_2 + a_1a_3 + a_2a_3)$, and for the second prism is $2(b_1b_2 + b_1b_3 + b_2b_3) = 2(xa_1xa_2 + xa_1xa_3 + xa_2xa_3) = x^2A$. The sides of the prism are in the ratio $1 : x$ and the total surface areas are in the ratio $1 : x^2$. Similarly, the volume of the first is $V = a_1a_2a_3$ and of the second is $xa_1xa_2xa_3 = x^3V$. The volumes are thus in the ratio $1 : x^3$.

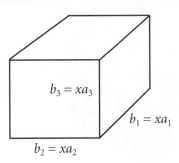

3.6 SOLVED PROBLEMS

1. Suppose the diameter of the earth is roughly 0.003 of the diameter of the sun. Find the ratios of the surface areas and volumes of the earth to that of the sun.

   Solution: $E = 0.003S$. Surface area $E = (0.003)^2 \times$ surface area S; Volume $E = (0.003)^3 \times$ Volume S.

   Hence, the two ratios are 9×10^{-6} for the surface areas and 27×10^{-9} for the volumes.

2. Find the area of a circle formed when a plane passes 12 units from the center of a sphere with radius 15 units.

   Solution: From the figure, the radius r of the cross-sectional circle can be found by the Law of Pythagoras $r^2 = 15^2 - 12^2 = 225 - 144 = 81$. Hence, $r = 9$. The resulting area is 81π.

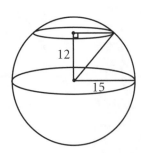

3. Given a right square pyramid with base edge 20 and lateral edge 26. Find its lateral area, total area, and volume.

Solution: Notice $l = \sqrt{26^2 - 10^2} = 24$. Hence, the lateral area $= \frac{1}{2}pl = \frac{1}{2}80 \cdot 24 = 960$.

But, area of base + lateral area $= 20^2 + 960 = 1360 =$ total area. In right $\triangle ABC$, $AB^2 = l^2 - BC^2 = 24^2 - 10^2 = 576 - 100 = 476$. Hence, $AB = \sqrt{476} = 2\sqrt{119}$. This means that $V = \frac{1}{3}(2\sqrt{119})(20^2) = \frac{800\sqrt{119}}{3}$.

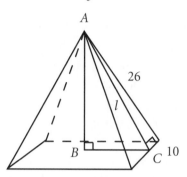

4. Find the lateral area of a right cone with radius of base r and lateral slant l.

Solution: If one draws on a piece of paper a sector OAB of a circle with radius l and center O so that $\overline{OA}$ and $\overline{OB}$ overlap, the figure formed is a right circular cone with radius r, and slant height l. The circumference of the base of the cone is the length of the arc of the sector, determined by $\angle AOB = \theta$, and $2\pi l$ is the circumference of the circle O:

$$\frac{\theta}{360}(2\pi l) = 2\pi r; \quad \frac{\theta}{360} = \frac{2\pi r}{2\pi l} = \frac{r}{l}.$$

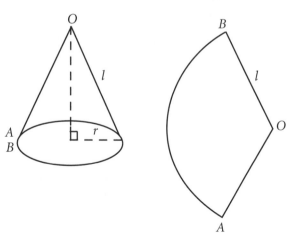

The lateral area of the cone equals the area of the curved surface of the cone:

$$\frac{\theta}{360}(\pi l^2) = \frac{r}{l}(\pi l^2) = \pi r l.$$

3.6 UNSOLVED PROBLEMS

1. Given that the volume of a sphere with radius r equals the volume of a cone with height 3 and radius r, find r.

2. A hollow wooden box with no lid has a base of 20 by 13 and a height of 8. If the thickness of the box is 0.5, what is the amount of wood needed to make the box? (All units are in cm.)

3. Find the volume of a solid, which consists of a square pyramid with side x(cm) and height 3cm, and a half sphere of radius $\dfrac{x}{2}$ cm joined to the base of the pyramid.

4. An open tank with a square horizontal section should hold 100m³ of liquid. If the side of the square section is x (neglect the thickness of the tank), find an expression in x for the total surface area of the tank.

5. Suppose the volume of a cube C_1 is tripled to give cube C_2 with a surface area of 20. Find the surface area of C_1.

6. A sector of a circle with radius 6 has an angle of 120°. It is bent to make a cone. Find the radius of the base of the cone and its vertical angle (angle at vertex).

7. Find the capacity of a bucket 12cm in diameter at the top and 8cm in diameter at the bottom and 10cm deep.

8. Find the mass of a cylindrical iron pipe 2m long and 10cm in external diameter, if the metal is 1cm thick and has a density of 7.8 g cm^{-3}.

SECTION 3.7

REFLECTIONS, ROTATIONS, AND TRANSLATIONS OF POINTS, LINES, AND POLYGONS IN THE PLANE

Euclidean geometry deals with static plane and three-dimensional figures, while transformational geometry deals with movement of figures either in the plane or in space. This section deals with movement of figures in the plane. The most convenient way to represent movement involves the use of matrices.

Matrix Algebra

A matrix is a $m \times n$ array of numbers into m rows and n columns. The matrix $\begin{pmatrix} a & b & c \\ d & e & f \end{pmatrix}$ is a 2×3, with 2 rows and 3 columns. To add (subtract) two matrices, they must be of the same dimension (have the same number of rows and columns). You add (subtract) the matrix term by term. For example, $\begin{pmatrix} 1 & 2 & 3 \\ 4 & 5 & 6 \end{pmatrix} + \begin{pmatrix} -3 & -2 & -1 \\ -6 & -5 & -4 \end{pmatrix} = \begin{pmatrix} -2 & 0 & +2 \\ -2 & 0 & +2 \end{pmatrix}$.
To multiply a matrix by a scalar you multiply each term in the matrix by a scalar. For example, $5\begin{pmatrix} -2 & -3 \\ -1 & 5 \end{pmatrix} = \begin{pmatrix} -10 & -15 \\ -5 & 25 \end{pmatrix}$.

Matrix Multiplication

Consider the equation $x' = 2x + y$ and $y' = x + 3y$. These transformations can move any point (x, y) in the plane, to the point (x', y'), which means $(1, 2)$ maps into $(4, 7)$.

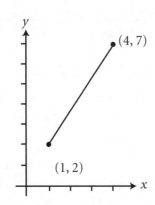

In general, we write the transformation of the plane in the form: $x' = ax + by$; $y' = cx + dy$. Alternatively, we can write this transformation in terms of the array $\begin{pmatrix} a & b \\ c & d \end{pmatrix}$ and define $\begin{pmatrix} x' \\ y' \end{pmatrix} = \begin{pmatrix} a & b \\ c & d \end{pmatrix}\begin{pmatrix} x \\ y \end{pmatrix}$; $\begin{pmatrix} x' \\ y' \end{pmatrix} = \begin{pmatrix} ax + by \\ cx + dy \end{pmatrix}$. The concept of matrix multiplication can be generalized in the case of 2×2 matrices. Suppose $T_1 = (x, y) \rightarrow (x', y')$ and $T_2 = (x', y') \rightarrow (x'', y'')$ where $T_1 = \begin{pmatrix} a & b \\ c & d \end{pmatrix}$ and $T_2 = \begin{pmatrix} \alpha & \beta \\ \gamma & \delta \end{pmatrix}$, then

$$x'' = \alpha(ax + by) + \beta(cx + dy) = (\alpha a + \beta c)x + (\alpha b + \beta d)y$$
$$y'' = \gamma(ax + by) + \delta(cx + dy) = (\gamma a + \delta c)x + (\gamma b + \delta d)y$$

which is the matrix $\begin{pmatrix} \alpha a + \beta c & \alpha b + \beta d \\ \gamma a + \delta c & \gamma b + \delta d \end{pmatrix}$.

This suggests the following definition: $\begin{pmatrix} \alpha & \beta \\ \gamma & \delta \end{pmatrix}\begin{pmatrix} a & b \\ c & d \end{pmatrix} = \begin{pmatrix} \alpha a + \beta c & \alpha b + \beta d \\ \gamma a + \delta c & \gamma b + \delta d \end{pmatrix}$.

In general, to multiply matrix A and matrix B the number of columns of matrix A must be equal to the number of rows of matrix B. In this case, the product of two matrices A and B is a matrix C whose element in the ith row and jth column is

$$c_{ij} = a_{i1}b_{1j} + a_{i2}b_{2j} + a_{i3}b_{3j} + \ldots + a_{in}b_{nj}$$

If $A = n \times m$ and $B = m \times k$, then the dimension of the product matrix $A \times B$ is $n \times k$.

Reflections

A reflection of the plane in the x-axis preserves all the x-values of each point in the plane and changes the sign of the y-values (similarly for reflection in the y-axis): $x = x'$ and $y - y'$. The matrix operator is given by $\begin{pmatrix} 1 & 0 \\ 0 & -1 \end{pmatrix}\begin{pmatrix} x \\ y \end{pmatrix} = \begin{pmatrix} x \\ -y \end{pmatrix}$.

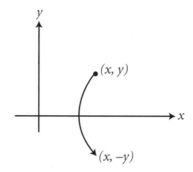

Size Transformation

A size transformation of the plane multiplies the x-value of each element in the plane by a constant, and the y-value of each element by a constant. Consider: $x' = 2x$; $y' = 3y$, which transforms the square $A(1, 1)$, $B(2, 1)$, $C(2, 2)$, $D(1, 2)$ into $A'(2, 3)$, $B'(4, 3)$, $C'(4, 6)$, $D'(2, 6)$. The matrix operator is given by $\begin{pmatrix} 2 & 0 \\ 0 & 3 \end{pmatrix}\begin{pmatrix} x \\ y \end{pmatrix} = \begin{pmatrix} 2x \\ 3y \end{pmatrix}$.

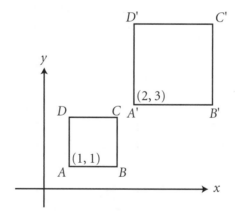

Rotation

A rotation of the plane holds one point fixed, and rotates all the other points around this point by a fixed number of degrees. A rotation of 90° counterclockwise around the origin takes the square

$$A(1, 1),\ B(3, 1),\ C(3, 3),\ D(1, 3)\ \text{into}\ A'(-1, 1),\ B'(-1, 3),\ C'(-3, 3),\ D'(-3, 1).$$

The matrix operator for this operation is given by $\begin{pmatrix} 0 & -1 \\ 1 & 0 \end{pmatrix}\begin{pmatrix} x \\ y \end{pmatrix} = \begin{pmatrix} -y \\ x \end{pmatrix}$.

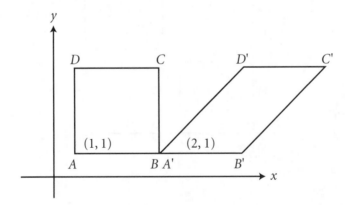

Similarly, a rotation of 180° around the origin takes each point $\begin{pmatrix} x \\ y \end{pmatrix}$ into $\begin{pmatrix} -x \\ -y \end{pmatrix}$. The matrix operator for this operation is given by $\begin{pmatrix} -1 & 0 \\ 0 & -1 \end{pmatrix}\begin{pmatrix} x \\ y \end{pmatrix} = \begin{pmatrix} -x \\ -y \end{pmatrix}$.

Shear

A shear keeps one of the variables constant while it changes the other according to some fixed rule. The shear $x' = x + y$; $y' = y$ transforms $A(1, 1)$, $B(2, 1)$, $C(2, 2)$, $D(1, 2)$ into $A'(2, 1)$, $B'(3, 1)$, $C'(4, 2)$, $D'(3, 2)$.

Translation

A translation (sometimes called a glide) moves each point (x, y) to $(x + a, y + b)$. For example, $T(2, 3)$ the translation by $(2, 3)$ transforms the square $A(1, 1)$, $B(3, 1)$, $C(3, 3)$, $D(1, 3)$ into $A'(3, 4)$, $B'(5, 4)$, $C'(5, 6)$, $D'(3, 6)$. This transformation is expressed most clearly as a matrix sum $\begin{pmatrix} x \\ y \end{pmatrix} + \begin{pmatrix} a \\ b \end{pmatrix} = \begin{pmatrix} x + a \\ y + b \end{pmatrix}$.

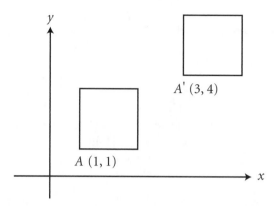

3.7 SOLVED PROBLEMS

1. Describe the transformation defined by $\begin{pmatrix} 0 & 1 \\ -1 & 0 \end{pmatrix}$.

   Solution: Notice $\begin{pmatrix} 0 & 1 \\ -1 & 0 \end{pmatrix}\begin{pmatrix} x \\ y \end{pmatrix} = \begin{pmatrix} y \\ -x \end{pmatrix}$. This transformation represents a rotation of 90° clockwise around the origin. This transformation transforms the square $A(1, 1)$, $B(3, 1)$, $C(3, 3)$, $D(1, 3)$ into $A'(1, -1)$, $B'(1, -3)$, $C'(3, -3)$, $D'(3, -1)$.

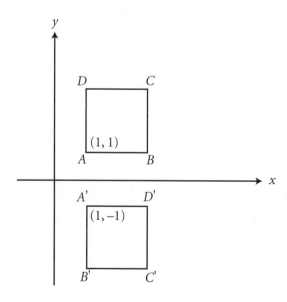

3. Describe the transformation defined by $\begin{pmatrix} 3 & -3 \\ -1 & 1 \end{pmatrix}$.

Solution: Notice $\begin{pmatrix} 3 & -3 \\ -1 & 1 \end{pmatrix}\begin{pmatrix} x \\ y \end{pmatrix} = \begin{pmatrix} 3x - 3y \\ -x + y \end{pmatrix}$. Every point in the transformation satisfies the equation $x' = -3y'$. Hence, the unit square is "squashed" into points on the line $x' = -3y'$. Notice that the points on the line $-3y = x$ stay on the line $-3y' = x'$. This means the line $-3y = x$ remains fixed under this transformation. This line defines the fixed line (eigenvector) of the transformation.

4. Show that if the transformation $\begin{pmatrix} a & b \\ c & d \end{pmatrix}$ takes the points $(1, 0)$ into $(5, 2)$ and $(0, 1)$ into $(-1, 3)$, then $\begin{pmatrix} a & b \\ c & d \end{pmatrix} = \begin{pmatrix} 5 & -1 \\ 2 & 3 \end{pmatrix}$ (knowing the images of the unit vectors in a transformation gives an easy way of determining the matrix transformation).

Solution: Consider the image of $(0, 1)$ and $(1, 0)$ under the transformation $\begin{pmatrix} a & b \\ c & d \end{pmatrix}$

We get: $\begin{pmatrix} a & b \\ c & d \end{pmatrix}\begin{pmatrix} 1 \\ 0 \end{pmatrix} = \begin{pmatrix} a \\ c \end{pmatrix}$; $\begin{pmatrix} a & b \\ c & d \end{pmatrix}\begin{pmatrix} 0 \\ 1 \end{pmatrix} = \begin{pmatrix} b \\ d \end{pmatrix}$. If the image of $(1, 0)$ is $(5, 2)$ it fol-

lows that $a = 5$ and $c = 2$. Similarly, if the image of $(0, 1)$ is $(-1, 3)$ it follows that $b = -1$ and $d = 3$. Hence, the transformation is $\begin{pmatrix} 5 & -1 \\ 2 & 3 \end{pmatrix}$.

6. Find the matrix which represents reflection in $y = x$.

Solution: Under this reflection $(1, 0) \rightarrow (0, 1)$ and $(0, 1) \rightarrow (1, 0)$. In other words, the x and y coordinates interchange. Hence, the matrix is given by $\begin{pmatrix} 0 & 1 \\ 1 & 0 \end{pmatrix}$.

7. Find the matrix for a shear with the x-axis invariant and $(0, 1) \rightarrow (-3, 1)$.

Solution: Notice $(1, 0)$ goes into $(1, 0)$ while $(0, 1)$ goes into $(-3, 1)$. Hence, the matrix of the transformation is given by $\begin{pmatrix} 1 & -3 \\ 0 & 1 \end{pmatrix}$.

8. Find the image of the unit square $A(0, 0)$, $B(1, 0)$, $C(1, 1)$ and $D(0, 1)$ under the matrix transformation $\begin{pmatrix} 3 & -1 \\ -1 & 2 \end{pmatrix}$. Compare the area of the square to the area of the new parallelogram.

Solution:

$\begin{pmatrix} 3 & -1 \\ -1 & 2 \end{pmatrix}\begin{pmatrix} 0 \\ 0 \end{pmatrix} \rightarrow \begin{pmatrix} 0 \\ 0 \end{pmatrix}$; $\begin{pmatrix} 3 & -1 \\ -1 & 2 \end{pmatrix}\begin{pmatrix} 1 \\ 0 \end{pmatrix} \rightarrow \begin{pmatrix} 3 \\ -1 \end{pmatrix}$; $\begin{pmatrix} 3 & -1 \\ -1 & 2 \end{pmatrix}\begin{pmatrix} 1 \\ 1 \end{pmatrix} \rightarrow \begin{pmatrix} 2 \\ 1 \end{pmatrix}$; $\begin{pmatrix} 3 & -1 \\ -1 & 2 \end{pmatrix}\begin{pmatrix} 0 \\ 1 \end{pmatrix} \rightarrow \begin{pmatrix} -1 \\ 2 \end{pmatrix}$.

The area of the new parallelogram is $A = 4 \cdot 3 - ($Area 1 + Area 2 + Area 3 + Area 4 +

Area 5 + Area 6). $A = 12 - \left(\dfrac{1}{2} \cdot 3 \cdot 1 + \dfrac{1}{2} \cdot 1 \cdot 2 + 1 \cdot 1 + \dfrac{1}{2} \cdot 1 \cdot 3 + \dfrac{1}{2} \cdot 1 \cdot 2 + 1 \cdot 1 \right) = 5$.

Notice that $\begin{vmatrix} 3 & -1 \\ -1 & 2 \end{vmatrix} = 6 - 1 = 5$. The area of the parallelogram is 5 times larger (the value of the determinent of the matrix) than the area of the given square.

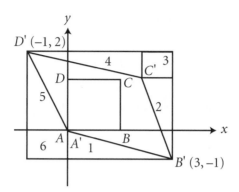

9. Suppose the origin is invariant under a linear transformation. Give the equations of this transformation.

Solution: If $\begin{pmatrix} a & b \\ c & d \end{pmatrix} \begin{pmatrix} 0 \\ 0 \end{pmatrix} \rightarrow \begin{pmatrix} 0 \\ 0 \end{pmatrix}$ then a, b, c, d may be any real numbers. In other words, the equations of this transformation are given by $x' = ax + by$ and $y' = cx + dy$.

10. Any vector whose direction is unchanged after a transformation is called an eigen-vector of the transformation. The factor by which its length is changed is called the eigenvalue of the vector. Describe the eigenvectors and corresponding eigenvalues for $\begin{pmatrix} 1 & 0 \\ 0 & -1 \end{pmatrix}$ and for $\begin{pmatrix} k & 0 \\ 0 & 1 \end{pmatrix}$.

Solution: The transformation $\begin{pmatrix} 1 & 0 \\ 0 & -1 \end{pmatrix}$ is a reflection in the x-axis, so the vectors $(1, 0)$ and $(0, 1)$ remain unchanged. The corresponding eigenvalues are 1 and -1. The transformation $\begin{pmatrix} k & 0 \\ 0 & 1 \end{pmatrix}$ has the eigenvectors $(1, 0)$ and $(0, 1)$ with the corresponding eigenvalues k and 1.

3.7 UNSOLVED PROBLEMS

1. Show that transformations of reflection, rotation, and translation preserve distance.

2. Show that the determinant of the transformation $\begin{pmatrix} 6 & 3 \\ 2 & 1 \end{pmatrix}$ is zero. What is the scale factor of the area for this transformation (i.e., consider the image of the unit square)? From this result, what might you guess to be the relation between the determinant of a transformation and the area scale factor of the transformation?

3. Describe the line(s) that remain constant after the transformation $A = \begin{pmatrix} 1 & 0 \\ 0 & -1 \end{pmatrix}$.

   For what values of γ will $Ax = \gamma x$ under this transformation (γ is called the eigenvalue of the matrix transformation $\begin{pmatrix} 1 & 0 \\ 0 & -1 \end{pmatrix}$).

4. Describe geometrically the transformation $\begin{pmatrix} 3 & 0 \\ 0 & 1 \end{pmatrix}$.

5. Describe the fixed lines of the transformation $A = \begin{pmatrix} 3 & 0 \\ 0 & 1 \end{pmatrix}$, find the values of λ such that $Ax = \lambda x$.

6. Determine the point(s) (x, y) in the transformation in problem 5 such that $A(x, y) = \lambda(x, y)$.

7. Determine the transformation for a rotation of the plane of 120° counterclockwise around the origin.

8. Given the regular hexagon $ABCDEF$, with center O at origin. Determine:

   a) $R_{180°}(E)$ (i.e., image of E under rotation of 180° around the origin)

   b) Reflection (D) in line EB

   c) Rotate point E 180° about O and then reflect in line EB.

9. Investigate some general properties of the matrix $\begin{pmatrix} 6 & 2 \\ 3 & 1 \end{pmatrix}$ by investigating what happens to the unit square.

10. Find an eigenvector for $\begin{pmatrix} 4 & 2 \\ 2 & 1 \end{pmatrix}$.

Locus	A figure that consists of all points, and only those points, which satisfy one or more conditions

SECTION 3.8

CONSTRUCTIONS AND LOCI

Classical construction in Euclidean geometry requires the use of a straight edge and compass. Such constructions involve the concept of locus, or path. The locus of a point traces out a path as it moves in the plane according to certain conditions. The concept of locus is connected with that of functions and relations. A locus may define a function or relation, and conversely, a function or relation may define a locus. A locus (plural *loci*) problem may satisfy not only one, but more than one condition—an intersection of loci. This section summarizes the most frequently asked locus problems in the following table.

TABLE 3.2

Given an angle, construct an angle congruent to it. 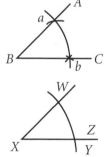	Draw ray $\overrightarrow{XY}$. Using B as a center draw an arc intersecting $\overrightarrow{AB}$ at a and $\overrightarrow{BC}$ at b. Reproduce this arc with X as center intersecting $\overrightarrow{XY}$ at Z. With compass centered at b draw an arc through a. Reproduce the arc with center at Z to find intersection W. Draw $\overrightarrow{XW}$. (Notice $\triangle ABC \cong \triangle WXY$ by SSS $\cong$ SSS; hence $\angle X \cong \angle B$.)
Given a line segment $\overline{AB}$, construct a perpendicular bisector of the segment. 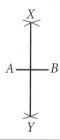	Let $\overline{AB}$ be given, with center at A draw an arc more than $\dfrac{1}{2}AB$; with center at B repeat this procedure using the same compass setting. Call the resulting intersections X and Y. Draw $\overline{XY}$ (figure $AXBY$ is a rhombus with diagonals $\overline{AB}$ and $\overline{XY}$, hence $\overline{AB} \perp \overline{XY}$).

(continues)

TABLE 3.2	Continued

At a given point on a circle construct a tangent to the circle. 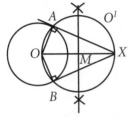	A tangent is perpendicular to a radius at the point of tangency (see Unsolved Problems). Given circle O with point P on the circle. Draw a line passing through O and P. Construct through point P a line perpendicular to this line (see Solved Problems). This line is the required tangent.
Given a point outside a given circle construct a tangent to the circle.	Given circle O with point X outside of O. Find M, the midpoint of OX. Let M be the center of circle O′ with radius OM. Circles O, O′ intersect at A and B, $m\angle OAX = m\angle OBX = 90°$ since OX is a diameter of circles O′. Hence, $\overline{XA}$ and $\overline{XB}$ are the required tangents.
Given a line segment. Divide it into a given number of congruent segments. 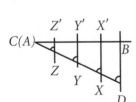	Let AB be the given line segment. Suppose we want to divide it into 4 segments. Take another line segment $\overline{CD}$ which we draw so it is divided into four equal segments, with C placed on A, with $\angle DAB$ any acute angle. Draw a line through B and D. Reproduce $\angle D$ at points X, Y and Z to give X′, Y′, Z′ (Notice: $\triangle XAX' \sim \triangle YAY' \sim \triangle ZAZ' \sim \triangle DAB$ with $DX = XY = YZ = ZA$. Hence, $BX' = X'Y' = Y'Z' = Z'A$.)
Given three line segments with lengths a, b, c. We want to construct segment x so that $\dfrac{a}{b} = \dfrac{c}{x}$. 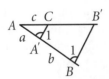	Draw $\overline{AB}$ with segments of length $a = AA'$ and $b = A'B$. Draw $\overrightarrow{AB'}$. On side $\overrightarrow{AB'}$ mark off C so that $AC = c$. Draw $\overrightarrow{A'C}$ to create $\angle 1$. Reproduce $\angle 1$ at point B. The segment $CB' = x$. (Notice: $\triangle ACA' \sim \triangle AB'B$.)

3.8 SOLVED PROBLEMS

1. Given a line segment, construct a segment congruent to the given segment.

   Solution: Let $\overline{AB}$ be a given line segment. Draw line l_1 (with length bigger than AB). With center at A draw arc AB. With any point on l_1 as center reproduce $\overline{AB} \cong \overline{A'B'}$, so that $AB = A'B'$.

A B

A' B' l_1

2. Given a point on a line construct the perpendicular to the line at the given point.

   Solution: Let line $\overleftrightarrow{l_1}$ be given, and P a point on $\overleftrightarrow{l_1}$ with length bigger than AB). With compass centered at P draw an arc intersecting $\overleftrightarrow{l_1}$ at X and Y. Draw two larger arcs with the same radii and centers, first at X and then at Y. Find point A, the intersection of the two arcs. Draw $\overline{AP}$. (Notice: $\triangle XAP \cong \triangle YAP$ by SSS. Hence, $m\angle APX = m\angle APY = 90°$.)

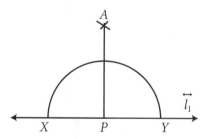

         A

                         $\overleftrightarrow{l_1}$

X P Y

3. Draw any triangle. Find the center of the circumscribed circle around the triangle.

   Solution: Let $\triangle ABC$ be given. Draw $\perp$ bisectors for $\overline{CB}$, $\overline{AC}$, and $\overline{AB}$. Consider a circle with center at P, and radius equal to $PC = PB = PA$. (Notice: If the $\perp$ bisectors of two sides intersect at point P, the $\perp$ bisector of the third must also pass through P.) This point determines all points equidistant from three fixed points. The radius of the circumscribed circle is the distance of P to any vertex of the triangle.

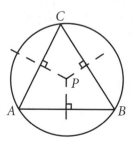

         C

          P

A B

4. Given a line segment of length s. Construct a line segment of length $s\sqrt{3}$.

Solution: Let a line segment of length s be given, double its length to $\overline{AB}$. Construct an equilateral $\triangle ABC$ with sides equal to $2s$. Drop a perpendicular $\overline{CX}$, from C to $\overline{AB}$ (Notice: $\triangle ACX$ is a 60°, 30° right triangle). Hence, $CX = s\sqrt{3}$.

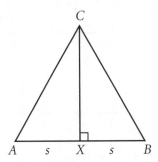

5. Given $\triangle ABC$ with medians $\overline{AX}$, $\overline{BY}$, and $\overline{CZ}$. If $BY = x^2 + 1$ and $PB = x + 2$, find x.

Solution: The medians meet at a point two-thirds the lengths of any median (see Unsolved Problems). Hence, $\dfrac{2}{3}(x^2 + 1) = x + 2$ or $2x^2 + 2 = 3x + 6$; $2x^2 - 3x - 4 = 0$, which means $x = \dfrac{3 \pm \sqrt{9 + 32}}{4} = \dfrac{3 + \sqrt{41}}{4}$. Notice that $3 - \sqrt{41} < 0$. Hence, the value of x is, $x = \dfrac{3 + \sqrt{41}}{4}$.

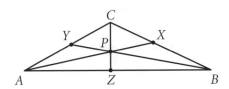

6. Given triangle $\triangle ABC$, construct the circle inscribed in this triangle.

Solution: Draw angle bisectors for $\angle A$, $\angle B$, and $\angle C$ which intersect at P. The fact that these lines intersect at the same point is similar to the argument in Solved Problem 3. (The angle bisectors are equidistant from sides of the angles, construction 2. Hence, P is equidistant from all the sides of the triangle. The circumscribed circle has P as a center and distance to any side of the triangles as radius.)

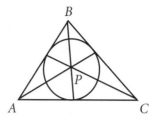

7. Given line segments of length a and b. Find a segment of length x that is the mean proportion between a and b.

Solution: Draw line segment $\overline{AB}$ divided by point X into segments of length a and length b. Through X construct a perpendicular to $\overline{AB}$. Find midpoint M of $\overline{AB}$. Draw a circle with center at M and radius $MA = MB$. Find the intersection Z of perpendicular and this circle. $\overline{ZX}$ is the required segment. (Notice: $\triangle AZB$ is a right triangle with altitude drawn to the hypotenuse $\overline{AB}$; hence $\overline{ZX}$ is the mean proportion between AX and XB.)

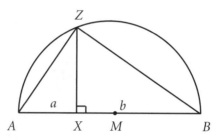

8. Draw an ellipse using a loose thread of length l that is greater than the distance between two points A and B, which are the foci of the ellipse. How might you define the ellipse in terms of A, B, and the length of the thread?

Solution: Take the thread and attach its ends to A and B. The thread is pulled by a pencil point, which is moved so that it produces the required ellipse. The locus of points the sum of whose distances from two fixed points is constant, is an ellipse.

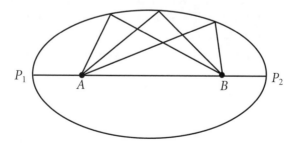

9. Create a wheel out of cardboard and allow it to roll along a length of floor against a sheet of paper that is taped onto a wall adjacent to the floor. Mark a point P on the wheel and describe its path.

Solution: The curve is called a cycloid.

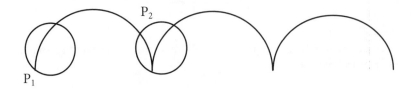

10. Find the locus of points in space at a distance r from a fixed point p.

Solution: The locus is a sphere with radius r and center p.

3.8 UNSOLVED PROBLEMS

1. Given a point outside a given line, construct the perpendicular to the line from this point.

2. Through a point outside a given line, construct the line ∥ to the given line (this construction reflects the famous parallel postulate of Euclid).

3. Construct a regular octagon.

4. Show a radius of a circle is ⊥ to a tangent line at the point of tangency. (Hint: use indirect proof.)

5. Construct an equilateral triangle using a circle. (Hint: first construct a regular hexagon.)

6. Suppose a dog runs around in a circle in an elevator chasing its tail. Describe the locus of the figure traced out by the dog as the elevator goes up.

7. Find the locus of the latch of a gate that swings 180°.

8. Find the locus of points equidistant from the endpoints of a line segment $\overline{AB}$.

9. Attach a wire to the top of a vertical pole so that the wire is longer than the pole. Find the locus of the wire if it is taut as it rotates around the top of the pole to a point on the horizontal ground.

10. Find locus of centers of circles tangent to a given point P on a given line l.

CHAPTER FOUR

Trigonometry

Circular or trigonometric functions play a central role in the theory of functions. Historically, trigonometry was developed to solve practical problems in geometry. It provided indirect ways to measure lengths and distances. From a more abstract perspective, trigonometric relations allow one to re-write many mathematical expressions in alternate forms. Trigonometric functions frequently permit one to express algebraic relationships in forms that allow for an ease of manipulation.

The nature of classical trigonometry means that the topics studied in it are fairly well defined. This chapter explores these fundamental concepts including definitions, identities, the sine and cosine laws, geometrical applications, and complex numbers. The chapter places a heavy emphasis on the relationship between geometry and trigonometry and the mastering of identities needed for basic calculus.

GLOSSARY OF TERMS

One degree	The measure of an angle that is 1/360 of the circumference of a circle
One radian	$\dfrac{180}{\pi}$ degrees
sinθ (sine)	If θ is an acute angle in a right triangle then $$\sin\theta = \frac{\text{side opposite}\,\theta}{\text{hypotenuse of the right triangle}}$$ Let $\overrightarrow{OP}$ generate (counterclockwise), the angle θ in a circle with its center at the origin, starting at the positive half of the of the x-axis. Suppose P has the coordinates (x, y) on the circle, then $\sin\theta = \dfrac{y}{\sqrt{x^2 + y^2}}$
cosθ(cosine)	$\sin\left(\dfrac{\pi}{2} - \theta\right)$
tanθ(tangent)	$\dfrac{\sin\theta}{\cos\theta}$
cotθ(cotangent)	$\dfrac{1}{\tan\theta}$
secθ(secant)	$\dfrac{1}{\cos\theta}$
cscθ(cosecant)	$\dfrac{1}{\sin\theta}$

SECTION 4.1

RADIAN MEASURE, BASIC TRIGONOMETRIC FUNCTIONS OF THE RIGHT TRIANGLE AND UNIT CIRCLE, SPECIAL ANGLES

Angles may be measured in degrees; one degree equals 1/360 of a complete rotation of a circle. This concept of a degree requires a somewhat arbitrary division of the circumference of a circle by 360. A radian is a more intuitive sense of angle measure. Consider any circle of radius r. An angle of 1 radian (or 1) defines a central angle in the circle that intersects a length of r units on the circumference of a circle.

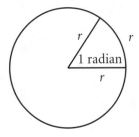

Radians and Degrees

The circle has a circumference of $2\pi r$ and a circle angle measures $360°$. We have 2π radian $= 360°$,

$$1 \text{ radian} = \frac{180°}{\pi} \quad \text{or} \quad \frac{\pi}{180°} \text{ radians} = 1°$$

In other words, π radians equals $180°$. Other frequently occurring measures include:

TABLE 4.1

degrees		radians
30°	30/180 = 1/6	$\dfrac{\pi}{6}$
45°	45/180 = 1/4	$\dfrac{\pi}{4}$
60°	60/180 = 1/3	$\dfrac{\pi}{3}$
90°	90/180 = 1/2	$\dfrac{\pi}{2}$
120°	120/180 = 2/3	$\dfrac{2\pi}{3}$
135°	135/180 = 3/4	$\dfrac{3\pi}{4}$
150°	150/180 = 5/6	$\dfrac{5\pi}{6}$
180°	180/180 = 1	π

Notice that $3°$ equals $\dfrac{\pi}{60}$ radians, since $\dfrac{3}{180} = \dfrac{1}{60}$; similarly, $5°\,30' = 5\dfrac{1}{2}° = \dfrac{11\pi}{360}$ radians since $\dfrac{5\dfrac{1}{2}}{180} = \dfrac{11}{60}$. To change radians to degrees we use the same principle: multiply by $180°$ and divide by π. (Radian and degree measures are interchangeable.)

Length of Arc and Area of Sector

Suppose that a circular sector of radius r and angle θ has arc length l and area A.

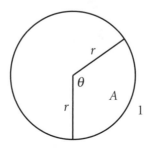

The angle 2π generates a circle. We can find the area of a sector of this circle by considering the proportion that the angle of this sector makes with 2π. A particular sector defined by an angle of θ radians has an area $= \dfrac{\theta}{2\pi} \cdot r^2\pi = \dfrac{\theta r^2}{2}$. Its arc length is found in a similar way: arc length of a sector $= \dfrac{\theta}{2\pi} \cdot 2r\pi = \theta r$.

Sine and Cosine as Circular Functions

Suppose that a circle of unit radius is centered at $(0, 0)$ in a Cartesian coordinate system. Suppose, furthermore, that point P rotates counterclockwise around the circle so that $\angle POA$ defines an angle θ.

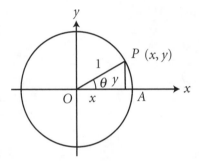

Then the coordinates of $P(x, y)$ define $x = \dfrac{x}{1} = \cos\theta$; $y = \dfrac{y}{1} = \sin\theta$.

More specifically, in a right triangle $\cos\theta = \dfrac{\text{adjacent side}}{\text{hypotenuse}}$ while $\sin\theta = \dfrac{\text{opposite side}}{\text{hypotenuse}}$.

The graphs of the functions $y = \sin\theta$, $y = \cos\theta$ follow from this definition by plotting the lengths of the sine and cosine against θ, as θ changes from 0 to 2π.

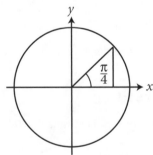

The measure of $\sin\theta$ when $\theta = \dfrac{\pi}{4}$

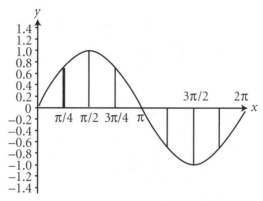

The plot of $y = \sin \theta$ with the measure of $\sin \frac{\pi}{4}$ emphasized

It is clear that both $y = \sin \theta$ and $y = \cos \theta$ repeat in every 2π interval. Hence, we call these functions periodic, with period 2π. The following is the graph for $y = \sin \theta$:

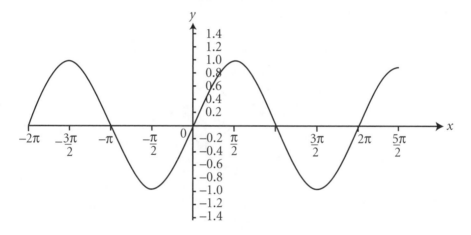

The following is the graph for $y = \cos \theta$:

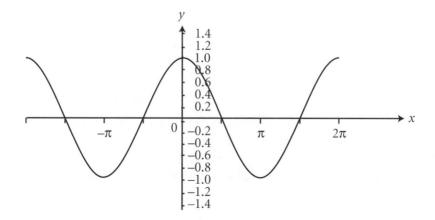

In particular, $\sin \pi = \sin(\pi + 2\pi) = \sin 3\pi = 0$ or $\cos \dfrac{\pi}{2} = \cos\left(\dfrac{\pi}{2} + 2\pi\right) = \cos \dfrac{5\pi}{2} = 0$.

We can also obtain a number of relations by simply noticing certain symmetries from the unit circle.

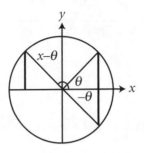

$$\sin \theta = \sin (\pi - \theta)$$
$$\sin (-\theta) = -\sin \theta$$

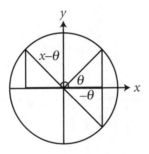

$$\cos \theta = \cos (-\theta)$$
$$\cos (\pi - \theta) = -\cos \theta$$

Similarly, the graph of $y = \cos \theta$ is a shift of $y = \sin \theta$ by $\dfrac{\pi}{2}$. We conclude:

$$\sin \theta = \cos\left(\dfrac{\pi}{2} - \theta\right)$$

$$\cos \theta = \sin\left(\dfrac{\pi}{2} - \theta\right)$$

One further note, while graphs of trigonometric functions may frequently be represented with angle measure in degrees on the x-axis, clearly these graphs make little conceptual sense, since degrees are not actual lengths. The graphs of $y = \cos \theta$ and $y = \sin \theta$ make more sense if θ is measured in radians, since a radian represents a real number.

Tangent

The tangent may be defined as: $\tan \theta = \dfrac{\sin \theta}{\cos \theta}$.

Alternately, we can define $\tan \theta = \dfrac{y}{x} = \dfrac{\text{side opposite to angle } \theta \text{ in right triangle } POA}{\text{side adjacent to angle } \theta \text{ in right triangle } POA}$.

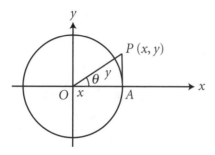

The tangent may also be defined from the unit circle where $\overline{OP}$ now defines a tangent $\overline{PA}$ drawn to the circle at point A. Once again, $\tan \theta = PA = $ slope of $\overline{OP}$ (also the length of $\overline{PA}$). The graph for the tangent follows. It has a period of π, as would be expected of the graph of a slope (e.g., slope of lines only have distinctive values between 0 and π).

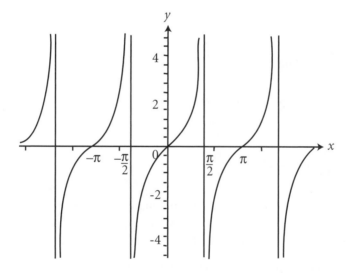

Notice $\dfrac{\pi}{2} + n\pi$ $(n \in Z)$ define vertical asymptotes for $y = \tan \theta$. Consequently, $\tan \dfrac{\pi}{2} + n\pi$ $(n \in Z)$ does not exist; alternatively, $\tan \theta = \dfrac{y}{x}$ does not exist for $x = 0$.

Other functions: csc θ, sec θ, cot θ.

We define the co-functions by the following:

$$\csc \theta = \frac{1}{\sin \theta} \qquad \sec \theta = \frac{1}{\cos \theta} \qquad \cot \theta = \frac{1}{\tan \theta}$$

The definition allows us to deduce the properties of these three functions from the original functions. For example, $\sec \theta = \dfrac{1}{\cos \theta} = \dfrac{1}{\sin\left(\dfrac{\pi}{2} - \theta\right)} = \csc\left(\dfrac{\pi}{2} - \theta\right)$ which means

$\sec \dfrac{\pi}{6} = \csc \dfrac{\pi}{3}$, since the angles are complementary. The same relationships hold between the $\tan \theta$ and $\cot \theta$.

Pythagorean Identities

By the Law of Pythagoras we have $x^2 + y^2 + r^2$ for any right triangle with legs x and y, and with hypotenuse r. From the previous definitions of trigonometric functions it follows that:

1. $\dfrac{x^2}{r^2} + \dfrac{y^2}{r^2} = 1$, or $\cos^2 \theta + \sin^2 \theta = 1$

2. $1 + \dfrac{y^2}{x^2} = \dfrac{r^2}{x^2}$, or $\tan^2 \theta + 1 = \sec^2 \theta$

3. $\dfrac{x^2}{y^2} + 1 = \dfrac{r^2}{y^2}$, or $\cot^2 \theta + 1 = \csc^2 \theta$

4.1 SOLVED PROBLEMS

The solutions of the following are given either in radians or degrees.

1. Derive values of the trigonometric functions for 45°, 30°, and 60°.

   Solution: Notice that in isosceles right triangle we have that

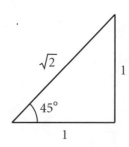

$\sin 45° = \dfrac{1}{\sqrt{2}} = \dfrac{\sqrt{2}}{2}$; $\cos 45° = \dfrac{1}{\sqrt{2}} = \dfrac{\sqrt{2}}{2}$; $\tan 45° = \dfrac{1}{1} = 1$. We can also use an equila-

teral triangle to define the value of the trigonometric functions for 30° and 60°.

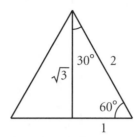

$\sin 30° = \dfrac{1}{2}$; $\cos 30° = \dfrac{\sqrt{3}}{2}$; $\tan 30° = \dfrac{1}{\sqrt{3}} = \dfrac{\sqrt{3}}{3}$; $\sin 60° = \cos 30° = \dfrac{\sqrt{3}}{2}$

$\cos 60° = \sin 30° = \dfrac{1}{2}$ which means $\tan 60° = \sqrt{3}$.

Using the definitions of the co-functions we can also find:

$$\csc 45° = \sqrt{2} \qquad \csc 30° = 2 \qquad \csc 60° = \dfrac{2}{3}\sqrt{3}$$

$$\sec 45° = \sqrt{2} \qquad \sec 30° = \dfrac{2}{3}\sqrt{3} \qquad \sec 60° = 2$$

$$\cot 45° = 1 \qquad \cot 30° = \sqrt{3} \qquad \cot 60° = \dfrac{1}{\sqrt{3}} = \dfrac{\sqrt{3}}{1}$$

2. Find the values of the trigonometric functions for the angles 0°, 90°, 180°, 270°.

   Solution: We use the definition of sine, cosine, tangent and consider a point on the unit circle for the appropriate angle:

$$\sin 0° = \dfrac{y}{r} = \dfrac{0}{1} = 0 \qquad\qquad \sin 90° = \dfrac{y}{r} = \dfrac{1}{1} = 1$$

$$\cos 0° = \dfrac{x}{r} = \dfrac{1}{1} = 1 \qquad\qquad \cos 90° = \dfrac{x}{r} = \dfrac{0}{1} = 0$$

$$\tan 0° = \dfrac{y}{x} = \dfrac{0}{1} = 0 \qquad\qquad \tan 90° = \dfrac{y}{x} = \dfrac{1}{0}\,\text{undefined}$$

$$\sin 180° = \dfrac{y}{r} = \dfrac{0}{1} = 0 \qquad\qquad \sin 270° = \dfrac{y}{r} = \dfrac{-1}{1} = -1$$

$$\cos 180° = \dfrac{x}{r} = \dfrac{-1}{1} = -1 \qquad \cos 270° = \dfrac{x}{r} = \dfrac{0}{1} = 0$$

$$\tan 180° = \dfrac{y}{x} = \dfrac{0}{1} = 0 \qquad\qquad \tan 270° = \dfrac{y}{x} = \dfrac{-1}{0}\,\text{undefined}$$

3. Find one value x such that $\cos 5 = -\cos x$.

   Solution: Notice that $\dfrac{3\pi}{2} < 5 < 2\pi$, which means an angle of 5 lies in quadrant IV, or $\cos 5 > 0$. If $\cos 5 = -\cos x$, then $\cos x = -\cos 5$, which means $\cos x < 0$. Pick angle x in quadrant II, which has $2\pi - 5$ as a reference angle. It follows that one value is $x = 5 - \pi$.

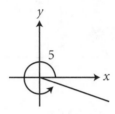

4. Suppose a gear rotates at 5 rotations per second. Express its speed in terms of degrees and radians per second.

   Solution: 5 rotations $= 5 \cdot 360° = 1800°$/sec or $5 \cdot 2\pi = 10\pi$/sec.

5. In the same situation, what is the speed of the wheel per radian?

   Solution: The wheel rotates 1800°/sec or $\dfrac{1}{1800}$ seconds every 1°; similarly it takes $\dfrac{1}{10\pi}$ seconds to travel 1 radian.

6. Suppose a gear goes 1 radian in 1 minute. How many degrees does it go in 1 second?

   Solution: π radian $= 180°$; 1 radian $= \dfrac{180°}{\pi}$. Since the gear goes 1 radian/minute, it goes $\dfrac{180}{\pi}$ degrees/minute, or $\dfrac{180}{\pi}$ degrees/60 seconds, which means $\dfrac{3}{\pi}$ degrees/second.

7. Find one possible solution x, y, z in radians if $\cos^2(x^2 + y^2) + \sin^2(z^2) = 1$

   Solution: Notice that $\cos^2 A + \sin^2 A = 1$, which means that when $x^2 + y^2 = z^2$, the given expression holds true. But $x^2 + y^2 = z^2$ is a general expression for Pythagorean triplets. Choose $x = 3$, $y = 4$, $z = 5$.

8. Solve for x, if $\sin^2 x + \cos^2 x + \tan^2 x = 1$.

   Solution: $\sin^2 x + \cos^2 x = 1$ and since $1 + \tan^2 x = \sec^2 x$, we can choose any value for x for which $\tan x$ and $\sec x$ are defined. Choose $x = 0$.

9. Graph the equation traced by the point (x, y) where $x = 5 + \cos \theta$ and $y = -1 + 5\sin \theta$ for any θ.

   Solution: $5\cos \theta = x - 2$ and $5\sin \theta = y + 1$; hence, $25(\sin^2 \theta + \sin^2 \theta) = (x - 2)^2 + (y + 1)^2$ or $25 = (x - 2)^2 + (y + 1)^2$. The equation describes a circle with center at $(2, -1)$ and radius 5.

10. Find the error in the following argument:

For all values of x, $\cos^2 x = 1 - \sin^2 x$, $(1 + \cos x)^2 = [1 + (1 - \sin^2 x)^{1/2}]^2$. Let $x = \pi$; $(1 - 1)^2 = [1 + (1 - 0)^{1/2}]^2$; $0 = 4$.

Solution: The fact that $\cos^2 x = 1 - \sin^2 x$, does not mean $\cos x = \sqrt{1 - \sin^2 x}$ (the cosine function takes on both positive and negative values, not simply positive values). The theory of equations does not assert that you have equivalent equations if you take squares (or square roots) of variables in equations. For example, $-\sqrt{x} = 5$ has no solution, although $\left(-\sqrt{x}\right)^2 = 25$ would seem to imply $x = 25$.

4.1 UNSOLVED PROBLEMS

1. If $\csc x - \cot x = \dfrac{1}{3}$ find values for $\csc x$ and $\cot x$.

2. Solve the equation $3\tan^2 \theta - 5\sec \theta + 1 = 0$.

3. Solve for θ if $\sec^2 \theta - \sin^2 \theta - \cos^2 \theta - \tan^2 \theta = 0$.

4. Express in terms of $\sin \theta$ and $\cos \theta$: $\tan\left(\dfrac{3\pi}{2} + \theta\right)$.

5. Show that: $\dfrac{\sin x}{\sec x + 1} + \dfrac{\sin x}{\sec x - 1} = 2\cot x$.

6. Solve for all x such that $\sin x - \cos x = 1$.

7. Prove: $\sin^2 \theta - \tan^2 \theta = -(\tan^2 \theta)(\sin^2 \theta)$.

8. Find $f(x, y) = 0$, if $x = 5\sin \theta$ and $y = \cos \theta$.

9. Eliminate θ from the equations $x = 2 + 3\tan \theta$, $y = 1 + \sec \theta$ to get a relationship between x and y.

10. Give a polynomial equation that describes the curve traced by $x = \tan \theta - \sin \theta$, $y = \tan \theta + \sin \theta$.

11. Graph: $\sin^2 x + \cos^2 y = 0$.

12. Prove: $\dfrac{1}{\csc x + \cot x} = \csc x - \cot x$.

| OF TERMS

Law of Cosines	Given $\triangle ABC$ with sides a, b, c
	$a^2 = b^2 + c^2 - 2bc \cos A$
	$b^2 = a^2 + c^2 - 2ac \cos B$
	$c^2 = a^2 + b^2 - 2ab \cos C$
Law of Sines	Given $\triangle ABC$ with sides a, b, c
	$\dfrac{a}{\sin A} = \dfrac{b}{\sin B} = \dfrac{c}{\sin C}$
$y = A \sin x$	$\lvert A \rvert$ is the amplitude of the function
$y = \sin Ax$	$\left\lvert \dfrac{2\pi}{A} \right\rvert$ is the period of the function
$y = \sin(x - A)$	A is the phase shift of the function
Asymptotes for $y =$ tan x and $y =$ sec x	Vertical asymptotes for the function occur at $x = \dfrac{\pi}{2} + n\pi, (n \in Z)$
Asymptotes for $y =$ cot x and $y =$ csc x	Vertical asymptotes for the function occur at $x = n\pi, (n \in Z)$

SECTION 4.2

LAWS OF SINES, COSINES, AND GRAPHS OF TRIGONOMETRIC FUNCTIONS

It is clear that some combinations of side and angle produce a unique triangle. For example, three sides (SSS), construct only one triangle. Similarly, two sides and an included angle (SAS) construct only one triangle. These theorems suggest that relationships exist between the lengths of the sides of a triangle and its angles. Consider acute triangle ABC, with altitude h drawn from vertex C to side c.

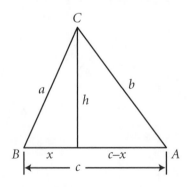

Law of Sines

The Law of Sines states: $\sin B = \dfrac{h}{a}$ or $a \sin B = h$; $\sin A = \dfrac{h}{b}$ or $b \sin A = h$; $a \sin B = b \sin A$; $\dfrac{a}{\sin A} = \dfrac{b}{\sin B}$. Similarly, drawing an altitude from either vertex B or A gives: $\dfrac{a}{\sin A} = \dfrac{b}{\sin B} = \dfrac{c}{\sin C}$. These arguments hold for any triangle.

Law of Cosines

From the diagram it also follows by the Law of Pythagoras that $h^2 = a^2 - x^2$; $h^2 = b^2 - (c-x)^2$. We can conclude: $a^2 - x^2 = b^2 - (c-x)^2$; $a^2 - x^2 = b^2 - c^2 + 2cx - x^2$; $a^2 + c^2 - 2cx = b^2$. But $x = a \cos B$. Hence, we obtain one form of the Law of Cosines: $b^2 = a^2 + c^2 - 2ac \cos B$. Using the other corresponding altitudes we have three cases: $a^2 = b^2 + c^2 - 2bc \cos A$; $b^2 = a^2 + c^2 - 2ac \cos B$; $c^2 = a^2 + b^2 - 2ab \cos C$.

To calculate the six parts of a unique triangle from any three given parts we can either use the Law of Sines or Law of Cosines. The Law of Sines can be used when you have an angle and a side opposite (ASA), while the Law of Cosines can be used in all other cases (SSS, SAS).

Example: Given $\triangle ABC$ with $a = 4$, $b = 3$ and $c = 2$ (SSS). Using the Law of Cosines we find: $4^2 = 3^2 + 2^2 - 2 \cdot 3 \cdot 2 \cdot \cos A$, or $-.25 = \cos A$. Hence, $A = 104°$ (A must be in the second quadrant). Now use the Law of Sines (since we have side a and angle A opposite): $\dfrac{4}{\sin 104°} = \dfrac{3}{\sin B} = \dfrac{2}{\sin C}$; $\sin B = \dfrac{3}{4}\sin 104° = .724$; $\sin C = \dfrac{1}{2}\sin 104° = .484$. But both B and C must be acute, since A is obtuse. Hence, $B = 47°$ and $C = 29°$. (Check $47 + 29 + 104 = 180$).

From the following figure it is clear how the remaining case SSA can produce two distinct triangles: one acute, one obtuse. This is known as the ambiguous case, which produces 0, 1, or 2 solutions.

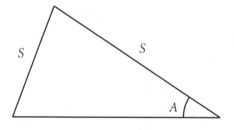
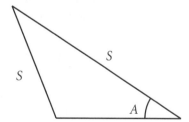

Graphs of Trigonometric Functions

From the graphs for $y = \sin x$, $y = \cos x$, $y = \tan x$, one obtains the graphs of the remaining three trigonometric functions:

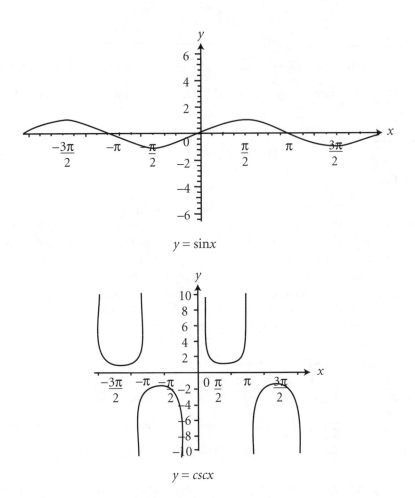

$$y = \sin x$$

$$y = \csc x$$

Notice that $y = \csc x$ repeats with a period of 2π. While the amplitude of $y = \sin x$ is 1, the graph $y = \csc x$ has infinite amplitude. In particular, $x = n\pi$, $n \in Z$ serves as asymptote for the function. The graph for $y = \sec x$ simply shifts the graph of $y = \csc x$ by a phase of $\pi/2$. This follows since $y = \cos x$ shifts $y = \sin x$ by a phase of $\pi/2$.

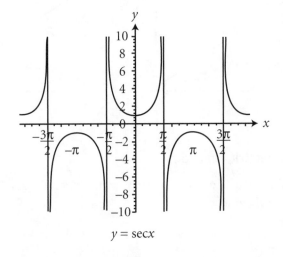

$$y = \sec x$$

The reciprocal relationship between $y = \tan x$ and $y = \cot x$ produces the graph for $y = \cot x$, with a period of π, and asymptotes at $\dfrac{\pi}{2} + n\pi$ $(n \in Z)$:

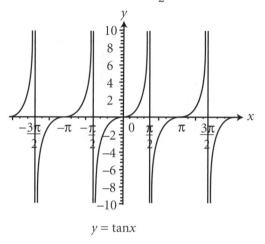

$y = \tan x$

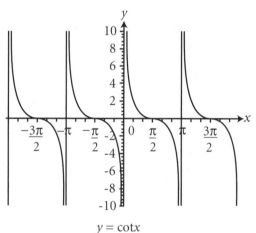

$y = \cot x$

Consider the graph $y = A \sin (Bx + C)$. Notice the height of the graph (amplitude) is $|A|$, while the period is $\left|\dfrac{2\pi}{B}\right|$ and its shift from the graph $y = \sin x$ is $\dfrac{-C}{B}$. These transformations can be clearly seen in a specific example. Graph $y = -3\sin\left(2x + \dfrac{\pi}{6}\right)$:

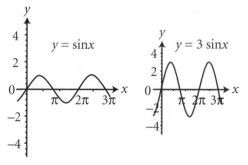

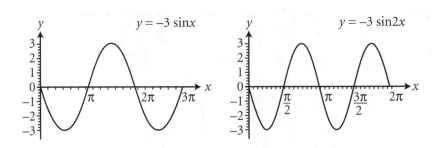

Notice $y = -3\sin\left(2x + \dfrac{\pi}{6}\right)$ completes one cycle from $0 = 2x + \dfrac{\pi}{6}$ to $2\pi = 2x + \dfrac{\pi}{6}$ or from $-\dfrac{\pi}{12}$ to $\dfrac{11\pi}{12}$.

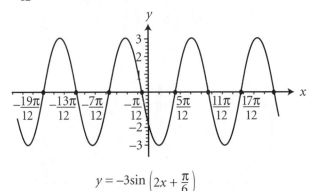

$$y = -3\sin\left(2x + \dfrac{\pi}{6}\right)$$

Hence, there is a shift of $-\dfrac{\pi}{12} = \dfrac{C}{B}$.

4.2 SOLVED PROBLEMS

1. In $\triangle ABC$ $a = 4$, $b = 3$, and $c = 2$. Solve the triangle.

   Solution: Use the Law of Cosines:

   $$a^2 = b^2 + c^2 - 2bc\cos A;\ 4^2 = 3^2 + 2^2 - 2\cdot 3\cdot 2\cdot\cos A;$$
   $$16 = 9 + 4 - 12\cos A;\ 25 = \cos A,\ \text{or } A \approx 105°.$$

   We have one side ($a = 4$) and the angle opposite $A = 105°$. We can use the Law of Sines twice to find angle B and C, or use it once to find angle B or C, and then use the fact that all angles must add up to $180°$ to find the other angle. Since $\dfrac{b}{\sin B} = \dfrac{a}{\sin A}$;

   $\dfrac{3}{\sin B} = \dfrac{4}{\sin 105°} = \dfrac{4}{\sin 75°};\ B = \dfrac{3\sin 75°}{4} = .726$ or $B \approx 46°$ (since B cannot be obtuse).

   So, $C = 180° - (46° + 105°) = 180° - 151° = 29°$.

2. Show that the area of a $\triangle$ can be expressed as $A = \dfrac{1}{2}ab\sin C$.

Solution: In the accompanying triangle notice that $h = a \sin C$, where h is the altitude drawn from angle B to side b.

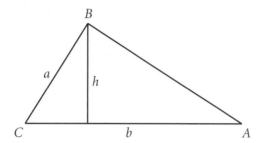

The area of the triangle is given by $A = \dfrac{1}{2} bh$, or $A = \dfrac{1}{2} ab \sin C$.

3. Solve the triangle $\triangle ABC$ for which $b = 30$, $a = 5$ and $A = 45°$.

   Solution: This situation results in the ambiguous case SSA when we may have no solution, one solution or two solutions. By the Law of Sines: $\dfrac{a}{\sin A} = \dfrac{b}{\sin B}$; $\dfrac{5}{\sin 45°} = \dfrac{30}{\sin B}$; $3\sqrt{2} = \sin B$, which is impossible. Hence, there is no solution.

4. In problem 3, what values should the side a have so that precisely one solution will exist?

   Solution: One solution will exist when $\sin B = 1$, or $a = 15\sqrt{2}$.

5. Prove Heron's formula for the area of $\triangle ABC$: $A = \sqrt{s(s-a)(s-b)(s-c)}$, where $s = \dfrac{a+b+c}{2}$.

   Solution: By problem 2 we have $A = \dfrac{1}{2} cb \sin A = \sqrt{\dfrac{1}{4} c^2 b^2 \sin^2 A}$. However, $\sin^2 A = 1 - \cos^2 A$. Hence, $A = \sqrt{\dfrac{1}{4} c^2 b^2 (1 - \cos^2 A)} = \sqrt{\left[\dfrac{1}{2} bc(1 - \cos A)\right]\left[\dfrac{1}{2} bc(1 + \cos A)\right]}$.

   Notice:
   $$b^2 + c^2 - a^2 = 2bc \cos A$$
   $$\frac{b^2 + c^2 - a^2}{4} = \frac{bc \cos A}{2}$$
   $$\frac{b^2 + c^2 - a^2}{4} + \frac{1}{2} bc = \frac{1}{2} bc(1 + \cos A)$$
   $$\frac{1}{4}(b^2 + c^2 - a^2 + 2bc) = \frac{1}{2} bc(1 + \cos A)$$
   $$\frac{1}{4}\left[(b+c)^2 - a^2\right] = \frac{1}{2} bc(1 + \cos A)$$
   $$\left[\frac{1}{2}(b + c - a)\right]\left[\frac{1}{2}(b + c + a)\right] = \frac{1}{2} bc(1 + \cos A)$$

In a similar way it follows that:

$$\frac{1}{2}bc(1-\cos A) = \left[\frac{1}{2}(a-(b-c))\right]\left[\frac{1}{2}(a+(b-c))\right] = \left[\frac{1}{2}(a-b+c)\right]\left[\frac{1}{2}(a+b-c)\right].$$

Let $s = \dfrac{a+b+c}{2}$. These two expressions can be written as:

$$\frac{1}{2}bc(1+\cos A) = s(s-a)$$

$$\frac{1}{2}bc(1-\cos A) = (s-b)(s-c)$$

Hence, we can conclude that $A = \sqrt{s(s-a)(s-b)(s-c)}$.

4.2 UNSOLVED PROBLEMS

1. Find θ $(0 \le \theta \le \pi)$ such that $\cos \theta = -.73$.

2. Interpret $\tan \theta = -3$ in terms of the unit circle.

3. Using the unit circle, solve pictorially for x in terms of α; $\sin x = \sin \alpha$.

4. Using the unit circle, solve pictorially: $\cos \theta = -.5$.

5. Express the solutions in Problem 4 in set notation.

6. Prove: $\tan (x + 180°) = \tan x$.

7. Solve for $\triangle ABC$: $a = 5$, $B = 30°$, $C = 80°$.

8. Two cargo ships left New York at 8.00 A.M. One goes 18 knots (18 nautical miles per hour) to Natal, Brazil (E 45°S), and another at 21 knots to Southhampton, UK (E 15°N). How far will they be from each other in 4 hours? (Assume the earth is flat!)

9. Graph the function $y = -1 + 2\cos 3x$.

10. Graph: $y = -\sin\left(3x - \dfrac{\pi}{2}\right)$, $y = \cos 3x$. What can we conclude from these graphs?

11. If one rotates the point (x, y) by θ degrees, using $(0, 0)$ as the center of rotation, show that $(x, 0) \rightarrow (x \cos \theta, x \sin \theta)$.

12. If one rotates the point (x, y) by θ degrees using $(0, 0)$ as the center of rotation, show that $(0, y) \rightarrow (-y \sin \theta, y \cos \theta)$.

sin(x ± y)	$\sin(x \pm y) = \sin x \cos y \pm \cos x \sin y$
cos(x ± y)	$\cos(x \pm y) = \cos x \cos y \mp \sin x \sin y$
tan(x ± y)	$\tan(x \pm y) = \dfrac{\tan \pm \tan y}{1 \mp \tan x \tan y}$
sin 2x	$\sin 2x = 2 \sin x \cos x$
cos 2x	$\cos 2x = \cos^2 x - \sin^2 x$
sin $\frac{1}{2}$ x	$\sin \dfrac{1}{2} x = \pm \sqrt{\dfrac{1 - \cos x}{2}}$
cos $\frac{1}{2}$ x	$\cos \dfrac{1}{2} x = \pm \sqrt{\dfrac{1 + \cos x}{2}}$
sin A + sin B	$\sin A + \sin B = 2 \sin \left(\dfrac{A+B}{2} \right) \cos \left(\dfrac{A-B}{2} \right)$
sin A − sin B	$\sin A - \sin B = 2 \cos \left(\dfrac{A+B}{2} \right) \sin \left(\dfrac{A-B}{2} \right)$
cos A + cos B	$\cos A + \cos B = 2 \cos \left(\dfrac{A+B}{2} \right) \cos \left(\dfrac{A-B}{2} \right)$
cos A − cos B	$\cos A - \cos B = -2 \sin \left(\dfrac{A+B}{2} \right) \sin \left(\dfrac{A-B}{2} \right)$

SECTION 4.3

IDENTITIES FOR SUMS OF ANGLES, DOUBLE ANGLES, HALF ANGLES, AND SUMS OF SINES AND COSINES

One important property of trigonometric functions is their ability to transform into other trigonometric functions. (Consider them changlings!) This property is crucial in the investigation of integrals and trigonometric equations. This section examines the most common trigonometric identities that facilitate such transformations.

Sum and Difference of Angles: sin($\theta \pm \varphi$) and cos($\theta \pm \varphi$)

Consider the rotation of a point $P(x, y)$ on the unit circle around the origin O through an angle α to give a new value of $P'(x', y')$.

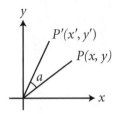

This rotation transforms the point $(1, 0)$ into $(\cos \alpha, \sin \alpha)$, while it maps the point $(0,1)$ into $(-\sin \alpha, \cos \alpha)$.

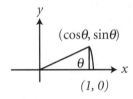

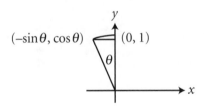

Hence, the matrix transformation for this rotation is given by $\begin{pmatrix} \cos\alpha & -\sin\alpha \\ \sin\alpha & \cos\alpha \end{pmatrix}$. In other words, $\begin{pmatrix} x' \\ y' \end{pmatrix} = \begin{pmatrix} \cos\alpha & -\sin\alpha \\ \sin\alpha & \cos\alpha \end{pmatrix}\begin{pmatrix} x \\ y \end{pmatrix}$.

Let $\alpha = \theta + \varphi$. Notice that a rotation by θ then φ is the same as a rotation by $(\theta + \varphi)$. Hence, the following matrix equation holds: $T(\alpha) = T(\theta + \varphi) = T(\theta)\ T(\varphi)$.

Hence, $\begin{pmatrix} \cos(\theta+\varphi) & -\sin(\theta+\varphi) \\ \sin(\theta+\varphi) & \cos(\theta+\varphi) \end{pmatrix} = \begin{pmatrix} \cos\theta & -\sin\theta \\ \sin\theta & \cos\theta \end{pmatrix}\begin{pmatrix} \cos\varphi & -\sin\varphi \\ \sin\varphi & \cos\varphi \end{pmatrix}$

$= \begin{pmatrix} \cos\theta\cos\varphi - \sin\theta\sin\varphi & -\sin\theta\cos\varphi - \cos\theta\sin\varphi \\ \sin\theta\cos\varphi + \cos\theta\sin\varphi & \cos\theta\cos\varphi - \sin\theta\sin\varphi \end{pmatrix}$

or $\sin(\theta + \varphi) = \sin\theta\ \cos\varphi + \cos\theta\ \sin\varphi$
$\cos(\theta + \varphi) = \cos\theta\ \cos\varphi - \sin\theta\ \sin\varphi$

If we replace φ by $-\varphi$, and remember that $\cos(-\varphi) = \cos \varphi$, and $\sin(-\varphi) = -\sin \varphi$, we have:

$$\sin(\theta - \varphi) = \sin \theta \cos\varphi - \cos \theta \sin\varphi$$
$$\cos(\theta - \varphi) = \cos \theta \cos\varphi + \sin \theta \sin\varphi$$

Double and Half Angles

If you let $\varphi = \theta$ in $\sin(\theta + \varphi) = \sin \theta \cos\varphi + \cos \theta \sin\varphi$, you then obtain:
$\sin 2\theta = \sin \theta \cos \theta + \cos \theta \sin \theta$; $\sin 2\theta = 2 \sin \theta \cos \theta$.

In a similar way you get: $\cos 2\theta = \cos^2 \theta - \sin^2 \theta$.

To find the half angle formulas use the identity $1 = \cos^2 \theta + \sin^2 \theta$ and then add (subtract) the formula for $\cos 2\theta$ to get:

$$\cos 2\theta = \cos^2 \theta - \sin^2 \theta; \qquad 1 - \cos 2\theta = 2\sin^2 \theta; \qquad \frac{1 - \cos 2\theta}{2} = \sin^2 \theta;$$

$$\pm\sqrt{\frac{1 - \cos 2\theta}{2}} = \sin \theta. \text{ Similarly, } \pm\sqrt{\frac{1 + \cos 2\theta}{2}} = \cos\theta. \text{ Substituting } \frac{x}{2} = \theta$$

we get $\sin\frac{1}{2}x = \pm\sqrt{\frac{1 - \cos x}{2}}, \quad \cos\frac{1}{2}x = \pm\sqrt{\frac{1 + \cos x}{2}}.$

Sum and Difference of Sines and Cosines

One of the most crucial sets of formulas comes by adding and subtracting the formula for the sum and difference of angles:

$$\sin(\theta + \varphi) = \sin \theta\cos\varphi + \cos \theta\sin\varphi$$
$$\sin(\theta - \varphi) = \cos \theta\cos\varphi - \sin \theta\sin\varphi$$

to get

$$\sin(\theta + \varphi) + \sin(\theta - \varphi) = 2 \sin \theta\cos\varphi$$
$$\sin(\theta + \varphi) - \sin(\theta - \varphi) = 2 \cos \theta\sin\varphi$$

If we let $\theta + \varphi = A$ and $\theta - \varphi = B$, we get that $\dfrac{A + B}{2} = \theta$ and $\dfrac{A - B}{2} = \varphi$ It follows that:

$$\sin A + \sin B = 2\sin\left(\frac{A + B}{2}\right)\cos\left(\frac{A - B}{2}\right)$$

$$\sin A - \sin B = 2\cos\left(\frac{A + B}{2}\right)\sin\left(\frac{A - B}{2}\right)$$

In a similar way,

$$\cos A + \cos B = 2\cos\left(\frac{A+B}{2}\right)\cos\left(\frac{A-B}{2}\right)$$

$$\cos A - \cos B = -2\sin\left(\frac{A+B}{2}\right)\sin\left(\frac{A-B}{2}\right)$$

4.3 SOLVED PROBLEMS

1. Find sin 75° in radical form.

   Solution: $75° = 45° + 30°$. Then $\sin 75° = \sin(45° + 30°) = \sin 45° \cos 30° + \cos 45° \sin 30°$

   $$= \frac{1}{\sqrt{2}} \cdot \frac{\sqrt{3}}{2} + \frac{1}{\sqrt{2}} \cdot \frac{1}{2} = \frac{\sqrt{3}+1}{2\sqrt{2}} = \frac{\sqrt{2}(\sqrt{3}+1)}{4}.$$

2. Prove: $\tan(x + y) = \dfrac{\tan x + \tan y}{1 - \tan x \tan y}$

   Solution: $\tan(x + y) = \dfrac{\sin(x+y)}{\cos(x+y)} = \dfrac{\sin x \cos y + \cos x \sin y}{\cos x \cos y - \sin x \sin y} = \dfrac{\dfrac{\sin x \cos y}{\cos x \cos y} + \dfrac{\cos x \sin y}{\cos x \cos y}}{1 - \dfrac{\sin x \sin y}{\cos x \cos y}}$

   $$= \frac{\tan x + \tan y}{1 - \tan x \tan y}.$$

3. Find the value of $\sin(45° + A) - \sin(45° - A)$.

   Solution:
   $$\sin(45° + A) - \sin(45° - A) = 2\cos 45° \sin A = \frac{2\sqrt{2}}{2}\sin A = \sqrt{2}\sin A = \sqrt{2}\sin A.$$

4. What is the amplitude of the function $f(x) = 4\cos\theta + 3\sin\theta$?

   Solution: Notice that $4\cos\theta + 3\sin\theta$ is a form of $R\cos(x-y) = R\cos x \cos y + R\sin x \sin y$. In this case $R\cos y = 4$, $R\sin y = 3$, $R^2 = 25$, $R = 5$.

5. What is the period and phase difference of the function $f(x) = 4\cos\theta + 3\sin\theta$?

   Solution: $R\cos(x - y) = R\cos x \cos y + R\sin x \sin y$. In this case $R = 5$ (see Problem 4), which means $\cos y = \dfrac{4}{5}$, $y = \arccos\dfrac{4}{5}$; $\sin y = \dfrac{3}{5}$, $y = \arcsin\dfrac{3}{5}$ Thus, $R\cos(x - y)$ has a period of 360°, and a phase shift of $\arccos\dfrac{4}{5}(\approx 37°)$.

6. Solve the equation $\cos 2\,\theta = 3 - 7\cos\theta$ for $0 \le \theta < 360$.

   Solution: Since $\cos 2\,\theta = 2\cos^2\theta - 1$, it follows that $2\cos^2\theta - 1 = 3 - 7\cos\theta$;

   $2\cos^2\theta + 7\cos\theta - 4 = 0$; $(2\cos\theta - 1)(\cos\theta + 4) = 0$; $\cos\theta = \dfrac{1}{2}$ or $\cos\theta = -4$
   (which is impossible). Thus $\theta = 60°,\ 300°$.

7. Find the area of a regular octagon with side 20.

   Solution: The value of h (the apothem) can be found using cotangent: $\cot 22.5° = \dfrac{h}{10}$

   or $h = 10\cot 22.5°$. It follows that the area of the octagon is $8\left(\dfrac{1}{2} \cdot 20 \cdot 10\cot 22.5°\right) =$
   $800\cot 22.5° = 1931$.

8. Solve: $\tan 3\,\theta = \dfrac{2\sin\theta\cos\theta}{\cos^2\theta - \sin^2\theta}$.

   Solution: $\tan 3\,\theta = \dfrac{\sin 2\,\theta}{\cos 2\,\theta} = \tan 2\,\theta$. Hence, $3\,\theta = 2\,\theta + n\pi,\ n \in Z;\ \theta = n\pi,\ n \in Z$.

9. Suppose $\sin x = \sin y$. Find all solutions of x in terms of y.

   Solution: If $\sin x = \sin y$, then $x = y$, or $x = \pi - y$. The more general solution of x in terms of y is given by adding $2n\pi$ onto each of these simple solutions: $x = 2n\pi + y$ or $x = 2n\pi + \pi - y = (2n + 1)\pi - y$.

10. Prove: $(\csc\theta + 1)(\csc\theta - 1) = \cot^2\theta$.

    Solution: $(\csc\theta + 1)(\csc\theta - 1) = \csc^2\theta - 1 = \dfrac{1}{\sin^2\theta} - 1 = \dfrac{1 - \sin^2\theta}{\sin^2\theta} = \dfrac{\cos^2\theta}{\sin^2\theta} = \cot^2\theta$.

11. Prove: $\dfrac{\sin(x + y)}{\cos x\cos y} = \tan x + \tan y$.

    Solution: $\dfrac{\sin x\cos y + \cos x\sin y}{\cos x\cos y} = \tan x + \tan y$; $\dfrac{\sin x}{\cos x} + \dfrac{\sin y}{\cos y} = \tan x + \tan y$;
    $\tan x + \tan y = \tan x + \tan y$.

12. a) Show: $\sin x\cos x = \dfrac{\tan x}{\sec^2 x}$ b) Show: $\cos^2 x - \sin^2 x = \dfrac{1 - \tan^2 x}{\sec^2 x}$.

    Solution:

    a) $\dfrac{\tan x}{\sec^2 x} = \dfrac{\dfrac{\sin x}{\cos x}}{\sec^2 x} = \dfrac{\sin x}{\cos x} \cdot \cos^2 x = \sin x\cos x$

    b) $\dfrac{1 - \tan^2 x}{\sec^2 x} = \dfrac{1 - \tan^2 x}{1 + \tan^2 x} = \dfrac{1 - \dfrac{\sin^2 x}{\cos^2 x}}{1 + \dfrac{\sin^2 x}{\cos^2 x}} = \dfrac{\cos^2 x - \sin^2 x}{\cos^2 x + \sin^2 x} = \cos^2 x - \sin^2 x$.

13. a) Show: $\tan 2\,\theta = \dfrac{2\tan\theta}{1 + \tan^2\theta}$.

    b) If $t = \tan\dfrac{\theta}{2}$, show $\sin\theta = \dfrac{2t}{1 + t^2}$, $\cos\theta = \dfrac{1 - t^2}{1 + t^2}$.

Solution:

a) Notice that $\tan(x + y) = \dfrac{\tan x + \tan y}{1 - \tan x \tan y}$. Let $x = y = \theta$. It follows that

$$\tan 2\,\theta = \frac{2\tan \theta}{1 - \tan^2 \theta}.$$

b) Let $t = \tan\dfrac{\theta}{2}$.

We have: $\sin \theta = 2\sin\dfrac{\theta}{2}\cos\dfrac{\theta}{2} = 2\dfrac{\tan\dfrac{\theta}{2}}{\sec^2\dfrac{\theta}{2}} = 2\dfrac{\tan\dfrac{\theta}{2}}{1 + \tan^2\dfrac{\theta}{2}} = \dfrac{2t}{1 + t^2}$.

Similarly, $\cos \theta = \cos^2\dfrac{\theta}{2} - \sin^2\dfrac{\theta}{2} = \dfrac{1 - \tan^2\dfrac{\theta}{2}}{\sec^2\dfrac{\theta}{2}} = \dfrac{1 - t^2}{1 + t^2}$.

14. Find the area of a regular polygon of n sides inscribed in a circle with radius r.

Solution: Consider a central angle $\angle A$ in the circle that is circumscribed around the polygon. If $\angle A$ intersects one side of the polygon, then $m\angle A = \dfrac{2\pi}{n}$. Therefore, the

area of polygon $= n\left[\dfrac{1}{2}\left(r\cos\dfrac{2\pi}{2n}r\sin\dfrac{2\pi}{2n}\right)\right]\cdot 2$ and (since $\sin 2\,\theta = 2\cos \theta \sin \theta$): area

of a polygon $= n\dfrac{1}{2}r^2\left(\sin\dfrac{2\pi}{n}\right) = \dfrac{1}{2}nr^2\left(\sin\dfrac{2\pi}{n}\right)$.

4.3 UNSOLVED PROBLEMS

1. Show: $\tan 3x = \dfrac{3\tan x - \tan^3 x}{1 - 3\tan^2 x}$.

2. Show: $\cos 3x = 4\cos^3 x - 3\cos x$.

3. Prove: $\cos 4A = 8\cos^4 A - 8\cos^2 A + 1$.

4. Solve: $\sin 3\theta = \cos \theta$ $(0 \le \theta \le 360°)$.

5. Using trigonometric identities find $\sin 15°$.

6. Express $\cos 5x - \cos 3x$ as a product of trigonometric functions.

7. Expand $\tan(\pi + x)$ in terms of $\tan x$.

8. A circular cone with base radius r and slant height l unrolls into a circular sector. Find the angle of this sector.

9. Solve the equation $\cos \theta + 2\sin \theta = 2$ for $0 \le \theta \le \dfrac{\pi}{2}$.

10. Drop a perpendicular from the point $P(\sin t, \cos t)$ to the x-axis. Show the length of the segment from P to $(0, 1)$ is given by $2\sin\dfrac{t}{2}$.

11. Prove that if A, B, C are angles of a triangle, $\sin A + \sin B + \sin C = 4\cos\dfrac{A}{2}\cos\dfrac{B}{2}\cos\dfrac{C}{2}$.

Pole	The origin
Polar axis	A horizontal ray with end point at the pole and coincident with the positive x-axis
Polar coordinates (r, θ)	Polar coordinate of a point P, where r is the distance of the pole to P, and θ is the angle between the polar axis and $\overrightarrow{OP}$.
$r(\cos \theta + i\sin \theta)$	The trigonometric form of the complex number $a + bi$ where $\cos \theta = \dfrac{a}{r} = \dfrac{a}{\sqrt{a^2 + b^2}}$ and $\sin \theta = \dfrac{b}{r} = \dfrac{b}{\sqrt{a^2 + b^2}}$
r	The modulus of a complex number, $r = \sqrt{a^2 + b^2}$
$z^n = r^n(\cos n\,\theta + i\sin n\,\theta)$	De Moivre's Theorem for any complex number $z = a + bi$

SECTION 4.4

POLAR COORDINATES, APPLICATIONS OF DE MOIVRE'S THEOREM

Polar Coordinates

We usually use the Cartesian coordinate system to locate points in a plane. Other systems of coordinates exist, but perhaps the most important is polar coordinates.

Let P be any point in the plane (in which we have the Cartesian coordinate system). Draw $\overrightarrow{OP}$, the ray connecting P to the origin O.

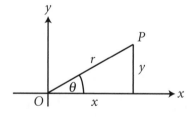

The origin O is also called the pole and $\overrightarrow{OP}$ is called the radius vector. If r is the length of $\overrightarrow{OP}$, and θ is the angle $\overrightarrow{OP}$ makes with the polar-axis, we say that P has the polar coordinates (r, θ). We allow multiple representations for the same point. For example, the polar coordi-nates: $(2, 60°)$, $(2, 420°)$, $(2, -300°)$, $(-2, 240°)$, $\left(2, \dfrac{\pi}{3} + 2n\pi\right)$ all represent the same point. When we superimpose a Cartesian coordinate system with a polar system, each point in the plane can be represented by its Cartesian coordinate (x, y) or by polar coordinate (r, θ). If $r > 0$, we have the fundamental relation between the Cartesian and polar coordinate of a point: $x = r\cos \theta$ and $y = r\sin \theta$, which means $x^2 + y^2 = r^2$.

133

For example, to find the polar coordinate of $(-1, \sqrt{3})$, notice that $r^2 = (-1)^2 + (\sqrt{3})^2 = 4$, or $r = 2$. This means that $\cos\theta = -\dfrac{1}{2}$, $\sin\theta = \dfrac{\sqrt{3}}{2}$, or $\theta = 120°$. One suitable choice for a polar coordinate is $(2, 120°)$ or $\left(2, \dfrac{2}{3}\right)$.

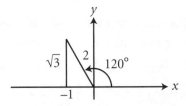

Alternatively, we can have an equation in Cartesian form and transform it into polar form. Consider the equation of a circle of radius 5 with center at $(0, 0)$: $x^2 + y^2 = 25$.

If we substitute $x = r\cos\theta$, $y = r\sin\theta$, we get the equation in polar form:

$$r^2(\cos^2\theta + \sin^2\theta) = 25 \text{ or } r = 5.$$

In this way, polar coordinates may help simplify a complicated Cartesian equation. More generally, consider a circle with center at (x_1, y_1) and radius a:

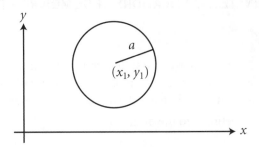

Consider the polar coordinates of the fixed point (x_1, y_1) to be (C, γ). This means that $(r\cos\theta - C\cos\gamma)^2 + (r\sin\theta - C\sin\gamma)^2 = a^2$.

Simplifying this equation we get:

$$r^2\cos^2\theta - 2rC\cos\theta\cos\gamma + C^2\cos^2\gamma + r^2\sin^2\theta - 2rC\sin\theta\sin\gamma + C^2\sin^2\gamma = a^2 \text{ or}$$

$$r^2(\cos^2\theta + \sin^2\theta) - 2rC(\cos\theta\cos\gamma + \sin\theta\sin\gamma) + C^2 = a^2$$

which means that $r^2 - 2rC\cos(\theta - \gamma) + C^2 = a^2$.

Trigonometric Form of Complex Numbers: De Moivre's Theorem

Consider a complex number in the plane with coordinates $(a, b) = a + bi$. Notice that $a + bi$ may be written in polar form of (r, θ) where $r = \sqrt{a^2 + b^2}$, and $a = r\cos\theta$, $b = r\sin\theta$, where θ is the angle made between r and the positive half of the x-axis. The trigonometric form of $a + bi = r\cos\theta + ir\sin\theta = r(\cos\theta + i\sin\theta)$.

The number r is called the modulus and θ is called the argument of $a + bi$. Notice that if

$$z_1 = r_1(\cos\theta_1 + i\sin\theta_1) \text{ and } z_2 = r_2(\cos\theta_2 + i\sin\theta_2), \text{ we have:}$$

$$z_1 \cdot z_2 = r_1 r_2(\cos\theta_1 + i\sin\theta_1)(\cos\theta_2 + i\sin\theta_2)$$

$$= r_1 r_2\left[(\cos\theta_1\cos\theta_2 - \sin\theta_1\sin\theta_2) + i(\sin\theta_1\cos\theta_2 + \cos\theta_1\sin\theta_2)\right]$$

$$= r_1 r_2\left[\cos(\theta_1 + \theta_2) + i\sin(\theta_1 + \theta_2)\right]. \text{ This result suggests the following two-part theorem:}$$

Let $z_1 = r_1(\cos\theta_1 + i\sin\theta_1)$ and $z_2 = r_2(\cos\theta_2 + i\sin\theta_2)$, then

$$z_1 \cdot z_2 = r_1 r_2\left[\cos(\theta_1 + \theta_2) + i\sin(\theta_1 + \theta_2)\right]; \frac{z_1}{z_2} = \frac{r_1}{r_2}\left[\cos(\theta_1 - \theta_2) + i\sin(\theta_1 - \theta_2)\right].$$

To raise a complex number to a power, repeat the multiplication rule and use mathematical induction to get **De Moivre's Theorem**: $z^n = r^n(\cos n\,\theta + i\sin n\,\theta)$.

For example, consider $(1+i\sqrt{3})^{10}$. Notice $r^2 = 1 + 3 = 4$ or $r = 2$. Similarly, $\sin\theta = \frac{\sqrt{3}}{2}$ and $\cos\theta = \frac{1}{2}$, which makes $\theta = \frac{\pi}{3}$. The trigonometric form of $1 + \sqrt{3}i$ can be written as $1 + \sqrt{3}i = 2\left(\cos\frac{\pi}{3} + i\sin\frac{\pi}{3}\right)$. By DeMoivre's Theorem we have:

$$(1+\sqrt{3}i)^{10} = 2^{10}\left(\cos\frac{10\pi}{3} + i\sin\frac{10\pi}{3}\right) = 1024\left(\cos\frac{10\pi}{3} + i\sin\frac{10\pi}{3}\right)$$

$$= 1024(-1 - \sqrt{3}) = -1024 - 1024\sqrt{3}.$$

De Moivre's Theorem can be used to find the nth root of a complex number. Assume that the nth power of some complex number solves the equation $c^n = z$. In other words, if $c = a(\cos\theta + i\sin\theta)$, $c^n = a^n(\cos n\,\theta + i\sin n\,\theta)$ or $z = a^n(\cos n\,\theta + i\sin n\,\theta)$. It follows that, if z is known, we can find the modulus of c by taking the nth root of the modulus of z, and we can also find the argument of c by dividing the argument of z by n. In general, (replacing θ with $\theta + 2k\pi$, where $k = 0, 1, 2, \ldots$), we have that for a positive integer n, the complex number $z = r(\cos\theta + i\sin\theta)$ has n distinct roots:

$$r^{\frac{1}{n}}\left(\cos\frac{\theta + 2k\pi}{n} + i\sin\frac{\theta + 2k\pi}{n}\right), \text{ where } k = 0, 1, 2, \ldots, n - 1$$

For example, to find the square root of i, first place i in trigonometric form $i = 1\left(\cos\frac{\pi}{2} + i\sin\frac{\pi}{2}\right)$. Hence, the square roots of i are given by:

$$i^{\frac{1}{2}} = 1^{\frac{1}{2}}\left(\cos\frac{\pi}{4} + i\sin\frac{\pi}{4}\right) = \sqrt{2} + i\sqrt{2} \text{ or } i^{\frac{1}{2}} = 1^{\frac{1}{2}}\left(\cos\frac{5\pi}{4} + i\sin\frac{5\pi}{4}\right) = -\sqrt{2} - i\sqrt{2}.$$

Notice that the both roots have a magnitude of 1 and are evenly distributed around the unit circle.

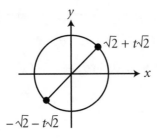

4.4 SOLVED PROBLEMS

1. Which of the following represents the same point(s) $((-r, \theta)$ reflects (r, θ) in the origin): $\left(2, \dfrac{\pi}{3}\right), \left(-2, -\dfrac{5\pi}{3}\right), \left(2, -\dfrac{\pi}{3}\right), \left(-2, \dfrac{\pi}{3}\right)$

   Solution:

   $$\left(2, \frac{\pi}{3}\right) = \left(2\cos\frac{\pi}{3}, 2\sin\frac{\pi}{3}\right) = (1, \sqrt{3}); \quad \left(-2, -\frac{5\pi}{3}\right) = \left(-2\cos\frac{5\pi}{3}, -2\sin\frac{5\pi}{3}\right) = (1, \sqrt{3})$$

   $$\left(2, -\frac{\pi}{3}\right) = \left(2\cos\left(-\frac{\pi}{3}\right), 2\sin\left(-\frac{\pi}{3}\right)\right) = (1, -\sqrt{3}); \quad \left(-2, \frac{\pi}{3}\right) = \left(-2\cos\frac{\pi}{3}, -2\sin\frac{\pi}{3}\right) = (-1, -\sqrt{3})$$

   Clearly, $\left(2, \dfrac{\pi}{3}\right) = \left(-2, -\dfrac{5\pi}{3}\right)$.

2. Find the equation of the line $y = 2x$ in polar form.

   Solution: The line has a slope of 2 and passes through the origin. In other words, the equation of the line is $\theta = \tan^{-1} 2, y = r\sin\theta; x = r\cos\theta$.

3. Find the polar form of $(-\sqrt{2}, \sqrt{2})$.

   Solution: The distance of $(-\sqrt{2}, \sqrt{2})$ from the origin is $r^2 = 4$ or $r = 2$, while the radius vector makes an angle of $\dfrac{3\pi}{4}$ with the polar-axis. Hence, the polar form is $\left(2, \dfrac{3\pi}{4}\right)$.

4. Show the polar equation of a line l containing the point P with polar coordinates (r, α) where $\overline{OP}$ is perpendicular to l, is $x\cos\alpha + y\sin\alpha = r$.

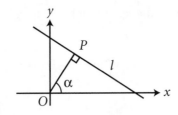

Solution: Notice that the Cartesian coordinates of P are $(r\cos\alpha, r\sin\alpha)$, which means the slope of line l must be $-\dfrac{\cos\alpha}{\sin\alpha}$ (i.e., the negative reciprocal of slope of $\overrightarrow{OP}$). Hence, $x\cos\alpha + y\sin\alpha = k$ To determine k, notice again that $(r\cos\alpha, r\sin\alpha)$ is a point on the line such that: $r\cos\alpha \cdot \cos\alpha + r\sin\alpha\sin\alpha = k$ or $r = k$. Hence, $x\cos\alpha + y\sin\alpha = r$.

5. Sketch the equation $\left\{(r, \theta)\middle| r > 0, \dfrac{\pi}{2} < \theta < \pi \right\}$.

Solution: Notice that any point P in the second quadrant belongs to this solution set.

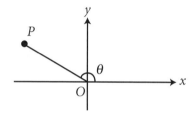

6. If $z_1 = r_1(\cos\theta_1 + i\sin\theta_1)$ and $z_2 = r_2(\cos\theta_2 + i\sin\theta_2)$ show that: $\dfrac{z_1}{z_2} = \dfrac{r_1}{r_2}\big[\cos(\theta_1 - \theta_2) + i\sin(\theta_1 - \theta_2)\big]$.

Solution: $\dfrac{z_1}{z_2} = \dfrac{r_1(\cos\theta_1 + i\sin\theta_1)}{r_2(\cos\theta_2 + i\sin\theta_2)} = \dfrac{r_1}{r_2} \cdot \dfrac{(\cos\theta_1 + i\sin\theta_1)(\cos\theta_2 - i\sin\theta_2)}{(\cos\theta_2 + i\sin\theta_2)(\cos\theta_2 - i\sin\theta_2)}$

$\qquad = \dfrac{r_1}{r_2} \cdot \dfrac{(\cos\theta_1\cos\theta_2 + \sin\theta_1\sin\theta_2 + i(\sin\theta_1\cos\theta_2 - \cos\theta_1\sin\theta_2)}{\cos^2\theta_2 + \sin^2\theta_2}$

$\qquad = \dfrac{r_1}{r_2}\big[\cos(\theta_1 - \theta_2) + i\sin(\theta_1 - \theta_2)\big]$.

7. Derive the identities: $\cos3\,\theta = 4\cos^3\theta - 3\cos\theta$, $\sin3\,\theta = 3\sin\theta - 4\sin^3\theta$.

Solution: Using De Moivre's Theorem:

$\cos3\,\theta + i\sin3\,\theta = (\cos\theta + i\sin\theta)^3 = (\cos^3\theta - 3\cos\theta\sin^2\theta) + i(3\cos^2\theta\sin\theta - \sin^3\theta)$.

Hence, $\cos3\,\theta = \cos^3\theta - 3\cos\theta\sin^2\theta = \cos^3\theta - 3\cos\theta(1 - \cos^2\theta) = 4\cos^3\theta - 3\cos\theta$

and $\sin3\,\theta = 3\cos^2\theta\sin\theta - \sin^3\theta = 3(1 - \sin^2\theta)\sin\theta - \sin^3\theta = 3\sin\theta - 4\sin^3\theta$.

8. Prove: $(\cos\theta + i\sin\theta)^n = \cos n\,\theta + i\sin n\,\theta$, if n is an integer $n < 0$, and if $n = \dfrac{p}{q}$.

Solution: If n is a negative integer, let $m = -n$. Then $(\cos\theta + i\sin\theta)^n = \dfrac{1}{(\cos\theta + i\sin\theta)^m}$

$$= \frac{1}{\cos m\,\theta + i\sin m\,\theta} = \frac{\cos m\,\theta - \sin m\,\theta}{\cos^2 m\,\theta + \sin^2 m\,\theta} = \cos m\,\theta - \sin m\,\theta = \cos(-m\,\theta) + i\sin(-m\,\theta)$$

$$= \cos n\,\theta + i\sin n\,\theta.$$

b) If $n = \dfrac{p}{q}$ where p and q are integers, then

$$(\cos\frac{p}{q}\theta + \sin\frac{p}{q}\theta)^q = \cos p\,\theta + i\sin p\,\theta = (\cos\theta + i\sin\theta)^p. \text{ Hence,}$$

$$\cos\frac{p}{q}\theta + \sin\frac{p}{q}\theta = (\cos\theta + i\sin\theta)^{\frac{p}{q}}.$$

9. Let $z^5 - 1 = (z - z_1)(z - z_2)\ldots(z - z_5)$ Suppose that $z_1 = 1$, $z_k = z_{k-1}(\cos\theta + i\sin\theta)$. Find θ.

Solution: The five roots of 1 form a regular pentagon with roots at the vertices:
$$\theta = \frac{2\pi}{5}.$$

4.4 UNSOLVED PROBLEMS

1. Suppose $(-r, \theta)$ satisfies a polar equation $r = f(\theta)$ whenever (r, θ) satisfies the equation. What can we deduce about $r = f(\theta)$?

2. Find the Cartesian coordinate for the polar coordinate $(\pi, 2\pi)$.

3. Find the polar coordinate for $(-1, \sqrt{3})$.

4. Solve: $z^6 - 1 = 0$.

5. Show: $z^n - 1 = (z - 1)(z - z_1)(z - z_1^2)\ldots(z - z_1^{n-1})$

where $z_1 = \cos\dfrac{2\pi}{n} + i\sin\dfrac{2\pi}{n}$ for $n \in I$.

6. Let $1, w, w^2, w^3, \ldots, w^6$ be the seven roots of 1. What is the relationship between w^r and w^{n-r}?

7. Solve: $z^3 = i$.

8. Describe the locus of complex numbers z such that $|z - 1 - i| = 1$.

9. Find the locus of complex number z such that $|z - 1| = |z|$.

CHAPTER FIVE

Functions

The concept of functions permeates mathematics from its most elementary ideas (e.g., counting on fingers) to the most complex (e.g., any research journal in mathematics has plenty of these). This chapter explores some of the most fundamental ideas of functions in the context of basic definitions, graphs, transformations, composition of functions, and inverse functions. It reviews material on algebraic and trigonometric functions, and the basic properties of inverse trigonometric, exponential, and logarithmic functions.

OF TERMS

$A \times B$	The Cartesian cross-product A and B consists of (a, b) such that $a \in A$ and $b \in B$
$f : A \rightarrow B$	A function from A to B consists of elements $(a, b) \; \varepsilon \; A \times B$ such that for every $a \in A$ there exists precisely one $b \in B$
Domain of function $f : A \rightarrow B$	The set A
Range of function $f : A \rightarrow B$	All b in B such that $f(a) = b$ for some a in A
One-to-one or injective function	A function $f : A \rightarrow B$ such that whenever (a_1, b) and (a_2, b) are elements of f, then $a_1 = a_2$
Onto or surjective function:	A function $f : A \rightarrow B$ such that for any $b \in B$ there exists at least one $a \in A$ such that $(a, b) \in f$
Bijective or one-to-one and onto function:	A function $f : A \rightarrow B$ which is both injective and surjective
Greatest Integer Function	$y = [x]$ (the greatest integer less than or equal to x)
Absolute Value Function	$y = |x|$ (the distance of x from the origin)
Quadratic Function	$y = Ax^2 + Bx + C$ for some real numbers A, B and C

SECTION 5.1

FUNCTIONS AND THEIR GRAPHS

Perhaps the most central concept in all mathematics is the concept of a function. This chapter explores the basic definition and properties of functions. A **relation** on sets A and B is any subset of the Cartesian Cross-Product $A \times B$. A **function**: $f : A \rightarrow B$ is a relation on $A \times B$, such that for every $a \in A$ there exists precisely one $b \in B$, such that (a, b) is an element of f. The **domain** of a function refers to the input of the function, the values to which the function rule is applied. The **range** of a function refers to the output of the function, the values to which the function maps the elements in the domain.

Types of Functions

One-to-one (injective) $f: A \to B$ is a one-to-one (injective) function if f is a function such that whenever (x_1, b) and (x_2, b) are elements of f then $x_1 = x_2$. **Onto (surjective)** $f: A \to B$ is an onto function if f is a function such that for any $b \in B$ there exists some $a \in A$ such that (a, b) is an element of f. A **one-to-one and onto (bijective) function** $f: A \to B$ is a one-to-one and onto (bijective).

Various Representations for Functions

Functions are frequently represented in diagrams. Consider the following set diagram

for the function consisting of the elements $\{(a, x), (b, x), (c, x)\}$:

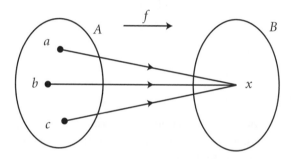

Algorithmic representations of functions frequently are given by "rules"; for example, $f: Z \to Z$ (where Z is a set of integers) such that $f(x) = 2x$ for any $x \in Z$ or $y = 2x$. This representation may also be graphed as a representation of points on a line.

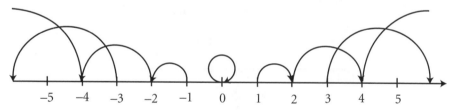

Alternatively, a function may be given by a table of values that indicate specific "points" belonging to the function and the corresponding pattern of these points:

$$f: R \to R \ (R = \{\text{real numbers}\}), f: x \to 2x \text{ or } f(x) = 2x \text{ or } y = 2x$$

x	0	1	−1
y	0	2	−2

A graphic representation can be drawn from a table of values and often allows for one to see important properties of a function. For example, if you graph $y = 2x$ and $y = x$ on a Cartesian coordinate system the slope (angle of inclination) of the line $y = 2x$ will be greater than the slope for the line $y = x$. Notice that the following graph fails to define a function $f : X \rightarrow Y$ (x_1 has images ($y_1 \neq y_2 \neq y_3$) by the vertical line test:

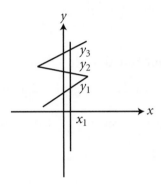

Step Functions

Consider the step function $[x] = y$. Define it by $y =$ the value of the greatest integer less than or equal to x. The step function defines a "broken" line. Some texts also call this function the *floor function*, denoted $\lfloor x \rfloor$.

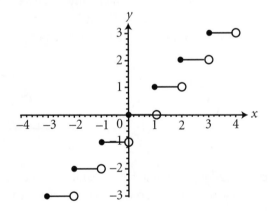

Absolute Value Functions

The graph of the absolute value gives a "broken" line. Consider the function $y = |x|$.

x	0	1	−1	2	−2
y	0	1	1	2	2

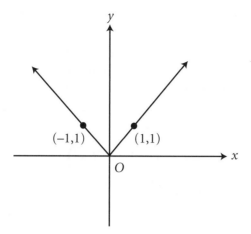

Quadratic Functions

A quadratic function is defined, in general, by the equation:
$Ax^2 + By^2 + Cxy + Dx + Ey + F = 0$, where A, B, C, D, E and F are real numbers. One of the most basic quadratics is the parabola $y = ax^2 + bx + c$. Consider a specific case of a parabola, $y = x^2$.

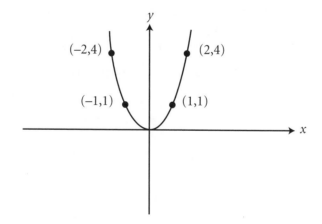

Let $y = ax^2 + bx + c$. Completing the square gives: $y = a\left(x + \dfrac{b}{2a}\right)^2 + \left(c - \dfrac{b^2}{4a}\right)$. In particular, when $x = \dfrac{-b}{2a}$ we have either a minimum for y (if $a > 0$) or a maximum value for y (if $a < 0$). In other words, the axis of symmetry for a parabola $y = ax^2 + bx + c$ is $x = \dfrac{-b}{2a}$.

5.1 SOLVED PROBLEMS

1. The following relationship (an arrow between elements) indicates, "is a brother of" for a set of boys and girls. How many members of the set are girls? If a family consists of brothers and sisters related to each other, what is the largest size family?

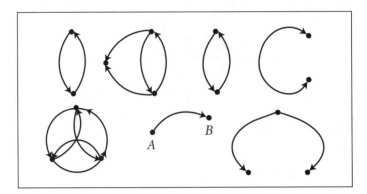

Solution: If an arrow goes from point A to B, it means A is a brother of B. If an arrow then does not go from B to A, it means B is not a brother of A (B is a sister of A). A total of six such points exist with this property: seven families exist with the largest being four and the smallest two.

2. Let {a, b, c, d, e} be a set of sides of a pentagon lettered in order. The relation "is perpendicular to" for this set gives the ordered pairs {(a, e), (b, c), (c, b), (e, d), (d, e), (e, a)}. Draw and label a pentagon illustrating this set.

Solution: The following gives one solution to the problem:

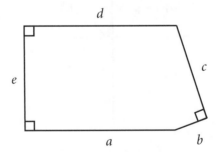

3. Let S be a set of people. R is a relation on S such that for every $x \in S$, xRx. Which of the following relations best fits their description: sings with? lives next door to? is the sister of ? is the parent of ? has the same name as?

Solution: The phrase that makes best sense if xRx is "has the same name as."

4. In the following scheme, the sequence of numbers 1, 5, 13, ... annotates a set of fractions with equal numerators and denominators. What is the next number in this sequence?

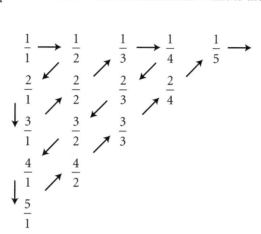

Solution: This diagram indicates: $1 \to \frac{1}{1}; 5 \to \frac{2}{2}; 13 \to \frac{3}{3}...$ In this scheme the next equivalent value for 1 will occur at $\frac{4}{4}$. The next number in the sequence is 25.

5. Consider the function $f: F \to N$ defined in the following arrow diagram:

$$F\{\frac{1}{1} \quad \frac{1}{2} \quad \frac{2}{1} \quad \frac{3}{1} \quad \frac{2}{2} \quad \frac{1}{3} \quad ... \quad p \quad ...\}$$
$$\downarrow \quad \downarrow \quad \downarrow \quad \downarrow \quad \downarrow \quad \downarrow \qquad\quad \downarrow$$
$$N\{1, \quad 2, \quad 3, \quad 4, \quad 5, \quad 6, \quad ... \quad q \quad ...\}$$

Find p such that $F(p) = 30$.

Solution: Notice in this scheme (see Figure 1.10) $\frac{2}{7}$ is the 30th term; $p = \frac{2}{7}$.

6. Two sets A, B are called **equivalent** iff a bijective mapping may be defined from $f: A \to B$. Show that the number of even integers is equivalent to the number of integers. Suggest a definition we might use for a set to be infinitely large.

Solution: Define $f: Z \to Z$ by $f: x \to 2x$. Notice: f is a properly defined mapping. In addition, each even number $2x$ comes from exactly one number x (f is onto). If two even numbers are equal $2x_1 = 2x_2$ then $x_1 = x_2$ (f is one-to-one). Hence, the set of even integers is equivalent to of all integers. This property suggests the following **definition**: a set S is infinitely large if a bijective mapping exists from S onto a proper subset of S.

7. A set is called **countable** iff it is equivalent to the set of positive integers. Show that the set of all positive rational numbers is countable.

Solution: Consider the scheme introduced in problem 5.

8. Graph: $y = -|x - 2|$.

Solution:

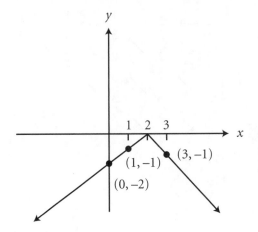

9. Describe the graph of $y = -2x^2 + x - 3$.

Solution: The equation describes a parabola with turning point $-\dfrac{1}{2(-2)} = x$ and the y intercept at $y = -3$. The parabola is turned down.

10. The trajectory of a ball when thrown is given by $y = -t^2 + 8t$ after t seconds. Find its maximum height. After how many seconds does it hit the ground?

Solution:

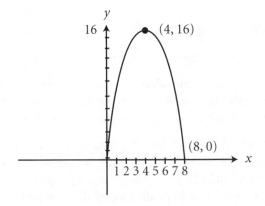

The graph of the trajectory is given in the figure. The turning point is at $x = 4$; maximum height $f(4) = -16 + 32 = 16$. The ball hits the earth when $y = 0$, after 8 seconds.

11. Graph the following step function: $y = [x^2]$.

Solution:

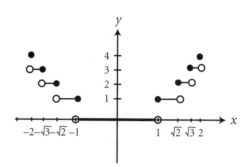

12. Find the range and domain for $y = \sqrt{x}$ and graph it.

Solution: The domain of the function consists of $x \geq 0$. The range is $y \geq 0$.

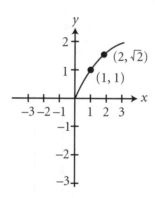

13. Find the range of and domain of the function $y = \dfrac{x}{|x|}$ and graph it.

Solution: Notice $x \neq 0$; while y takes on only two values: $1, -1$.

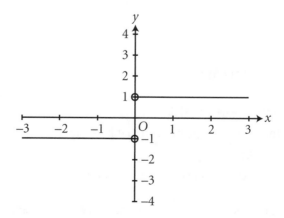

14. Give the graph and find the range and domain for $y = [2x + 1]$.

Solution: In this case the range and domain are precisely as in problem 2.

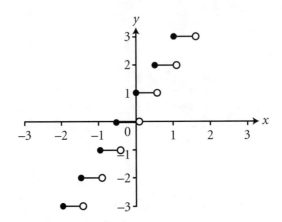

15. Give the graph and find the range and domain for $y = \dfrac{1}{1-x}$.

Solution: x may be any value except 1, and y will never equal 0, since the function may be re-written as: $y = yx$ or $x = \dfrac{1-y}{-y}$.

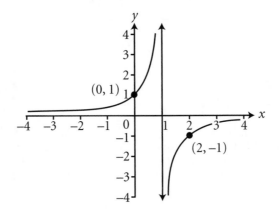

5.1 UNSOLVED PROBLEMS

1. Sketch the graph $y + |y| = x + |x|$.
2. Determine the area in the plane such that $|x| + |y| \le 5$.
3. Graph: $y - 2 = \sqrt{x-1}$.
4. Determine whether the following is a function: $(x+3)^2 + (y+2)^2 = 9$.
5. Consider the function $f(x) = \dfrac{|x|}{x}$. Find the range and domain of $f(x)$.
6. If $f(x) = x^2 + 1$, find $f(\tan x)$.

7. If $f(x) = x^2 + 9$ and $g(x) = \sqrt{x+4}$, find $(-f(0))^{-g(0)}$.

8. Determine a "proper" domain, which allows the following expressions to be functions:

   a) $f(x) = \sqrt{x^{-1}}$;   b) $f(x) = \sqrt[3]{\dfrac{|x+1|}{x+1}}$.

9. Find the range and domain for $y = \dfrac{1}{(x-1)(x-2)}$.

10. Find the range and domain of $y = [\sin x]$.

SECTION 5.2

TRANSFORMATIONS OF FUNCTIONS

Functions may be transformed by equations similar to those used in transformations for the Euclidian plane. The most common of such transformations involve translations and size transformations. We consider how functions change when they are moved in directions parallel to the x- and y-axis, and how to alter the basic shapes of functions by size transformations. These transformations provide a visual vocabulary that help organize functions into families.

Basic Transformations

Consider the table of values $y = f(x)$ for a function:

x	x_1	x_2	x_3
$f(x)$	$f(x_1)$	$f(x_2)$	$f(x_3)$

For a new function $y - b = f(x - a)$ make the substitutions $x' = x - a$ and $y' = y - b$. Then, $y - b = f(x - a)$ becomes $y' = f(x')$ where $x = x' + a$ and $y = y' + b$ or $f(x) = f(x') + b$. For the table of value of $y' = f(x')$ we have:

x'	x_1'	x_2'	x_3'
$f(x')$	$f(x_1')$	$f(x_2')$	$f(x_3')$

Corresponding to this is the table of values for $y = f(x)$:

x	$x_1' + a$	$x_2' + a$	$x_3' + a$
$f(x)$	$f(x_1') + b$	$f(x_2') + b$	$f(x_3') + b$

For example, $y = x^2$ and $y - 2 = (x - 3)^2$. For the function $y = x^2$:

x	0	1	2	3	4	−1	−2
x^2	0	1	4	9	16	1	4

The table for the new function $y - 2 = (x - 3)^2$ is given by:

x	$0 + 3$	$1 + 3$	$2 + 3$	$3 + 3$	$4 + 3$	$-1 + 3$	$-2 + 3$
$(x - 3)^2 + 2$	$0 + 2$	$1 + 2$	$4 + 2$	$9 + 2$	$16 + 2$	$1 + 2$	$4 + 2$

This table denotes a function that shifts $y = x^2$ by 3 units to the right and 2 units up.

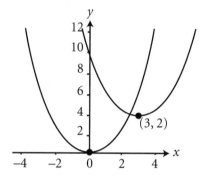

Similarly, $y + b = f(x + a)$ will represent a shift of the actual function $y = f(x)$ by a units to the left and b units down. Size transformations of a function "squash" and "stretch" the original function. Once again, consider $y = x^2$:

x	0	1	−1	2	−2	3	−3
y	0	1	1	4	4	9	9

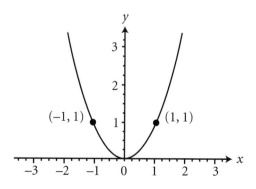

It can be "squashed" horizontally by a factor of 2 by the transformation $y = f(2x)$ to give a new table of values for f. The values that we once had at $x = 2$ now occur at $x = 1$.

x	0	1	-1	2	-2	3	-3
y	0	4	4	16	16	36	36

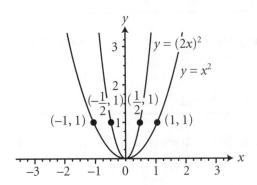

Similarly, the transformation $y = f\left(\dfrac{x}{2}\right)$ "stretches" the original function $y = f(x)$. The values for f at $x = 2$ now occur at $x = 1$. Using our example $y = x^2$, we obtain the graph for $y = f\left(\dfrac{x}{2}\right)$:

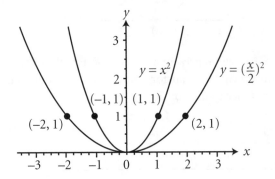

In a similar way, we "stretch" the y value of the original function by a factor of 2 with the transformation $y = 2f(x)$ (or $\dfrac{1}{2}y = f(x)$), and "squash" the y value by a factor of $\dfrac{1}{2}$ with the transformation $y = \dfrac{1}{2}f(x)$ (or $2y = f(x)$).

5.2 SOLVED PROBLEMS

1. Graph the following $y = x^2$, $y = x^3$, $y = x^3 - 2x^2$, $y = |x|$, $y = [x]$, $x^2 + y^2 = 1$, $y = \dfrac{x^2}{4 - x}$, $y = 10x$, $y = \log x$.

   Solution: The following are some of the basic families of graphs. They may be obtained by a table of values and some basic algebraic manipulations, or by using the graphing calculator. (Note: For a quadratic polynomial it is sufficient to have 3 points.)

a)

x	0	−2	2
x^2	0	4	4

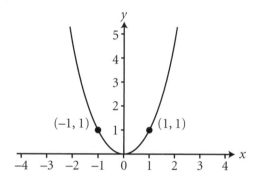

b)

x	−2	−1	0	1	2
x^3	−8	−1	0	1	8

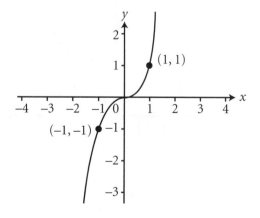

c)

x	-1	0	1	2	3
$x^3 - 2x^2$	$(-1)^3 - (2)$ $(-1)^2 = -3$	$0^3 - 2(0)^2$ $= 0$	$1^3 - 2(1)^2$ $= -1$	$2^3 - 2(2)^2 =$ $= 0$	$3^3 - 2(3)^2$ $= 9$

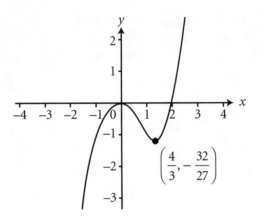

$$\left(\frac{4}{3}, -\frac{32}{27}\right)$$

d)

x	-2	-1	0	1	2
$|x|$	2	1	0	1	2

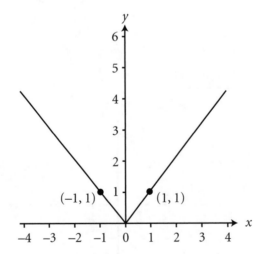

$(-1, 1)$ $(1, 1)$

e)

x	$-3 \le x \le -2$	$-2 \le x \le -1$	$-1 \le x \le 0$	$0 \le x \le 1$	$1 \le x \le 2$	$2 \le x \le 3$
$[x]$	-3	-2	-1	0	1	2

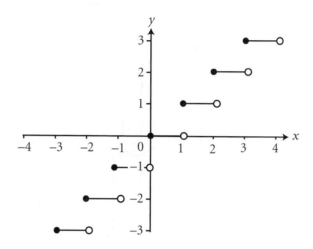

f)

x	1	-1	0	0
$x^2 + y^2 = 1$	0	0	1	-1

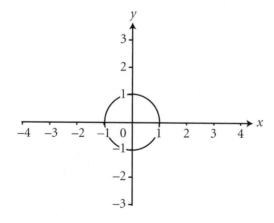

g)

x	0	1	−1	2	−2
$y = \dfrac{x^2}{4-x}$	0	$\dfrac{1}{3}$	$\dfrac{1}{5}$	2	$\dfrac{2}{3}$

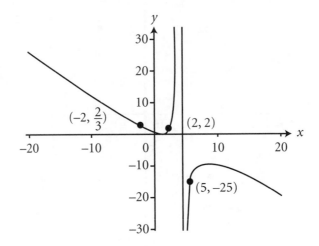

In particular, notice that $x \to 4$, $y \to \pm \infty$, also notice that $y = \dfrac{x}{\dfrac{4}{x} - 1} \approx -x - 4$ as x

gets increasingly large. Thus $y = x - 4$ is a line to which the graph approaches as $x \to \infty$, or $x \to -\infty$. To determine the values y takes, solve (e.g., to determine the range of the function) for x in terms of y: $y(4 - x) = x^2$ or $x^2 + xy - 4y = 0$.

Solve this by the quadratic formula with $a = 1$, $b = y$, $c = -4y$. The discriminant of the quadratic formula is $y^2 + 16y$, which must be nonnegative to have real solutions. $y^2 + 16y \ge 0$; $y(y + 16) \ge 0$, which means $y \ge 0$ or $y \le -16$.

h)

x	0	1	−1	2
$10x$	1	10	.1	100

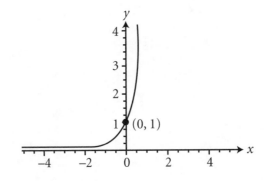

i)

x	1	.1	100	.01
$y = \log x$	0	−1	2	−2

In particular, notice as $x \to 0$, $y \to -\infty$.

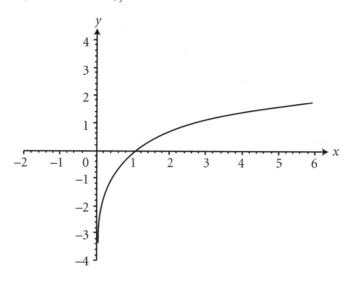

2. Graph: $y = |x - 2|$.

   Solution: $y = |x - 2|$ is a translation of $y = |x|$ so that $x = x' - 2$.

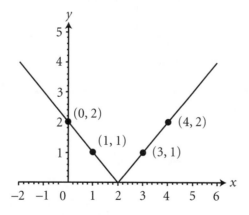

3. Graph: $(x - 2)^2 + (y - 3)^2 = 1$.

   Solution: Notice y is a translation $x \to x - 2$ and $y \to y - 3$ of the unit circle $x^2 + y^2 = 1$.

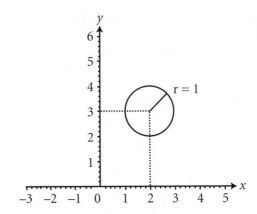

4. Using the concepts of translation and dilations, the following graph represents an equation of the form $y = a(x - b)^3 + c$:

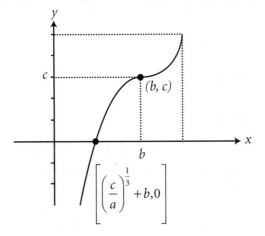

Solution: Using this information graph $y - 3 = 2(x - 2)^3$.

Solution: The new graph is a translation of $y = x^3$ to the point $(2, 3)$, dilated by a factor 2: $y - 3 = 2(x - 2)^3$.

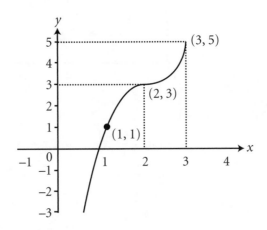

5. Graph: $y = \sqrt{x}$,

Solution: Notice the graph for $y = x^2$.

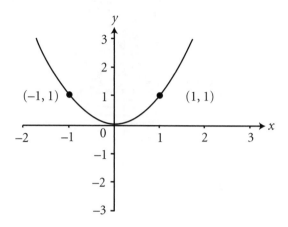

To create the graph $y = \sqrt{x}$, interchange the x and y axis in $y = x^2$, and then only take values for $y \geq 0$.

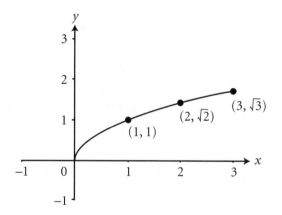

6. Give values for $f(x, y) = (x^2 + y, x^2 - y^2)$ when $x = 1, y = 1; x = 1, y = 2$. What is the cross section of the relation $z^2 = x^2 + x^2$ for any value z_0 of z?

Solution: $x = 1, y = 1$ then $f(1, 1) = (2, 0); x = 1, y = 2$ then $f(1, 2) = (3, -3)$. Notice for $z = z_0$ (constant), $x^2 + y^2 = z_0^2$, which is a circle of radius z_0. This means $z^2 = x^2 + x^2$ is the equation of the "mathematical" cone.

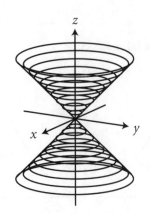

5.2 UNSOLVED PROBLEMS

1. Graph: $y - 3 = 2|x - 1|$.

2. Using the concept of translation describe the function $y - 3 = \sqrt{x - 2}$.

3. Find the equation for the following function if $y = x^3$ is given by the bold line:

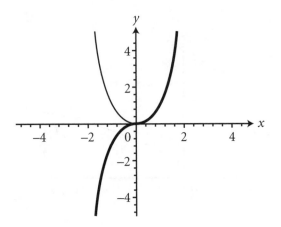

4. Graph the following function: $y = \dfrac{x - 1}{x + 1}$.

5. If $f(x) = y$ is represented by the following graph, graph $f(x + 3) = y$:

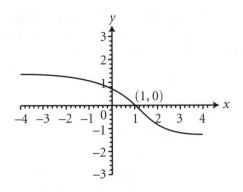

6. Graph: $y = -\sqrt{1-x^2}$.

7. Graph: $(y - x^3)(y - x^2) = 0$.

8. Graph: $2y(2x - 3y + 1) - 3x(2x - 3y + 1) + 2x - 3y + 1 = 0$.

9. Consider $\dfrac{f(x+h) - f(x)}{h}$ when $f(x) = x^2$. This quantity is called the difference quotient. Give a geometric interpretation of this difference quotient.

$(f \circ g)(x)$(composition)	Let $f: A \to B$ and $g: B \to C$ be two functions then $(f \circ g): A \to C$ such that $(f \circ g)(x) = f(g(x))$
$f^{-1}(x)$(inverse)	f^{-1} is the inverse of $f: A \to B$ iff f^{-1} is properly defined on B and $f(f^{-1}(x)) = f^{-1}(f(x)) = x$ for all x
$y = \arcsin x = \sin^{-1} x$	$\sin y = x; -1 \le x \le 1$ (domain); $-\dfrac{\pi}{2} \le y \le \dfrac{\pi}{2}$ (range)
$y = \arccos x = \cos^{-1} x$	$\cos y = x; -1 \le x \le 1$ (domain); $0 \le y \le \pi$ (range)
$y = \arctan x = \tan^{-1} x$	$\tan y = x; -\infty < x < \infty$(domain); $-\dfrac{\pi}{2} < y < \dfrac{\pi}{2}$ (range)
$y = \text{arc} \cot x = \cot^{-1} x$	$\cot y = x; -\infty < x < \infty$(domain); $0 < y < \pi$ (range)
$y = \text{arc} \sec x = \sec^{-1} x$	$\sec y = x.$ Domain: $(-\infty, -1] \cup [1, \infty)$
	Range: $\left[0, \dfrac{\pi}{2}\right) \cup \left(\dfrac{\pi}{2}, \pi\right]$
$y = \text{arc} \csc x = \csc^{-1} x$	$\csc y = x.$ Domain: $(-\infty, -1] \cup [1, \infty)$
	Range: $\left[-\dfrac{\pi}{2}, 0\right) \cup \left(0, \dfrac{\pi}{2}\right]$
Logarithm of x to base "a"	$y = \log_a x$ iff $a^y = x$
Laws of Logarithms	$\log AB = \log A + \log B$
	$\log \dfrac{A}{B} = \log A - \log B$
	$\log A^n = n \log A$
Laws of Exponents	$a^x \cdot a^y = a^{x+y}, a > 0$
	$\dfrac{a^x}{a^y} = a^{x-y}$
	$(a^x)^n = a^{nx}$

SECTION 5.3

COMPOSITE AND INVERSE FUNCTIONS

Given a function $f: A \to B$ and a function $g: B \to C$, so that the range values of f may be used as the domain values of g. Define the **composition** of functions f by g as a function such that $x \to g(f(x))$. Consider a function g defined on a set A where $g: A \to A$ and $g(x) = x$ for all $x \in A$. This function g is called the **identity function**. In particular, if g is the identity function then $f \circ g = g \circ f = f$ for f defined on A.

Suppose $f: A \to B$ is 1–1 (injective). Consider a function $f^{-1}: f^{-1}(B) \to A$ such that $f(f^{-1}(x)) = f^{-1}(f(x)) = x$. (Notice $f \circ f^{-1} = f^{-1} \circ f = id$). The function f^{-1} is called the **inverse function** of f. Diagrammatically:

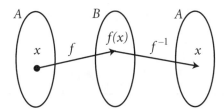

Another way one may explain an inverse function is by examining a table of values. The inverse function for f is that function which "inverts" the table of values. If you have a table of values for f, you can the invert it to define f^{-1} (if f^{-1} is a function). If you invert this inverse table, you will get back the original table of values for f. A convenient graphical interpretation of inverse function for f also exists: the inverse for f is a reflection of the graph of f in the line $y = x$.

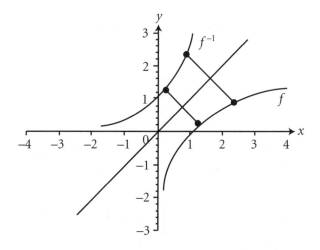

5.3 SOLVED PROBLEMS

1. Consider $f(x) = 3x - 5$ and $g(x) = x^2 + 2$. Find $(f \circ g)(x) = f(g(x))$ and $g \circ f(x) = g(f(x))$. Is composition commutative over the set of functions?

   Solution: Notice $f(g(x)) = f(x^2 + 2) = 3(x^2 + 2) - 5$, while $g(f(x)) = g(3x - 5) = (3x - 5)^2 + 2$. Clearly, $f \circ g \neq g \circ f$; the operation of composition of functions is not commutative over the set of functions.

2. Consider the function $y = x^2$. Does it have an inverse function?

   Solution: Consider the graph for $y = x^2$.

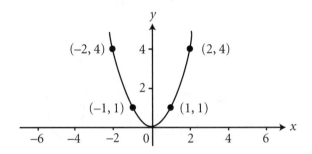

   Reflect the curve through the line $y = x$. The resulting relation, $y^2 = x$, is clearly not a function, since for every $x > 0$ there exists two values y_1 and y_2 such that $x \to y_1$ and $x \to y_2$.

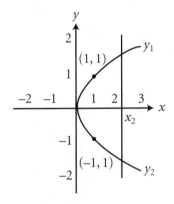

3. Consider the function $f(x) = 2x - 5$. Define f^{-1} and show $f \circ f^{-1} = f^{-1} \circ f = id$.

   Solution: If $f(x) = 2x - 5$, then the inverse function is $x = \dfrac{y+5}{2}$ or $f^{-1}(x) = \dfrac{x+5}{2}$.

   Hence, $f \circ f^{-1} = f\left(\dfrac{x+5}{2}\right) = 2\left(\dfrac{x+5}{2}\right) - 5 = x$; $f^{-1} \circ f = f^{-1}(2x - 5) = \dfrac{2x - 5 + 5}{2} = x$.

4. Find the equation of the inverse function for $Ax + By + C = 0$. Show that the product of the slope of the resulting line m_1 and the slope of the given line m equals 1.

Solution: The equation of the inverse function for $Ax + By + C = 0$ is given by:

$Ay + Bx + C = 0$. The slope of this inverse is $m_1 = -\dfrac{B}{A}$. The slope of the given line

is $m = -\dfrac{A}{B}$. Notice $m_1 \cdot m = \left(-\dfrac{B}{A}\right)\left(-\dfrac{A}{B}\right) = 1.$

5. Describe an appropriate domain and range for the inverse function for $y = \sin x$.

   Solution: Consider the graph for $y = \sin x$.

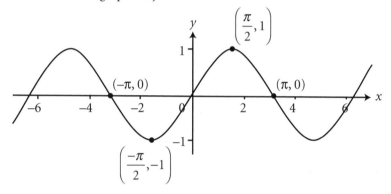

The inverse of this function would be represented graphically by a reflection of $y = \sin x$ in the line $y = x$, or $y = \arcsin x$:

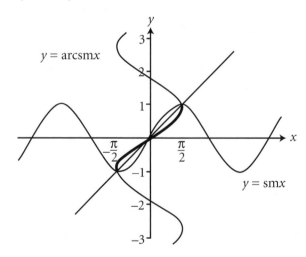

The indicated portion of the inverse relation could define a function. In other words, $y = \arcsin x$ for $-1 \le x \le 1$ (domain) and $\dfrac{\pi}{2} \le y \le \dfrac{\pi}{2}$ (range) (interchange the x and y axis).

6. Prove that, if the inverse function for f exists, it must be unique (assume composition of functions is an associative operation).

   Solution: Assume f_1^{-1} and f_2^{-1} are both inverses for f. By definition of the inverse

   function: $f_1^{-1} = f_1^{-1} \circ id = f_1^{-1} \circ (f \circ f_2^{-1}) = (f_1^{-1} \circ f) \circ f_2^{-1} = id \circ f_2^{-1} = f_2^{-1}.$

7. Let $f(x) = 3x - 5$ and $g(x) = \dfrac{x+5}{3}$. Graph $(f \circ g)(x)$.

   Solution: Notice $f^{-1} = g$, which means $f \circ g = id$. In other words, $(f \circ g)(x) = x$.

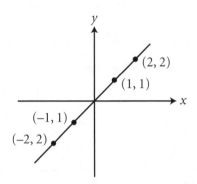

8. If $f(x) = x^3$ find the domain of the inverse function f^{-1}, if it exists.

   Solution: If $y = x^3$, the inverse is $x = y^3$ or the function $y = x^{\frac{1}{3}}$, which exists for all real x.

9. Consider a clock. Define $f(1) = 12$, the number of distinct numbers you touch when you move around a clock in steps of 1 starting at 12. Define $f(2) = 6$, which is the number of distinct numbers you touch when you move around the clock in steps of 2, and so on. Find the range of f. What can you say about n if $f(n) = 12$?

   Solution: When you move in steps of 1 around the clock you land on all the numbers: 1, 2, 3, 4, 5, 6, 7, 8, 9, 10, 11, 12. Hence, $f(1) = 12$. When you move in steps of 2 around the clock, you get 2, 4, 6, 8, 10, 12. Hence, $f(2) = 6$. Similarly, $f(3) = 4, f(4) = 3, f(6) = 2$. By similar argument, when you move in steps of 5 starting at 12 you get 5, 10, 3, 8, 1, 6, 11, 4, 9, 2, 7, 12. In other words, $f(5) = 12, f(7) = 12, f(8) = 3, f(9) = 4, f(10) = 6, f(11) = 12, f(12) = 1$. Notice $f(n) = 12$ if $(n, 12) = 1$.

10. Let $f(x) = x^2$ and $g(x) = x + 1$. When does $f \circ g = g \circ f$?

    Solution: $f \circ g = f(x + 1) = (x + 1)^2$; $g \circ f = f(x^2) = x^2 + 1$; if $(x + 1)^2 = x^2 + 1$, then $x = 0$.

11. Give a family of functions for which the graph of f^{-1} gives the same picture as the graph for f.

    Solution: The relationship holds when the reflection of f in $y = x$ does not change the graph for f. Take any line perpendicular to $y = x$, for example, $y = -x$ or $y = k - x$ for $k \in Z$.

12. Let $f(x) = x^2$, $g(x) = 3x - 2$. Find $(f \circ g^{-1})(x)$.

    Solution: If $g(x) = 3x - 2$, then $g^{-1}(x) = \dfrac{x+2}{3}$. Consequently, $(f \circ g^{-1})(x) = \left(\dfrac{x+2}{3}\right)^2$.

13. Find $\cos(\arcsin b)$ where $0 \le \arcsin b \le \dfrac{\pi}{2}$.

    Solution: From the following right triangle, it follows that $\cos(\arcsin x) = \sqrt{1-b^2}$.

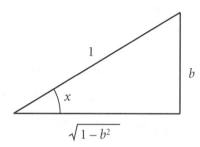

14. Solve: $3^{5x-1} = 2^{7x-8}$.

    Solution: Taking logarithms of both sides of the equation we have:

    $$(5x+1)\log 3 = (7x-8)\log 2; \ 5x\log 3 - 7x\log 2 = \log 3 - 8\log 2; \ x = \frac{\log 3 - 8\log 2}{5\log 3 - 7\log 2}.$$

15. Solve $x^{x^{x^{x^{\cdots}}}} = 2$.

    Solution: Since the values of x's form an infinite repetitive set, you can remove one x from the set and still have the same set. Hence, $x^2 = 2$ or $x = \sqrt{2}$.

16. Assume growth of certain population (t is in days) follows the function $y = ae^{kt}$. After 3 days there are 10,000 new babies born, and after 5 days there are 15,000 new babies. How many new babies will there be after 10 days?

    Solution: Notice $10{,}000 = ae^{3k}$ and $15{,}000 = ae^{5k}$. It follows that $a = \dfrac{10{,}000}{e^{3k}}$ and $15{,}000 = \dfrac{10{,}000}{e^{3k}}e^{5k}$. This yield $15{,}000 = 10{,}000 \, e^{2k}$ or $\dfrac{15{,}000}{10{,}000} = e^{2k}$, which means

    $\ln\dfrac{15}{10} = \ln e^{2k}; \ \ln\dfrac{3}{2} = 2k; \ k = \dfrac{1}{2}\ln\dfrac{3}{2}.$ This yields $a = \dfrac{10{,}000}{e^{\frac{3}{2}\ln\frac{3}{2}}} = \dfrac{10{,}000}{e^{\ln(\frac{3}{2})^{\frac{3}{2}}}}$, or $a = \dfrac{10{,}000}{\left(\dfrac{3}{2}\right)^{\frac{3}{2}}}$.

    The growth equation is $y = \dfrac{10{,}000}{\left(\dfrac{3}{2}\right)^{\frac{3}{2}}} e^{\ln\left(\frac{3}{2}\right)^{\frac{t}{2}}} = \dfrac{10{,}000}{\left(\dfrac{3}{2}\right)^{\frac{3}{2}}} \cdot \left(\dfrac{3}{2}\right)^{\frac{t}{2}}.$

    After ten days we have $y = \dfrac{10{,}000}{\left(\dfrac{3}{2}\right)^{\frac{3}{2}}} e^{\frac{5}{2}(\ln 3 - \ln 2)} \approx 41{,}335$

17. On the Richter scale the magnitude M of earthquake with intensity I is $M = \log_{10} \dfrac{I}{I_0}$

where I_0 is the initial intensity used for computation, $I_0 = 1$. The 1998 Loma Prieta quake in the San Francisco Bay Area registered 7.0, while the 1999 Ismail quake in Turkey registered 7.4. How much more intense was the Ismail quake than the Loma Prieta quake?

Solution: For the Ismail quake $7.4 = \log_{10} I \Rightarrow I = 10^{7.4} = 25{,}000{,}000$.

For the Loma Prieta quake $7.0 = \log_{10} I \Rightarrow I = 10^{7.0} = 10{,}000{,}000$.

Taking the ratio $\dfrac{25{,}000{,}000}{10{,}000{,}000} = 2.5$. An increase of .4 on the Richter scale provides a quake that is 2.5 times as intense.

5.3 UNSOLVED PROBLEMS

1. If the graph of an equation does not change shape when it is reflected in $y = x$, then we say the resulting figure is its own inverse. Which of the following figures are not self-inverses: a) unit circle b) $(y - x^2)(y^2 - x) = 0$; c) $x^2 + \dfrac{y^2}{4} = 1$; d) $xy = 1$?

2. Consider a relation on $\{a_1, a_2, a_3, a_4\}$. If a connection starts at a_i and goes to a_j the term has the matrix value of 1. Find the inverse of the following matrix:

	a_1	a_2	a_3	a_4
a_1	0	1	0	0
a_2	1	0	1	1
a_3	1	1	0	1
a_4	0	0	0	0

Find the matrix that indicates the connections that start at a_j and go to a_i (transpose).

3. Consider the function $y = \sqrt{1 - x^2}$. Does it have an inverse? If it does, define it.

4. If functions f and g have inverse, show $(f \circ g)^{-1} = g^{-1} \circ f^{-1}$.

5. Let f be a function defined by the following diagram:

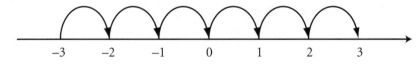

Let g be a function defined by:

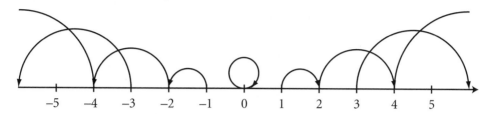

Draw a diagram for $f \circ g$ and $g \circ f$.

6. Suppose $f \circ g = g \circ f$. Show that $(f \circ g)^n = f^n \circ g^n$.

7. Show that the inverse of the relation $(y - \sin x)(y - \arcsin x) = 0$ on the interval $-1 \le x \le 1$ is itself.

8. Solve the following equation using a graphic calculator: $29(3^{x-6}) = 5$.

9. Solve the following equation: $\log_5 x + \log_5 (x - 2) = \log_5 x$.

10. Solve the following equation for θ so that $0 < \theta < 2\pi$: $\cos^2\theta - 3\sin\theta = 1$.

CHAPTER SIX

Statistics

Statistics is relevant to a wide range of areas in science, social sciences, and the humanities. Topics covered in a standard statistics course are well defined and sometime presuppose a knowledge of calculus to investigate continuous probability distributions. Sections 1 through 4 of this chapter use discrete mathematics in the treatment of data representation, measures of central tendency, and discrete probability distributions. Section 5 introduces some calculus in its discussion of continuous probability distributions.

Statistics	The theory of information, with inference as its objective
Samples	Collections of observations gathered from populations
Relative frequency distribution	The portion of the total number of measurements falling into each interval

SECTION 6.1

PROBABILITY AND STATISTICS

Both the relative frequency distribution and the frequency histogram allow us to interpret data graphically and analytically. Assume that we made 10 measurements: 2.08, 2.28, 2.47, 2.75, 3.01, 2.22, 2.45, 2.52, 2.41, and 2.62. To determine the relative frequency we need to divide the axis of measurements into subintervals, with the stipulation that all measurements fall inside the whole interval. Relative frequency is determined by finding the fraction of the total number of measurements that fall into each interval. For example, the fraction of measurements between 2.25 and 2.45, namely, 2.28, 2.41, and 2.42 is $\frac{3}{10} = 0.3$, which is represented in the following relative frequency distribution:

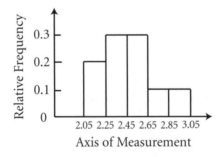

Consider the following list of monthly rentals in a suburban town:

Monthly Rentals ($)	Number of Units	Monthly Rentals ($)	Number of Units
600–799	4	1,400–1,599	42
600–800	9	1,600–1,799	22
1,000–1,199	11	1,800–1,999	16
1,200–1,399	20	2,000–2,199	7

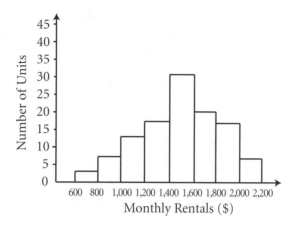

To create a histogram for this information, we assume that the class frequencies (the number of units) are scaled on the y-axis. The probability that certain rentals are being paid also relates directly to the area of the rectangles above that rental. For example, the probability of a rental being between $1,400 and $1,600 is the area of the histogram between $1,400 and $1,600 divided by the total area of the histogram. Symbolically:

$$P(\$1400 < x < \$1600) = \frac{\left(\text{Area}_{1400}^{1600}\right)}{\left(\text{Area}_{600}^{2200}\right)}$$

$$= \frac{42 \cdot (200)}{4(200) + 9(200) + 11(200) + 20(200) + 42(200) + 22(200) + 16(200) + 7(200)} = \frac{42}{131}$$

Such calculation reiterates the important connection between area and probability.

In terms of this example, four individuals pay between $600 and $799; they are in the class $600–$799. Alternately, we may interpret this histogram to mean that four individuals all pay $700 rentals per month. The histogram also allows a visual representation for some basic generalizations about the collected data: the greatest number of rents occurs around $1,500 (between $1,400–$1,599); the lowest rental is around $700 (between $600–$800); most of the rentals occur between $1,200 and $1,800.

6.1 SOLVED PROBLEMS

1. Construct a frequency histogram from the following data set:

1,170	1,817	1,821	729
1,112	790	9,990	535
531	7,950	8,750	1,412
1,635	652	1,252	1,785

Solution: To determine a reasonable class interval for the histogram, first determine the highest (1,817) and lowest (531) score, then create a reasonable number of class intervals (approximately five) in this problem.

$$\text{Suggested Class Interval} = \frac{\text{Highest} - \text{Lowest}}{\text{Number of Class Intervals}} = \frac{1,817 - 531}{5} = \frac{1,286}{5} \approx 250.$$

To summarize the data:

Data ($)	Frequency
500–749	3
750–999	4
1,000–1,249	3
1,250–1,499	1
1,500–1,740	2
1,750–1,999	3

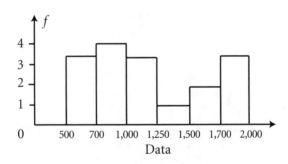

2. The scores on an exam were arranged into the following distribution:

Scores	Number of Scores
100–119	6
120–139	17
140–159	38
160–179	15
180–199	4

Represent the distribution in the form of a histogram. Interpret the following features of the histogram: lowest score, highest score; intervals where most scores occur, and intervals that have the largest concentration of scores.

Solution:

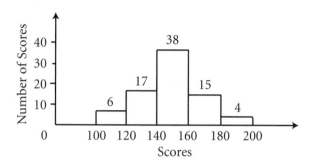

1. Lowest scores around 110 (midpoint of first interval); high scores are around 190 (midpoint of last interval).
2. The interval 140–160 contains most number of scores.
3. Largest concentration of scores occurs between 120 and 180.

6.1 UNSOLVED PROBLEMS

1. The following data measuring the time taken for workers to perform an assembly project for construction equipment were collected, using two methods:

Time in minutes	5–7	8–10	11–12	13–15	16–18
Number studied (Method 1)	126	426	1,060	286	108

It was more difficult to collect data for workers who used Method 2, which required the workers to be monitored at the actual site where the equipment would be used:

Time in minutes	5–7	8–10	11–12	13–15	16–18
Number studied (Method 2)	4	11	25	7	3

Using histograms (percentage frequencies), show which method is more efficient.

2. Using the histograms approximate the probability that someone could take approximately six minutes to perform this task using Method 1 or using Method 2.

3. Quiz grades in a physics class of 15 pupils are the following: 72, 67, 70, 66, 59, 60, 64, 66, 63, 70, 74, 66, 71, 64, 69. Graph the data in a histogram (frequency distribution). From looking at the histogram what are some general remarks you may make about these scores?

4. Consider the grades on the same physics quiz for a second class of 20 pupils: 46, 53, 45, 56, 61, 63, 66, 67, 68, 68, 69, 71, 72, 72, 73, 75, 77, 78, 80, 74. Graph the data in a histogram (frequency distribution). From looking at the histogram what are some general remarks you may make about these scores? Compare the graphs of these scores with the graphs in problem 3.

Permutation	An ordered arrangement of n objects, taken r at a time
Combination	A selection of n objects without regard of order taken r at a time
An experiment	A process by which an observation is made
A simple event	An event that cannot be decomposed
A discrete sample space	A set of objects containing a finite or countable number of sample points
Pascal's Triangle	Combinations of numbers arranged in sequences of rows. The nth row consists of n items taken k at a time, where $k = 0, 1, \ldots, n$ (the vertex of the triangle, 0 items taken 0 at a time, equals 1)
Binomial Theorem	The general result for determining the expansion $(a + b)^n$

SECTION 6.2

COUNTING TECHNIQUES, BINOMIAL EXPANSION, AND PASCAL'S TRIANGLE

Permutations and Combinations

The binomial expansion and the closely related topic of Pascal's Triangle are of central importance in sequences and series. Before developing these topics we need to consider the number of ways of arranging objects in a set, *permutations*, and the number of ways of choosing a number of objects from a set, *combinations*.

Fundamental Counting Principle

If an action a_1 is performed in n_1 ways and an action a_2 can be performed in n_2 ways, the number of ways both actions can be done successively is $n_1 n_2$ ways.

Permutations

In how many ways can you arrange five books on a shelf? Choose one book for the first position on the shelf; then one of the remaining four for the next position, and so on. The total number of permutations is $5 \times 4 \times 3 \times 2 \times 1 = 5! = 120$. More generally, the number of permutations of n different objects into n places is

$_nP_n = n(n-1)(n-2)\ldots 1 = n!$ In how many ways we could arrange five books into three positions? We have $_5P_3 = 5 \cdot 4 \cdot 3$ so that $_5P_3 = \dfrac{5 \cdot 4 \cdot 3}{2 \cdot 1} = \dfrac{5!}{2!}$. In general, the number of permutations of n items in r places, without repetition is, $_nP_r = \dfrac{n(n-1)(n-2)\ldots 1}{(n-r)(n-r-1)\ldots 1}$ or $_nP_r = \dfrac{n!}{(n-r)!}$ and with repetition $_nP_r = n^r$.

Combinations

If we have a set of n different objects, in how many ways can we choose r objects out of them (irrespective of the order)? For example, suppose we have five people and we want to find out how many committees of three we can choose from these five people. If we represent the people by p_1, p_2, p_3, p_4, p_5 then the number or combinations (i.e., number of distinct committees) of three ($_5C_3$), can be obtained by noticing that the number of possible arrangements of three people, is $_5P_3 = 5 \cdot 4 \cdot 3$, while the number of distinct arrangements of a given group of three number is $_3P_3 = 3 \cdot 2 \cdot 1$. The number of "distinct" permutations can then be found by dividing all the possible arrangements by the number of repetitions possible for each arrangement: $\dfrac{5 \cdot 4 \cdot 3}{1 \cdot 2 \cdot 3} = {_5C_3}$. More specifically, consider the following lists:

$P_1P_2P_3$	$P_1P_2P_4$	$P_1P_2P_5$	$P_1P_3P_4$	$P_1P_3P_5$	$P_1P_4P_5$
$P_1P_3P_2$	$P_1P_4P_2$	$P_1P_5P_2$	$P_1P_4P_3$	$P_1P_5P_3$	$P_1P_5P_4$
$P_2P_3P_1$	$P_2P_4P_1$	$P_2P_5P_1$	$P_3P_4P_1$	$P_3P_5P_1$	$P_4P_5P_1$
$P_2P_1P_3$	$P_2P_1P_4$	$P_2P_1P_5$	$P_3P_1P_4$	$P_3P_1P_5$	$P_4P_1P_5$
$P_3P_1P_2$	$P_4P_2P_1$	$P_5P_1P_2$	$P_4P_1P_3$	$P_5P_1P_3$	$P_5P_1P_4$
$P_3P_2P_1$	$P_4P_1P_2$	$P_5P_2P_1$	$P_4P_3P_1$	$P_5P_3P_1$	$P_5P_4P_1$

$P_2P_3P_4$	$P_2P_3P_5$	$P_2P_4P_5$	$P_3P_4P_5$
$P_2P_4P_3$	$P_3P_5P_3$	$P_2P_5P_4$	$P_3P_5P_4$
$P_3P_4P_2$	$P_3P_5P_2$	$P_4P_5P_2$	$P_4P_3P_5$
$P_3P_2P_4$	$P_3P_2P_5$	$P_4P_2P_5$	$P_4P_3P_5$
$P_4P_2P_3$	$P_5P_2P_3$	$P_5P_2P_4$	$P_5P_3P_4$
$P_4P_3P_2$	$P_5P_3P_2$	$P_5P_4P_2$	$P_5P_4P_3$

We can rewrite $_5C_3$ as $_5C_3 = \dfrac{_5P_3}{3!}$. To generalize: $_nC_r = \dfrac{_nP_r}{r!} = \dfrac{n!}{(n-r)!r!}$.

Frequently $_nC_r$ is written as $\dbinom{n}{r}$ or $C(n, r)$ so $\dbinom{n}{r} = C(n,r) = {_nC_r} = \dfrac{_nP_r}{r!} = \dfrac{n!}{(n-r)!r!}$.

Pascal's Triangle and the Binomial Theorem

We can now look at the sequence of coefficients, which arise from $(a + b)^n$. For successive values of n, we see that:

$$(a+b)^0 = 1; (a+b)^1 = 1a + 1b; (a+b)^2 = 1a^2 + 2ab + 1b^2$$

$$(a+b)^3 = 1a^3 + 3a^2b + 3ab^2 + 1b^3$$

$$(a+b)^4 = 1a^4 + 4a^3b + 6a^2b^2 + 4ab^3 + 1b^4$$

$$(a+b)^5 = 1a^5 + 5a^4b + 10a^3b^2 + 10a^2b^3 + 5ab^4 + 1b^5$$

If we notice the position of the numerical coefficients, we obtain an array known as Pascal's Triangle.

$$
\begin{array}{ccccccccccc}
&&&&& 1 &&&&& \\
&&&& 1 && 1 &&&& \\
&&& 1 && 2 && 1 &&& \\
&& 1 && 3 && 3 && 1 && \\
& 1 && 4 && 6 && 4 && 1 & \\
1 && 5 && 10 && 10 && 5 && 1
\end{array}
$$

Also notice that each row is made up of combinations of $\begin{pmatrix} n \\ r \end{pmatrix}$. For example,

$$
\begin{array}{ccccccccccc}
&&&&& \binom{1}{0} &&&&& \\
&&&& \binom{1}{0} && \binom{1}{1} &&&& \\
&&& \binom{2}{0} && \binom{2}{1} && \binom{2}{2} &&& \\
&& \binom{3}{0} && \binom{3}{1} && \binom{3}{2} && \binom{3}{3} && \\
& \binom{4}{0} && \binom{4}{1} && \binom{4}{2} && \binom{4}{3} && \binom{4}{4} & \\
\binom{5}{0} && \binom{5}{1} && \binom{5}{2} && \binom{5}{3} && \binom{5}{4} && \binom{5}{5}
\end{array}
$$

In the expression for $(a + b)^n$, as we decrease the power of the ath term by 1, we increase the number of the bth combination by 1. This relationship suggests the Binomial Theorem:

$$(a+b)^n = \binom{n}{0}a^n + \binom{n}{1}a^{n-1}b + \binom{n}{2}a^{n-2}b^2 + \binom{n}{3}a^{n-3}b^3 + \ldots + \binom{n}{n-1}ab^{n-1} + \binom{n}{n}b^n.$$

(Proof of the Binomial Theorem is usually done by mathematical induction: see Chapter 9.)

6.2 SOLVED PROBLEMS

1. Calculate in how many ways can three prizes be awarded to a class of 20 students if (a) there is a rule that no student can have more than one prize, (b) no such rule holds.

   Solution:

   a) Prize 1 can be chosen 20 ways, prize 2 can be chosen 19 ways, prize 3 can be chosen 18 ways. Hence, the total number of ways the three prizes can be chosen is $_{20}P_3 = 20 \cdot 19 \cdot 18$.

   b) If no such rule exists each prize can be chosen in 20 different or 20^3 ways.

2. In how many ways can you arrange the letters in the word *Connecticut*?

   Solution: The number of distinct arrangements will equal the total number of possible arrangements, divided by the number of repetitions possible for each distinct arrangement. The number of distinct arrangements is $\dfrac{11!}{3!\,2!\,2!}$.

3. In how many ways can a congressional committee of three Republicans and two Democrats can be chosen from six Republicans and eight Democrats?

   Solution: $\dbinom{6}{3}\dbinom{8}{2}$.

4. Prove that $\dbinom{n+1}{r} = \dbinom{n}{r-1} + \dbinom{n}{r}$.

   Solution: Notice that the word "or" indicates addition. For example, to choose r objects out of $n + 1$ we can *either* choose "the first" and then the other $r - 1$ from the remaining n, *or* not choose "the first" but choose all the r from the remaining n.

5. Find the first three terms of $(1 - 2x)^{10}$ expanded in ascending powers of x.

   Solution: $(1 - 2x)^{10} = 1^{10} + \dbinom{10}{1}1^9(-2x) + \dbinom{10}{2}1^8(-2x)^2 + \ldots = 1 - 20x + 180x^2$.

6. Evaluate $(.998)^{10}$ to four decimal places using the binomial expansion.

   Solution: Consider the previous expansion for $(1 - 2x)^{10}$; let $x = .001$, so $(.998)^{10} = [1 - 2(.001)]^{10} = 1 - 20(.001) + 180(.001)^2 + \ldots = 1 - .02 + .000180 \approx .9802$.

7. Find the b^5 term in the expansion for $(a - 2b)^8$.

   Solution: $_8C_5 a^{8-5}(-2b)^5 = 56a^3(-2b)^5 = -1792a^3b^5$.

8. Show $\dbinom{n}{0} + \dbinom{n}{1} + \dbinom{n}{2} + \ldots \dbinom{n}{n} = 2^n$.

Solution: $(a+b)^n = \binom{n}{0}a^n + \binom{n}{1}a^{n-1}b + \ldots \binom{n}{n}b^n$. Let $a = b = 1$. This means

$$2^n = \binom{n}{0} + \binom{n}{1} + \binom{n}{2} + \ldots \binom{n}{n}.$$

9. Find the number of subsets of a set that has 10 elements.

   Solution: Notice the total number of subsets can be expressed as: *Total number of subsets = subsets with 0 elements + subsets with 1 element + … subsets with 10 elements.* The number of subsets with one element means the number of ways you can choose from 10 elements, sets with 1 distinct element. Total number of subsets is

   $$\binom{10}{0} + \binom{10}{1} + \binom{10}{2} + \ldots \binom{10}{10} = 2^{10}.$$

10. Assume that using an alphabet consisting of 32 letters (Russian), the letters are arranged in groups of six letters called *words.*

    a) Find the number of words with six letters not allowing a repetition of letters.

    b) Find the number of words with six letters allowing a repetition of letters.

    Solution:

    a) The number of different words containing each letter no more than once is:
    $$\frac{32!}{(32-6)!} = \frac{32!}{26!} = 32 \cdot 31 \cdot 30 \cdot 29 \cdot 28 \cdot 27 = 652,458,240$$

    b) $32^6 = 1,073,741,824$, which is the number of different words with repetition of letters.

11. Find the number of samples of six fuses that can be selected from a lot of 100 fuses.

    Solution: Using the formula for the number of combinations with $n = 100$ and $r = 6$ we obtain the following number of samples: $\binom{100}{6} = \frac{100!}{6!(100-6)!} = 1,192,052,400.$

6.2 UNSOLVED PROBLEMS

1. What is the sum of the coefficients of the expression $(x + y)^8$?

2. Consider a line drawn from the vertex of Pascal's Triangle, "perpendicular" to "its base." Give one property of this line in relation to the numbers in the triangle.

3. Place the first term of Pascal's Triangle at the origin of a Cartesian coordinate system. Continue the following pattern to give the third row of the triangle:

$$\binom{1}{0} \to (-1, 1) \quad \binom{1}{1} \to (1, 1) \quad \binom{2}{0} \to (-2, 2) \quad \binom{2}{1} \to (0, 2) \quad \binom{2}{2} \to (2, 2)$$

What is the relationship between the values of Pascal's Triangle at $(-3, 5)$ and $(3, 5)$?

4. Continue the pattern in the previous problem. Let n be a positive integer.

   Calculate $\displaystyle\sum_{x=-n}^{n} (x, n)$.

5. Expand the trinomial $(1 - x - x^2)^5$ as far as x^2.

6. Use the expansion $(1 + x)^n$ to find $\dbinom{n}{0} - \dbinom{n}{1} + \dbinom{n}{2} + \ldots (-1)^n \dbinom{n}{n}$.

7. Find: $n + \dfrac{n(n-1)}{1} + \dfrac{n(n-1)(n-2)}{1 \cdot 2} + \ldots + \dfrac{n(n-1)\ldots(1)}{1 \cdot 2 \ldots (n-1)}$.

8. Find the constant term in the expansion of $\left(2x + \dfrac{1}{x^2}\right)^3$.

9. Use the binomial Theorem to evaluate: $(2.001)^8$ to 6 significant figures.

OF TERMS

Probability of an event *P(E)*	The ratio of the number of favorable events to the total number of possible outcomes (or number of samples in sample space): $$P(E) = \frac{\text{number of favorable outcomes}}{\text{number of total possible outcomes}}$$
Contingency table	A table illustrating all possible outcomes
Probability of independent events *A* and *B*	$P(A \cap B) = P(A) \cdot P(B)$
Probability of the union of events *A* and *B*	$P(A \cup B) = P(A) + P(B) - P(A \cap B)$
Conditional probability of an event *A*, given that an event *B* occurred	$P(A/B) = \dfrac{P(A \cap B)}{P(B)}; \quad P(B) \neq 0$
Bayes' Rule (The conditional probability B$_j$/A where A $\subset$ (B$_1$ ∪ B$_2$ . . . ∪ B$_n$))	$P(B_j/A) = \dfrac{P(A \cap B_j)}{P(A)} = \dfrac{P(B_j)P(A/B_j)}{\displaystyle\sum_{i=1}^{k} P(B_j)P(A/B_j)}$

SECTION 6.3

CONTINGENCY TABLES; DISCRETE AND COMPOUND PROBABILITIES

Some Basic Concepts

An experiment is a process for which an observation is made. A *simple event* is an event that cannot be decomposed. A simple event is also called a *sample point* or an *outcome*. The *sample space* associated with an experiment is the set consisting of all possible sample points. A *discrete sample space* is one that contains a finite or countable number of sample points. The *probability of an event E*, which is subset of a finite sample space *S* of equally likely outcomes, is:

$$P(E) = \frac{\text{number of sample points in } E}{\text{number of sample points in } S}; \quad 0 \le P(E) \le 1.$$

Using this definition, it follows immediately that a complementary event E' (everything not in E) has a probability $P(E') = 1 - P(E)$. Define *mutually exclusive events* as events that cannot occur simultaneously (they have no sample points in common). *Probability of the union of events (events E_1 and E_2 are not mutually exclusive)* is: $P(E_1 \cup E_2) = P(E_1) + P(E_2) - P(E_1 \cap E_2)$. (Consider the formula for number of elements in the set $E_1 \cup E_2$ given the number of elements in set E_1 and set E_2.)

Compound events (A and B) can be illustrated by means of *probability*, or *contingency tables*. For example, suppose a card is drawn from a deck. Let A represent the choice of an ace, B the choice of a black card. Find $P(A)$, $P(A')$, $P(A \cap B)$, $P(A' \cap B)$, $P(A \cap B')$, $P(A' \cap B')$, $P(B)$, and $P(B')$. The solution of this problem may be most accurately represented with the following contingency table (notice the events are all independent):

	B	B'	
A	$P(A \cap B) = \dfrac{1}{26}$	$P(A \cap B') = \dfrac{1}{26}$	$P(A) = \dfrac{1}{13}$
A'	$P(A' \cap B) = \dfrac{6}{13}$	$P(A' \cap B') = \dfrac{6}{13}$	$P(A') = \dfrac{12}{13}$
	$P(B) = \dfrac{1}{2}$	$P(B') = \dfrac{1}{2}$	1

Conditional Probability and Independent Events

Two events A and B are defined as **independent** if $P(A \cap B) = P(A) \cdot P(B)$. **Conditional Probability** of an event A given the occurrence of an event B is given by the following formula: $P(A/B) = \dfrac{P(A \cap B)}{P(B)}$; $P(B) \neq 0$. Conditional probability of the event A is the probability of the event A, given that the other related event B occurred which may alter the outcome of the event A. The concept of conditional probability generalizes if one event S is composed of mutually exclusive events B_j as:

Bayes' Rule: If $S = B_1 \cup B_2 \cup B_3 \cup \dots \cup B_k$; $P(B_i \neq 0$; $P(B_i \cap B_j) = \emptyset$ if $i \neq j$, and A is a subset of S, then $P(A) = \displaystyle\sum_{i-1}^{k} P(B_i)P(A/B_i)$ or for the conditional probability

$$P(B_j/A) = \frac{P(A \cap B_j)}{P(A)} = \frac{P(B_j)P(A/B_j)}{\displaystyle\sum_{i=1}^{k} P(B_i)P(A/B_i)}.$$

6.3 SOLVED PROBLEMS

1. Find a contingency table for the choice of a black card, and the choice of club C.

   Solution:

	B	B'	
C	$\frac{1}{4}$	0	$\frac{1}{4}$
C'	$\frac{1}{4}$	$\frac{1}{2}$	$\frac{3}{4}$
	$\frac{1}{2}$	$\frac{1}{2}$	1

2. Five percent of a population is known to have disease A. If three people are chosen randomly from the population what is the chance that (a) all will have A, (b) none will have A, (c) at least one will have disease A? Assume that choosing any person who has disease A is not affected by those people previously chosen (the choice of individuals is an independent event).

   Solution: Since we can assume the events are independent, we get:

   a) $P(A \cap A \cap A) = \dfrac{1}{20} \cdot \dfrac{1}{20} \cdot \dfrac{1}{20} = 0.000125.$

   b) $P(A') = \dfrac{95}{100}$; So, $P(A' \cap A' \cap A') = \dfrac{95}{100} \cdot \dfrac{95}{100} \cdot \dfrac{95}{100} = \dfrac{(95)^3}{1,000,000} = 0.857375.$

   c) $P(\text{at least one have } A) = 1 - P(\text{none}) = 1 - 0.857 \approx .143.$

3. Let E_1 be the event: I draw a club from a deck of cards. Let E_2 be the event: I draw a black card from a deck of cards. Are E_1 and E_2 independent?

   Solution: $P(E_1) = \dfrac{1}{4}, P(E_2) = \dfrac{1}{2}, P(E_1 \cap E_2) = \dfrac{1}{4}.$ Notice $P(E_1 \cap E_2) \neq P(E_1) \cdot P(E_2).$
   Hence, E_1 and E_2 are not independent.

4. A test for a disease correctly diagnoses a person as having a disease with probability 0.85. The test will diagnose negatively a person without this disease with probability 0.85. If 1% of the people in a population have the disease, what is the chance that a person from this population who tests positive for the disease actually has the disease?

   Solution: Define an event D: a person has a disease, and an event T: a person is tested positively for a disease. Then the conditional probability that a person who was tested positively for a disease has, in fact, a disease is the following:

$$P(D/T) = \frac{P(D)P(T/D)}{P(D) \cdot P(T/D) + P(T/D') \cdot P(D')} = \frac{0.01 \cdot 0.85}{0.01 \cdot 0.85 + 0.15 \cdot 0.99} = 0.0541.$$

5. When tossing a fair die, what is the probability of getting an even number or a number more than 4?

Solution: Let A be an event "even number," and B be an event "number more than 4." We have: $P(A \cup B) = \frac{3}{6} + \frac{3}{6} - \frac{1}{6} = \frac{4}{6} = \frac{2}{3}.$

6.3 UNSOLVED PROBLEMS

1. Tom and Jane each throws a die.

T: Tom throws a 6.

J: Jane throws a 6.

Calculate $P(T)$, $P(J)$ and $P(T \cap J)$. Are these two events independent?

2. Allen and Barbara take a card from the deck.

A: Allen first picks a heart and does not put it back in the deck.

B: Barbara then picks a heart.

Calculate $P(A)$, $P(B)$ and $P(A \cap B)$. Are these two events independent?

3. Joe chooses a number at random between 1 and 200. Find the following probabilities:

E_1: The number is divisible by 4; E_2: The number is divisible by 10.

Are these events independent?

4. Draw a contingency table for the following:

A: the choice of a 10, from a deck of cards.

B: the choice of a red card.

Find: $P(A \cap B)$, $P(A)$, $P(A' \cap B)$, $P(A \cap B')$, $P(A' \cap B')$, $P(A')$, $P(B)$, $P(B')$.

5. Let A, B, and C be events such that A and B are independent, A and C as well as B and C are mutually exclusive, and $P(A) = \frac{1}{4}$; $P(B) = \frac{1}{6}$; $P(C) = \frac{1}{2}$. Find $P[(A \cap B)' \cup C]$.

6. Let R, S, and T be independent, equally likely events with common probability $\frac{1}{3}$. What is the probability $P(R \cup S \cup T)$?

7. An oil burner ignites by electric switch. The probability of clogging the oil burner during the heating season is 5%, while the probability of a broken electric switch is 1%. What is the probability that during the winter season the oil burner will need repair?

SECTION 6.4

MEASURES OF CENTRAL TENDENCY AND DISPERSION

Consider the following scores of 15 students made on a test with 35 questions (class A):

$$31, 27, 30, 27, 19, 20, 34, 23, 24, 25, 30, 33, 32, 26, 30$$

The statistical term for any such set is called a **population**. Three measures of central tendency are commonly used for some measure of location of elements in a population.

a) The **mode** is most frequently occurring score. In this case, 30 occurs more frequently than any other score. If two numbers occur most frequently, the population is bimodal. A population may have a number of different modes.

b) The **median** is the score, which is the middle value, if the scores in the population are arranged from lowest to highest. Suppose this is done for the test marks 19, 20, 23, 24, 25, 26, 27, 27, 30, 30, 30, 31, 32, 33, 34, then the median is 27, the eighth score. If there had been an even number of scores the median would be taken as halfway between the two middle values. Notice the median need not be a score in the population. (A similar calculation can be made for quartiles, deciles, etc.)

187

c) The **mean** is the score most frequently used as a measure of the central tendency. It represents the value that all the scores would have if their resulting sum would equal the sum of all the scores of the population. (The mean indicates the value of each score, when the sum-value of all the scores is evenly distributed.) In this case: $\dfrac{19+20+23+\ldots+34}{15}=\dfrac{411}{15}=27.4$. More generally, the mean of the n scores

$x_1, x_2, \ldots, x_n$ is $m=\bar{x}=\dfrac{1}{n}\sum_{i=1}^{n}x_i$.

Dispersion

A second class of students (class B) have the following scores on the same test:

8, 10, 15, 16, 18, 20, 24, 25, 28, 28, 28, 29, 30, 31, 32, 32, 33, 35, 35, 35

The total of these marks is 548, and therefore, this mean is $\dfrac{548}{20}=27.4$ (exactly the mean of class A). Clearly, the classes have performed very differently on the test: the spread of scores for class B is greater than for class A. The simplest measure of spread is **range**, which is the difference between the largest and the smallest values in the population. For class A the range is $34-19=15$, and for class B the range is $40-6=34$. When a population has an isolated extreme value, the range can give a distorted impression of the spread. To eliminate this problem the **interquartile range** is often used in preference of the range. It gives the value between the lower and the upperquartile. Hence, for class A: 20, 23, 24, 25, 26, 27, 27, 30, 30, 30, 31, 32, 33, 34. Interquartile range is $31-24=7$. Another way to calculate the spread is by calculating the average difference from the mean. For example, subtracting the mean of the distribution, 27.4, from each score in class A: $-8.4, -7.4, \ldots$.

The average of such coded scores is 0, which clearly must always be the case if you consider: $\displaystyle\sum_{i=1}^{n}(x_i-\bar{x})=\left(\sum_{i=1}^{n}x_i\right)-n\bar{x}; =n\bar{x}-n\bar{x}=0.$

One way to overcome this problem is by squaring these differences and taking their average. We call this number the **variance**. To compensate by the squaring of the difference we can take the square root of the variance to get the standard deviation.

Notationally, $S^2=\dfrac{1}{n}\displaystyle\sum_{i=1}^{n}(x_i-\bar{x})^2$ is called the variance of the population.

Similarly, $S=\sqrt{\dfrac{1}{n}\displaystyle\sum_{i=1}^{n}(x_i-\bar{x})^2}$ is called the standard deviation of the population.

To calculate S^2 more readily, notice:

$$S^2 = \frac{1}{n}\sum_{i=1}^{n}(x_i - \bar{x})^2 = \frac{1}{n}\sum_{i=1}^{n}\left(x_i^2 - 2x_i(\bar{x}) + (\bar{x})^2\right)$$

$$= \frac{1}{n}\left[\sum_{i=1}^{n}x_i^2 - \sum_{i=1}^{n}2x_i(\bar{x}) + \sum_{i=1}^{n}(\bar{x})^2\right] = \frac{1}{n}\left[\sum_{i=1}^{n}x_i^2 - 2(\bar{x})n(\bar{x}) + n(\bar{x})^2\right]$$

$$= \frac{1}{n}\left[\sum_{i=1}^{n}x_i^2\right] - \frac{1}{n}\left[2(\bar{x})n(\bar{x}) - n(\bar{x})^2\right] = \frac{1}{n}\sum_{i=1}^{n}x_i^2 - (\bar{x})^2.$$

In summary, $S^2 = \dfrac{1}{n}\sum_{i=1}^{n}(x_i - \bar{x})^2 = \left(\dfrac{1}{n}\sum_{i=1}^{n}x_i^2\right) - (\bar{x})^2.$

Coding Series

To facilitate calculations, scores can be coded. This allows calculations to be performed with relatively small numbers and then recoded to find the mean and variance for the original population. In general, if you multiply each score by a factor of λ, and increase it by a, it follows that for the new scores $y_r = \lambda x_r + a$,

$$\bar{x}_y = \frac{1}{n}\sum y_n = \frac{1}{n}\sum(\lambda x_n + a) = \frac{1}{n}\lambda\sum x_n + \frac{1}{n}\sum a = \frac{1}{n}\lambda n\bar{x} + \frac{1}{n}na = \lambda\bar{x} + a.$$

Similarly,

$$S_y^2 = \frac{1}{n}\sum(y_r - \bar{x})^2 = \frac{1}{n}\sum\left[(\lambda x_r + a) - (\lambda\bar{x} + a)\right]^2 = \frac{1}{n}\sum(\lambda x_r - \lambda\bar{x})^2 = \lambda^2 S_x^2.$$

If $y = \lambda x + a$; $\bar{y} = \lambda\bar{x} + a$; $S_y^2 = \lambda^2 S_x^2$ or $S_y = \lambda S_x$.

Mathematical Expectation

What is the value, on average, you get in rolling a die? How many heads can you expect to appear when you toss a coin 100 times? The concept of mathematical expectation evolves from such considerations.

Suppose you place the numbers 1, 2, 3, 4, 5, 6 in a hat. The average of the set is given by $\dfrac{1+2+3+4+5+6}{6}$ or, $\dfrac{1}{6}(1)+\dfrac{1}{6}(2)+\dfrac{1}{6}(3)+\dfrac{1}{6}(4)+\dfrac{1}{6}(5)+\dfrac{1}{6}(6)$. In other words, a sensible definition for the expected value of this experiment is the following: $E(x) = P(1)(1) + P(2)(2) + P(3)(3) + \ldots P(6)(6)$ where $P(1)$, $P(2)$ ... $P(6)$ give the probability of picking out the numbers 1, 2, 3 ... 6. Using summation notation and letting $x_1 = 1, x_2 = 2, \ldots x_6 = 6$, we define $E(x) = \sum_{i=1}^{6}P(x_i)x_i$. These considerations give rise to the following definition:

Definition: The expectation of the random variable $X(s)$ on sample space S is equal to $E(x) = \sum_{s \in S} P(s)X(s)$ where $P(s)$ is the probability of s occurring in S.

6.4 SOLVED PROBLEMS

1. The temperatures in a controlled climate setting in a museum recorded in degrees (Celsius) during one day were as follows: 20.2, 20.4, 20.1, 20.2, 20.2, 20.3, 20.1, 20.5. Find the mean of these temperatures.

   Solution: Subtract 20.0 from each of these scores and divide the result by 0.10 to get 4, 1, 2, 2, 2, 3, 1, 5 (use the transformation $y = \dfrac{x - 20.0}{0.10}$). With these coded scores we calculate $\bar{y} = \dfrac{3 \cdot 2 + 4 + 2 \cdot 1 + 3 + 5}{8}$; $\bar{y} = 2.5$. Hence, $\bar{x} = 0.1(2.5) + 20.0 = 20.25$.

2. A random sample of 250 cans is taken from a machine shop. The measurements to the nearest 0.01mm of the cans are listed in the following table:

Diameter	Number
23.07–23.11	10
23.12–23.16	20
23.17–23.21	28
23.22–23.26	36
23.27–23.31	52
23.32–23.36	38
23.37–23.41	32
23.42–23.46	21
23.47–23.51	13

Graph the information in a histogram. Find the mean and standard deviation of this distribution. Draw a histogram from the data using the intervals one-half a unit more than the given data; assume all the elements in the interval occur at the midpoint of the interval.

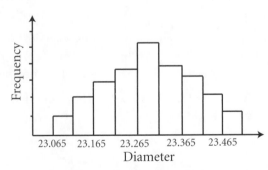

Solution: To code this data subtract 23 from each and multiply by 100 using the transformation $y = 100(x - 23)$ or $x = \dfrac{y}{100} + 23$. The calculation for mean and standard deviation can be performed with the following (simplified) data:

x_r	y_r	f_r	$f_r y_r$	$f_r y_r^2$
23.09	9	10	90	810
23.14	14	20	280	3920
23.19	19	28	532	10108
23.24	24	36	864	20736
23.29	29	52	1508	43732
23.34	34	38	1292	43982
23.39	39	32	1248	48672
23.44	44	21	924	40656
23.49	49	13	637	31213
		250	7375	243775

Using the coded scores we have: $m_y = \dfrac{7375}{250} = 29.5$; $S_y = \sqrt{\dfrac{243775}{250} - (29.5)^2}$ Hence, the value for $\bar{x} = \dfrac{29.5}{100} + 23 = 23.295$ and the value for $S_x = \dfrac{10.2}{100} = 0.102$.

3. A fair coin is tossed two times. Let X equal the random variable that assigns to an outcome the number of heads for the outcome (i.e., "X" assigns a real number to each possible outcome). Find $E(X)$.

Solution: Four outcomes are possible when a coin is tossed two times: HH, HT, TH, TT. Hence, the probability of each outcome is $\dfrac{1}{4}$, so $E(X) = \dfrac{1}{4}$ ((HH) + (HT) + (TH) + (TT)) $= \dfrac{1}{4}(2+1+1+0) = \dfrac{4}{4} = 1$. In other words, "on average" one can expect one head to appear.

4. When a pair of dice is rolled let X equal the sum of numbers that appear on the faces of the dice. Find the expected value for the sum.

Solution:

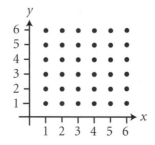

$$P(x = 2) = P(x = 12) = \frac{1}{36}; \quad P(x = 3) = P(x = 11) = \frac{2}{36} = \frac{1}{18}$$

$$P(x = 4) = P(x = 10) = \frac{3}{36}; \quad P(x = 5) = P(x = 9) = \frac{4}{36} = \frac{1}{9}$$

$$P(x = 6) = P(x = 8) = \frac{5}{36}; \quad P(x = 7) = \frac{6}{36} = \frac{1}{6}$$

Hence, the expectation for X is given by:

$$E(X) = \sum_{i=1}^{12} P(x_i)x_i = \frac{1}{36}(2+12) + \frac{1}{18}(3+11) + \frac{1}{12}(4+10) + \frac{1}{9}(5+9) + \frac{5}{36}(6+8) + \frac{1}{6}(7) = 7.$$

5. Let X be the random variable equal to the number of successes in n independent events, where the probability of success on one trial is p and the probability of failure is $q = 1 - p$. What is the probability of k successes in n events?

Solution: Consider how to obtain one success: $pqqq...q$.

But p can occur in any trial, hence the probability of obtaining one success is $_nC_1p^1q^{n-1}$. By a similar argument, the probability of obtaining two successes would be $ppqq...q$. In this case, the number of ways of obtaining two successes is $_nC_2$. Hence, the probability of two successes is $_nC_2p^2q^{n-2}$. In general $P(k,n) = _nC_kp^kq^{n-k}$.

6. Let X be the random variable equal to the number of successes in n independent trials, when the probability of success on one trial is p and the probability of failure is $q = 1 - p$. Find $E(X)$.

Solution:

$$E(X) = \sum_{k=1}^{n} P(X_K) \cdot k = \sum_{k=1}^{n} [C(n,k)p^kq^{n-k}] \cdot k \quad \text{(see problem 5)}$$

$$= \sum_{k=1}^{n} \frac{n!}{k!(n-k)!} \cdot k \; p^kq^{n-k} = \sum_{k=1}^{n} \frac{n(n-1)...(n-(k-1))}{1 \cdot 2...k} kp^kq^{n-k}$$

$$= \sum_{k=1}^{n} \left[\frac{n(n-1)...[n-k+1]}{1 \cdot 2...(k-1)} \right] \frac{1}{k} kp^kq^{n-k} = \sum_{k=1}^{n} \left[\frac{(n-1)...[n-k+1]}{1 \cdot 2...(k-1)} \right] \frac{n}{k} kp^kq^{n-k}$$

$$= \sum_{k=1}^{n} C(n-1,k-1)\frac{n}{k} \cdot kp^kq^{n-k}$$

Let $j = k - 1$ (j ranges from 0 to $n - 1$ when k ranges from 1 to n). By the Binomial Theorem: $np\sum_{j=0}^{n-1} C(n-1,j)p^jq^{n-1-j} = np(p+q)^{n-1} = np.$

7. Show: $E(ax + b) = aE(x) + b$.

Solution:

$$E(ax+b) = \sum_{i=1}^{n} P(x_i)(ax_i + b) = \sum_{i=1}^{n} P(x_i)ax_i + \sum_{i=1}^{n} P(x_i)b.$$

But, $\sum_{i=1}^{n} P(x_i) = 1$; hence, $E(ax+b) = \sum_{i=1}^{n} aP(x_i)x_i + b = a\sum_{i=1}^{n} P(x_i)x_i + b = aE(x) + b$

8. Let X be a random variable on a sample space S (e.g., "(X)"assigns a real number to each possible outcome). The variance of X is defined by: $V(X) = \sum_{x \in s}[X(s) - E(X)]^2 P(s)$

   where $E(X)$ is the expectation of X and $P(s)$ is the probability of s occurring in sample space S. Show: $V(X) = E(X^2) - [E(X)]^2 = \sigma^2$.

   Solution: $V(X) = \sum_{x \in s}[X(s) - E(X)]^2 P(s)$

   $$= \sum_{x \in s}[(X(s))^2 - 2E(X)(X(s)) + (E(X))^2]P(s)$$

   $$= \sum_{x \in s} P(s)(X(s))^2 - 2E(X)\sum_{x \in S} X(s)P(s) + [E(X)]^2 \sum_{x \in S} P(s)$$

   $$= E(X^2) - 2E(X)E(X) + [E(X)]^2 = E(X^2) + [E(X)]^2.$$

9. Find the expected value of hitting a bull's–eye on 100 trials if the probability of hitting a bull's–eye on one trial is 0.1, when it is assumed that each trial is independent of every other one.

   Solution: This situation defines a binomial distribution with $n = 100$, $p = 0.1$. Hence, $E(X) = np = (0.1)(100) = 10$.

6.4 UNSOLVED PROBLEMS

1. Consider the following data, which represents the frequency of an event occuring over a certain time interval.

0.5–1.5	11
1.5–2.5	19
2.5–3.5	23
3.5–4.5	14
4.5–5.5	10
5.5–10.5	15
10.5–20	8
	100

Create the histogram that codes the given scores so that the area of the rectangle in the histogram, rather than their heights, represents frequencies. Find the heights of the corresponding intervals.

2. Two dice were thrown 200 times and the frequency with which the scores occurred were recorded. What are the mean and standard deviation of the scores?

score	12	11	10	9	8	7	6	5	4	3	2
frequency	7	10	20	20	30	34	27	21	14	11	6

3. Create a histogram based on the following data, which record the age of death of individuals in a small village in central Asia. Mark the position of the mean and one standard deviation on either side of the mean.

life time	0–9	10–39	40–49	50–59	60–69	70–79	80–89
number of people	8	3	7	18	31	21	11

4. Find the probability of heads occurring if a biased coin is tossed and heads are three times as likely to occur than tails.

5. Suppose three is three times as likely to occur than any other number when rolling a biased die. What probability should be assigned to getting a three?

6. An alarm system is built with three backup components operating independently with .01 probability of failing during 100 hours. The system will still operate if any one of the three components operates.

   a) Find the probability that two of the three components will operate at least 100 hours.

   b) Find the probability that the alarm will operate at least 100 hours.

7. Using the definition of variance for a random variable, find the variance of random variable $X(t) = 1$, if the binomial trial is a success, and $X(t) = 0$ if it is a failure, where p is the probability of a success.

8. Ten printers were sold for $100 each from a large lot that is known to have 5% defectives. Find the expected net gain for the manufacturer if defective items will be returned for full refund.

OF TERMS

Binomial Law	$P(y) = \binom{n}{y} p^y q^{n-y}; y = 0, 1, 2, \dots n; 0 \le p \le 1$
Distribution function	$F(y) = P(Y \le y), -\infty < y < \infty$
Probability density function	$f(y) = \dfrac{dF(y)}{dy} = F'(y)$

SECTION 6.5

PROBABILITY DISTRIBUTIONS

Binomial Probability

An experiment is called binomial if it satisfies the following conditions:

1. The experiment consists of n independent identical trials.
2. Each trial results in exactly one of two outcomes (success or failure).
3. The probability of success is equal to p, and probability of failure is $q = 1 - p$.

The Binomial Law gives the probability that a discrete random variable Y assumes a value of y as: $P(y) = \binom{n}{y} p^y q^{n-y}; y = 0, 1, 2, \dots, n; 0 \le p \le 1$ with $E(y) = \mu = np$ (mean of distribution) and $\sigma^2 = V(Y) = npq$ (variance of distribution and 6 is the standard deviation of the distribution), where a discrete random variable Y is understood in a sense that it can assume only a finite or countably infinite number of distinct values

Probability Distributions for Continuous Random Variables (Requires Calculus)

A random variable Y is considered continuous if it can assume any value in a given interval. If Y is a continuous random variable, then the distribution function of Y, denoted as $F(y)$, is given by $F(y) = P(Y \le y), -\infty < y < \infty$. This gives the cumulative probability for all events such that $Y \le y$. If $F(y)$ is a distribution function, then

1. $\lim\limits_{y \to -\infty} F(y) = F(-\infty) = 0$

2. $\lim\limits_{y \to \infty} F(y) = F(\infty) = 1$

3. $F(y_b) \ge F(y_a)$; if $y_b > y_a$ ($F(y)$ is increasing).

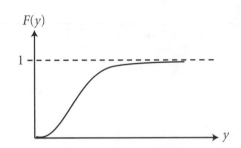

If $F(y)$ is a distribution function for a continuous random variable Y, then $f(y)$ is given by: $f(y) = \dfrac{dF(y)}{dy} = F'(y)$ wherever the derivative exits. The function $f(y)$ is called the probability density function for the random variable Y.

From the fundamental theorem of calculus it follows that $F(y) = \displaystyle\int\limits_{-\infty}^{y} f(t)dt$, which means the cumulative probability at y is the area under the density curve from $-\infty$ to y. The density function for the continuous random variable is an analog for the probability distribution $P(y)$ for the discrete random variable. The distribution function $F(y)$ for a continuous random variable is an analog of the probability $P(Y \leq y)$. The following are properties of density functions: $f(y) \geq 0$ (compare for discrete variable $P(y) \geq 0$) and the area under the curve to the x-axis is 1 $\left(\displaystyle\int\limits_{-\infty}^{\infty} f(t)dt = 1 \right)$. (Compare for discrete variable $\displaystyle\sum_{y} p(y) = 1$.

Mean and Variance of a Distribution

The distribution function (as well as the density) determines all the properties of a random variable completely. If density is known, then we can determine mean, variance and other characteristics (parameters) of the random variable. The mean is:

a) $\mu = \displaystyle\sum_{y_j} y_j P(y_j)$ (discrete distribution).

b) $\mu = \displaystyle\int\limits_{-\infty}^{\infty} tf(t)dt$ (continuous distribution).

The variance of the distribution is given by the following:

a) $V = \sigma^2 = \sum_{y_j}(y_j - \mu)^2 P(y_j)$ (discrete distribution).

b) $V = \sigma^2 = \int_{-\infty}^{\infty}(t - \mu)^2 f(t)dt$ (continuous distribution).

Normal Distribution

The normal distribution or *Gauss distribution* is defined as the distribution with the

density $f(y) = \dfrac{1}{\sigma\sqrt{2\pi}} e^{-\frac{1}{2}\left(\frac{y-\mu}{\sigma}\right)^2}$ and the statistical characteristics $E(Y) = \mu$; $V(Y) = \sigma^2$.

This is the familiar bell-shaped curve. The distribution function $F(y)$ can be obtained

by the integration $F(y) = \dfrac{1}{\sigma\sqrt{2\pi}} \int_{-\infty}^{y} e^{-\frac{1}{2}\left(\frac{t-\mu}{\sigma}\right)^2} dt$. Hence, the probability that a normal

random variable Y assumes any value in some interval $a < x \le b$ is the area under the density (bell) curve is given by:

$$P(a \le Y \le b) = F(b) - F(a) = \frac{1}{\sigma\sqrt{2\pi}} \int_{a}^{b} e^{-\frac{1}{2}\left(\frac{y-\mu}{\sigma}\right)^2} dy.$$

The empirical law shows that a large number of observed values of a normal random variable Y will be distributed as follows:

$$P(\mu - \sigma < Y \le \mu + \sigma) \approx 68\%$$
$$P(\mu - 2\sigma < Y \le \mu + 2\sigma) \approx 95\%$$
$$P(\mu - 3\sigma < Y \le \mu + 3\sigma) \approx 99.7\%$$

6.5 SOLVED PROBLEMS

1. Suppose that a lot of 200 electric bulbs contains 5% defectives. If a sample of six bulbs is tested, find a probability of observing at least one defective.

   Solution: $P = 1 - P(0) = 1 - \binom{6}{0}q^6 = 1 - (0.95)^6 = 0.265.$

2. Let Y have the density function $f(y) = c(1 - y^2)$ if $-1 \le y \le 1$, zero otherwise.

   a) Find the constant c that makes it a probability density function.

   b) Find the distribution function.

c) Find the probabilities $P(-1/4 \le Y \le 1/4)$, and $P(-1/4 \le Y \le 1.5)$.

d) Find y such that $P(|Y| \le y) = 0.95$.

Solution:

a) $c \int\limits_{-1}^{1} (1 - t^2) dt = \dfrac{4}{3} c = 1; \Rightarrow c = 0.75.$

b) $F(y) = 0.75 \int\limits_{-1}^{y} (1 - t^2) dt = 0.5 + 0.75y - 0.25y^3; \; -1 \le y \le 1$

$F(y) = 1; \; |y| > 1$

c) $P\left(-\dfrac{1}{4} \le Y \le \dfrac{1}{4}\right) = F\left(\dfrac{1}{4}\right) - F\left(-\dfrac{1}{4}\right) = 0.75 \int\limits_{-1/4}^{1/4} (1 - t^2) dt = 0.368$

$P(-\dfrac{1}{4} \le Y \le 1.5) = F(1.5) - F\left(-\dfrac{1}{4}\right) = 0.75 \int\limits_{-1/4}^{1} (1 - t^2) dt = 0.684$

d) $P\left(|Y| \le y\right) = F(y) - F(-y) = 1.5y - 0.5y^3 = 0.95$

$1.5y - 0.5y^3 = 0.95; \; y \approx 0.811$

6.5 UNSOLVED PROBLEMS

1. A box of 24 alarm clocks contains four that are defective. If four alarm clocks are randomly selected for an inspection, what is the probability that
   a) all four are defective?
   b) at most one is defective?
   c) exactly two are defective?

2. Let Y possess the following density function, for some constant c:

$$f(y) = \begin{cases} c(3 - y) & 0 \le y \le 3 \\ 0 & \text{elsewhere} \end{cases}$$

   a) Find: c.
   b) Find: $F(y)$.
   c) Find: $P(0.5 \le Y \le 1.5)$; $P(-0.5 \le Y \le 1)$.

3. Let Y possess the following density function, for some constant c:

$$f(y) = \begin{cases} y + 1 & -1 \le y < 0 \\ e^{-cy} & 0 \le y < \infty \end{cases}$$

a) Find: c.
b) Find: $F(y)$.
c) Find: $P(-1 \le Y \le -0.5)$.
d) Find: $P(-1 \le Y \le 1)$.
e) Find: $P(1 \le Y \le 2)$.

CHAPTER SEVEN

Vectors and Conic Sections

This chapter expands the discussion of linear function to lines and planes in three dimensions. Three-dimensional figures are usually described by vectors. In addition, from the perspective of classical analytical geometry, the chapter covers general second-degree equations: conic sections (circles, parabolas, ellipses, and hyperbolas). It defines a conic section according to specific geometric principles (e.g., the circle is the locus of points at a fixed distance from a fixed point). The chapter then examines some general geometric characteristics of conics, and introduces the concept of eccentricity as a principle applicable to all conics.

Vector in the plane	A quantity $\vec{v} = (a, b)$ has magnitude and direction; for example, a force exerted on a body
Scalar multiple of a vector	A scalar multiple t of a vector (a, b) is the vector (ta, tb)
Line	A line in two dimensions has the general form $y = mx + b$ where m is the direction (slope) of the line and b is the y intercept of the line. In three dimensions the equation of the line is $\vec{r} = t\vec{m} + \vec{b}$, where $\vec{m}$ is the direction of the line, t is a scalar multiple of $\vec{m}$ and $\vec{b}$ is a point on the line
Plane	The locus of all lines in space through a given point (x_0, y_0, z_0) and perpendicular to a given line (or perpendicular to a line parallel to the given line). It has the general form $Ax + By + Cz + D = 0$
Dot product of vectors $\vec{a}$ and $\vec{b}$	$\vec{a} \cdot \vec{b} = \|\vec{a}\|\|\vec{b}\|\cos\theta$ where θ is the angle between $\vec{a}$ and $\vec{b}$ (n.b. the dot product of two vectors is a scalar)

SECTION 7.1

VECTORS

Vectors

Vectors are the quantities that have magnitude and direction. You add vectors by the **triangle law** of addition: place the "tail" of the first vector onto the "head" of the second vector. The sum is the vector that starts from the tail of the first vector, and goes to the head of the second vector. For example, $\vec{a} + \vec{b} = \vec{c}$.

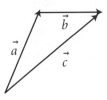

The **parallelogram law** for vector addition (an alternate form of the triangle law) represents the sum of two vectors $\vec{a}$ and $\vec{b}$ as the diagonal of the parallelogram formed by $\vec{a}$ and $\vec{b}$.

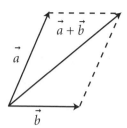

The negation of a vector reverses its direction, while multiplication of a vector by a positive scalar λ keeps the same direction but multiplies the magnitude by λ. Notice that vector addition is associative and commutative:

$$\vec{a} + (\vec{b} + \vec{c}) = (\vec{a} + \vec{b}) + \vec{c}$$
$$\vec{a} + \vec{b} = \vec{b} + \vec{a}$$

while scalar multiplication is distributive:

$$(\alpha + \beta)\vec{a} = \alpha\vec{a} + \beta\vec{a}$$
$$\alpha(\vec{a} + \vec{b}) = \alpha\vec{a} + \alpha\vec{b}$$

(The proofs of these statements follow immediately from the definitions of scalar multiplication.)

Dot Product

Let $\vec{a}$ and $\vec{b}$ be two vectors with magnitude $|\vec{a}| = a$ and $|\vec{b}| = b$ with an angle θ between them. We define the dot product as $\vec{a} \cdot \vec{b} = |\vec{a}||\vec{b}|\cos\theta$.

Notice that, $\vec{a} \cdot \vec{b} = |\vec{a}|(|\vec{b}|\cos\theta) = |\vec{a}|$ (projection of $\vec{b}$ onto $\vec{a}$).

Some immediate results follow from these definitions:

a) $\vec{a} \cdot \vec{a} = |\vec{a}||\vec{a}|\cos\theta = a^2 \cos 0 = a^2$

b) $\vec{a} \cdot \vec{b} = \vec{b} \cdot \vec{a}$

c) If $\vec{a}$ and $\vec{b}$ are nonzero vectors and $\vec{a} \cdot \vec{b} = 0 \Rightarrow \cos\theta = 0$ or $\theta = \dfrac{\pi}{2}$ (if the dot product of two nonzero vectors is zero, then the vectors are perpendicular).

Notice also,

d) $\vec{a} \cdot (\alpha \vec{b}) = \alpha(\vec{a} \cdot \vec{b})$ for scalar α

e) $(\vec{a} + \vec{b}) \cdot \vec{c} = \vec{a} \cdot \vec{c} + \vec{b} \cdot \vec{c}$ and $\vec{a} \cdot (\vec{b} + \vec{c}) = \vec{a} \cdot \vec{b} + \vec{a} \cdot \vec{c}$ (draw the figures)

A convenient form for the scalar product follows from these remarks. Let

$$\vec{a} = a_1 i + a_2 j + a_3 k = (a_1, a_2, a_3)$$
$$\vec{b} = b_1 i + b_2 j + b_3 k = (b_1, b_2, b_3)$$

be two vectors expressed in terms of unit vectors $\vec{i} = (1, 0, 0)$, $\vec{j} = (0, 1, 0)$, and $\vec{k} = (0, 0, 1)$. By definition:

$$\vec{a} \cdot \vec{b} = (a_1 \vec{i} + a_2 \vec{j} + a_3 \vec{k}) \cdot (b_1 \vec{i} + b_2 \vec{j} + b_3 \vec{k})$$
$$= a_1 b_1 + a_2 b_2 + a_3 b_3$$

since $\vec{i}, \vec{j}, \vec{k}$ are $\perp$ to each other, and

$$\vec{i} \cdot \vec{i} = \vec{j} \cdot \vec{j} = \vec{k} \cdot \vec{k} = 1$$

Lines in Space

Suppose P_0 is a point, represented by vector $\vec{r_0}$. Consider a straight line that passes through P_0 in the direction of $\vec{\mu}$. It follows that for any point $\vec{r} = (x, y, z)$ on this line $\vec{r} = \vec{r_0} + \lambda(\vec{\mu})$ (where λ is a scalar), which is the **vector form** of the equation of a line.

Hence, $(x, y, z) = (x_0, y_0, z_0) + \lambda(l, m, n)$ where $r_0 = (x_0, y_0, z_0)$ and $\vec{\mu} = (l, m, n)$. Alternately, you have the **parametric form** of the equation of the line:

$$x = x_0 + \lambda l$$
$$y = y_0 + \lambda m$$
$$z = z_0 + \lambda n$$

or

$$\frac{x - x_0}{l} = \frac{y - y_0}{m} = \frac{z - z_0}{n},$$

which gives the **Cartesian form** of the equation of a line passing through (x_0, y_0, z_0) in the direction of (l, m, n).

Planes

A normal to the plane is a line perpendicular to the plane. Suppose that the normal to the plane is in the direction $\vec{n}$ so that $\vec{n} \cdot (\vec{r} - \vec{r_0}) = 0$ or $\vec{n} \cdot \vec{r} = \vec{n} \cdot \vec{r_0}$ ($\vec{r_0}$ is the position vector of the point r_0). This equation is called the **normal form** of the plane, where r_0 is a fixed point in the plane and r is any point in the plane. Let $\vec{n} = ai + bj + ck$ be a normal to a plane. It follows that $(ai + bj + ck) \cdot (xi + yj + zk) = \vec{n} \cdot \vec{r_0}$ where $\vec{n} \cdot \vec{r_0}$ is a constant $-d$. In other words, $ax + by + cz + d = 0$. This is called the Cartesian form of the equation of a plane.

7.1 SOLVED PROBLEMS

1. Find the equation of the "line" passing through $(1, 2)$ $(2, -3)$ with "holes" at $x = 3, 4$.

   Solution: The equation of a line passing through $(1, 2)$ and $(2, -3)$ is given by the two-point form:

   $$y - 2 = -\frac{5}{1}(x - 1) \text{ or}$$

   $$y - 2 = -5(x - 1)$$

   The required equation will not have values at $x = 3$ and $x = 4$. Hence, one solution to the problem is given by:

   $$\frac{(y - 2)(x - 3)(x - 4)}{(x - 3)(x - 4)} = -5(x - 1).$$

   Alternately, we can also write:

   $$y - 2 = -\frac{5(x - 1)(x - 3)(x - 4)}{(x - 3)(x - 4)}.$$

2. Show that the general linear equation $Ax + By + C = 0$ is an equation of a straight line.

   Solution:

   Case 1 Suppose $B = 0$. The equation reduces to $x = -\frac{C}{A}$, which is the equation of a line $\perp$ to the x-axis, passing through $\left(-\frac{C}{A}, 0\right)$.

   Case 2 Suppose $B \neq 0$. The equation reduces to $y = -\frac{A}{B}x - \frac{C}{A}$, which is the equation of a line with slope $-\frac{A}{B}$ passing through $\left(0, -\frac{C}{A}\right)$.

3. Consider the line $y = x$. What does the transformation of the plane defined by $\begin{bmatrix} 0 & 1 \\ 1 & 0 \end{bmatrix}$ do to this line?

    Solution: Notice $\begin{bmatrix} 0 & 1 \\ 1 & 0 \end{bmatrix}\begin{bmatrix} x \\ y \end{bmatrix} = \begin{bmatrix} y \\ x \end{bmatrix}$ for any point (x, y) in the plane. In other words, the transformation reflects each point on the plane in the line $y = x$. Hence, the points on the line $y = x$ remain constant. (The transformation does not affect the graph of $y = x$.)

4. Find the Cartesian equation of the line joining points $(1, 2, 3)$ and $(4, 5, 6)$.

    Solution: Notice the direction vector of the line is given by: $(4 - 1, 5 - 2, 6 - 3) = (3, 3, 3)$ or $(1, 1, 1)$. Hence, the vector equation is $r = r_0 + \lambda(1, 1, 1) = (1, 2, 3) + \lambda(1, 1, 1) = (1 + \lambda, 2 + \lambda, 3 + \lambda)$. In parametric form: $x = 1 + \lambda, y = 2 + \lambda, z = 3 + \lambda$. In Cartesian form: $x - 1 = y - 2 = z - 3$.

5. Find the Cartesian form for the equation of a plane passing through the point $(1, 2, 3)$ perpendicular to the line: $r = (3, 4, 5) + \lambda(3, 2, 1)$.

    Solution: The direction vector of the line is given by $(3, 2, 1)$. The vector from $(1, 2, 3)$ to any point on the plane (x, y, z) is given by: $(x - 1, y - 2, z - 3)$. By assumption, these two vectors must be perpendicular. It follows that their dot product must be zero, or $3(x - 1) + 2(y - 2) + 1(z - 3) = 0$. In standard form we get: $3x + 2y + z = 10$.

6. Show that the midpoint between the endpoint of a vector A and the endpoint of vector B is given by: $\vec{C} = \dfrac{1}{2}(\vec{A} + \vec{B})$.

    Solution: Consider vector $\overrightarrow{BA}$ with O as an origin (see diagram).

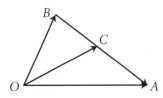

    Notice $\overrightarrow{OC} = \vec{B} + \dfrac{1}{2}\overrightarrow{(BA)} = \vec{B} + \dfrac{1}{2}(\vec{A} - \vec{B}) = \dfrac{1}{2}\vec{A} + \dfrac{1}{2}\vec{B}$.

7. Find the midpoint of the vector joining $(3, 5, -6)$ and $(-1, 2, -3)$.

    Solution:

    Midpoint P is given by: $P = (x, y, z) = \dfrac{1}{2}[(3, 5, -6) + (-1, 2, -3)] = \left(1, \dfrac{7}{2}, -\dfrac{9}{2}\right)$.

8. Find the angle between the two planes $x + y + z = 0$ and $2x + 3y + 4z = 0$.

Solution: The direction of the normals to these planes are $(1, 1, 1)$ and $(2, 3, 4)$. The angle between these two normals is also the angle between the two planes. Hence, by the dot product:

$$\cos\theta = \frac{\vec{a}\cdot\vec{b}}{|\vec{a}||\vec{b}|} = \frac{(1, 1, 1)\cdot(2, 3, 4)}{\sqrt{3}\cdot 29} = \frac{(2+3+4)\sqrt{87}}{87} = \frac{9\cdot\sqrt{87}}{87}; \theta = \cos^{-1}\left(\frac{9\sqrt{87}}{87}\right) \approx 15.2°.$$

9. Show that the distance of point $P_1(x_1, y_1, z_1)$ to the plane $Ax + By + Cz + D = 0$ is given by: $\dfrac{\left|Ax_1 + By_1 + Cz_1 + D\right|}{\sqrt{A^2 + B^2 + C^2}}$.

Solution: The length of the projection of P_1 (x_1, y_1, z_1) in the direction of the normal (A, B, C) to the plane, gives the distance of (x_1, y_1, z_1) to the plane. Notice that the foot of the perpendicular from (x_1, y_1, z_1) to the plane $Ax + By + Cz + D = 0$ is given by: $(x_1, y_1, z_1) \pm p\dfrac{\vec{n}}{n}$, where p is the distance of (x_1, y_1, z_1) to the plane and $n = \sqrt{A^2 + B^2 + C^2}$ ($\pm p$ depends on the direction of $\vec{n}$). But this point lies in the plane. Hence, $\vec{n}\cdot\left[(x_1, y_1, z_1)\pm p\dfrac{\vec{n}}{n}\right] + D = 0$. This implies

$$\vec{n}\cdot(x_1, y_1, z_1)\pm p\frac{n^2}{n} + D = 0 \text{ or } \vec{n}\cdot(x_1, y_1, z_1)\pm pn + D = 0 \text{ or } \pm pn = -\vec{n}\cdot(x_1, y_1, z_1) - D.$$

Hence, $|p| = \dfrac{\left|\vec{n}\cdot(x_1, y_1, z_1) + D\right|}{n}$. But, $\vec{n}\cdot(x_1, y_1, z_1) = Ax_1 + By_1 + Cz_1$ and

$n = \sqrt{A^2 + B^2 + C^2}$; so $|p| = \dfrac{\left|Ax_1 + By_1 + Cz_1 + D\right|}{\sqrt{A^2 + B^2 + C^2}}$.

10. Show that the diagonals of a rhombus are perpendicular.

Solution: Consider the rhombus formed by vectors $\vec{a}$ and $\vec{b}$ (see diagram) so that $|\vec{a}| = |\vec{b}|$.

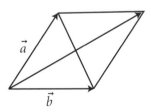

One diagonal of the rhombus is given by $\vec{a}+\vec{b}$, the other by $\vec{a}-\vec{b}$. This means $(\vec{a}+\vec{b})\cdot(\vec{a}-\vec{b}) = |\vec{a}|^2 - |\vec{b}|^2 = 0$. Hence, $(\vec{a}+\vec{b})$ is perpendicular to $(\vec{a}-\vec{b})$.

7.1 UNSOLVED PROBLEMS

1. The point M is the midpoint of side $\overline{BC}$ in $\triangle ABC$. For simplicity, let M be located at the origin where M is the midpoint of $\overline{BC}$, which lies on the x-axis.
   Show that: $(AB)^2 + (AC)^2 = 2\left((AM)^2 + (MC)^2\right)$.

2. Show that the distance from point (x_1, y_1) to line $Ax + By + C = 0$ is given by:
   $$\frac{\left|Ax_1 + By_1 + C\right|}{\sqrt{A^2 + B^2}}.$$

3. Find the equation of the bisector(s) of the angle(s) formed by the lines $3x - 2y - 5 = 0$ and $x + y + 7 = 0$.

4. Suppose $Ax + By + C = 0$ and $A_1x + B_1y + C_1 = 0$ and $AB_1 - A_1B = 0$. What do you know about these lines?

5. A tetrahedron has a horizontal equilateral triangular base of 12cm and its sloping edges are 8cm. Find the angle of inclination of the sloping edge to the horizontal.

6. Show that the diagonals of a parallelogram bisect each other.

7. Find the angle between planes $4x + 3y + 2z = 0$ and $x + 2y + 3z = 0$.

8. Find the angle between $\dfrac{x-2}{3} = \dfrac{y-1}{2} = \dfrac{z-3}{4}$ and the plane $4x + 3y + 2z + 2 = 0$.

9. Find the distance from the plane $2x + 3y + z + 1 = 0$ to the point $(1, 1, 1)$.

10. Resolve vector $\vec{a}$ into two components $\vec{a_1}$ and $\vec{a_2}$, one parallel to, and the other perpendicular to a nonzero vector $\vec{b}$.

SECTION 7.2

CONIC SECTIONS

A mathematical cone consists of both top and bottom sections. Cross-sections of this cone produce conic sections. There are four standard conic sections (circle, parabola, ellipse, and hyperbola) along with three degenerate conic sections (point, line, two intersecting lines). This section deals with material relating to the four standard conic sections.

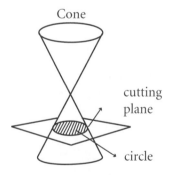

A plane that cuts a cone parallel to the base of the cone produces a **circle**.

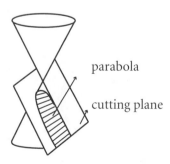

A plane that cuts a cone parallel to a plane tangent to the cone produces a **parabola**.

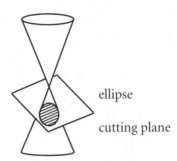

ellipse

cutting plane

A plane that is non-parallel to the base of the cone that cuts only the top or the bottom produces an **ellipse**.

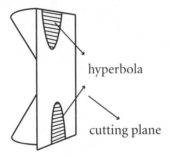

hyperbola

cutting plane

A plane that cuts both the top and the bottom parts of the cone produces a **hyperbola**.

Circles

Consider the locus of points equidistant from a fixed point $(0, 0)$ in a plane. By the Law of Pythagoras $x^2 + y^2 = r^2$ for any point (x, y) at a fixed distance from $(0, 0)$. The resulting figure is a circle with center $(0, 0)$ and radius r. Suppose one translates the center of this circle to (a, b). The resulting translation is described by:

$$x - a = x_0$$
$$y - b = y_0$$

where x and y represent the translated variables x_0 and y_0. Hence, the equation of a circle with center at (a, b) and radius r is: $(x - a)^2 + (y - b)^2 = r^2$.

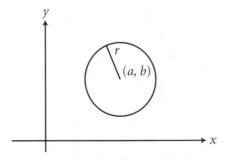

Parabolas

Consider the locus of points equidistant from a fixed point (focus) and a fixed line (directrix). If the fixed point is $(p, 0)$, because the midpoint between $(-p, 0)$ and $(p, 0)$ is a point on the parabola, the fixed line must be $x = -p$. (This choice of position for the parabola is called the standard position.)

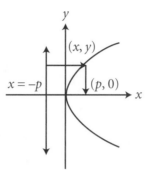

In other words, $(x - p)^2 + y^2 = (x + p)^2$ or $x^2 - 2xp + p^2 + y^2 = x^2 + 2xp + p^2$; $y^2 = 4px$. This parabola has focus at $(p, 0)$ and a directrix at $y = -p$.

Ellipses

Consider the locus of points the sum of whose distance from two fixed points is a constant.

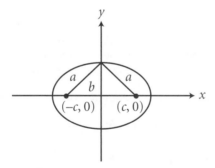

Let $(-c, 0)$ and $(c, 0)$ be these two fixed points (foci). Suppose $2a$ is equal to the fixed sum, then the equation of the ellipse in standard form is

$$\sqrt{(x+c)^2 + y^2} + \sqrt{(x-c)^2 + y^2} = 2a$$

$$\sqrt{(x+c)^2 + y^2} = 2a - \sqrt{(x-c)^2 + y^2}$$

$$(x+c)^2 + y^2 = 4a^2 - 4a\sqrt{(x-c)^2 + y^2} + (x-c)^2 + y^2$$

$$4cx - 4a^2 = -4a\sqrt{(x-c)^2 + y^2}$$

$$a^2 - cx = a\sqrt{(x-c)^2 + y^2}$$

Squaring again, we get: $a^4 - 2a^2 cx + c^2 x^2 = a^2 (x^2 - 2xc + c^2) + a^2 y^2$;

$(a^2 - c^2)x^2 + a^2 y^2 = a^2 (a^2 - c^2)$ or $\dfrac{x^2}{a^2} + \dfrac{y^2}{a^2 - c^2} = 1$. Since $a > c$ (see figure) we can let

$b = \sqrt{a^2 - c^2}$, or $\dfrac{x^2}{a^2} + \dfrac{y^2}{b^2} = 1$, where $2b$ is the length of the minor axis of the ellipse, $2a$

is the length of the major axis and $(\pm c, 0)$ are the foci of the ellipse $(c = \sqrt{a^2 - b^2})$.

Hyperbolas

Consider the locus of points the difference of whose distances from two fixed points is constant.

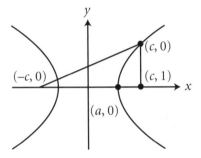

Let $(c, 0)$ and $(-c, 0)$ be these two fixed points (foci). The equation of the hyperbola in the standard form is: $\sqrt{(x+c)^2 + y^2} - \sqrt{(x-c)^2 + y^2} = 2a$. We simplify exactly as in the equation of the ellipse, except in the case of the hyperbola $c^2 - a^2 > 0$. Hence, the equation of the hyperbola is $\dfrac{x^2}{a^2} - \dfrac{y^2}{c^2 - a^2} = 1$, or $\dfrac{x^2}{a^2} - \dfrac{y^2}{b^2} = 1$ where $b = \sqrt{c^2 - a^2}$.

(Notice that this value is analogous to the ellipse where $b^2 + c^2 = a^2$.)

One characteristic of the hyperbola that is not shared with other conic sections is that each hyperbola has a pair of asymptotes. The asymptotes of a hyperbola are the two lines that "contain" the hyperbola. The equation of the hyperbola $\dfrac{x^2}{a^2} - \dfrac{y^2}{b^2} = 1$ may be written as $y^2 = \dfrac{b^2}{a^2}x^2 - b^2$. For large values of x, $\dfrac{b^2}{a^2}x^2 - b^2 \approx \dfrac{b^2}{a^2}x^2$. Therefore, as $x \to \infty$,

$y^2 \to \dfrac{b^2}{a^2}x^2$ or $y = \pm\dfrac{b}{a}x$, which gives the asymptotes of the hyperbola. In general, the

equation $\left(\dfrac{x}{a} - \dfrac{y}{b}\right)\left(\dfrac{x}{a} + \dfrac{y}{b}\right) = 0$ gives the equations of both asymptotes (alternately

$b^2 x^2 - a^2 y^2 = 0$).

The $xy = c^2$ form of a hyperbola

The hyperbola $\dfrac{x^2}{a^2} - \dfrac{y^2}{b^2} = 1$ has two asymptotes: $\dfrac{x}{a} - \dfrac{y}{a} = 0$ and $\dfrac{x}{a} + \dfrac{y}{a} = 0$. In other words, two asymptotes are perpendicular since the product of their slopes is -1 (i.e., the asymptotes are perpendicular since the slopes are negative reciprocals of each other).

Consider the hyperbola $x^2 - y^2 = a^2$ and rotate it by 45° (or half of the angle of intersection of the asymptotes). The units x and y under this transformation are mapped into the following: $(1,0) \rightarrow \left(\dfrac{1}{\sqrt{2}}, \dfrac{1}{\sqrt{2}} \right)$ and $(0,1) \rightarrow \left(-\dfrac{1}{\sqrt{2}}, \dfrac{1}{\sqrt{2}} \right)$.

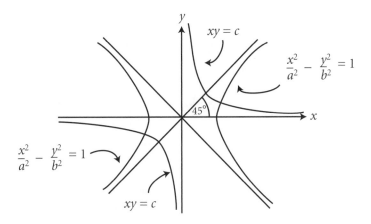

The matrix describing this transformation is:

$$\begin{pmatrix} x' \\ y' \end{pmatrix} = \begin{pmatrix} \dfrac{1}{\sqrt{2}} & -\dfrac{1}{\sqrt{2}} \\ \dfrac{1}{\sqrt{2}} & \dfrac{1}{\sqrt{2}} \end{pmatrix} \begin{pmatrix} x \\ y \end{pmatrix} \qquad \begin{aligned} \Rightarrow \; x' &= \frac{1}{\sqrt{2}}(x - y) \\[2mm] \Rightarrow \; y' &= \frac{1}{\sqrt{2}}(x + y) \end{aligned}$$

Hence, the equation $x^2 - y^2 = a^2$ transforms into $2(x'y') = (x^2 - y^2)$, or $2x'y' = a^2$. Let $c^2 = \dfrac{1}{2}a^2$, and you have the second standard form for the hyperbola: $xy = c^2$. The asymptotes of this parabola are $x = 0$ and $y = 0$. An alternate form for this equation can also be considered in parametric form. Let $x = ct$ and $y = \dfrac{c}{t}$. It follows that $xy = c^2$. In summary: $xy = c^2$ gives a hyperbola with the x and y axis as asymptotes, as do the parametric equation $x = ct$ and $y = \dfrac{c}{t}$.

Alternatively, conic sections may also be defined in terms of eccentricity $\left(e = \dfrac{c}{a} \right)$; in the case of the ellipse and hyperbola the eccentricity the directrices to be defined as $d = \dfrac{a}{e}$.

(The properties of eccentricity are included in the following table without detailed explanations.) The following chart gives the major properties of ellipse, hyperbola, and parabola:

Curve	Ellipse	Hyperbola	Parabola
Equation	$\dfrac{x^2}{a^2}+\dfrac{y^2}{b^2}=1$	$\dfrac{x^2}{a^2}-\dfrac{y^2}{b^2}=1$	$y^2=4cx$
Center	$(0,0)$	$(0,0)$	$(0,0)$
Focii	$(\pm c,0)=\left(\pm\sqrt{a^2-b^2},0\right)$	$(\pm c,0)=\left(\pm\sqrt{a^2+b^2},0\right)$	$(c,0)$
Vertices	$(\pm a,0)(0,\pm b)$	$(\pm a,0)$	$(0,0)$
Directrices $\left(d=\dfrac{a}{e}\right)$	$x=a^2\big/\sqrt{a^2-b^2}$	$x=a^2\big/\sqrt{a^2+b^2}$	$x=-c$
Eccentricity $\left(e=\dfrac{c}{a}\right)$	$\dfrac{c}{a}=\sqrt{a^2-b^2}\big/a$	$\dfrac{c}{a}=\sqrt{a^2+b^2}\big/a$	1
Asymptotes	—	$b^2x^2-a^2y^2=0$	—

7.2 SOLVED PROBLEMS

1. Describe the locus of points satisfying: $x^2+y^2-8x+2y-8=0$.

   Solution: The equation is of the form $(x-a)^2+(y-b)^2=r^2$ which is a circle. More specifically, $x^2-8x+16+y^2+2y+1=25$ or $(x-4)^2+(y+1)^2=5^2$. The equation is a circle with center at $(4,-1)$ and radius 5.

2. Show that the locus of points P such that $PA=2PB$, where A is $(-a,0)$ and B is $(a,0)$, is a circle. (This circle is sometimes called the Circle of Apollonius.)

   Solution: Let $P(x,y)$ be any point satisfying the required condition. Hence,

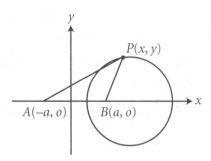

$$\sqrt{(x+a)^2+y^2}=2\sqrt{(x-a)^2+y^2}\,;\ (x+a)^2+y^2=4[(x-a)^2+y^2];$$

$$x^2+2ax+a^2+y^2=4x^2-8ax+4a^2+4y^2;\ 0=3x^2+3y^2-10ax+3a^2;$$

$0 = x^2 + y^2 - \dfrac{10a}{3}x + a^2.$ Hence, it is a circle with center at $\left(\dfrac{5a}{3}, 0\right)$ and radius

$\sqrt{\dfrac{25a^2}{9} - 0^2} = \dfrac{4}{3}a.$

3. Find the equation of the tangent to $x^2 + y^2 - 2x + 4y - 3 = 0$ at $\left(1, 2(1+\sqrt{2})\right)$.

    Solution: The standard form of this circle is $(x-1)^2 + (y-2)^2 = 8$; its center is $(1, 2)$, its radius is $2\sqrt{2}$. Hence, the radius through $\left(1, 2(1+\sqrt{2})\right)$ has no slope $(\Delta x = 0)$. In other words, the line perpendicular to this radius must be parallel to the x-axis, which means $y = 2(1+\sqrt{2})$.

4. Identify the following conic section, describe its relevant geometric properties (i.e. center, focus, directrix, etc.): $(x-2)^2 + 8(y-3) = 0$.

    Solution: The conic is of the form $y = a(x-h)^2 + k$, the equation of a parabola with a vertex at $(2, 3)$; $4p = -8$ or $p = -2$. Its focus is at $(2, 1)$; its directrix is $y = 2 + 3 = 5$.

5. Find the equation of a parabola with its vertex at the origin and focus $(-2, 0)$.

    Solution: This parabola has the form $y^2 = 4px$ with $p = -2$; hence $y^2 = -8x$.

6. Find the equation of a parabola with focus at $(3, 3)$ and directrix $x = -3$.

    Solution: The parabola has the vertex $(0, 3)$. It has the standard form $y^2 = 4px$ with $p = 3$. It is the equation $y^2 = 12x$.

7. Determine a parametric equation for the parabola $y^2 = 4ax$.

    Solution: Let $x = at^2$ and $y = 2at$ for some value t. Notice: $y^2 = 4a^2t^2 = 4a(at^2) = 4ax$. In other words, for all values of t, the point $(at^2, 2at)$ lies on the parabola $y^2 = 4ax$. One parametric representation is given by: $x = at^2$, $y = 2at$.

8. Determine the equation of a chord of a parabola $x = at^2$ and $y = 2at$ connecting points P_1 and P_2, on the parabola with parameter values of t_1 and t_2.

    Solution:

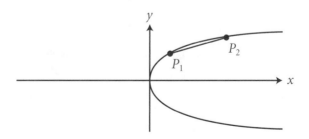

Thus, the slope of $\overline{P_1 P_2}$ is $\dfrac{\Delta y}{\Delta x} = \dfrac{2at_1 - 2at_2}{at_1^2 - at_2^2} = \dfrac{2a(t_1 - t_2)}{a(t_1 - t_2)(t_1 + t_2)} = \dfrac{2}{t_1 + t_2}.$

The line passing through P_1 with this slope has the equation (point-slope form of a line) $\dfrac{y - 2at_1}{x - at_1^2} = \dfrac{2}{t_1 + t_2}$, which means $2x - (t_1 + t_2)y + 2at_1t_2 = 0$.

9. Find the equation of the tangent to the parabola defined in terms of parameter t at point $P = (x, y)$.

Solution: Consider the equation of the chord P_1P_2 when point P_1 coincides with point P_2 so $2x - (t_1 + t_2)y + 2at_1t_2 = 0$ (problem 8); $2x - 2ty + 2at^2 = 0$, or $x - ty + at^2 = 0$.

10. Define the eccentricity of an ellipse as the ratio $e = \dfrac{c}{a}$. (The eccentricity of a conic indicates how "far off" the conic is from being a circle, which is the conic with an eccentricity of 0). Find the eccentricity of the ellipse: $4x^2 + y^2 - 8x + 4y - 8 = 0$.

Solution: $4x^2 + y^2 - 8x + 4y = 8$; $4(x^2 - 2x) + y^2 + 4y = 8$ or

$4(x^2 - 2x + 1) + (y^2 + 4y + 4) = 16$. In standard form we have: $\dfrac{(x-1)^2}{4} + \dfrac{(y+2)^2}{16} = 1.$

This is an equation of an ellipse with center at $(1, -2)$, with foci $(1, -2 - 2\sqrt{3})$ and $(1, -2 + 2\sqrt{3})$ and vertices $(1, -6)$ and $(1, 2)$. Hence, the eccentricity

$e = \dfrac{c}{a} = \dfrac{2\sqrt{3}}{4} = \dfrac{\sqrt{3}}{2}$. (Notice $0 < e < 1$ for every ellipse, since $c < a$.)

11. Find the inequality corresponding to the area between $x^2 + y^2 = 1$ and $\dfrac{x^2}{4} + \dfrac{y^2}{1} = 1$.

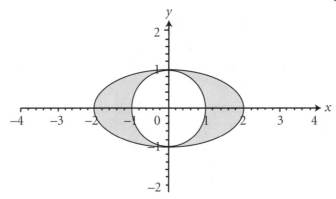

Solution: Clearly the area is outside the circle, and inside the ellipse, which means it consists of all (x, y) such that $x^2 + y^2 > 1$ and $\dfrac{x^2}{4} + \dfrac{y^2}{1} < 1$ (for example let $x = \dfrac{3}{2}$ and $y = 0$).

12. Cut the ellipse $\dfrac{x^2}{a^2} + \dfrac{y^2}{b^2} = 1$ into two halves such that each half will give a function $(a > b)$.

Solution: If $a > b$ then the ellipse will have its major axis on the x axis. Two resulting functions will be given by: $y = \sqrt{b^2\left(1 - \dfrac{x^2}{a^2}\right)}$ and $y = -\sqrt{b^2\left(1 - \dfrac{x^2}{a^2}\right)}$.

13. Find the foci and eccentricity of a hyperbola with the two asymptotes $y - 2x = 0$ and $y + 2x = 0$.

    Solution: We have the equation of the hyperbola as $(y - 2x)(y + 2x) = 1$ or $y^2 - 4x^2 = 1$.

    In standard form: $y^2 - \dfrac{x^2}{\frac{1}{4}} = 1$. Hence, $e = \dfrac{c}{a} = \dfrac{\sqrt{5}}{1} = \sqrt{5}$ while the two foci are

    given by $(0, \pm c)$, or since $c^2 = a^2 + b^2 = 1 + \dfrac{1}{4} = \dfrac{5}{4}$, we have $\left(0, \pm \dfrac{\sqrt{5}}{2}\right)$.

14. Find the asymptotes for the hyperbola $\dfrac{(x-1)^2}{9} - \dfrac{(y+4)^2}{16} = 1$. At what point do these asymptotes intersect?

    Solution: The two asymptotes are given by: $\dfrac{(x-1)}{3} + \dfrac{(y+4)}{4} = 0$

    and $\dfrac{(x-1)}{3} - \dfrac{(y+4)}{4} = 0$. Clearly, the asymptotes intersect at the center of the

    hyperbola $(1, -4)$.

15. Classify the following conic $Ax^2 + Cy^2 + Dx + Ey + F = 0$ given $A = C$, $AC = 0$, $AC > 0$, $AC < 0$.

    Solution:

    If $A = C$ the conic is of the form $x^2 + y^2 + \dfrac{D}{A}x + \dfrac{E}{A}y + \dfrac{F}{A} = 0$; it is a circle.

    If $AC = 0$ $(A \neq C)$ then either $A = 0$ or $C = 0$, which means if the conic is of the form $Cy^2 + Dx + Ey + F = 0$ or $Ax^2 + Dx + Ey + F = 0$, then it is a parabola.

    If $AC > 0$ then either $A > 0$ and $C > 0$, or $A < 0$ and $C < 0$, which means if the conic is of the form $Ax^2 + Cy^2 + Dx + Ey + F = 0$ where A and C have the same sign, then it is an ellipse.

    If $AC < 0$ $(A \neq C)$ then A and C are opposite in sign which means if the conic is of the form $Ax^2 - |C|y^2 + Dx + Ey + F = 0$ or $-|A|x^2 - Cy^2 + Dx + Ey + F = 0$ (so that x^2 and y^2) are of the opposite signs, then it is a hyperbola.

7.2 UNSOLVED PROBLEMS

1. Show that at any point P on a parabolic mirror if a ray of light is parallel to the axis of the parabola, then it passes through the focus of the parabola. (This describes the property of a magnifying glass that allows one to focus length into a point, and hence create an intense source of heat.)

2. Find the equation of the circle passing through $(4, 5)$, $(2, -1)$, and $(0, 1)$.

3. Find the equation of the conic $x = a\cos\theta$, $y = b\sin\theta$. Identify the curve.

4. Find the area of an ellipse with major axis a and minor axis b.

5. Graph a hyperbola $\dfrac{(x-h)^2}{a^2} - \dfrac{(y-k)^2}{b^2} = 1$. Find the equation of its asymptotes.

6. Rotate the hyperbola $xy = 1$ by $-\dfrac{\pi}{4}$. Find the resulting equation.

7. Given that the value $B^2 - 4AC$ remains invariant under rotation in the general conic $Ax^2 + Bxy + Cy^2 + Dx + Ey + F = 0$. Identify the conic: $x^2 - 2xy + y^2 - x - y = 0$.

8. A student argues that a circle is not a conic; her teacher argues that it is a conic. Give a reason for each point of view.

9. The point $(1, 0)$ on the circle $x^2 + y^2 = 1$ moves "s" units around the circumference in a counterclockwise direction. Find the coordinates of the point at which it stops.

CHAPTER EIGHT

Calculus

Calculus is central to any sophisticated understanding of mathematics. The subject also has enormous numbers of practical applications in the physical sciences. Because of the central role calculus plays in both mathematics and science, the topics covered in a calculus course are quite standard. This chapter gives only a brief sketch of the highlights of first year calculus. The material in it provides a selection of the type of problems that students are most frequently asked to solve in such a course. The chapter follows the convention of most first year calculus courses, in which major theorems are explained but not usually proven.

$\lim\limits_{x \to a} f(x) = L$	The value for f is as close to L as you like, for all x in a specified interval around a ($x \neq a$)
$\lim\limits_{x \to a} f(x) = \infty$	The value for f gets as large as you like, for all x in a specified interval around a ($x \neq a$)
If $\lim\limits_{x \to a} f(x) = A$ and $\lim\limits_{x \to a} f(x) = B$ then $A = B$	If the limit of a function exists, it is unique
If $f(x) = c$ then $\lim\limits_{x \to a} f(x) = c$	The limit of a constant value is the constant
$\lim\limits_{x \to a} cf(x) = c \lim\limits_{x \to a} f(x)$	The limit of a constant times a function is the constant times the limit of the function
$\lim\limits_{x \to a} f(x) \pm g(x) = \lim\limits_{x \to a} f(x) \pm \lim\limits_{x \to a} g(x)$ $\lim\limits_{x \to a} f(x) \cdot g(x) = \lim\limits_{x \to a} f(x) \cdot \lim\limits_{x \to a} g(x)$	The limit of the sum (difference) and product of two functions is the sum (difference) and product of their limits assuming that both functions have finite limits
$\lim\limits_{x \to a} \dfrac{f(x)}{g(x)} = \dfrac{\lim\limits_{x \to a} f(x)}{\lim\limits_{x \to a} g(x)}$ $(\lim\limits_{x \to a} g(x) \neq 0)$	The limit of the quotient of two functions is the quotient of the limits of the functions (the limit of the denominator $\neq 0$ and both functions have finite limits)

SECTION 8.1

LIMITS AND THEIR PROPERTIES

The concept of a limit is central to understanding calculus and more advanced topics in analysis. Historically, this concept was understood intuitively long before Cauchy developed a precise definition for it in the 19th century. For example, the Chinese (among others) knew centuries before the development of the calculus that the limit of the area of a regular polygon with n-sides, as n approached a larger and larger number, would give the area of a circle. In particular, for a regular polygon:

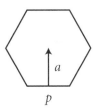

$A = \dfrac{1}{2}ap$, where a is the apothem and p is the perimeter of the polygon. Consider

$\lim\limits_{n \to \infty} A = \lim\limits_{n \to \infty} \dfrac{1}{2}ap$. As the number of the sides gets increasingly large, the polygon approaches a circle. In addition, the apothem approaches the radius, and the perimeter of the polygon approaches the circumference of the circle $2\pi r$.

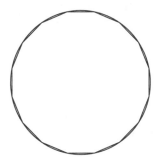

The area of the polygon approaches the area of the circle; or $A_0 = \dfrac{1}{2}(\pi r)r = \pi r^2$.

With this example as a model we see that the $\lim\limits_{x \to \infty} f(x) = L$ "roughly" means that $f(x)$ gets very close to the value L, as x gets very large. Closely related to this idea is the expression: $\lim\limits_{x \to a} f(x) = L$. It means that $f(x)$ gets as close as one would like to the quantity L, whenever x is in a specified interval around a ($x \neq a$). Intuitively, $\lim\limits_{x \to 2}(2x^2 + 1) = 9$. In certain cases the limit of a function can be found by "substitution methods"—i.e., one "substitutes" the quantity approached in the expression to obtain the desired limit. Consider, $\lim\limits_{x \to 3}(2x + 1) = 7$ or $\lim\limits_{x \to \frac{\pi}{2}} \sin x = 1$. In other situations, substitution results in one or more indeterminate forms. Other methods of calculation may then allow one to find the required limit. For example, if you substitute $x = 2$ to find the $\lim\limits_{x \to 2} \dfrac{x^2 - 4x + 4}{x^2 - 4}$, you get the indeterminate form $\dfrac{0}{0}$. Alternatively, if we factor the expression and cancel common factors, we find: $\lim\limits_{x \to 2} \dfrac{(x - 2)(x - 2)}{(x - 2)(x + 2)} = \lim\limits_{x \to 2} \dfrac{(x - 2)}{(x + 2)} = 0.$

Properties of Limits

The following theorems allow for easier evaluations of limits of complex expressions. Most "ring true" from an intuitive point of view; some are more difficult than others to actually prove. Formal proofs are omitted here but may be found in a standard calculus text.

Theorem on limits

1. If $\lim\limits_{x \to a} f(x) = A$ and $\lim\limits_{x \to a} f(x) = B$ then $A = B$.

2. If $f(x) = c$, then $\lim\limits_{x \to a} f(x) = c$.

   Suppose $\lim\limits_{x \to a} f(x) = A$ and $\lim\limits_{x \to a} g(x) = B$.

3. Let c be any constant, then $\lim\limits_{x \to a} cf(x) = cA$.

4. $\lim\limits_{x \to a} (f(x) \pm g(x)) = \lim\limits_{x \to a} f(x) \pm \lim\limits_{x \to a} g(x) = A \pm B$.

5. $\lim\limits_{x \to a} (f(x) \cdot g(x)) = \lim\limits_{x \to a} f(x) \cdot \lim\limits_{x \to a} g(x) = A \cdot B$.

6. Suppose $\lim\limits_{x \to a} g(x) \neq 0$, then $\lim\limits_{x \to a} \dfrac{f(x)}{g(x)} = \dfrac{\lim\limits_{x \to a} f(x)}{\lim\limits_{x \to a} g(x)} = \dfrac{A}{B}$.

7. Power rule: $\lim\limits_{x \to a} [f(x)]^n = [\lim\limits_{x \to a} f(x)]^n$.

Definition of Infinity

The concept of a limit gives rise to the idea of infinity, a condition indicating that a number may be as "large" as one likes. More formally, define $\lim\limits_{x \to a} f(x) = \infty$ to mean the following: for any number N, as large as you like to choose, $|f(x)| > N$ (f is unbounded), whenever x is close to a ($x \neq a$). The definition for $-\infty$ follows exactly the same reasoning.

8.1 SOLVED PROBLEMS

1. Find the following limits:

   a) $\lim\limits_{x \to \infty} \dfrac{x-1}{x+1}$

   b) $\lim\limits_{x \to \infty} \dfrac{6x^2 + 2x + 1}{3x^2 + x - 1}$

   c) $\lim\limits_{x \to \infty} \dfrac{2x^3 + 1}{x^2 + 5}$

   Solution:

   a) $\lim\limits_{x \to \infty} \dfrac{x-1}{x+1} = \lim\limits_{x \to \infty} \dfrac{1 - \dfrac{1}{x}}{1 + \dfrac{1}{x}} = \dfrac{1}{1} = 1$

   b) $\lim\limits_{x \to \infty} \dfrac{6x^2 + 2x + 1}{3x^2 + x - 1} = \lim\limits_{x \to \infty} \dfrac{6 + \dfrac{2}{x} + \dfrac{1}{x^2}}{3 + \dfrac{1}{x} - \dfrac{1}{x^2}} = \dfrac{6}{3} = 2$

c) $\lim\limits_{x\to\infty}\dfrac{2x^3+1}{x^2+5}=\lim\limits_{x\to\infty}\dfrac{2x+\dfrac{1}{x^2}}{1+\dfrac{5}{x^2}}=\lim\limits_{x\to\infty}\dfrac{2x}{1}=\infty$ (the expression gets as large as you like).

2. Find the following limits by whatever methods possible.

a) $\lim\limits_{x\to16}\dfrac{x-16}{\sqrt{x}-16}$

b) $\lim\limits_{x\to16}\dfrac{\sqrt{x}-4}{x-16}$

c) $\lim\limits_{x\to2}\dfrac{x^3-8}{x^2-4}$

Solution:

a) $\lim\limits_{x\to16}\dfrac{x-16}{\sqrt{x}-16}=\lim\limits_{x\to16}\dfrac{(x-16)}{\sqrt{x}-16}\cdot\dfrac{\sqrt{x}-16}{\sqrt{x}-16}=\lim\limits_{x\to16}\dfrac{x-16}{x-16}\left(\sqrt{x}-16\right)=\lim\limits_{x\to16}\sqrt{x}-16=0$

b) $\lim\limits_{x\to16}\dfrac{\sqrt{x}-4}{x-16}=\lim\limits_{x\to16}\dfrac{\sqrt{x}-4}{x-16}\cdot\dfrac{\sqrt{x}+4}{\sqrt{x}+4}=\lim\limits_{x\to16}\dfrac{x-16}{x-16}\cdot\dfrac{1}{\sqrt{x}+4}=\lim\limits_{x\to16}\dfrac{1}{\sqrt{x}+4}=\dfrac{1}{8}$

c) $\lim\limits_{x\to2}\dfrac{x^3-8}{x^2-4}=\lim\limits_{x\to2}\dfrac{(x-2)(x^2+2x+4)}{(x-2)(x+2)}=\lim\limits_{x\to2}\dfrac{x^2+2x+4}{x+2}=3$

3. Find the following one-sided limits ($x\to1^-$ means that x approaches 1 from the left; $x\to1^+$ means that x approaches 1 from the right): $\lim\limits_{x\to0^-}\dfrac{1+|x|}{1-x}$; $\lim\limits_{x\to0^-}\tan(x+|x|)$.

Solution: For all $x<0$, $|x|=-x$. Hence, $\lim\limits_{x\to0^-}\dfrac{1+|x|}{1-x}=\lim\limits_{x\to0^-}\dfrac{1-x}{1-x}=1.$

For all $x>0$, $|x|=x$. Hence, $\lim\limits_{x\to0^+}\tan(x+|x|)=\lim\limits_{x\to0^+}\tan(x+x)=\lim\limits_{x\to0^+}\tan2x=0.$

5. Find: $\lim\limits_{x\to0}\dfrac{1}{x^2}$.

Solution: From an intuitive perspective, for any number N, no matter how large, when x gets sufficiently close to 0, $\dfrac{1}{x^2}$ will be larger than N. In this case we write:

$\lim\limits_{x\to0}\dfrac{1}{x^2}=\infty.$

6. Find: $\lim\limits_{x\to0}\dfrac{1}{x}$.

Solution: When x approaches 0 from the right, $\dfrac{1}{x}$ gets infinitely large, positively; if x approaches 0 from the left, $\dfrac{1}{x}$ gets infinitely large, negatively. Hence, no limit exists.

7. Given $f(x) = x^2$ find $\lim\limits_{h \to 0} \dfrac{f(x+h) - f(x)}{h}$. (This quantity is called the derivative and represents the slope of the tangent to the curve at any point; see diagram.)

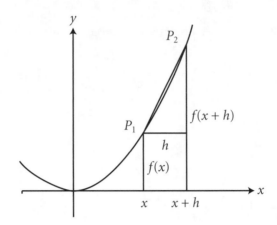

Solution:

$$\lim_{h \to 0} \frac{f(x+h) - f(x)}{h} = \lim_{h \to 0} \frac{(x+h)^2 - x^2}{h} = \lim_{h \to 0} \frac{x^2 + 2hx + h^2 - x^2}{h} = \lim_{h \to 0}(2x + h) = 2x.$$

8.1 UNSOLVED PROBLEMS

Find the following limits if they exist:

1. $\lim\limits_{x \to \frac{\pi}{2}} [\sin x]$ (The greatest integer function for $\sin x$)

2. $\lim\limits_{x \to 3^+} \dfrac{\sqrt{x^2 - 9}}{x + 3}$

3. $\lim\limits_{x \to 3^-} \dfrac{\sqrt{x^2 - 9}}{x + 3}$

4. $\lim\limits_{x \to 0} \dfrac{x}{|x|}$

5. $\lim\limits_{x \to 0^-} \dfrac{x}{|x|}$

6. $\lim\limits_{x \to 4} \dfrac{x^2 - 16}{x^3 - 64}$

7. $\lim\limits_{x \to 1} \dfrac{|x - 1|}{1 + x}$

8. $\lim\limits_{x \to \frac{\pi}{2}} \tan x$

9. $\lim\limits_{x\to 2}(\cos x+|\cos x|)$

10. $\lim\limits_{x\to\pi}\cos[x]$ where ($[x]$ = greatest integer function)

11. If $f(x) = \dfrac{x^5}{|x|}$, is it true that $\lim\limits_{x\to 0}\left|f(x)\right| = \left|\lim\limits_{x\to a} f(x)\right|$?

12. If $f(x) = \dfrac{x}{|x|}$ is it true that $\lim\limits_{x\to 0}\left|f(x)\right| = \left|\lim\limits_{x\to 0} f(x)\right|$?

$f(x)$ is continuous at $x = a$	$\lim\limits_{x \to a} f(x) = f(a)$
$f'(x) = \dfrac{dy}{dx}$	The derivative of a function at a point gives the slope of the tangent to the function at the point
The power rule	$f(x) = x^n$ then $f'(x) = nx^{n-1}$
Chain rule	$\dfrac{dy}{dx} = \dfrac{dy}{dz} \cdot \dfrac{dz}{dx}$
Fundamental formulas for differentiation	Derivative formulas for algebraic, trigonometric, inverse trigonometric, logarithmic and exponential functions

SECTION 8.2

CONTINUITY AND DERIVATIVES

Continuity

From an intuitive perspective a function is continuous if you can draw its graph without taking the pencil off the paper, or chalk off the board: no jumps, no skips. In other words, a function is continuous if the value it takes on at a point is the value it approaches as you get very near the point. Continuity may therefore be defined in terms of limits.

A function $f(x)$ is **continuous** at the interior point $x = c$ in its domain if $\lim\limits_{x \to c} f(x) = f(c)$. A function is continuous at the endpoints of [a, b] if $\lim\limits_{x \to a^+} f(x) = f(a)$ or $\lim\limits_{x \to b^-} f(x) = f(b)$.

The Derivative

Another basic concept defined in terms of limits is that of the derivative. Let $f(x) = y$ be a function. If the following limit exists it is called the **derivative** of f at x: $\lim\limits_{h \to 0} \dfrac{f(x+h) - f(x)}{h} = f'(x) = \dfrac{dy}{dx} = \dfrac{df}{dx}$. The derivative gives the general expression for the slope of tangents to a curve.

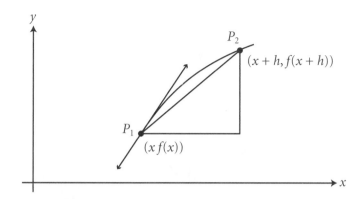

Notice that $\dfrac{f(x+h)-f(x)}{h}$ gives the slope of the secant line joining P_1 and P_2, both points on $y=f(x)$. In the limit as $h \to 0$ we can "intuitively see" that this chord becomes a tangent. Hence, we define the slope of a tangent to the curve $y = f(x)$ at x_1 to be the value of the derivative $f'(x)$ at x_1 (e.g. $f'(x_1)$). The following rules exist for the differentiation of algebraic functions f and g.

Rules for Differentiation

Power Rule	If $f(x) = x^n$ then $\dfrac{df}{dx} = nx^{n-1}$
Chain Rule	Suppose $y = f(g(x))$ then $\dfrac{dy}{dx} = \dfrac{dy}{dg} \cdot \dfrac{dg}{dx}$
Sum and Difference Rule	$\dfrac{d(f \pm g)}{dx} = \dfrac{df}{dx} \pm \dfrac{dg}{dx}$
Product Rule	$\dfrac{d(fg)}{dx} = f\dfrac{dg}{dx} + g\dfrac{df}{dx}$
Quotient Rule	$\dfrac{d(f/g)}{dx} = \dfrac{1}{g^2}\left(g\dfrac{df}{dx} - f\dfrac{dg}{dx} \right)$

Continuity and Derivative

The properties of continuity and differentiability are closely related. Consider the function $y = |x|$ at $x = 0$. For the derivative to exist at the point we need to find: $\lim\limits_{h \to 0} \dfrac{|0+h|-|0|}{h}$

$= \lim\limits_{h \to 0} \dfrac{|h|}{h}$. If $h < 0$, then this limit is -1; if $h > 0$, then the limit is 1. Hence, no such limit exists (limits are unique). This means that the function $f(x) = |x|$ does not have a derivative (i.e., no slope for a tangent line) at $x = 0$. From the diagram it is clear that at $x = 0$ the graph comes to "a point," and no tangent exists. But clearly the limit: $\lim\limits_{x \to 0} |x| = 0$, which means the function $y = |x|$ is continuous at $x = 0$.

A function can be continuous at a point, but have no derivative at that point.

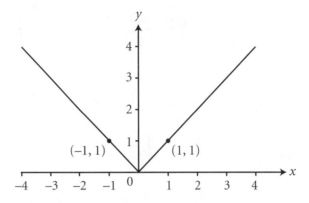

Consider the converse of this statement. Suppose f is differentiable at x, then $\lim\limits_{z \to x} \dfrac{f(z) - f(x)}{z - x} = f'(x)$ (let $z = x + h$ in the definition of derivative). Notice that

$f(z) - f(x) = \dfrac{f(z) - f(x)}{(z - x)}(z - x)$. By hypothesis $\lim\limits_{z \to x} \dfrac{f(z) - f(x)}{z - x} = f'(x)$ and $\lim\limits_{z \to x}(z - x) = 0$.

Hence, by the product rule for limits: $\lim\limits_{z \to x}(f(z) - f(x)) = f'(x) \cdot 0 = 0$. We conclude that $\lim\limits_{z \to x} f(z) = f(x)$, or that the function is continuous at x. This proves one of the most important relationships between differentiability and continuity: **If a function is differentiable at $x = a$, then it is continuous at $x = a$.**

The Mean-Value Theorem (and Rolle's Theorem)

The Mean-Value Theorem for derivatives plays an extremely important role in differential calculus and its applications. It explains a connection between a slope of a secant between two points a and b on a continuous function, and a derivative of the function at some intermediate point $a < c < b$ on $[a, b]$. The Mean-Value Theorem follows from the following:

> **Rolle's Theorem:** Suppose we have a function defined over a closed interval $[a, b]$.

Let a, b be two numbers such that $a < b$. Let f be a function continuous on $[a, b]$ and differentiable on (a, b). If $f(a) = f(b) = 0$ then there exists at least one point c, $a < c < b$ such that $f'(c) = 0$. (One usually proves Rolle's Theorem in advanced calculus).

Consider the following graph:

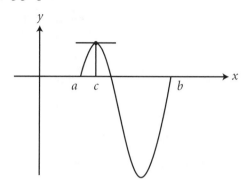

Rolle's Theorem can be used to prove the Mean-Value Theorem.

Mean-Value Theorem

If a function $f(x)$ is continuous on $[a, b]$ and differentiable on (a, b), then there is at least one point c, $a < c < b$ such that $f'(c) = \dfrac{f(b) - f(a)}{b - a}$.

   Proof: Let $g(x)$ represent a linear function whose graph is the secant line connecting points $(a, f(a))$ and $(b, f(b))$. Then the slope of this secant line will be $m = \dfrac{f(b) - f(a)}{b - a}$. The difference of two functions $f(x) - g(x)$ satisfies the conditions of Rolle's Theorem. By Rolle's Theorem there must be at least one point in (a, b) such that $f'(c) - g'(c) = 0$, thus $f'(c) = g'(c)$. Since g is a linear function, its derivative is equal to its slope. We conclude that $f'(c) = \dfrac{f(b) - f(a)}{b - a}$.

Differentials

Consider a curve $g = (x)$ with a derivative $f'(x) = \dfrac{dy}{dx}$ at point (x, y). From the figure below the quantity dy can be calculated, where dx is a given quantity. This quantity is called the differential dy. While the differential dy is reminiscent of the quantity $\dfrac{dy}{dx}$, clearly it has a completely different meaning than the derivative. Alternately, $\Delta y \approx dy = f'(x)dx$.

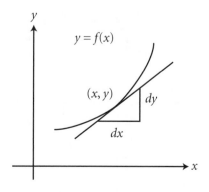

Implicit Differentiation

If we have a function $f(x, y) = 0$, we may assume that it implicitly defines y as a function of x, for all values of x for which there is a unique y such that $f(x, y) = 0$.

We may find the derivative of $g = f'(x)$ from this more general equation. For example, $x^2 + y^2 = 25$ or $\dfrac{d(x^2)}{dx} + \dfrac{d(y^2)}{dx} = 0$. Using the chain rule: $2x + 2y\dfrac{dy}{dx} = 0$, it means $\dfrac{dy}{dx} = \dfrac{-x}{y}, y \neq 0$. This formula gives the slopes of tangent lines for the function $y = \sqrt{25 - x^2}$ (or for the function $y = -\sqrt{25 - x^2}$). The expression $\dfrac{d(y^2)}{dx} = 2y\dfrac{dy}{dx}$ makes no sense unless we assume that y is a function of x, and then can apply general rules of differentiation to obtain the result. In implicit differentiation we assume that a functional relationship exists between y and x, in some neighborhood of (a,b), at which we are looking for the derivative. The matter of when and how such an equation implicitly defines differentiability is a topic for more advanced calculus.

A Special Limit for sin x

The differentiation of trigonometric functions depends on a key limit: $\lim\limits_{x \to 0}\dfrac{\sin x}{x} = 1$.

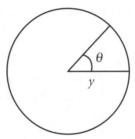

Consider the area of a sector of a circle with radius r subtended by an angle of θ radians. The area of the sector is given by: $\dfrac{\theta}{2\pi} = \dfrac{A}{\pi r^2}$. In other words, $\dfrac{\theta r^2}{2} = A$. If the radius of the circle is $r = 1$ then $A = \dfrac{\theta}{2}$ (see the sector in the accompanying diagram with radius $r = 1$). Notice that

K_1 (area of $\triangle OAB$) $< K_2$ (area of sector subtended by θ) $< K_3$ (area of $\triangle OCD$). Using the definition of trigonometric functions we have: $OA = \cos \theta$, $AB = \sin \theta$, $DC = \tan \theta$. Hence,

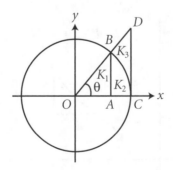

$$\frac{1}{2}\sin\theta\cos\theta < \frac{\theta}{2} < \frac{1}{2}\tan\theta; \quad \frac{1}{2}\sin\theta\cos\theta < \frac{\theta}{2} < \frac{1}{2}\frac{\sin\theta}{\cos\theta}; \cos\theta < \frac{\theta}{\sin\theta} < \frac{1}{\cos\theta}.$$

But $\lim_{\theta\to 0}\cos\theta = \lim_{\theta\to 0}\frac{1}{\cos\theta} = 1$, which means $\lim_{\theta\to 0}\frac{\theta}{\sin\theta} = 1 = \lim_{\theta\to 0}\frac{\sin\theta}{\theta}$.

Derivative of $y = \sin x$

By the definition of the derivative of $y = \sin x$, $\dfrac{dy}{dx} = \lim_{\Delta x\to 0}\dfrac{\sin(x + \Delta x) - \sin x}{\Delta x}$

$$= \lim_{\Delta x\to 0}\frac{2\cos\left(\dfrac{2x + \Delta x}{2}\right)\sin\left(\dfrac{\Delta x}{2}\right)}{\Delta x} = \lim_{\Delta x\to 0}\frac{\cos\left(x + \dfrac{\Delta x}{2}\right)\sin\left(\dfrac{\Delta x}{2}\right)}{\dfrac{\Delta x}{2}}.$$

But $\lim_{\Delta x\to 0}\dfrac{\sin\left(\dfrac{\Delta x}{2}\right)}{\dfrac{\Delta x}{2}} = 1$, since $\lim_{h\to 0}\dfrac{\sin(h)}{h} = 1$. Hence, $\dfrac{dy}{dx} = \cos x$.

Differentiation of $\cos x$, $\tan x$, $\cot x$, $\csc x$, $\sec x$

$$\cos x = \sin\left(\frac{\pi}{2} - x\right), \text{ which means } \frac{dy}{dx} = \frac{d\left(\sin\dfrac{\pi}{2} - x\right)}{dx} = -\cos\left(\frac{\pi}{2} - x\right) = -\sin x;$$

Suppose $\tan x = \dfrac{\sin x}{\cos x}$. By the quotient rule:

$$\frac{dy}{dx} = \frac{\cos x(\cos x) + \sin x(\sin x)}{\cos^2 x} = \frac{\cos^2 x + \sin^2 x}{\cos^2 x} = \frac{1}{\cos^2 x} = \sec^2 x; \; y = \tan x, \frac{dy}{dx} = \sec^2 x.$$

The derivatives for the other trigonometric function follow similarly. In general,

$$y = \sin x, \frac{dy}{dx} = \cos x; \qquad y = \cos x, \frac{dy}{dx} = \sin x; \qquad y = \tan x, \frac{dy}{dx} = \sec^2 x;$$

$$y = \csc x, \frac{dy}{dx} = -\csc x\cot x; \qquad y = \sec x, \frac{dy}{dx} = \sec x\tan x; \qquad y = \cot x, \frac{dy}{dx} = \csc^2 x.$$

Derivatives of Inverse Trigonometric Functions

If $y = \sin^{-1}x$ then $\sin y = x$ and $(\cos y)\dfrac{dy}{dx} = 1$; $\quad \dfrac{dy}{dx} = \dfrac{1}{\cos y}$.

Notice that if $y = \sin^{-1}x$, it follows that $\cos y = \dfrac{\sqrt{1-x^2}}{1}$. Hence, $\dfrac{dy}{dx} = \dfrac{1}{\sqrt{1-x^2}}$.

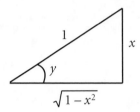

Suppose $y = \cos^{-1}x$, then $\cos y = x$ and $(-\sin y)\dfrac{dy}{dx} = 1$; $\quad \dfrac{dy}{dx} = \dfrac{-1}{\sin y}$.

Notice that, if $y = \cos^{-1}x$, then $\sin y = \sqrt{1-x^2}$; $\quad \dfrac{dy}{dx} = -\dfrac{1}{\sqrt{1-x^2}}$.

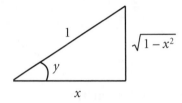

Suppose $y = \tan^{-1}x$, then $\tan y = x$ and $\sec^2 y\dfrac{dy}{dx} = 1$; $\quad \dfrac{dy}{dx} = \dfrac{1}{\sec^2 y}$.

But $\sec^2 y = 1 + x^2$. Hence, $\dfrac{dy}{dx} = \dfrac{1}{1+x^2}$.

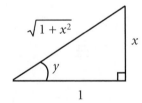

Suppose $y = \cot^{-1}x$ then $\cot y = x$ and $\dfrac{dy}{dx}(-\csc^2 y) = 1$; $\quad \dfrac{dy}{dx} = -\dfrac{1}{\csc^2 x}$.

But $\csc^2 y = \dfrac{1+x^2}{1}$. Hence, $\dfrac{dy}{dx} = -\dfrac{1}{1+x^2}$.

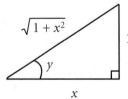

Suppose $y = \sec^{-1}x$, then $\sec y = x$ and $(\sec y \tan y)\dfrac{dy}{dx} = 1$; $\dfrac{dy}{dx} = \dfrac{1}{\sec y \tan y}$. But

$\tan^2 y = \sec^2 - 1 = x^2 - 1$. Hence, $\tan y = \pm\sqrt{x^2 - 1}$. By definition of $\sec^{-1}x = y$,

where we take y to be in $\left[0, \dfrac{\pi}{2}\right)$ or $\left(\dfrac{\pi}{2}, \pi\right]$. Therefore, $\tan y$ is positive, which means that

$\dfrac{dy}{dx} = \dfrac{1}{\tan y \sec y} = \dfrac{1}{|x|\sqrt{x^2 - 1}}$. By a similar argument, it follows that if $y = \csc^{-1}x$,

$\dfrac{dy}{dx} = -\dfrac{1}{|x|\sqrt{x^2 - 1}}$, where we take y to be in $\left[-\dfrac{\pi}{2}, 0\right)$ or $\left(0, \dfrac{\pi}{2}\right]$.

Derivatives of Logarithmic and Exponential Functions

The logarithmic function (or natural logarithm) is the area under the curve $y = \dfrac{1}{t}$ between 1 and x.

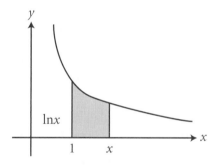

In terms of a definite integral, $\ln x = \displaystyle\int_1^x \dfrac{1}{t}\,dt$, $x > 0$. From the Fundamental Theorem of calculus, later in this chapter, we obtain that: $\dfrac{d(\ln x)}{dx} = \dfrac{1}{x}$ for $x > 0$.

Exponential Functions

Define: $y = e^x$ as inverse function of $y = \ln x$. The function $y = e^x$ has the following properties:

1. $e^x > 0$ for all x (Notice the range of e^x is the domain of $y = \ln x$)
2. $\ln(e^x) = x$ (In other words $y = e^x$ is the inverse of $y = \ln x$)
3. $e^{\ln x} = x$ (Same reasoning as in no. 2)
4. $\dfrac{d(e^x)}{dx} = e^x$ (Let $y = e^x$ then $\ln y = x$ or $\dfrac{1}{y}\dfrac{dy}{dx} = 1$, hence $\dfrac{dy}{dx} = y = e^x$)
5. $\dfrac{d}{dx}a^x = a^x \ln a$; $a > 1$ (A similar argument as in no. 4.)

8.2 SOLVED PROBLEMS

1. Show that all polynomial functions are continuous.

   Solution: Notice from our theorem on limits, for any polynomial
   $a_n x^n + a_{n-1} x^n - 1 + \ldots + a_0 = P(x)$,

   $$\lim_{x \to c} P(x) = \lim_{x \to c}(a_n x^n + a_{a-1} x^{n-1} + \ldots + a_1 x + a_0)$$

   $$= \lim_{x \to c} a_n \cdot \lim_{x \to c} x^n + \lim_{x \to c} a_{n-1} \cdot \lim_{x \to c} x^{n-1} + \ldots + \lim_{x \to c} a_1 \cdot \lim_{x \to c} x + \lim_{x \to c} a_0$$

   $$= a_n c^n + a_{n-1} c^{n-1} + \ldots + a_1 c + a_0.$$

   Hence, $\lim_{x \to c} P(x) = P(c)$.

2. Find $f'(x)$ if $f(x) = \sqrt{9 - x^2}$ using the definition of the derivative.

   Solution: $\displaystyle\lim_{h \to 0} \frac{f(x+h) - f(x)}{h} = \lim_{h \to 0} \frac{\sqrt{9 - (x+h)^2} - \sqrt{9 - x^2}}{h}$

   $$= \lim_{h \to 0} \frac{\sqrt{9 - (x+h)^2} - \sqrt{9 - x^2}}{h} \cdot \frac{\sqrt{9 - (x+h)^2} + \sqrt{9 - x^2}}{\sqrt{9 - (x+h)^2} + \sqrt{9 - x^2}}$$

   $$= \lim_{h \to 0} \frac{9 - (x+h)^2 - (9 - x^2)}{h(\sqrt{9 - (x+h)^2} + \sqrt{9 - x^2})} = \lim_{h \to 0} \frac{-2xh - h^2}{h(\sqrt{9 - (x+h)^2} + \sqrt{9 - x^2})}$$

   $$= \lim_{h \to 0} \frac{-2x}{\sqrt{9 - (x+h)^2} + \sqrt{9 - x^2}} - \lim_{h \to 0} \frac{h}{\sqrt{9 - (x+h)^2} + \sqrt{9 - x^2}}$$

   $$= \frac{-2x}{2\sqrt{9 - x^2}} = \frac{-x}{\sqrt{9 - x^2}} = -x(9 - x^2)^{-\frac{1}{2}}.$$

3. Prove the power rule for differentiation for all positive integral values of n: $f'(x) = nx^{n-1}$.

   Solution: Assume that Newton's Binomial expansion holds for all positive n:

   $(x+h)^n = x^n + nx^{n-1} \cdot h + \dfrac{n(n-1)}{1 \cdot 2} x^{n-2} h^2 + \ldots + h^n$. By the definition of the derivative:

   $$f'(x) = \lim_{h \to 0} \frac{f(x+h) - f(x)}{h} = \lim_{h \to 0} \frac{(x+h)^n - x^n}{h}$$

   $$= \lim_{h \to 0} \frac{x^n + nx^{n-1}h + \dfrac{n(n-1)}{1 \cdot 2} x^{n-2}h^2 + \ldots + h^n - x^n}{h}$$

   $$= \lim_{h \to 0}(nx^{n-1} + \frac{n(n-1)}{1 \cdot 2} x^{n-2}h + \ldots + h^{n-1}) \text{ (assume the power rule for all values of } n)$$

   $$= nx^{n-1}$$

4. Let $y = \dfrac{1}{x}$. Find $f'(x)$.

   Solution: Notice that $f'(x) = \displaystyle\lim_{h \to 0} \frac{\dfrac{1}{x+h} - \dfrac{1}{x}}{h} = \lim_{h \to 0} \frac{x - (x+h)}{h \cdot x \cdot (x+h)} = \frac{-1}{x \cdot (x+h)} = -x^{-2}.$

5. Suppose $y = f(g(x))$, and $u = g(x)$ is the intermediary value between x and y. If x increases by Δx, u increases by Δu and y increases by Δy. Show: $\dfrac{dy}{dx} = \dfrac{dy}{du} \cdot \dfrac{du}{dx}$ (Chain Rule).

   Solution: Notice that $\dfrac{\Delta y}{\Delta x} = \dfrac{\Delta y}{\Delta u} \cdot \dfrac{\Delta u}{\Delta x}$. As $\Delta x \to 0$, $\Delta u \to 0$ and $\Delta y \to 0$, we have

   $\dfrac{\Delta y}{\Delta x} \to \dfrac{dy}{dx}$; $\dfrac{\Delta y}{\Delta u} \to \dfrac{dy}{du}$; $\dfrac{\Delta u}{\Delta x} \to \dfrac{du}{dx}$. Hence, $\dfrac{dy}{dx} = \dfrac{dy}{du} \cdot \dfrac{du}{dx}$.

6. Let $y = (x^2 + x + 1)^3$. Find $\dfrac{dy}{dx}$.

   Solution: Using the Chain Rule, we find: $y' = 3(x^2 + x + 1)^2 \cdot (2x + 1)$.

7. Given $xy = x^2 y + y^2 + 2$. Find $\dfrac{dy}{dx}$.

   Solution: Using implicit differentiation we have: $y + x\dfrac{dy}{dx} = 2xy + x^2\dfrac{dy}{dx} + 2y\dfrac{dy}{dx}$ or $\dfrac{dy}{dx} = \dfrac{2xy - y}{x - x^2 - 2y}$.

8. Let $y \cos x = x \sin y$. Find $\dfrac{dy}{dx}$.

   Solution: $\dfrac{dy}{dx}\cos x + y(-\sin x) = \sin y + x\cos y\dfrac{dy}{dx}$ or $\dfrac{dy}{dx} = \dfrac{y\sin x + \sin y}{\cos x - x\cos y}$.

9. Let the graph of $f(x)$ be given by the following: $f(x) = \sin x$; $0 \le x \le \pi$. Where will the following inequality $\dfrac{-f'(x)}{f''(x)} \ge 0$ be satisfied in this interval?

   Solution: $f(x) = \sin x$, $f'(x) = \cos x$, $f''(x) = -\sin x$. Hence, $\dfrac{-f'(x)}{f''(x)} = \cot x \ge 0$ will be satisfied only in the interval $0 < x \le \dfrac{\pi}{2}$.

10. Find $\dfrac{dy}{dx}$ if $y = e^{\sin^2 x}$.

    Solution: $\dfrac{dy}{dx} = \dfrac{d(\sin^2 x)}{dx} \cdot e^{\sin^2 x} = e^{\sin^2 x} \cdot 2\sin x \cos x$.

11. Show that $y = ae^{kt}$ satisfies the differential equation $\dfrac{dy}{dx} = ky$.

    Solution: $y = ae^{kt}$, $\dfrac{dy}{dx} = kae^{kt} = ky$.

12. Find $\dfrac{dy}{dx}$ if $y = e^{xy}$.

    Solution: $\dfrac{dy}{dx} = e^{xy}\left(x\dfrac{dy}{dx} + y\right)$; $\dfrac{dy}{dx} - xe^{xy}\dfrac{dy}{dx} = ye^{xy}$; $\dfrac{dy}{dx}(1 - xe^{xy}) = ye^{xy}$; $\dfrac{dy}{dx} = \dfrac{ye^{xy}}{1 - xe^{xy}}$.

13. Find $\dfrac{dy}{dx}$ when $y = \tan^{-1}(e^x)$.

    Solution: $\dfrac{dy}{dx} = \dfrac{1}{1 + (e^x)^2} \cdot e^x = \dfrac{e^x}{1 + e^{2x}}$.

14. Find $\dfrac{dy}{dx}$ when $y = \ln(\sin(\cos x))$.

Solution: $y = \ln(\sin(\cos x))$; $\dfrac{dy}{dx} = \dfrac{1}{\sin(\cos x)} \cdot \cos(\cos x)(-\sin x)$.

15. Using the logarithmic differentiation, find the derivative of $y = x^x$.

Solution: $\ln y = x \ln x$; $\dfrac{1}{y} \cdot \dfrac{dy}{dx} = \ln x + 1$. Hence, $\dfrac{dy}{dx} = x^x (\ln x + 1)$.

16. Find the equation of the tangent to the curve $y = x^2 + x + 2$ at $x = 2$.

Solution: Notice that $(2, 8)$ is on the curve and $\dfrac{dy}{dx} = 2x + 1$; $f'(2) = 5$. Hence, the equation of the tangent is $y - 8 = 5(x - 2)$.

8.2 UNSOLVED PROBLEMS

1. Assume that y is an implicit function of x. Use the chain rule to find the derivative for $x^2 y + xy^2 + y^2 = 0$.

2. Given $\dfrac{d(x^n)}{dx} = nx^{n-1}$ for $n \; \varepsilon \; Z^+$, use implicit differentiation to show that $\dfrac{d(x^n)}{dx} = nx^{n-1}$ for $n \in Z$.

3. Prove the power rule for the general case $y = x^n$ where n is any rational number.

4. Given the family of curves $y^2 + (x - c)^2 = c^2$ for any value of c. Show that if f is a differentiable function whose graph is a subset of this family, then $y = f(x)$ satisfies the differential equation: $1 + (y')^2 = \left(\dfrac{x}{y} + y' \right)^2$.

5. Write the equation of the tangent to the curve $y = x^3 - 12x + 5$ at the point $(1, f(1))$.

6. Find the value of the derivative function $g = |x + 1|$ at $x = -1$.

7. Find the expression $\dfrac{f(x+h) - f(x)}{h}$ at $x = 2$, for the curve $f(x) = x|x + 1|$. Using this expression, find the derivative of y at $x = 2$.

8. Using the differentials, approximate $(16.03)^{1/2}$.

9. Find $\dfrac{dy}{dx}$ when $y = 10^x$.

10. Find $\dfrac{dy}{dx}$ when $y = \log_b x$.

11. Find $\dfrac{dy}{dx}$ when $y = x e^{x^e}$.

12. Find $\dfrac{dy}{dx}$ when $y = \ln(\ln x)$.

13. Find $\dfrac{dy}{dx}$ when $y = \ln(\tan e^x)$.

14. Find $\dfrac{dy}{dx}$ using logarithmic differentiation $y = (x^3 + 1)^2 (x^2 + 1)^3$.

15. If $y = \cos^x x$, find $\dfrac{dy}{dx}$.

GLOSSARY OF TERMS

L'Hospital's Rule	If $\lim_{x \to a} f(a) = 0$ and $\lim_{x \to a} g(x) = 0$, then $\lim_{x \to a} \dfrac{f(x)}{g(x)} = \lim_{x \to a} \dfrac{f'(x)}{g'(x)}$
Related rates problems	Problems that express the change of one variable with respect to another variable
Minima-maxima problems	Problems that involve optimization, usually by considering the derivatives of a function
Newton's method	A technique for finding approximate solutions to equations that are not easily solvable by simple formulas

SECTION 8.3

APPLICATIONS OF DERIVATIVES

L'Hospital's Rule

Evaluations of limits may sometimes involve the indeterminate forms: $\dfrac{0}{0}, \dfrac{\infty}{\infty}, 0 \cdot \infty$, $\infty - \infty, 0^0, \infty^0$, and 1^∞. These cases may be best solved by L' Hospital's Rule: Let f and g be differentiable in an interval about a with a excluded and suppose $\lim_{x \to a} f(a) = 0$ and $\lim_{x \to a} g(x) = 0$. Suppose $g'(x) \neq 0$ in this neighborhood (notice the similarity to the Mean-Value Theorem). Then $\lim_{x \to a} \dfrac{f(x)}{g(x)} = \lim_{x \to a} \dfrac{f'(x)}{g'(x)}$, if the limit on the right-hand side of this equation exists. (The formal proof of L'Hospital's Rule follows from the extended Mean-Value Theorem and can be found in more advanced texts.)

Related Rates and Rates of Change

Related rates problems arise when some physical, biological or other law relates values changing in time. Usually a problem is concerned with finding a rate difficult to measure by using others that are easier to measure. The following are common forms of related value problems: several variables (x, y, z) or (x, y), related to each other by some given equation; variables are implicit functions of some parameters (usually, time); a related rate $\dfrac{dx}{dt}$ or $\dfrac{dy}{dt}$ is found through the given rate, using implicit differentiation and the chain rule. The following general guidelines help in solving related rates problems: clearly understand the geometrical and/or physical nature of the problem; draw appropriate figure(s); describe the relationship between the components of the problem with the appropriate function(s); implicitly differentiate the function(s) with respect to time;

substitute known quantities relevant to the problems in the resulting derivative(s) expression(s), and then solve for the unknowns.

Applied Minima-Maxima Problems

Minima and maxima problems arise in an optimization process: for example, when we need to find a shape of a cylinder of maximum volume made from an aluminum plate of the given area. The following procedure to solve maxima and minima problems can be followed: determine which variable is to be maximized or minimized; identify geometrical, physical and other laws that connect the variables involved, and write their mathematical expressions; differentiate implicitly or explicitly with respect to the dependent variable and set the derivative equal to zero and solve; use additional equations to establish relations between the parameters maximizing or minimizing the value in question, and then check by evaluating the second derivative (or some alternate test) for the type of extremum sought.

Using Derivatives to Approximate Roots of the Functions (Newton's Method)

Analytic formulas for roots exist for a rather restricted class of algebraic equations: linear, quadratic, cubic, and quadric equations. Some elementary trigonometric and transcendental equations can also be solved analytically. In many interesting cases analytic solutions do not exist, or are very difficult to obtain, and roots should be found by numerical methods. One of these methods is called Newton's method (the Newton-Raphson method). The method is based on linearization of the function $f(x)$ and finding n successive x-intercepts of tangent lines instead of the function itself. It is represented graphically in the following figure:

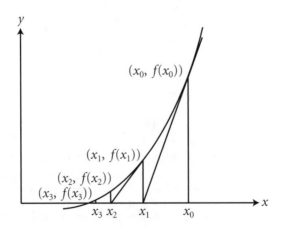

Analytically, we use a formula for the tangent line at x_0 : $f(x) = f(x_0) + f'(x_0)(x - x_0)$, to determine the first value of the x-interception. If we set $f(x) = 0$, then $x_1 = x_0 - \dfrac{f(x_0)}{f'(x_0)}$.

We obtain the nth approximation as $x_{n+1} = x_n - \dfrac{f(x_0)}{f'(x_0)}$.

Convergence of Newton's method

Newton's method converges if the following theorem from calculus is applicable: $\left|\dfrac{f(x)\cdot f''(x)}{[f'(x)]^2}\right|<1$ for all x in some interval containing the root $x=r$. (Where $f''(x)$ is the second derivative.) Note that Newton's method depends on the choice of the initial point x_0. If $f'(x_0)=0$, then Newton's method stops, and another starting point should be chosen. Also, it is possible that Newton's procedure will converge to a root, but it may be not the root we were looking for, as illustrated in the following graph. The procedure for finding roots by Newton's method can be extremely sensitive to the choice of the starting point.

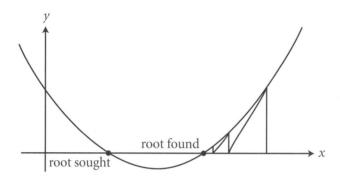

8.3 SOLVED PROBLEMS

1. $\displaystyle\lim_{x\to0}\frac{\sin^2 x}{1-\cos x}$

　　Solution: By L'Hospital's Rule $\displaystyle\lim_{x\to0}\frac{\sin^2 x}{1-\cos x}=\lim_{x\to0}\frac{2\sin x\cos x}{\sin x}=\lim_{x\to0}2\cos x=2.$

2. $\displaystyle\lim_{x\to\infty}x\left(\tan^{-1}x-\frac{\pi}{2}\right)$

　　Solution: Notice that L'Hospital's Rule also applies in the case of $\dfrac{\infty}{\infty}$ (this result requires a bit more difficulty in proving L'Hospital's Rule than for the form $\dfrac{0}{0}$; it is usually done in advanced calculus).

$$\lim_{x\to\infty}x\left(\tan^{-1}x-\frac{\pi}{2}\right)=\lim_{x\to\infty}\frac{\frac{1}{2}\pi-\tan^{-1}x}{-x^{-1}}=\lim_{x\to\infty}\frac{-\frac{1}{x^2+1}}{x^{-2}}=\lim_{x\to\infty}\frac{-x^2}{x^2+1}=\lim_{x\to\infty}\frac{-2x}{2x}=-1.$$

3. $\displaystyle\lim_{x\to0}(\sin x)^x$

　　Solution:

Consider $y=(\sin x)^x$; $\ln y=x\ln(\sin x)$; $\displaystyle\lim_{x\to0}(\ln y)=\lim_{x\to0}\frac{\ln\sin x}{x^{-1}}=\lim_{x\to0}\frac{\frac{1}{\sin x}\cos x}{-x^{-2}}$

$=\displaystyle\lim_{x\to0}\frac{-x^2}{\sin x}\cdot\cos x=\lim_{x\to0}\frac{-x^2\cdot\cos x}{\sin x}=0$; hence, $\displaystyle\lim_{x\to0}\ln y=0\Rightarrow\lim_{x\to0}(\sin x)^x=1.$

4. $\lim\limits_{x\to\infty}\left(1+\dfrac{1}{x}\right)^x$

Solution:

Let $y=\left(1+\dfrac{1}{x}\right)^x$; $\ln y = x\ln\left(1+\dfrac{1}{x}\right)$. Hence, $\lim\limits_{x\to\infty}\ln y = \lim\limits_{x\to\infty}x\ln\left(1+\dfrac{1}{x}\right)$

$=\lim\limits_{x\to\infty}\dfrac{\ln\left(1+\dfrac{1}{x}\right)}{x^{-1}}=\lim\limits_{x\to\infty}\dfrac{\ln\left(1+\dfrac{1}{x}\right)}{x^{-1}}=\lim\limits_{x\to\infty}\dfrac{\ln(x+1)-\ln x}{x^{-1}}=\lim\limits_{x\to\infty}\dfrac{\dfrac{1}{x+1}-\dfrac{1}{x}}{-x^{-2}}=\lim\limits_{x\to\infty}\dfrac{\dfrac{x-(x+1)}{x(x+1)}}{-\dfrac{1}{x^2}}$

$=\lim\limits_{x\to\infty}\dfrac{-1}{x(x+1)}\cdot(-x^2)=\lim\limits_{x\to\infty}\dfrac{x}{x+1}=\lim\limits_{x\to\infty}\dfrac{1}{1}=1$ If $\lim\limits_{x\to\infty}\ln y = 1$, then $\lim\limits_{x\to\infty}y=e^1=e$.

5. $\lim\limits_{x\to\infty}xe^{\frac{1}{x}}$

Solution: $\lim\limits_{x\to\infty}xe^{1/x}=\infty$ (no L'Hospital's rule is needed).

6. $\lim\limits_{x\to 0}\left(\dfrac{1}{1-e^x}-\dfrac{1}{x}\right)$

Solution: $\lim\limits_{x\to 0}\left(\dfrac{1}{1-e^x}-\dfrac{1}{x}\right)=\lim\limits_{x\to 0}\dfrac{x-1+e^x}{x(1-e^x)}=\lim\limits_{x\to 0}\dfrac{1+e^x}{1-xe^x-e^x}=\infty$

7. $\lim\limits_{x\to 0^+}x^x$

Solution: Let $y=x^x$; $\ln y = x\ln x$. Hence, $\lim\limits_{x\to 0^+}y=\lim\limits_{x\to 0^+}x\ln x = \lim\limits_{x\to 0^+}\dfrac{\ln x}{\dfrac{1}{x}}=\lim\limits_{x\to 0^+}\dfrac{\dfrac{1}{x}}{-\dfrac{1}{x^2}}$

$=\lim\limits_{x\to 0}\dfrac{-x^2}{x}=\lim\limits_{x\to 0^+}(-x)=0$, then $\lim\limits_{x\to 0^+}\ln y = 0 \Rightarrow \lim\limits_{x\to 0}y=e^0=1$.

8. Let x and y be differentiable functions of t and let $S=\sqrt{x^2+y^2}$ be the distance between points $(x,0)$ and $(0,y)$ in the (x,y) plane. How does $\dfrac{dS}{dt}$ relate to $\dfrac{dx}{dt}$ and $\dfrac{dy}{dt}$?

Solution: Differentiating the expression $S=\sqrt{x^2+y^2}$ we obtain:

$$\frac{dS}{dt}=\frac{1}{2\sqrt{x^2+y^2}}\left(2x\frac{dx}{dt}+2y\frac{dy}{dt}\right)=\frac{1}{\sqrt{x^2+y^2}}\left(x\frac{dx}{dt}+y\frac{dy}{dt}\right).$$

9. A conical container is being filled with a liquid. The radius of the cone of the liquid is changing at the rate of 0.1 ft/min and the height of the liquid is changing at the rate of 0.2 ft/min. Find the rate of change of the volume of the cone of liquid when $r=2$ and $h=3$.

Solution: The volume of the cone is given by: $V = \dfrac{\pi}{3}r^2h$. Differentiate this expression with respect to time and subsitute $r = 2$ and $h = 3$: $\dfrac{dV}{dt} = \dfrac{\pi}{3}\left[2rh\dfrac{dr}{dt} + r^2\dfrac{dh}{dt}\right] = \dfrac{\pi}{3}[2 \cdot 2 \cdot 3 \cdot (.1) + 2^2 \cdot (.2)] = \dfrac{\pi}{3}(2) = \dfrac{2\pi}{3}$.

10. Suppose a stone is dropped into a pond. Find the rate of change of the area of the resulting concentric circles at the time the outer ripple has the radius of 1.

Solution: The area of a circle is given by $A = \pi r^2$. Hence, the change of area with respect to time is given by $\dfrac{dA}{dt} = 2\pi r\dfrac{dr}{dt}$. The rate of change of this area when $r = 1$ is $2\pi\dfrac{dr}{dt}$.

11. Suppose a cylindrical tank has a fixed radius and the height of the water in the tank is decreasing at the rate of 1 ft/min. How quickly is the tank draining?

Solution: The volume of a cylinder is given by $V = \pi r^2h$. Differentiate this expression with respect to t: $\dfrac{dV}{dt} = \pi\left[2rh\dfrac{dr}{dt} + r^2\dfrac{dh}{dt}\right]$. Notice that $\dfrac{dr}{dt} = 0$ since the radius is a constant and $\dfrac{dh}{dt} = -1$ ft/min. Hence, $\dfrac{dV}{dt} = \pi r^2(-1) = \pi r^2$ ft/min.

12. Suppose that $r(x)$ is the revenue from selling x items and $c(x)$ is the cost of manufacturing x items while $p(x) = r(x) - c(x)$ is the profit from selling x items. Let $\dfrac{dr}{dx}, \dfrac{dc}{dx}, \dfrac{dp}{dx}$ be marginal revenue, marginal cost, marginal profit, correspondingly. Suppose that $r(x) = 3x$; $c(x) = x^3 - 9x^2 + 18x$. Is there an x that maximizes the profit?

Solution: $p(x) = r(x) - c(x)$; $p'(x) = r'(x) - c'(x) = 3 - 3x^2 + 18x - 18$; $-3x^2 + 18x - 15 = 0$; $x^2 - 6x + 5 = 0$, so $x = 1$ or $x = 5$. To find out which of the two solutions brings a maximum profit, we find the second derivative: $p''(x) = -6x + 18$ and evaluate it. At $x = 1$, $p''(x) > 0$ which gives a minimum. At $x = 5$, $p''(x) < 0$ which gives a maximum. Thus, $x = 5$ provides a maximum profit, and $x = 1$ provides a minimum profit (loss).

13. Use Newton's method to estimate the real solution of the equation $x^3 + 3x + 1 = 0$.

Solution: $y = x^3 + 3x + 1$; start with $x_0 = 0$ and find the second approximation. Notice: $y' = 3x^2 + 3$ and $x_{n+1} = x_n - \dfrac{x_n^3 + 3x_n + 1}{3x_n^2 + 3}$. It follows that

$$x_0 = 0;\ x_1 = -\frac{1}{3};\ x_2 = -\frac{1}{3} - \frac{-\dfrac{1}{27} - 1 + 1}{\dfrac{1}{3} + 3} = -\frac{1}{3} + \frac{1}{90} \approx -0.322$$

14. Consider the following graph. Explain why in this instance Newton's method will not work to find the root closest to x_1 (start the approximation process at x_1).

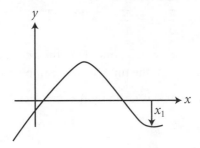

Solution:

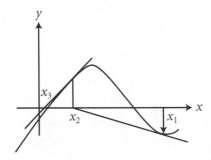

Notice the process approaches a root but it is not the root intended (x_0).

8.3 UNSOLVED PROBLEMS

1. Using L'Hospital's Rule find the following:

a) $\lim\limits_{x \to \infty} \dfrac{3x^2 + 2x - 1}{x^2 + 3x - 2}$

b) $\lim\limits_{x \to 0} \dfrac{e^{-\frac{1}{x}}}{x}$

c) $\lim\limits_{x \to \infty} \dfrac{x^{10}}{e^x}$

d) $\lim\limits_{x \to \infty} \dfrac{e^x}{x}$

e) $\lim\limits_{x \to \infty} \dfrac{\sin(e^x - 1)}{x}$

f) $\lim\limits_{x \to 0} e^{\frac{\sin(e^x - 1)}{x}}$

2. The area A of a triangle with sides of length a and b enclosing an angle of measure θ is $A = \frac{1}{2}ab\sin\theta$. How fast will the area change when $\theta = \frac{\pi}{4}$, if θ is changing at the constant rate of $0 \cdot 1\,\text{rad}\big/\text{sec}$ and $a = 1$, $b = 2$?

3. A spherical balloon is inflated with helium at the rate of $270\ \dfrac{ft^3}{min}$. How fast is the balloon's radius increasing when the radius is 4 ft?

4. Jim and Bill are walking on straight streets that meet at right angles. Jim approaches the intersection at $6\dfrac{ft}{sec}$, while Bill moves away from the intersection at $3\dfrac{ft}{sec}$. At what rate is the distance between them changing when Jim is 12 ft away from the intersection and Bill is 5 ft away from the intersection?

5. Suppose the cost of producing an item (x) is given by the equation: $y = x + \dfrac{16}{x}$. Find the value of x that will give a minimum cost. Find this cost.

6. Find the decimal approximation of $\sqrt{2}$ using Newton's method (two decimal places).

7. Explain why Newton's method does not work for the following function (start with x_1).

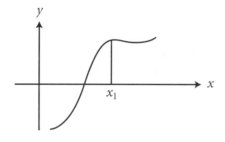

Indefinite integral	The antiderivative of a function
Definite integral	A limit of infinite sums that frequently represent areas and volumes
Fundamental Theorem	The theorem that allows one to evaluate the definite integral by using indefinite integrals
Numerical integration	Methods that allow for approximations of definite integrals

SECTION 8.4

INTEGRATION

The indefinite integral (the antiderivative) involves finding a function from its derivative. In this section we find formulas for antiderivatives. We then examine the Fundamental Theorem of calculus that relates definite integrals to areas and volumes. Proofs of the theorems in this section usually are presented in advanced calculus textbooks.

Definition

A function $F(x)$ is called an antiderivative of a function $f(x)$ if $F'(x) = f(x)$ for all x in the domain of f. The set of all antiderivatives is denoted as an indefinite integral, $\int f(x)dx = F(x) + c$ where c is an arbitrary constant. The function $f(x)$ is called the integrand and x is a variable of integration. A table of elementary integrals can be created by simply differentiating some functions. For example, we know that $\frac{d}{dx}(x + c) = 1$ thus, $\int dx = x + c$. For trigonometric functions $\frac{d}{dx}(\sin kx) = x \cos kx$, which means $\int \cos kx dx = \frac{\sin kx}{k} + c$. It is best to memorize the list of elementary integrals that follows.

Indefinite integrals

Basic Integration Formulas

$\int x^n dx$	$= \dfrac{x^{n+1}}{n+1} + c, \ n \neq -1, \ n$ rational
$\int \sin kx \ dx$	$= -\dfrac{\cos kx}{k} + c$
$\int \cos kx \ dx$	$= \dfrac{\sin kx}{k} + c$
$\int \sec^2 x \ dx$	$= \tan x + c$
$\int \csc^2 x \ dx$	$= -\cot x + c$
$\int \sec x \tan x \ dx$	$= \sec x + c$
$\int \csc x \cot x \ dx$	$= -\csc x + c$
$\int \dfrac{1}{x} dx$	$= \ln x + c$
$\int e^x dx$	$= e^x + c$

Algebra of Antiderivatives

The following rules hold for the indefinite integrals:

1. *Constant Multiple Rule* $\int kf(x) \ dx = \int f(x) \ dx$ where k is a constant.

2. *Sum and Difference Rule* $\int [f(x) \pm g(x)] dx = \int f(x) \ dt \pm \int g(x) \ dx$.

CAUTION! There is no general rule for the integral of the product of two functions. In many cases, it is rather difficult to figure out what function should be differentiated to give an integrand. In some of the cases, a change of variable or substitution can transform the integral so that it can be evaluated or found in the table.

The Method of Substitution in Integration

If we can find an appropriate substitution $u = g(x)$ such that the integrand can be represented in the form $f(g(x))g'(x)$, then the following formula can be used: $\int f(g(x))g'(x) \ dx = \int f(u) \ du = F(u) + c = F(g(x)) + c$ and then, returning to the variable of x, we will have final expression in terms of x. It is necessary to understand that applying substitution does not guarantee that we can evaluate the original integral. Sometimes it requires a second substitution or leads to a function whose indefinite integral does not exist in elementary functions, such as, $\int e^{x^2} dx$, $\int \dfrac{\sin x}{x}$. Fortunately, these types of integrals are rarely encountered in textbooks.

How to Find an Appropriate Substitution

In many textbooks differentiation is addressed as the "technique of differentiation" while integration is called "the art of integration," since there are no definite rules how to recognize proper substitutions or figure out other methods of integration that will work better. When we see an integrand that looks very complicated, we want to find a substitution that absorbs the most complicated expression. We need to make sure that within the integrand there is a function that will serve as a derivative of this substitution. For example: $\int \sin^4 x \cos x \, dx$.

We know that the derivative of $\sin x$ is $\cos x$ and vise versa, the derivative of $\cos x$ is $(-\sin x)$. We will use a substitution $u = \sin x$, since $du = \cos x \, dx$ and the integral can be introduced in a simpler form: $\int \sin^4 x \cos x \, dx = \int u^4 du = \dfrac{u^5}{5} + c = \dfrac{\sin^5 x}{5} + c$. In general, if a function of $\sin x$ and $\cos x$ is present as a factor then we can represent an integral in the following form: $\int f(\sin x)\cos x \, dx = \int f(u) \, du$ or $\int f(\cos x)\sin x \, dx = -\int f(u) \, du$.

Definite Integrals

The definite integral as a limit of a Riemann Sum

It is clear that the area under the curve can be estimated by partitioning the interval (a, b) into (for simplicity's sake) equal parts, and building rectangles on these partitions as shown in the following figure:

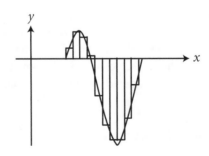

Let f be a function defined on (a, b). If for the partition P the number c_k is arbitrarily chosen on $[x_{k-1}, x_k]$ and there exists a number I such that $\lim\limits_{\|P\|\to 0} \sum\limits_{k=1}^{n} f(c_k)\Delta x = I$, where $\|P\|$ is the norm of the partition for any choice of c_k, then f is called integrable, and I is a definite integral of f over (a, b). The following theorem holds:

Integrability of Continuous Functions

All continuous functions are integrable, that is, if $f(x)$ is continuous on (a, b), then the definite integral $\int_a^b f(d)dx$ exists.

The Fundamental Theorem of Calculus

The Fundamental Theorem of Calculus connects the derivatives of the function to the problem of finding the area under the function. At first this is a rather surprising result. The concept of determining slope of the tangent to a function appears to have no relationship to the problems of finding the area between a function and the x-axis. On closer inspection the concepts of differentiating and integrating (finding slopes and tangents and finding areas under the curves) simply turn out to be "inverse operations."

Fundamental Theorem of Calculus (Part 1)

If the function $f(x)$ is continuous on $[a, b]$ then the function $F(x) = \int_a^x f(t)\,dt$ has a derivative at every point of $[a, b]$: $\dfrac{dF}{dx} = \dfrac{d}{dx}\int_a^x f(t)\,dt = f(x)$. The theorem actually says that every continuous function has an antiderivative. Note: when the upper and (or) lower limits are functions of x, namely: $F(x) = \int_{g(x)}^{h(x)} f(t)\,dt$, the derivative can be evaluated using the chain rule: $\dfrac{dF}{dx} = f(h(x)) \cdot h'(x) - f(g(x)) \cdot g'(x)$.

The Fundamental Theorem of Calculus
(Part 2: The Integral Evaluation Theorem)

If a function $f(x)$ is continuous at every point in $[a, b]$ and F is one of the antiderivatives of f, then $\int_b^a f(x)\,dx = F(a) - F(b)$. This formula is one of the most powerful formulas in calculus. It tells us that any definite integral of a continuous function can be evaluated easily, as soon as an antiderivative is known.

The Mean-Value Theorem for definite integrals

If f is continuous on (a, b) then there is some point $c \in (a, b)$ such that $f(c) = \dfrac{1}{b-a}\int_a^b f(x)\,dx$ (the average value of f over $[a, b]$).

Example: Find the average value of the function $f(x) = 2 - x$ on $(0, 2)$. Also find the point in $(0, 2)$ where f actually takes on this value.

Notice $\bar{f}(x) = \dfrac{1}{2}\int_{0}^{2}(2-x)\,dx = \dfrac{1}{2}\left(2x - \dfrac{x^2}{2}\right)\Bigg|_{0}^{2} = \dfrac{1}{2}\left(4 - \dfrac{4}{2}\right) = \dfrac{1}{2}\cdot 2 = 1$, so that the av-

erage value of $f(x) = 2 - x$ over $[0, 2]$ is 1. The point where the function assumes this value can be found from an equation $2 - x = 1$ which has a solution $x = 1$. Now we consider the

Applications of Definite Integrals

Finding the area

The area of the region between two figures such that $f(x) \geq g(x)$ is

$A = \int_{a}^{b}[f(x) - g(x)]dx$. To find area between two curves we:

1. Graph the functions to determine which curve is higher and which is lower

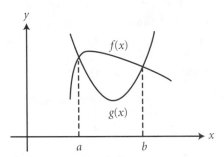

2. Find the limits of integration as points of intersection of the curves
3. Write a formula for $f(x) - g(x)$ and simplify it (as much as possible)
4. Evaluate the integral $\int_{a}^{b}[f(x) - g(x)]dx$, which is the sought area.

Volumes of solids of revolution

The volume of solids of revolution is given by the formula:

$\int_{a}^{b}\pi\left\{[R(x)]^2 - [r(x)]^2\right\}dx$ (see solved problems for derivation of formula),

where $R(x)$ is the outer radius, and $r(x)$ is the inner radius.

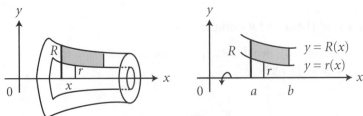

To find volumes of the solids of revolution (Washer method):

1. Draw the region and identify the cross-section that will be created by rotating this region about the given line
2. Find the limits of integration
3. Identify external and internal radii of the cross-section
4. Integrate to find the volume.

Other common methods for integration include: "shells": $V = 2\pi \int_a^b x\, f(x)dx$ and "disks":
$$V = \pi \int_a^b \left[(f(x)) \right]^2 dx.$$

Numerical Integration

Numerical approximations using derivatives and involving integrals are frequently used to calculate quantities that otherwise might be difficult to find. Increasingly, with the use of graphic calculators and advanced software, these types of approximations have become less important in elementary calculus. Nevertheless, these classical techniques deserve mentioning, as they are used in special numerical methods. We will present here only one of the most elementary numerical methods for the integral evaluation.

The Trapezoidal Rule

Consider a function $y = f(x)$. Let n be a positive integer and take $h = \dfrac{b-a}{n}$. If we write $y_i = f(a + ih)$ for $i = 1, 2, 3, \ldots n$, we can approximate the integral $\int_a^b f(x)dx$ by a sum of areas of trapezoids: $\int_a^b f(x)dx = \dfrac{h(y_0 + y_1)}{2} + \dfrac{h(y_1 + y_2)}{2} + \ldots + \dfrac{h(y_{n-2} + y_{n-1})}{2} + \dfrac{h(y_{n-1} + y_n)}{2}.$

Simplifying this expression we get:

$$\int_a^b f(x)dx \approx \left(\frac{y_0}{2} + \frac{y_1}{2} + \frac{y_1}{2} + \frac{y_2}{2} + \frac{y_2}{2} + \ldots + \frac{y_{n-1}}{2} + \frac{y_{n-1}}{2} + \frac{y_n}{2} \right) h$$

$$= \left(\frac{y_0}{2} + y_1 + y_2 + y_3 + \ldots + y_n + \frac{y_n}{2} \right) h.$$

8.4 SOLVED PROBLEMS

1. $\int \left(\dfrac{1}{x^2} - x^2 - \dfrac{1}{3} \right) dx$

   Solution: $\int \left(x^{-2} - x^2 - \dfrac{1}{3} \right) dx = -\dfrac{1}{x} - \dfrac{x^3}{3} - \dfrac{1}{3}x + c$

2. $\int 2x(1 - x^{-3}) dx$

   Solution: $\int (2x - 2x^{-2}) dx = \dfrac{2x^2}{2} + \dfrac{2}{x} + c = x^2 + \dfrac{2}{x} + c$

3. $\int \sin^2 x \, dx$

   Solution: $\int \dfrac{1 - \cos 2x}{2} dx = \int \left(\dfrac{1}{2} - \dfrac{\cos 2x}{2} \right) dx = \dfrac{x}{2} - \dfrac{\sin 2x}{4} + c$

4. $\int \cos^2 x \, dx$

   Solution: $\int \dfrac{1 + \cos 2x}{2} dx = \int \left(\dfrac{1}{2} + \dfrac{\cos 2x}{2} \right) dx = \dfrac{x}{2} + \dfrac{\sin 2x}{4} + c$

5. $\int \dfrac{x \, dx}{\sqrt{x^2 + 1}}$

   Solution: Substituting $\sqrt{x^2 + 1} = u$, we have $du = \dfrac{2x}{2\sqrt{x^2+1}} dx = \dfrac{x \, dx}{\sqrt{x^2+1}}$, then

   $\int du = u + c = \sqrt{x^2 + 1} + c.$

6. $\int x^{\frac{1}{2}} \sin(x^{\frac{3}{2}} + 1) dx$

   Solution: We use a substitution $x^{\frac{3}{2}} + 1 = u$; $du = \dfrac{3}{2} x^{\frac{1}{2}} dx$, then $\dfrac{2}{3} \int \sin u \, du =$

   $-\dfrac{2}{3} \cos u + c = -\dfrac{2}{3} \cos(x^{\frac{3}{2}} + 1) + c.$

7. $\int \dfrac{1}{t^2} \sin \dfrac{1}{t} \cos \dfrac{1}{t} dt$

   Solution: First, we use a substitution $\dfrac{1}{t} = u$, then $du = -\dfrac{1}{t^2} dt$. It leads to

   $\int \dfrac{1}{t^2} \sin \dfrac{1}{t} \cos \dfrac{1}{t} dt = -\int \sin u \cos u \, du.$ Now we can use the following substitution:

   $\cos u = v; \, dv = -\sin u du$ and $\int -\sin u \cos u du = \int v dv = \dfrac{v^2}{2} + c = \dfrac{\cos^2 \left(\dfrac{1}{t} \right)}{2} + c.$

8. Express as a definite integral: $\displaystyle\lim_{\|P\| \to 0} \sum_{k=1}^{n} x_k^3 \Delta x_k$, where P is a Δx_k partition of $(-1, 2)$ and $x_k \varepsilon \Delta x_k$.

   Solution: The limiting case will give the following integral: $\displaystyle\int_{-1}^{2} x^3 \, dx.$

9. Graph the integrand and use the notion of area to evaluate $\int\limits_{-1}^{1}|x|\,dx = 1.$

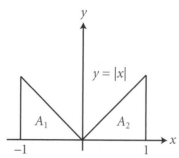

Solution: The graph shows that the areas A_1 and A_2 are equal. But $A_1 = 1\cdot 1\cdot\dfrac{1}{2}$. Thus, the integral is equal to 1.

10. $\int\limits_{-2}^{2}\sqrt{4 - x^2}\,dx = 2\pi.$

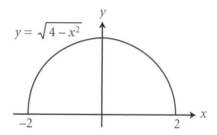

Solution: The area of the semicircle is equal to $\dfrac{1}{2}(\pi r^2) = \dfrac{1}{2}(\pi\cdot 4) = 2\pi.$

11. (Evaluating area using antiderivatives.) Find the area of the region bounded between the x-axis and the graph of the function $f(x) = x^2 + 2x - 3$.

Solution: Find the points of intersection with the x-axis: $f(x) = x^2 + 2x - 3 = (x + 3)(x - 1)$; the zeroes are $x = -3$; $x = 1$. We integrate over the interval $(-3, 1)$ and take the absolute value. $A = \left|\int\limits_{-3}^{1}(x^2 + 2x - 3)dx\right| = \left|\left(\dfrac{x^3}{3} + x^2 - 3x\right)\Big|_{-3}^{1}\right| = \dfrac{32}{3}$ (square units).

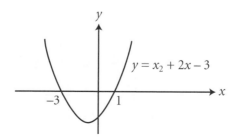

12. (The Fundamental Theorem of Calculus, Part 1.) Find the derivatives of the following integrals with variable limits:

a) $\dfrac{d}{dx}\displaystyle\int_0^{\sqrt{x}}\sqrt{1+t^2}\,dt$; b) $\dfrac{d}{d\theta}\displaystyle\int_{\sec\theta}^{\tan\theta}\sec t\,dt$.

Solution:

a) $\dfrac{d}{dx}\displaystyle\int_0^{\sqrt{x}}\sqrt{1+t^2}\,dt = \sqrt{1+(\sqrt{x})^2}\cdot\dfrac{1}{2\sqrt{x}} = \dfrac{1}{2}\sqrt{\dfrac{1+x}{x}}$

b) $\dfrac{d}{d\theta}\displaystyle\int_{\sec\theta}^{\tan\theta}\sec t\,dt = \sec(\tan\theta)\cdot\sec^2\theta - \sec(\sec\theta)\cdot\sec\theta\cdot\tan\theta$

13. Use a substitution to find an antiderivative and then apply the Fundamental Theorem to evaluate the integral $\displaystyle\int_0^{\frac{\pi}{4}}\sin x\cos^2 x\,dx$.

Solution: Substitute $\cos x = u$. The new limits of integration are: $x = 0$; $u = \cos 0 = 1$;

$x = \dfrac{\pi}{4}$; $u = \cos\dfrac{\pi}{4} = \dfrac{\sqrt{2}}{2}$, so $\displaystyle\int_0^{\frac{\pi}{4}}\sin x\cos^2 x\,dx = -\int_1^{\frac{\sqrt{2}}{2}}u^2\,du = -\dfrac{u^3}{3}\Bigg|_1^{\frac{\sqrt{2}}{2}} = -\dfrac{\left(\dfrac{\sqrt{2}}{2}\right)^3}{3} + \dfrac{1}{3}$

$= \dfrac{4-\sqrt{2}}{12}$.

14. Suppose that $\displaystyle\int_0^x f(t)\,dt = x^3 - 4x^2$. Find $f(x)$.

Solution: By the Fundamental Theorem of Calculus, $\dfrac{d}{dx}\displaystyle\int_1^x f(t)dt = f(x)$, so from the given equation $\dfrac{d}{dx}\displaystyle\int_1^x f(t)dt = 3x^2 - 8x$. Thus, $f(x) = 3x^2 - 8x$.

15. Find the area of the region enclosed by the parabola $y = 4 - x^2$ and the line $y = -3x$.

Solution: Find the points of intersection: $4 - x^2 = -3x$; $x^2 - 3x - 4 = 0$ which means $(x-4)(x+1) = 0$; $x = 4$; $x = -1$, (limits of integration). The expression $f(x) - g(x) = 4 - x^2 + 3x$. Thus, the area between the curves $= \displaystyle\int_{-1}^4(4 - x^2 + 3x)dx = \dfrac{125}{6}$ (square units).

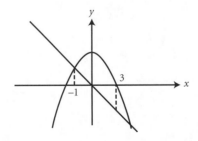

16. Find the volume generated by rotating the region enclosed between the curves $y = x^2 + 1$ and $y = 3 - x^2$ about the x-axis.

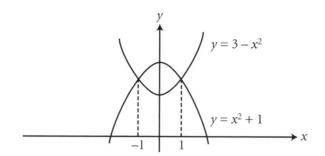

Solution: To find the limits of integration, solve the following: $x^2 + 1 = 3 - x^2$, or $2x^2 = 2$; $x = \pm 1$. External radius is $R(x) = 3 - x^2$; the internal one is $r(x) = x^2 + 1$. Set up the integral and find the volume: $V = \pi \int_{-1}^{1} [(3 - x^2)^2 - (x^2 + 1)^2]dx = \dfrac{32\pi}{3}$ (cubic units).

17. Use the trapezoidal rule to calculate $\displaystyle\int_1^2 \dfrac{dx}{x}$.

Solution: If we divide the interval $(1, 2)$ in 4 parts each with length $h = \dfrac{(2-1)}{4} = \dfrac{1}{4}$, we have $x_0 = 1$, $x_1 = \dfrac{5}{4}$, $x_2 = \dfrac{3}{2}$, $x_3 = \dfrac{7}{4}$, $x_4 = 2$. Since $y_i = \dfrac{1}{x_i}$, we have $y_0 = 1$, $y_1 = \dfrac{4}{5}$, $y_2 = \dfrac{2}{3}$, $y_3 = \dfrac{4}{7}$, $y_4 = \dfrac{1}{2}$. Hence, $\displaystyle\int_1^2 \dfrac{dx}{x} \approx \left(\dfrac{1}{2} + \dfrac{4}{5} + \dfrac{2}{3} + \dfrac{4}{7} + \dfrac{1}{4}\right)\dfrac{1}{4} \approx \dfrac{1171}{1680} \approx .697$

8.4 UNSOLVED PROBLEMS

1. $\displaystyle\int \tan^5 x \sec^2 x \, dx$

2. $\displaystyle\int \dfrac{1}{\sqrt{t}} \cos(\sqrt{t} + 3)dt$

3. $\displaystyle\int \dfrac{\cos\sqrt{\theta}}{\sqrt{\theta}\sin^2\sqrt{\theta}} d\theta$

4. $\displaystyle\int \dfrac{\sin x}{\cos x} dx$

5. $\displaystyle\int \dfrac{1}{1 + \cos x} dx$

6. $\int \sqrt{5t-1} \; dt$

7. $\int \dfrac{x}{(x^2+4)^4} dx$

8. $\int \csc^2 5x \; dx$

9. $\int x \sec^2(x^2) \tan(x^2) dx$

10. $\int \sec^3 x \tan x \; dx$

11. Find the area of the ellipse $\dfrac{x^2}{16}+\dfrac{y^2}{4}=1$

12. $\displaystyle\int_0^1 (x^3+3x^2) dx$

13. $\displaystyle\int_{-4}^2 |x| dx$

14. $\displaystyle\int_{\frac{\pi}{4}}^{\frac{\pi}{4}} \cos x \; dx$

15. Find the area of the region enclosed by the curves $y = x^2$ and $y = -x^2 + 4x$.

16. Find the volume of solid generated by revolving the region bounded by the parabola $y = x^2$, and lines $y = 0$, $x = 2$.

17. Compute using the trapezoidal rule:

a) $\displaystyle\int_{-2}^2 2^{-2} dx$ with $n = 4$; b) $\displaystyle\int_0^\pi \cos x \; dx$ with $n = 4$.

An infinite sequence	A number sequence, for example $a_n = \dfrac{1}{n}$; $S_n = \{a_n\}_{n=1}^{\infty}$ or $S = \{a_n\}$ is an ordered list of items
An infinite series	If $\{a_n\}$ is a sequence of numbers, an expression of the form $a_1 + a_2 + a_3 + \ldots + a_n + \ldots$ (also written as $\sum\limits_{n=1}^{\infty} a_n$)
Convergence tests for sequences and series	For sequences—the sum, difference, product and quotient laws, as well as the Sandwich Theorem; for series—the comparison, integral, ratio, root and Leibniz's tests (for positive series and alternating sign series)
Power series	$\sum\limits_{n=0}^{\infty} a_n x^n = a_0 + a_1 x + a_2 x^2 + \ldots a_n x^n + \ldots$
The interval of convergence for a power series	The values of x for which a power series converges

SECTION 8.5

SEQUENCES AND SERIES

The sequence $S = \{a_n\}$ is an ordered list of items. For example, consider a number sequence $S = \{a_n\}_{n=1}^{\infty}$ with an $a_n = \dfrac{1}{n}$. One of the most important questions is whether a sequence has a limit or not. Define the limit of the sequence as $\lim\limits_{n \to \infty} a_n = L$, if and only if for all $\varepsilon > 0$, there exists an N, such that $|a_n - L| < \varepsilon$ for all $n > N$. If the limit of sequence exists, the sequence is called convergent; otherwise it is called divergent. General theorems on sequences and corresponding tests for convergence are frequently proven in advanced calculus.

Bounded Sequences

A sequence S is called bounded from above by M when $a_n \leq M$ for all $n = 1, 2, 3, \ldots$ The constant M is called the upper bound. If $a_n \geq m$ for all $n = 1, 2, 3, \ldots$ the sequence is bounded from below, and m is called the lower bound. If $m \leq a_n \leq M$, then the sequence is bounded.

Limit Laws for Sequences

Let $\{a_n\}$ and $\{b_n\}$ be sequences of real numbers and let L_1 and L_2 be finite real numbers such that $\lim\limits_{n\to\infty} a_n = L_1$ and $\lim\limits_{n\to\infty} b_n = L_2$. The following rules hold:

$$\lim_{n\to\infty}(a_n \pm b_n) = L_1 \pm L_2; \quad \lim_{n\to\infty}\frac{a_n}{b_n} = \frac{L_1}{L_2} \ (\text{if } L_2 \neq 0); \quad \lim_{n\to\infty} K \cdot a_n = K \cdot L_1$$

The Sandwich Theorem of Sequences

If $\{a_n\}$, $\{b_n\}$, $\{c_n\}$ are sequences so that $\lim\limits_{n\to\infty} a_n = L$, $\lim\limits_{n\to\infty} c_n = L$ and $a_n \leq b_n \leq c_n$ then $\lim\limits_{n\to\infty} b_n = L$.

The Continuous Function Theorem for Sequences

If $\{a_n\}$ is a sequence of real numbers and $\lim\limits_{n\to\infty} a_n = L$, and a function f is defined for all n such that $f(n) = a_n$ then $\lim\limits_{n\to\infty} f(n) = f(L)$.

Continuous Extension of a Sequence

Let $f(x)$ be a function defined for all $x \geq n_0$ and $\{a_n\}$ be a sequence of real numbers such that $a_n = f(n)$ for all $n \geq n_0$. If $\lim\limits_{x\to\infty} f(x) = L$ then it follows that $\lim\limits_{n\to\infty} a_n = L$. This theorem allows us to apply very powerful methods involving continuous functions to find limits of discrete sequences.

Number Series with Nonnegative Terms

If $\{a_n\}$ is a sequence of numbers, an expression of the form $a_1 + a_2 + a_3 + \ldots + a_n + \ldots$ (also written as $\sum\limits_{n=1}^{\infty} a_n$) is called an infinite series, and a_n is the nth term of the series. When we analyze the series, we are trying to answer two questions: Is the sum of the series finite? (Is the series convergent?) If the series is convergent, what is the sum of the series? Two types of series with nonnegative terms, all $a_n > 0$, always have known sums: geometric series and telescoping series.

Geometric Series

$\sum\limits_{n=1}^{\infty} a \cdot r^{n-1}$ is convergent for $|r| < 1$ and divergent for $|r| \geq 1$. The sum of the geometric series if $|r| < 1$ is $\sum\limits_{n=1}^{\infty} a \cdot r^{n-1} = \dfrac{a}{1-r}$.

Telescoping Series

Any series that can be brought to the form $\sum_{n=1}^{\infty}[f(n)-f(n+1)]$, such that $\lim_{n\to\infty} f(n)=0$

has a sum $f(1)$. For example, the series $\sum_{n=1}^{\infty}\frac{1}{n(n+1)}=\sum_{n=1}^{\infty}\left(\frac{1}{n}-\frac{1}{n+1}\right)$ has a partial sum:

$$S_k=\left(1-\frac{1}{2}\right)+\left(\frac{1}{2}-\frac{1}{3}\right)+...+\left(\frac{1}{k}-\frac{1}{k+1}\right) \text{ and } \lim_{k\to\infty} S_k=1.$$

If a series is not one of these classical types, then to determine whether it is convergent or divergent we can use one of the following tests for a series with positive terms.

Tests for Convergence of Series

Direct Comparison Test

Let $\sum a_n$ be a series with nonnegative terms.
The series $\sum a_n$ converges if there is a convergent series $\sum b_n$, and $a_n < b_n$ for all $n > N$ (some integer).
The series $\sum a_n$ diverges if there is a divergent series $\sum c_n$ such that $a_n > c_n$ for all $n > N$.

Example: Is the series $\sum_{n=2}^{\infty}\frac{\ln n}{n^2}$ convergent or divergent?

$\frac{\ln n}{n^2} \le \frac{n^{\frac{1}{2}}}{n^2}=\frac{1}{n^{\frac{3}{2}}}$ for $n \ge 2$, and $\sum_{n=2}^{\infty}\frac{1}{n^{\frac{3}{2}}}$ is convergent,

which means that $\sum_{n=2}^{\infty}\frac{\ln n}{n^2}$ converges.

n^p test

The so-called *p*-series

$$\sum_{n=1}^{\infty}\frac{1}{n^p}=\frac{1}{1^p}+\frac{1}{2^p}+\frac{1}{3^p}+...+\frac{1}{n^p}+... \text{ where } p \text{ is a real con-}$$

stant, converges if $p > 1$ and diverges if $p \le 1$.

Example: Harmonic series $\sum_{n=1}^{\infty}\frac{1}{n}$ is divergent because

power of n is equal to 1, but it diverges very slowly.

Integral Test

If $\{a_n\}$ is a sequence with positive terms, and $a_n = f(n)$ and f is continuous, positive, decreasing function of x

for all $x \ge N$ (positive integer) then the series $\sum_{n=N}^{\infty} a_n$ and

the integral $\int_{N}^{\infty} f(x)dx$ are both convergent or both

divergent. $\left(\text{Define: } \int_{N}^{\infty} f(x)dx = \lim_{t\to\infty}\int_{N}^{t} f(x)dx \right)$

Example: Does the series $\displaystyle\sum_{n=1}^{\infty} \frac{1}{\sqrt{n} \cdot n}$ converge?

Applying the integral test for the continuous function

$f(x) = \dfrac{1}{x\sqrt{x}}$ we obtain $\displaystyle\int_{1}^{\infty} \frac{dx}{x\sqrt{x}} = \int_{1}^{\infty} x^{-\frac{3}{2}}dx = 2$ which

means that the series in question converges.

Ratio Test

Let $\displaystyle\sum a_n$ be a series with positive terms and suppose

that $\displaystyle\lim_{n\to\infty} \frac{a_{n+1}}{a_n} = \rho$. The series converges if $\rho < 1$, diverges

if $\rho > 1$, and the test is inconclusive (we need to use another test to reach a conclusion) if $\rho = 1$.

Example:

$\displaystyle\sum_{n=0}^{\infty} \frac{2^n}{n!}$ then $\dfrac{a_{n+1}}{a_n} = \dfrac{2^{n+1} \cdot n!}{(n+1)!2^n}$; $\displaystyle\lim_{n\to\infty} \frac{a_{n+1}}{a_n} = \lim_{n\to\infty} \frac{2}{n+1} = 0 < 1.$

The series converges.

The n-th Root Test

Let $\displaystyle\sum a_n$ be a series with nonnegative terms for $n > N$

and suppose that $\displaystyle\lim_{n\to\infty} \sqrt[n]{a_n} = \rho$. The series converges if

$\rho < 1$, diverges if $\rho > 1$, and the test is inconclusive if $\rho = 1$.

Example:

$\displaystyle\sum_{n=0}^{\infty} \frac{2^n}{n^n}$ then $\displaystyle\lim_{n\to\infty} \sqrt[n]{\frac{2^n}{n^n}} = \rho = 0 < 1.$ The series converges.

Alternating Series, Absolute and Conditional Convergence

A series with terms alternating in sign is called an alternating series. For example,
$\displaystyle\sum_{n=1}^{\infty} (-1)^n \frac{1}{n}$ is an alternating series. Alternating series can be written in the form:

$\displaystyle\sum_{n=1}^{\infty} (-1)^{n+1} u_n = u_1 - u_2 + u_3 - \ldots + (-1)^m u_m + \ldots$ where $u_n > 0$. The following test is

used to determine whether an alternating series converges or diverges.

The alternating series test (Leibniz's Test)

The series $\displaystyle\sum_{n=1}^{\infty} (-1)^{n+1} u_n = u_1 - u_2 + u_3 - \ldots + (-1)^m u_m + \ldots$ converges if all three of the

following conditions are satisfied: $u_n > 0$; $u_n \geq u_{n+1}$ for all $n \geq N$, where N is a positive
integer; $u_n \to 0$.

Example: The harmonic series $\sum_{n=1}^{\infty}(-1)^n\frac{1}{n}$ is convergent because all three conditions are satisfied.

Definition: A series $\sum a_n$ converges absolutely (is absolutely convergent) if the corresponding series of absolute values of all terms $\sum |a_n|$ converges. If a series converges, but not absolutely, it is called a conditionally convergent series.

Power Series

A power series can be represented as $\sum_{n=0}^{\infty}c_n x^n = c_0 + c_1 x + c_2 x^2 + \ldots + c_n x^n + \ldots$. An example of a power series is the geometric series: $\sum_{n=0}^{\infty}x^n = \frac{1}{1-x}$ if $|x| < 1$.

The Convergence Theorem for power series

Given a power series $\sum_{n=0}^{\infty}c_n(x-a)^n$ there are three possibilities:

1. The series is convergent for $|x - a| < R$ and divergent for $|x - a| > R$, and it may or may not converge for $x = a - R$ and $x = a + R$
2. The series converges for every x ($R = \infty$)
3. The series converges at $x = a$ and diverges elsewhere ($R = 0$).

Finding the interval of convergence

$\sum_{n=0}^{\infty}c_n(x-a)^n$ can be considered a number series, such that $c_n(x-a)^n = a_n$. If by the ratio test $\lim_{n\to\infty}\left|\frac{c_{n+1}(x-a)^{n+1}}{c_n(x-a)^n}\right| = \rho < 1$, then the interval of convergence can be determined from the following inequality $|x - a| < \lim_{n\to\infty}\left|\frac{c_n}{c_{n+1}}\right|$.

Taylor and Maclaurin series

The sum of the power series is a continuous function within the series' radius of convergence. The question is whether any continuous function having derivatives of all orders can be expressed as a power series? Let f be the function with derivatives of all orders on some interval containing $x = a$ as an interior point. Then the **Taylor series** generated by f at $x = a$ is $\sum_{k=0}^{\infty}\frac{f^{(k)}(a)}{k!}(x-a)^k = f(a) + f'(a)(x-a) + \frac{f''(a)}{2!}(x-a)^2 + \ldots$

$+\frac{f^n(a)}{n!}(x-a)^n + R_n(x)$ where $R_n(x)$ is a remainder. The **Maclaurin series** is a Taylor series generated by f at $x = 0$ and can be written in the following form:

$$\sum_{k=0}^{\infty}\frac{f^{(k)}(0)}{k!}x^k = f(0) + f'(0)x + \frac{f''(0)}{2!}x^2 + \ldots + \frac{f^{(n)}(0)}{n!}x^n + R_n(x).$$

The remainder $R_n(x)$ can be expressed as follows: $R_n(x) = \dfrac{f^{(n+1)}(c)}{(n+1)!}(x-a)^{n+1}$, where c is a point between a and x. The following table gives some of the most common Maclaurin series.

Basic Maclaurin series

$\dfrac{1}{1-x}$	$= 1 + x + x^2 + \cdots + x^n + \cdots = \displaystyle\sum_{n=0}^{\infty} x^n \quad (\lvert x \rvert < 1)$
$\dfrac{1}{1+x}$	$= 1 - x + x^2 - \cdots + (-x)^n + \cdots = \displaystyle\sum_{n=0}^{\infty} (-1)^n x^n \quad (x \lvert < 1)$
e^x	$= 1 + x + \dfrac{x^2}{2!} + \dfrac{x^3}{3!} + \cdots + \dfrac{x^n}{n!} + \cdots = \displaystyle\sum_{n=0}^{\infty} \dfrac{x^n}{n!} \quad \text{(for all real } x)$
$\sin x$	$= x - \dfrac{x^3}{3!} + \dfrac{x^5}{5!} - \cdots + (-1)^n \dfrac{x^{(2n+1)}}{(2n+1)!} + \cdots = \displaystyle\sum_{n=0}^{\infty} (-1)^n \dfrac{x^{2n+1}}{(2n+1)!} \quad \text{(all real } x)$
$\cos x$	$= 1 - \dfrac{x^2}{2!} + \dfrac{x^4}{4!} - \cdots + (-1)^n \dfrac{x^{2n}}{(2n)!} + \cdots = \displaystyle\sum_{n=0}^{\infty} (-1)^n \dfrac{x^{2n}}{(2n)!} \quad \text{(all real } x)$
$\ln(1+x)$	$= x - \dfrac{x^2}{2} + \dfrac{x^3}{3} - \cdots + (-1)^{n-1} \dfrac{x^n}{n} + \cdots = \displaystyle\sum_{n=1}^{\infty} (-1)^{n-1} \dfrac{x^n}{n} (-1 < x < 1)$

8.5 SOLVED PROBLEMS

Determine whether the following sequence $\{a_n\}$ converges or diverges:

1. $a_n = \dfrac{\ln n}{n}$

   Solution: Let $f(x) = \dfrac{\ln x}{x}$. Apply L'Hospital's Rule to get: $\lim\limits_{x \to \infty} \dfrac{\ln x}{x} = \lim\limits_{x \to \infty} \dfrac{\frac{1}{x}}{1} = 0$. Thus, the sequence $\{a_n\}$ converges.

2. $a_n = \dfrac{3^n}{2n}$

   Solution: Let $f(x) = \dfrac{3^x}{2x}$. Apply L'Hospital's Rule: $\lim\limits_{x \to \infty} \dfrac{3^x}{2x} = \lim\limits_{x \to \infty} \dfrac{3^x \ln 3}{2} = \infty$. Thus, the sequence $\{a_n\}$ diverges, since the nth term has no limit.

3. Apply logarithmic differentiation to find the limit of the sequence $\{a_n\}$ if $a_n = \left(1 + \dfrac{a}{n}\right)^n$.

   Solution: $f(x) = \left(1 + \dfrac{a}{x}\right)^x$; $\ln(f(x)) = x \cdot \ln\left(1 + \dfrac{a}{x}\right)$;

$$\lim_{x\to\infty} \ln(f(x)) = \lim_{x\to\infty} \frac{\ln\left(1+\dfrac{a}{x}\right)}{\dfrac{1}{x}} = \lim_{x\to\infty} \frac{\dfrac{1}{1+\dfrac{a}{x}} \cdot \left(-\dfrac{a}{x^2}\right)}{\left(-\dfrac{1}{x^2}\right)} = a. \text{ Thus, } \lim_{x\to\infty} \ln\left(f(x)\right) = a$$

and $\lim_{n\to\infty}\left(1+\dfrac{a}{n}\right)^n = e$.

4. Does the series $\displaystyle\sum_{n=1}^{\infty}(-1)^n \frac{1}{\sqrt{n+1}}$ converge absolutely, conditionally, or does it diverge?

   Solution: The series converges only conditionally; the series $\displaystyle\sum_{n=1}^{\infty}\frac{1}{\sqrt{n+1}}$ diverges (by the integral test).

5. Investigate the convergence or divergence for the series $\displaystyle\sum_{n=1}^{\infty}(-1)^n \frac{n!}{2^n}$.

   Solution: The series diverges because $\displaystyle\lim_{n\to\infty}\frac{n!}{2^n} = \infty$.

6. Find the interval of convergence of the following series $\displaystyle\sum_{n=1}^{\infty}\frac{(x-2)^n}{10^n}$.

   Solution: Notice $|x-2| \le \displaystyle\lim_{n\to\infty}\left|\frac{10^{n+1}}{10^n}\right| = 10;\ 2-10 < x < 2+10;\ -8 < x < 12.$ At the

   end point: $x = 12,\ \displaystyle\sum_{n=0}^{\infty}\frac{10^n}{10^n} = \sum_{n=0}^{\infty}1^n$ (series diverge). At the endpoint $x = -8$,

   $\displaystyle\sum_{n=0}^{\infty}\frac{(-1)^n \cdot 10^n}{10^n} = \sum_{n=0}^{\infty}(-1)^n$(series diverges). Thus, the interval of convergence is

   $(-8, 12)$.

7. Using the Maclaurin series for $f(x) = \sin x$, generate (a) the series for $f(x) = \sin 3x$, and (b) the series for $f(x) = \sin x^3$.

   Solution: a) Substitute $y = 3x$ into series $y = \sin x$ to get:

   $$\sin 3x = \sum_{n=0}^{\infty}(-1)^n \frac{(3x)^{2n+1}}{(2n+1)!} = \sum_{n=0}^{\infty}(-1)^n \frac{3^{2n+1}x^{2n+1}}{(2n+1)!}.$$

   Since the original series converges for $-\infty < 3x < \infty$, it follows that it is also converges for $-\infty < x < \infty$, so the newly created series converges for all x.

   b) Notice $\sin x = \displaystyle\sum_{R=0}^{\infty}\frac{(-1)^k}{(2k+1)!}x^{2k+1}$ for all x. Hence,

   $$\sin x^3 = \sum_{R=0}^{\infty}\frac{(-1)^k}{(2k+1)!}(x^3)^{2k+1} = \sum_{n=0}^{\infty}\frac{(-1)^k}{(2k+1)!}x^{6k+3} \text{ for all } x.$$

8.5 UNSOLVED PROBLEMS

Which of the sequences $\{a_n\}$ converge and which diverge?

1. $a_n = 2 + (0.2)^n$

2. $a_n = \dfrac{n^2 + 3n - 4}{n + 2}$

3. $a_n = \sqrt{\dfrac{4n}{n + 3}}$

4. $a_n = n^{\frac{1}{n}}$

5. $a_n = \dfrac{n}{2^n}$

Determine whether the following series converge absolutely, conditionally, or diverge:

6. $\displaystyle\sum_{n=1}^{\infty} \dfrac{(-2)^{n+1}}{n + 5^n}$

7. $\displaystyle\sum_{n=1}^{\infty} (-1)^{n+1} \dfrac{1}{n \ln n}$

8. $\displaystyle\sum_{n=2}^{\infty} (-1)^n \left(\dfrac{\ln n}{\ln n^2} \right)^n$

9. $\displaystyle\sum_{n=1}^{\infty} \dfrac{\cos n\pi}{n}$

10. $\displaystyle\sum_{n=1}^{\infty} (-1)^n (\sqrt{n+1} - \sqrt{n})$

11. Find the series' interval of convergence and, within the interval, the sum of the series as a function of x $\displaystyle\sum_{n=0}^{\infty} \dfrac{(x-1)^n}{4^n}$.

12. Find (a) the radius and interval of convergence, and for what values of x does $\displaystyle\sum_{n=0}^{\infty} \dfrac{nx^n}{n+2}$ converge (b) absolutely (c) conditionally?

13. Find the Taylor polynomial of order 3 generated by the following functions:
    a) $f(x) = \ln(1 + x)$ around $a = 0$
    b) $f(x) = \cos x$ around $a = \dfrac{\pi}{4}$.

14. Find the Maclaurin series for the following functions:

a) e^{-x}

b) $\dfrac{1}{1-x^2}$

c) $\sin\left(\dfrac{\pi}{2}x\right)$;

d) $e^{\frac{-x}{2}}$

CHAPTER NINE

Discrete Mathematics

Discrete mathematics deals with a wide range of subjects not continuous in nature. In this sense it forms a natural balance to topics in classical analysis. This chapter deals with some of the most basic topics in discrete mathematics: logic, set theory, propositional and set algebras, and relations. All of these topics are useful to classroom teachers in a wide variety of settings. For example, truth tables, one of the most elementary topics in logic, can be taught to students at all levels of secondary school—including students who may have difficulty with the traditional algebra, geometry, trigonometry, and analysis sequence.

OF TERMS

Proposition	A statement that is either true or false
Negation	$\sim p$ (not p)
Conjunction	$p \wedge q$ (p and q)
Disjunction	$p \vee q$ (p or q)
Implication	$p \rightarrow q$ (if p then q)
Bi-conditional	$p \leftrightarrow q$ (p if and only if q)
Set A	A set is an undefined term (sometimes it is referred to as a collection of objects)
Elements in A	The objects in a set ($a \in A$)
ϕ	The set that contains no elements
U	The set that contains all elements under discussion
$A \subseteq B$	A is a subset of B if and only if all the elements of A belong to B
$A \cup B$	The union of sets is a set that consists of all elements that occur in at least one of the sets
$A \cap B$	The intersection of sets is a set that consists of all elements that occur in both (all of) the sets
$A = B$	Two sets are equal if and only if they have the same elements
$A \cap B = \phi$	Two disjoint sets
A'	The complement of A consists of all elements in U not in A

SECTION 9.1

LOGIC, TRUTH TABLES, AND SETS

Rules of logic give precise meaning to mathematical statements. The definitions and "laws" of logic are useful in understanding a whole range of subjects including linguistics, electrical circuitry, computer programming, and programming languages.

Propositions

A proposition is a statement that is either true or false, but not both. For example, "today is Monday" is either true or false. In contrast, $x+1=3$ is not a proposition, since no specific value has been assigned to x to make the statement true or false. The truth value of the proposition indicates whether a proposition is true or false. Truth tables summarize the truth values of propositions.

Negation

Consider the proposition p. The symbol $\sim p$ is called the negation of p: the proposition $\sim p$ is read "not p." When proposition p is true, $\sim p$ is false; when proposition p is false, $\sim p$ is true. The truth table for $\sim p$ displays these results:

p	$\sim p$
T	F
F	T

Conjunction

Conjunction (and) joins two propositions. The symbol $\wedge$ is the symbol for conjunction. Conjunction is true only when p and q are both true. The truth table for conjunction summarizes these results:

p	q	$p \wedge q$
T	T	T
T	F	F
F	T	F
F	F	F

Disjunction

Disjunction ("or") joins two propositions, p, q. The symbol $\vee$ is the symbol for disjunction. Disjunction is only false when both propositions are false. The "or" operator is called the "inclusive or." It differs from the "exclusive or" ($\underline{\vee}$) that is frequently used in English. Compare the following: The door is opened or closed; If you have a $15,000 down payment or $50,000 in securities you can obtain a mortgage.

In the first case the "or" is exclusive, which means the door is open or closed but cannot be both open and closed. The second "or" is inclusive: you have $15,000, or if you have $50,000 in securities, or if you have both $15,000 and $50,000, you will obtain the mortgage. In mathematics the word "or" is *always inclusive*, unless otherwise indicated. For example, the roots to the quadratic equation $x^2 - 3x + 2 = 0$ are $x = 1$ or $x = 2$ (e.g., $x = 1$ or $x = 2$ or any of these answers). Disjunction has the following truth table:

p	q	$p \vee q$
T	T	T
T	F	T
F	T	T
F	F	F

If the exclusive "or" is used, it is represented by the symbol $\veebar$ and means that the proposition is true when exactly one of p and q is true, and false otherwise. It has the following truth table:

p	q	$p \veebar q$
T	T	F
T	F	T
F	T	T
F	F	F

Implication

"If p then q" is a basic mathematical expression used in the statement of numerous theorems. It has the logical representation $p \rightarrow q$. Implication is false only when the conclusion is false (q is false) and the antecedent (or premise p) is true. Implication has the following truth table:

p	q	$p \rightarrow q$
T	T	T
T	F	F
F	T	T
F	F	T

Once again, the meaning of the mathematical implication (if, then) differs a little from its standard meaning in English. "If it rains, then I'll bring my umbrella" is false if it rains and I do not bring my umbrella. If it doesn't rain, most English speakers would say that, the phrase does not have a true or false value. In contrast, in mathematics if it does not rain, we assume the implication is true if one brings an umbrella or not. The implication $p \rightarrow q$ can be expressed in number of different ways: If p then q; p is sufficient for q; p implies q; q necessarily follows from p (q is necessary for p); q whenever p; p only if q; q if p.

Bi-implication

Bi-implication, or the biconditional, is a logical connective not commonly used in English, but it is extremely important in mathematics. The connective $p \leftrightarrow q$ (if and only if, or iff) means that p and q have the same truth values; in other words, $(p \rightarrow q) \wedge (q \rightarrow p)$.

p	q	$p \leftrightarrow q$
T	T	T
T	F	F
F	T	F
F	F	T

Sets

Sets and operations on sets are closely related to truth functions. Given two sets A and B, the operation $A \cup B$ consists of all elements in at least one of the sets (compare with the "inclusive or," $\vee$). The operation $A \cap B$ consists of elements in both sets (compare with disjunction, $\wedge$). The Universal Set U contains all elements under discussion while the empty set ϕ contains no elements. The complement of a set A (A') consists of all elements in U not in A (compare with negation, ~). Two sets A and B are disjoint iff $A \cap B = \phi$. One set A is said to be a subset of a set B ($A \subseteq B$) iff every element of A is an element of B. Two sets A and B are said to be equal iff $A \subseteq B$ and $B \subseteq A$.

Venn Diagrams

Venn diagrams are visual representations for operations. Circles or other geometric figures are used to represent sets, and the areas of these figures, or parts of these figures, represent the operations between sets inside the universal rectangle U.

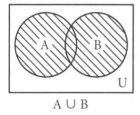

$A \cup B$

$A \cap B$

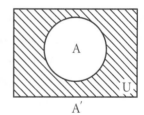

A'

9.1 SOLVED PROBLEMS

1. Translate the following sentence into an expression using propositions and language connectives: If it rains, I bring my umbrella, or, if it snows, I don't come.

   Solution: Let p = rains; q = bring umbrella; s = snows; c = come: $(p \rightarrow q) \vee (s \rightarrow {\sim}c)$

2. Explain the meaning of the following search terms on the Internet: a) diamond dealers *and* New York; b) diamond *and* gold dealers *and* New York ; c) diamond *and* gold dealers *and* New York *and* Amsterdam; d) diamond *and* gold dealers *and* New York *or* Amsterdam; e) diamond *or* gold dealers *and* New York *or* Amsterdam.

Solution: a) all diamond dealers in New York b) the dealers of diamonds and gold (both diamonds and gold) in New York c) dealers in both diamonds and gold with stores in both New York and Amsterdam d) dealers in diamonds and gold with stores in either New York City or Amsterdam e) dealer in diamonds or gold (or both) in New York or Amsterdam (or both).

3. Construct a truth table for the following proposition: $(p \lor q \lor r) \land (p \lor \sim q)$.

Solution:

p	q	r	$p \lor q \lor r$	$p \lor \sim q$	$(p \lor q \lor r) \land (p \lor \sim q)$
T	T	T	T	T	T
T	T	F	T	T	T
T	F	T	T	T	T
T	F	F	T	T	T
F	T	T	T	F	F
F	T	F	T	F	F
F	F	T	T	T	T
F	F	F	F	T	F

4. Assume $p \rightarrow q$ is an implicative. The converse is $q \rightarrow p$; the inverse is $\sim p \rightarrow \sim q$ and the contrapositive is $\sim q \rightarrow \sim p$. For the statement, if it rains, then I'll bring my umbrella, find the converse, inverse, and contrapositive.

Solution: Converse: If I bring my umbrella, then it will rain. Inverse: If it doesn't rain, then I will not bring my umbrella. Contrapositive: If I do not bring my umbrella, then it will not rain.

4. Write the following in the form $p \rightarrow q$:
   a) That you are in good health implies you take care of yourself.
   b) It is sufficient that you take care of yourself to be in good health.
   c) It is necessary to take care of yourself to be in good health.
   d) You will be in good health only if you take care of yourself.

   Solution: h = good health, c = take care: a) $h \rightarrow c$; b) $c \rightarrow h$; c) $h \rightarrow c$; d) $c \rightarrow h$.

5. What is the relationship between tables for $p \rightarrow q$ and $\sim q \rightarrow \sim p$?

   Solution: The truth tables have the same true and false values.

6. Find the set notation that describes the following Venn diagrams:

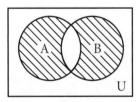

Solution: The shaded area represents all elements in *A* and not in *B*, $(A \cap B')$ or all the elements in *B* not in *A*, $(A' \cap B)$; in other words, $(A \cap B') \cup (A' \cap B)$.

9.1 UNSOLVED PROBLEMS

1. Give the truth tables for $(p \rightarrow q) \leftrightarrow (\sim q \rightarrow \sim p)$. What do you notice?

2. Write each of the following propositions in the form $p \rightarrow q$: a) It rains whenever the temperature suddenly drops; b) You will get into a good grad school if you have a high GPA; c) You will graduate only if you take finite math; d) If it rains then the garden doesn't need watering.

3. Construct a truth table for $p \wedge \sim p$. Compare it to the truth table in problem 1.

4. Suppose truth table for proposition *F* has all false entries. What operation will create a truth table with all true entries?

5. True or false: a) If $1 + 2 = 3$ then $2 + 2 = 4$; b) If $1 + 2 = 2$ then $2 + 2 = 4$;

   c) If $1 + 2 = 3$ then $2 + 1 = 1$: d) If $1 + 2 = 2$ then $2 + 2 = 1$.

6. Express the following in English: $(p \rightarrow q) \leftrightarrow (p \wedge q)$.

7. Consider the validity of the statement; If it rains, then I'll bring my umbrella iff if I do not bring my umbrella, then it does not rain.

8. Find set notation that describes the following Venn diagram:

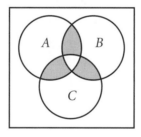

GLOSSARY | OF TERMS

Identity Law	$p \wedge T \leftrightarrow p, p \vee F \leftrightarrow p$ $A \cup \phi = A, A \cap U = A$
Domination Law	$A \cup U = U$ $A \cap \phi = \phi$
Idempotent Law	$p \vee p \leftrightarrow p$ $A \cup A = A, A \cap A = A$
Negation Law	$p \vee \sim p \leftrightarrow T, p \wedge \sim p \leftrightarrow F$
Commutative Laws	$p \vee q \leftrightarrow q \vee p, p \wedge q \leftrightarrow q \wedge p$ $A \cup B = B \cup A, A \cap B = B \cap A$
Associative Laws	$p \vee (q \vee r) \leftrightarrow (p \vee q) \vee r$ $p \wedge (q \wedge r) \leftrightarrow (p \wedge q) \wedge r$ $A \cup (B \cup C) = (A \cup B) \cup C$ $A \cap (B \cap C) = (A \cap B) \cap C$
Distributive Laws	$p \vee (q \wedge r) \leftrightarrow (p \vee q) \wedge (p \vee r)$ $p \wedge (q \vee r) \leftrightarrow (p \wedge q) \vee (p \wedge r)$ $A \cup (B \cap C) = (A \cup B) \cap (A \cup C)$ $A \cap (B \cup C) = (A \cap B) \cup (A \cap C)$
De Morgan's Laws	$\sim (p \vee q) \leftrightarrow \sim p \wedge \sim q$ $\sim (p \wedge q) \leftrightarrow \sim p \vee \sim q$ $(A \cup B)' = A' \cap B'$ $(A \cap B)' = A' \cup B'$

SECTION 9.2

BASIC ALGEBRAS OF PROPOSITIONS AND SETS

Logical equivalence may help to simplify logical expressions. This section discusses the basic logical equivalencies, which may be used, to evaluate more complex expressions. For example, to show $p \wedge q = \sim (\sim p \vee \sim q)$ (notice that $\leftrightarrow$ is frequently replaced by =), one can use De Morgan's Law and then the Law of Negation: $\sim (\sim p \vee \sim q) = \sim (\sim (p \wedge q)) = p \wedge q$.

Basic Logical Equivalence

One can also use truth tables to show that the following expressions are logically equivalent. These equivalences allow for substitutions in, and simplifications for, complete logical expressions. For example, consider the following proof of De Morgan's Law: $\sim (p \wedge q) \leftrightarrow \sim p \vee \sim q$ by showing that bi-implication is always true.

p	q	$p \wedge q$	$\sim(p \wedge q)$	$\sim p$	$\sim q$	$\sim p \vee \sim q$	$\sim(p \wedge q) \leftrightarrow (\sim p \vee \sim q)$
T	T	T	F	F	F	F	T
T	F	F	T	F	T	T	T
F	T	F	T	T	F	T	T
F	F	F	T	T	T	T	T

A similar set of relations for sets allows for simplification of set expressions.

9.2 SOLVED PROBLEMS

1. Define: $p - q = p \wedge \sim q$. Show: $\sim (p - q) = \sim p \vee q$.

   Solution: $\sim (p - q) = \sim (p \wedge \sim q) = \sim p \vee \sim (\sim q) = \sim p \vee q$.

2. Show: $\sim (p \vee (\sim p \wedge q)) = \sim p \wedge \sim q$.

   Solution: $\sim (p \vee (\sim p \wedge q)) = \sim p \wedge \sim (\sim p \wedge q) = \sim p \wedge (p \vee \sim q)$

   $= (\sim p \wedge p) \vee (\sim p \wedge \sim q) = F \vee (\sim p \wedge \sim q) = \sim p \wedge \sim q$.

3. Show: $\sim [\sim (p \vee q)] \vee \sim (p \vee q) = T$.

   Solution: $\sim [\sim (p \vee q)] \vee \sim (p \vee q) = (p \vee q) \vee \sim (p \vee q) = (p \vee q) \vee (\sim p \wedge \sim q)$

   $= (p \vee q \vee \sim p) \wedge (p \vee q \vee \sim q) = T$.

4. Show: $p \vee [\sim[\sim (p \vee q)] \vee \sim (p \vee q)] = T$.

   Solution: $p \vee \sim[\sim (p \vee q)] \vee (p \vee q) = p \vee [(p \vee q)] \vee \sim (p \vee q) = p \vee T = T$.

5. Prove: $(A \cap B)' = A' \cup B'$ (De Morgan's Law).

   Solution: Let $x \in (A \cap B)'$, then x is not in $A \cap B$, which means $x \notin A$ or $x \notin B$. Hence, $x \in A' \cup B'$. This shows $(A \cap B)' \subset (A' \cup B')$. Suppose $x \in A' \cup B'$, then $x \in A'$ or $x \in B'$, which means $x \notin A$ or $x \notin B$. Hence, $x \notin A \cap B$ or $x \in (A \cap B)'$. This shows $A' \cup B') \subset (A \cap B)'$.

6. Show: $[A \cup (B \cap C)]' = (C' \cup B') \cap A'$.

   Solution: $[A \cup (B \cap C)]' = A' \cap (B \cap C)'$ De Morgan's Law

   $\qquad\qquad\qquad\quad = A' \cap (B' \cup C')$ De Morgan's Law

   $\qquad\qquad\qquad\quad = (B' \cup C') \cap A'$ Communtative Law for intersections

   $\qquad\qquad\qquad\quad = (C' \cup B') \cap A'$ Communtative Law for unions

7. Show: $(A \cup (A' \cap B))' = A' \cap B'$.

   Solution: $(A \cup (A' \cap B))' = A' \cap (A' \cap B)'$ De Morgan's Law

   $\qquad\qquad\qquad\quad = A' \cap [(A')' \cup B']$ De Morgan's Law

   $\qquad\qquad\qquad\quad = A' \cap (A \cup B')$ Complementation

   $\qquad\qquad\qquad\quad = (A' \cap A) \cup (A' \cap B')$ Distributive Law

   $\qquad\qquad\qquad\quad = \phi \cup (A' \cap B')$ Complementation

   $\qquad\qquad\qquad\quad = A' \cap B'$ Identity Law

9.2 UNSOLVED PROBLEMS

1. Prove: $p \wedge (q \vee r) \equiv (p \wedge q) \vee (p \wedge r)$.

2. A tautology is a truth-value proposition that is always true. Prove:
   $[(p \vee q) \wedge (p \rightarrow r) \wedge (q \rightarrow r)] \rightarrow r$ is a tautology;
   $([(p \vee q) \wedge (p \rightarrow r) \wedge (q \rightarrow r)] \rightarrow r = T)$.

3. Prove: $(p \wedge q) \rightarrow (p \vee q)$ is a tautology.

4. Prove: $p \rightarrow q = {\sim} q \rightarrow {\sim} p$.

5. Prove: $p \vee (p \wedge q) = p \wedge (p \vee q)$.

6. Define $\forall x P(x)$ to mean $P(x)$ is true for all x in the universe of discourse. Define $\exists x P(x)$ to mean $P(x)$ is true for at least one element x in the universe of discourse. Let $P(x)$ be the statement $x^2 > 10$ with a universe of discourse $\{1, 2, 3, 4\}$. Find the value $\exists x P(x)$.

7. Let $P(x, y)$ be the statement $x + y = y + x$ for real numbers x and y. Find the truth value of $\forall x \forall y P(x)$.

8. An argument with premises $p_1, p_2 \ldots p_n$ and conclusion q is called valid if the implication $p_1 \wedge p_{2\ldots} \ldots \wedge p_n \rightarrow q$ is a tautology.

   Using truth tables show that the following expression is a tautology (This argument is sometimes called a *hypothetical syllogism* or *modus ponens*):

   $$[(p \rightarrow q) \wedge (q \rightarrow r)] \rightarrow (p \rightarrow r).$$

9. Prove: ${\sim} [({\sim} p \wedge q) \wedge ({\sim} p \wedge q)] \leftrightarrow (p \vee {\sim} q)$.

OF TERMS

Algorithm	A procedure one follows to solve a problem in a finite number of steps
Recursion formulas (function) f for a sequence $a_1, a_2, \ldots a_n$	$f(n) = a_n = f(a_{n-1}, a_{n-2}, \ldots a_{n-k})$
Principle of mathematical induction	If proposition $P(k)$ is true for $k = 1$, and if one assumes $P(k)$ is true for k implies $P(k)$ is true for $k + 1$, then P is true for all integers

SECTION 9.3

ALGORITHMS, RECURSION FORMULAS, AND INDUCTION

Algorithms

An algorithm is a finite set of instructions for performing a computation or for solving a problem. One of the most famous algorithms is the Euclidean algorithm of computing the greatest common divisor of two numbers. For example, a divisor of two numbers involves finding the prime factorization of these numbers. The product of all prime factors of minimum multiplicity forms the greatest common divisor. An alternate method involves the Euclidian algorithm. This algorithm rests on a straightforward observation. Suppose one wanted to calculate gcd (182, 287). First, divide 287 by 182 to obtain $287 = 1 \cdot 182 + 105$. Notice that any common divisor of 287 and 182 must also divide $105 = 287 - 1 \cdot 182$. Next, divide 182 by 105 to obtain $182 = 1 \cdot 105 + 77$. Again, $gcd(182, 105) = gcd(105, 77)$. Continue this process to obtain: $105 = 1 \cdot 77 + 28$; $77 = 2 \cdot 28 + 21$; $28 = 1 \cdot 21 + 7$; $21 = 3 \cdot 7$. Since 7 divides 21, it follows that $7 = gcd(7, 21) = gcd(28, 21) = gcd(105, 77) = gcd(182, 105) = gcd(287, 182)$, which solves the problem.

Recursion Formulas

Consider the following number patterns:

a) 1, 2, 3, 4, 5, 6, 7...

b) 1, 2, 3, 5, 8, 13, 21...

c) 1, 2, 4, 8, 16, 32, 64...

d) 1, 2, 6, 24, 120, 720...

The question arises whether we can state a general formula $f(n)$, for the nth term of all these sequences. For example by inspection ($n = 1, 2, 3, \ldots$)

a) $f(n) = n$

c) $f(n) = 2^{n-1}$

d) $f(n) = n!$

Others may be more difficult to derive: b) $f(n) = \dfrac{1}{\sqrt{5}}\left[\left(\dfrac{1+\sqrt{5}}{2}\right)^n - \left(\dfrac{1-\sqrt{5}}{2}\right)^n\right]$.

Alternately, this last sequence can be expressed as a recursion relation $a_n = a_{n-1} + a_{n-2}$. This section explores methods of defining functions in terms of closed and recurrence expressions.

Methods of Differences

Some basic identities allow some series to be expressed in functional notation. Consider $r^3 = \dfrac{1}{4}r^2[(r+1)^2 - (r-1)^2] = \dfrac{1}{4}r^2(r+1)^2 - \dfrac{1}{4}r^2[(r-1)^2$. Hence, $\displaystyle\sum_{r=1}^{100} r^3 = \dfrac{1}{4}(100)^2(101)^2$, which

hints at the general formula: $\displaystyle\sum_{r=1}^{n} r^3 = \left[\dfrac{1}{2}n(n+1)\right]^2 = \dfrac{1}{4}n^2(n+1)^2$ (see solved problems).

To prove these formulas one frequently uses the principle of mathematical induction.

Principle of Mathematical Induction

If proposition $P(k)$ is true for $k = 1$, and that if one assumes $P(k)$ is true for k and shows $P(k)$ is true for $k + 1$, then $P(k)$ is true for all positive integers.

Intuitively, one can consider the principle of mathematical induction as "the domino effect." Suppose dominos are placed close enough to each other so that if the nth domino falls, ($n + 1th$) domino also falls. Suppose you push the first domino, it falls; clearly, all the dominos will fall. For example, to prove $\displaystyle\sum_{1}^{n} 1 = n$ notice that the proposition is true for $k = 1$. Assume $\displaystyle\sum_{1}^{k} 1 = k$. If $\displaystyle\sum_{1}^{k} 1 = k$, then by adding 1 to each side we get:

$1 + \displaystyle\sum_{1}^{k} 1 = k + 1$; but $1 + \displaystyle\sum_{1}^{k} 1 = \displaystyle\sum_{1}^{k+1} 1$. Hence, $\displaystyle\sum_{1}^{k+1} = k + 1$ is also true. In other words,

$\displaystyle\sum_{1}^{n} 1 = n$ is true for all positive integers.

Recursion Relations

Find the sequence defined by the relation $a_{n+1} = 2a_n + 1$ with $a_1 = 1$. Find the formula for $f(n)$. Notice that $a_2 = 2a_1 + 1 = 2 \cdot 1 + 1 = 3$; $a_3 = 2a_2 + 1 = 2 \cdot 3 + 1 = 7$;

$a_4 = 2a_3 + 1 = 2 \cdot 7 + 1 = 15$. One obtains a sequence 1, 3, 7, 15, ... A ready conjecture is: $a_n = 2^n - 1$. Hence, $f(n) = 2^n - 1$. We can prove this proposition by mathematical induction. Suppose $a_k = 2^k - 1$, then $a_{k+1} = 2a_k + 1$ (by the recursion formula) $= 2(2^k + 1) + 1 = 2^{k+1} - 1$. Thus, if the conjecture is true for n it is true for $n + 1$. Notice that $a_1 = 2^1 - 1 = 1$. Hence, the conjecture is true for all positive integers n.

9.3 SOLVED PROBLEMS

1. Let S be the set defined by $4 \in S$; $x + y \in S$ if $x \in S$ and $y \in S$. Informally describe set S.

   Solution: S is the set of all positive integers divisible by 4: {4, 8, 12...}.

2. Prove $\displaystyle\sum_{r=1}^{n} r = \frac{n(n+1)}{2}$ for all positive integers n.

   Solution: Notice $f(1) = \dfrac{1(1+1)}{2} = 1$. Hence, the proposition is true for $k = 1$. Suppose

   $$\sum_{r=1}^{k} r = \frac{k(k+1)}{2}, \text{ then } (k+1) + \sum_{r=1}^{k} r = (k+1) + \frac{k}{2}(k+1); \sum_{r=1}^{k+1} r = (k+1)\left[1 + \frac{k}{2}\right]$$

   $$= \frac{(k+1)(k+2)}{2}. \text{ In other words, if we assume } f(k) \text{ is true for } k \text{ it follows that it is}$$

   true for $k + 1$.

3. Find the formula for $\displaystyle\sum_{r=1}^{n} \frac{1}{r(r+1)}$ given the difference identity $\dfrac{1}{r(r+1)} = \dfrac{1}{r} - \dfrac{1}{(r+1)}$.

   Solution: $\displaystyle\sum_{r=1}^{n} \frac{1}{r(r+1)} = 1 - \frac{1}{2} + \frac{1}{2} - \frac{1}{3} + \ldots \frac{1}{n} - \frac{1}{n+1}$. Hence, $\displaystyle\sum_{r=1}^{n} \frac{1}{r(r+1)} = 1 - \frac{1}{n+1}$

   $$= \frac{n+1-1}{n+1} = \frac{n}{n+1}.$$

4. Find $\displaystyle\sum_{r=1}^{n} r(r+1)$.

   Solution: Notice: $r(r+1) = \dfrac{1}{3} r(r+1)(r+2) - \dfrac{1}{3}(r-1)r(r+1)$. It follows that

   $$\sum_{r=1}^{n} r(r+1) = \frac{1}{3} n(n+1)(n+2), \text{ since all terms cancel, except the last term.}$$

5. Derive a formula for $\displaystyle\sum_{r=1}^{n} r^2$.

   Solution: The method of differences gives $r^2 = r(r+1) - r$.

   Hence, $\displaystyle\sum_{r=1}^{n} r^2 = \sum_{r=1}^{n} r(r+1) - r = \sum_{r=1}^{n} r(r+1) - \sum_{r=1}^{n} r = \frac{1}{3} n(n+1)(n+2) - \frac{n}{2}(n+1)$

   (from previous results) $= \dfrac{1}{6} n(n+1)[2(n+2) - 3] = \dfrac{1}{6} n(n+1)(2n+1)$.

6. Show: $f(x) = 1 + x + x^2 + x^3 + \ldots = \displaystyle\sum_{k=1}^{\infty} x^k = \frac{1}{1-x} \frac{1}{1-x}$ for $|x| < 1$.

   Solution: By long division: $\dfrac{1}{1-x} = 1 + x + x^2 + \ldots$. Hence, $\displaystyle\sum_{k=1}^{\infty} x^k = \frac{1}{1-x}$ for $|x| < 1$

9.3 UNSOLVED PROBLEMS

1. Give a recursive formula for $n!$

2. Use the principle of mathematical induction to prove $\displaystyle\sum_{k=0}^{n} ar^k = \frac{a - ar^{n+1}}{1 - r}$.

3. Use the principle of mathematical induction to prove: $\displaystyle\sum_{r=1}^{n} r^3 = \frac{1}{4}n^2(n + 1)^2 = f(n)$ (the sum of the first n cubes).

4. Use the principle of mathematical induction to prove $\displaystyle\sum_{r=1}^{n} r(r+1) = \frac{1}{3}n(n+1)(n+2)$.

   Also show: $\displaystyle\sum_{r=1}^{n}(2r-1)^2 = 4\sum_{r=6}^{n}r(r+1) - 8\sum_{r=1}^{n}r + \sum_{r=1}^{n}1$, and then find

   $1^2 + 3^2 + 5^2 + \ldots + 99^2$.

5. Let $U_{n+1} = (n + 1)U_n$ and $U_1 = 1$. Find $f(n) = U_n$.

6. Show that the sum of an integer and its square is an even number.

7. Use mathematical induction to show that n lines in the plane passing through the same point divide the plane into $2n$ parts.

8. Show by the method of mathematical induction that
   $1^2 + 2^2 + 3^2 \ldots + n^2 = \frac{1}{6}n(n + 1)(2n + 1)$.

9. Show by the method of mathematical induction that
   $\dfrac{1}{1 \times 2} + \dfrac{1}{2 \times 3} + \ldots + \dfrac{1}{n(n+1)} = \dfrac{n}{n+1}$.

10. Show by the method of mathematical induction that
    $1 + x + x^2 \ldots + x^{n-1} = \dfrac{1 - x^n}{1 - x}(x \neq 1)$.

OF TERMS

A relation between **A** and **B**	Any subset of $A \times B$
A relation on S	Any subset of $S \times S$
A relation R on S is reflexive	$\forall\, a \in S,\, aRa$
A relation R on S is symmetric	$\forall\, a,b \in S$, if aRb then bRa
A relation R on S is transitive	$\forall\, a,b,c \in S$, if aRb and bRc then aRc
A relation R on S is antisymmetric	$\forall\, a,b \in S$, if aRb then bRa only if $a = b$

SECTION 9.4

RELATIONS

Let A, B be a set. A binary relation from A to B is a subset of $A \times B$. More specifically, a binary relation on a set S is any subset of the Cartesian cross-product $S \times S$.

- A relation R on S is called **reflexive** if for $a \in S$, aRa.
- A relation R on S is called **symmetric** if for any a, b, $\in S$ if aRb then bRa.
- A relation R on S is called **transitive** in a binary relation for any a, b, $c \in S$ and if aRb and bRc then aRc.
- A relation R on set S is called **antisymmetric** if for all a, $b \in S$ if aRb then bRa only if $a = b$.

A relation that is reflexive, symmetric and transitive is called an **equivalence relation**.

Diagrams of Relations

Relation may be represented in a number of different ways, each having its unique strength. Consider $S = \{1, 2, 3, 4\}$ and the following diagram:

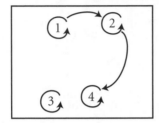

This relation is reflexive (but not symmetric or transitive): each element in S is related to itself. Consider the following relation on the same set:

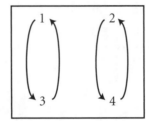

This relation is symmetric (but not reflexive or transitive). Finally, consider a third relation:

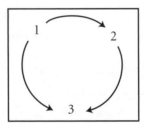

This relation is a transitive relation : aRb and bRc then aRc (but not reflexive, or symmetric).

Matrix Representation

Listing the set of elements in the relation may also represent relations. Consider a relation from $A = \{1, 2, 3\}$ to $B = \{2, 3\}$ containing (a, b), if $a \in A$ and $b \in B$ and $a < b$. A listing of these elements in R defines $R: \{(1, 2), (1, 3), (2, 3)\}$. Alternately, a pictorial representation may be made.

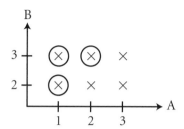

If such a pictorial representation is made with 0 representing a point not in R and 1 representing a point in R we get the following matrix:

$$\begin{bmatrix} 1 & 1 & 0 \\ 1 & 0 & 0 \end{bmatrix}$$

Alternately, suppose that the elements in A and B can be represented by numbers in increasing order, starting with the first row and column:

$$M = \begin{bmatrix} 1 & 1 \\ 1 & 0 \\ 0 & 0 \end{bmatrix}.$$

This means $\{(1, 1), (1, 2), (2, 1)\} \in R$.

9.4 SOLVED PROBLEMS

1. Suppose a relationship R is defined on $\{1, 2, 3, 4\} = S$ by the following:

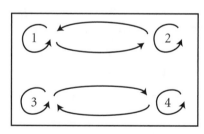

Is R reflexive, symmetric, transitive?

Solution: Notice $\{(1, 1), (2, 2), (3, 3), (4, 4)\}$. Hence, R is reflexive. Similarly, if $(a, b) \, \varepsilon \, R$ then $(b, a) \, \varepsilon \, R$; more specifically, $\{(1, 2), (2, 1), (3, 4), (4, 3)\} \subset R$. Hence, R is symmetric. Finally, $\{(1, 2), (2, 1), (1, 1)\} \subset R$, $\{(2, 1), (1, 2), (2, 2)\} \subset R$, $\{(3, 4), (4, 3), (3, 3)\} \subset R$ and $\{(4, 3), (3, 4), (4, 4)\} \subset R$. Hence, the relation is transitive.

2. Suppose the relation R on a set S is represented by the following matrix:

$$M_3 = \begin{bmatrix} 1 & 1 & 0 \\ 1 & 1 & 1 \\ 0 & 1 & 1 \end{bmatrix}$$

Is R reflexive and symmetric?

Solution: Notice the diagonal elements of the matrix all equal 1. Hence, the relation is reflexive. The matrix has reflective symmetry with respect to the main diagonal. Hence, the relation is symmetric.

3. Consider M_{R_1} and M_{R_2} representing matrices for the relations R_1 and R_2 on a set A. Define $M_{R_1 \vee R_2}$ as the relations representing the union of R_1 and R_2. Define $M_{R_1 \wedge R_2}$ as the relation representing the intersection of R_1 and R_2.

Let $M_{R_1} = \begin{bmatrix} 1 & 1 & 0 \\ 1 & 0 & 1 \\ 1 & 0 & 0 \end{bmatrix}$ and $M_{R_2} = \begin{bmatrix} 0 & 1 & 1 \\ 1 & 0 & 1 \\ 1 & 1 & 0 \end{bmatrix}$. Find $M_{R_1 \cup R_2}$ ($= M_{R_1} \vee M_{R_2}$) and $M_{R_1 \cap R_2}$ ($= M_{R_1} \wedge M_{R_2}$).

Solution: $M_{R_1 \cup R_2}$ defines the matrix in which 1 appears in either R_1 or R_2. Similarly, $M_{R_1 \cap R_2}$ defines a matrix in which 1 appears in both R_1 and R_2:

$$M_{R_1 \vee R_2} = \begin{bmatrix} 1 & 1 & 1 \\ 1 & 0 & 1 \\ 1 & 1 & 0 \end{bmatrix} \quad M_{R_1 \wedge R_2} = \begin{bmatrix} 0 & 1 & 0 \\ 1 & 0 & 1 \\ 1 & 0 & 0 \end{bmatrix}.$$

4. On the set $S = \{a, b, c\}$ define a relation: a) reflexive, not symmetric, transitive; b) not reflexive, symmetric, transitive; c) reflexive, symmetric, not transitive.

Solution: a) Consider the following figure. Clearly, since $(a, b) \in R$ but $(b, a) \notin R$, the relation is not symmetric. Since $\{(a, a), (b, b), (c, c)\} \subset R$, the relation is reflexive.

Since $\{(a, b), (b, c), (a, c)\} \subset R$, the relation is also transitive.

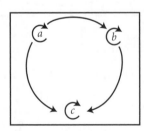

b) Consider the following figure. Clearly, since $(c, c) \notin R$ the relation is not reflexive. Since $\{(a, b), (b, a), (a, a), (b, b)\} \subset R$, the relation is symmetric and transitive.

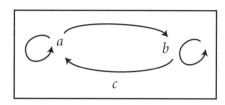

c) Consider the following figure. Notice that $\{(a, b), (b, c)\} \subset R$ but $(a, c) \notin R$. Hence, the relation is not transitive. Since $\{(a, a), (b, b), (c, c)\} \subset R$, the relation is reflexive. Since $\{(a, b), (b, a)\ (c, b), (b, c)\} \subset R$, the relation is symmetric.

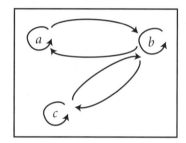

5. Let $\begin{bmatrix} 1 & 0 & 1 \\ 0 & 1 & 1 \\ 1 & 1 & 0 \end{bmatrix}$ represent a relation R on the set $A = \{1, 2, 3\}$. Define the elements

of R so the rows and columns can be represented by the integers in increasing order.

Solution: $R = \{(1, 1), (1, 3), (2, 2), (2, 3), (3, 1), (3, 2)\}$.

6. A path from a to b in the defined graph G_1 is a sequence of one or more "edges" $(X_0, X_1), (X_1, X_2), (X_2, X_3)\ldots(X_{n-1}, X_n)$ where $X_0 = a$ and $X_n = b$. The path is denoted by $X_0, X_1 \ldots X_n$ and has a length of n. Find the path between a and d in the following relation; what is its length?

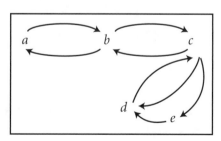

Notice $a \to b \to c \to d$; the path from a to d is given by a, b, c, d. It has length of 3.

7. Show that congruence defines an equivalence relation for figures in two-dimensional Euclidean space.

Solution: Let A be a two-dimensional figure. By definition of congruence: a) $A \cong A$; b) $A \cong B$ then $B \cong A$; c) If $A \cong B$ and $B \cong C$ then $A \cong C$.

Hence, $\cong$ is reflexive, symmetric, and transitive, which means it defines an equivalence relation for figures in two-dimensional Euclidean space.

9.4 UNSOLVED PROBLEMS

1. Represent each of the following relations on $\{1, 2, 3\}$ as a matrix in rows and columns so that elements of this set are in increasing order: $\{(1, 1), (1, 2), (2, 2)\}$.

2. Determine if the following relation is: reflexive, symmetric, transitive, antisymmetric.

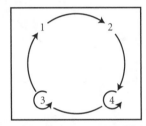

3. Draw a relation with directed graph for the set $B = \{a, b, c\}$ that is only antisymmetric. Give the matrix illustrating a property of antisymmetry.

4. A graph consists of a set of elements $(X_0, X_1), (X_1, X_2), (X_2, X_3) \ldots (X_k, X_0)$. Find the circuit(s) of elements starting with element a in the following relation (a circuit starts and finishes at the same element):

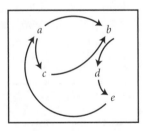

5. Let $M_{S_1} = \begin{vmatrix} 0 & 1 & 1 \\ 1 & 0 & 1 \\ 0 & 1 & 1 \end{vmatrix}$ and $M_{S_2} = \begin{vmatrix} 0 & 0 & 1 \\ 1 & 0 & 1 \\ 1 & 0 & 1 \end{vmatrix}$ be relations S_1 and S_2 on set A.

Find $M_{S_1} \wedge M_{S_2} = M_{S_1 \cap S_2}$ and $M_{S_1} \vee M_{S_2} = M_{S_1 \cup S_2}$.

6. Let (a, b) where a, b are real numbers, be a points on the coordinate axis. Define $(a, b) \, R \, (c, d)$ iff $ad = bc$. Show that this relation defines equivalence relation.

CHAPTER TEN

Linear Algebra

How can one solve systems of linear equations? This disarmingly simple question gives rise to a tremendous amount of mathematics. Chapter Ten touches on some of the most basic topics in linear algebra: matrix theory, solutions of systems of linear equations using matrices, and solutions of systems of linear equations using determinants. While all the topics are closely related, they form the basis for more advanced developments of the subject. They are fundamental to all of linear algebra.

OF TERMS

Matrix addition $A + B$	Add each of the corresponding terms in A and B (A and B must have the same dimension)
Matrix subtraction $A - B$	Subtract each of the corresponding terms in A and B (A and B must have the same dimension)
Scalar multiplication cA	Multiply each of the corresponding terms in A with c
Matrix multiplication $A \times B$	Assume matrix A is $m \times r$ dimensional and matrix B is $r \times n$ in dimension; multiply corresponding terms in ith row of A and a jth column of B, and add these products together to get the resulting $A \times B$ matrix, which is $m \times n$ dimensional
Transpose of matrix A	The transpose matrix A^T interchanges rows and columns of matrix A

SECTION 10.1

MATRIX OPERATIONS

Matrix Operations

Given matrix A and matrix B of equal dimensions, the matrix $A + B$ is found by adding each of the corresponding terms of A and B. Similarly, for $A - B$. The scalar product cA, for any matrix A is found by multiplying each term of matrix A by the scalar c. The matrix product $A \times B$ for A $(m \times r)$ and B $(r \times n)$ is the $m \times n$ matrix whose a_{ij} term is found by multiplying and adding together the elements in the ith row from A and the jth column from B:

$$A = \begin{pmatrix} 1 & 2 & 4 \\ 2 & 6 & 0 \end{pmatrix} \text{ and } B = \begin{pmatrix} 4 & 1 & 4 & 3 \\ 0 & -1 & 3 & 1 \\ 2 & 7 & 5 & 2 \end{pmatrix}$$

$$A \times B = \begin{pmatrix} 1 \cdot 4 + 2 \cdot 0 + 4 \cdot 2 & 1 \cdot 1 + 2(-1) + 4 \cdot 7 & 1 \cdot 4 + 2 \cdot 3 + 4 \cdot 5 & 1 \cdot 3 + 1 \cdot 2 + 4 \cdot 2 \\ 2 \cdot 4 + 6 \cdot 0 + 2 \cdot 0 & 2 \cdot 1 + 6(-1) + 0 \cdot 7 & 2 \cdot 4 + 3 \cdot 6 + 0 \cdot 5 & 2 \cdot 3 + 6 \cdot 1 + 0 \cdot 2 \end{pmatrix}$$

$$A \times B = \begin{pmatrix} 12 & 27 & 30 & 13 \\ 8 & -4 & 26 & 12 \end{pmatrix}.$$

Geometric Interpretations

In three dimensions, a linear transformation is defined by equations of the form:

$$x' = a_1 x + b_1 y + c_1 z$$
$$y' = a_2 x + b_2 y + c_2 z$$
$$z' = a_3 x + b_3 y + c_3 z$$

Geometrically, these three equations can be understood in terms of transformations of unit vectors (a direct analogy with two-dimensional transformations):

$$\begin{pmatrix} a_1 & b_1 & c_1 \\ a_2 & b_2 & c_2 \\ a_3 & b_3 & c_3 \end{pmatrix} \begin{pmatrix} 1 \\ 0 \\ 0 \end{pmatrix} \rightarrow \begin{pmatrix} a_1 \\ a_2 \\ a_3 \end{pmatrix}; \begin{pmatrix} a_1 & b_1 & c_1 \\ a_2 & b_2 & c_2 \\ a_3 & b_3 & c_3 \end{pmatrix} \begin{pmatrix} 0 \\ 1 \\ 0 \end{pmatrix} \rightarrow \begin{pmatrix} b_1 \\ b_2 \\ b_3 \end{pmatrix}; \begin{pmatrix} a_1 & b_1 & c_1 \\ a_2 & b_2 & c_2 \\ a_3 & b_3 & c_3 \end{pmatrix} \begin{pmatrix} 0 \\ 0 \\ 1 \end{pmatrix} \rightarrow \begin{pmatrix} c_1 \\ c_2 \\ c_3 \end{pmatrix}.$$

For example, a matrix that is a reflection in the xy plane ($z = 0$) so that: $(1, 0, 0) \rightarrow (1, 0, 0)$; $(0, 1, 0) \rightarrow (0, 1, 0)$; $(0, 0, 1) \rightarrow (0, 0, -1)$, is represented by

$$\begin{pmatrix} 1 & 0 & 0 \\ 0 & 1 & 0 \\ 0 & 0 & -1 \end{pmatrix}.$$

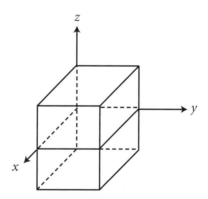

Similarly, a clockwise rotation of $90°$ ($-90°$) about the x-axis takes $(1, 0, 0) \rightarrow (1, 0, 0)$; $(0, 1, 0) \rightarrow (0, -1, 0)$; $(0, 0, 1) \rightarrow (0, 0, 1)$ is represented by the operator

$$\begin{pmatrix} 1 & 0 & 0 \\ 0 & -1 & 0 \\ 0 & 0 & 1 \end{pmatrix}.$$

10.1 SOLVED PROBLEMS

1. Describe a matrix rotation of $-90°$ and $90°$ around the z-axis (usually either transformation is just called a rotation of $90°$).

   Solution: The first transformation takes $(1, 0, 0)$ into $(0, -1, 0)$, while the second one takes $(0, 1, 0)$ into $(-1, 0, 0)$. The resulting matrix transformations are:

   $$A_1 = \begin{pmatrix} 0 & 1 & 0 \\ -1 & 0 & 0 \\ 0 & 0 & 1 \end{pmatrix} \quad A_2 = \begin{pmatrix} 0 & -1 & 0 \\ 1 & 0 & 0 \\ 0 & 0 & 1 \end{pmatrix}.$$

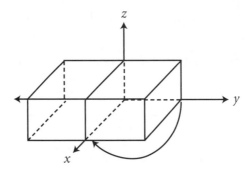

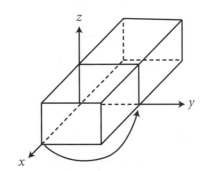

2. Follow the rotation of $90°$ around the z-axis which takes $(1, 0, 0)$ into $(0, -1, 0)$ by a rotation of $180°$ around the x-axis. What is the resulting matrix operator?

   Solution: The first operator has the matrix transformation $A_1 = \begin{pmatrix} 0 & 1 & 0 \\ -1 & 0 & 0 \\ 0 & 0 & 1 \end{pmatrix}$.

   The next operator takes the points $(1, 0, 0)$ into $(1, 0, 0)$ and $(0, 1, 0)$ into $(0, -1, 0)$

   and $(0, 0, 1)$ into $(0, 0, -1)$ and has the matrix transformation $A_2 = \begin{pmatrix} 0 & -1 & 0 \\ 1 & 0 & 0 \\ 0 & 0 & -1 \end{pmatrix}$.

Hence, the combined operation is done by A_2A_1, or

$$\begin{pmatrix} 1 & 0 & 0 \\ 0 & -1 & 0 \\ 0 & 0 & -1 \end{pmatrix} \begin{pmatrix} 0 & 1 & 0 \\ -1 & 0 & 0 \\ 0 & 0 & 1 \end{pmatrix} = \begin{pmatrix} 0 & 1 & 0 \\ 1 & 0 & 0 \\ 0 & 0 & -1 \end{pmatrix}.$$

3. Describe a simple geometric operation for the matrix operator $\begin{pmatrix} 0 & 1 & 0 \\ 1 & 0 & 0 \\ 0 & 0 & 1 \end{pmatrix}$.

Solution: In this case $(1, 0, 0) \rightarrow (0, 1, 0)$ and $(0, 1, 0) \rightarrow (1, 0, 0)$, which describes reflection in the line $y = x$, $z = 0$. The vector $(0, 0, 1) \rightarrow (0, 0, 1)$ stays the same. Hence, the matrix describes a reflection in the line $y = x$, $z = 0$.

4. In three dimensions, give the transformation that first scales with center at origin and a scale factor of 3, then reflects in the x-axis. Alternately, first give the transformation that reflects in the x-axis, then scales with center at origin and a scale factor of 3. Are there two sets of operations equivalent?

Solution: In the first case $(1, 0, 0) \rightarrow (3, 0, 0)$, $(0, 1, 0) \rightarrow (0, 3, 0)$ and $(0, 0, 1) \rightarrow (0, 0, 3)$ while $(1, 0, 0) \rightarrow (1, 0, 0)$, $(0, 1, 0) \rightarrow (0, -1, 0)$ and $(0, 0, 1) \rightarrow (0, 0, 1)$. Hence,

$$\begin{pmatrix} 1 & 0 & 0 \\ 0 & -1 & 0 \\ 0 & 0 & 1 \end{pmatrix} \begin{pmatrix} 3 & 0 & 0 \\ 0 & 3 & 0 \\ 0 & 0 & 3 \end{pmatrix} = \begin{pmatrix} 3 & 0 & 0 \\ 0 & -3 & 0 \\ 0 & 0 & 3 \end{pmatrix}.$$

In this second case $(1, 0, 0) \rightarrow (1, 0, 0)$, $(0, 1, 0) \rightarrow (0, -1, 0)$ and $(0, 0, 1) \rightarrow (0, 0, 1)$ while $(1, 0, 0) \rightarrow (3, 0, 0)$, $(0, 1, 0) \rightarrow (0, 3, 0)$ and $(0, 0, 1) \rightarrow (0, 0, 3)$. Hence,

$$\begin{pmatrix} 3 & 0 & 0 \\ 0 & 3 & 0 \\ 0 & 0 & 3 \end{pmatrix} \begin{pmatrix} 1 & 0 & 0 \\ 0 & -1 & 0 \\ 0 & 0 & 1 \end{pmatrix} = \begin{pmatrix} 3 & 0 & 0 \\ 0 & -3 & 0 \\ 0 & 0 & 3 \end{pmatrix}.$$

In other words, the two operations are equivalent.

5. In general, is a reflection followed by a rotation equivalent to a rotation followed by a reflection?

Solution: Reflect in the x-axis: $(1, 0, 0) \rightarrow (1, 0, 0)$; $(0, 1, 0) \rightarrow (0, -1, 0)$; $(0, 0, 1) \rightarrow (0, 0, 1)$. Rotate 90° around the z-axis, so $(1, 0, 0) \rightarrow (0, -1, 0)$; $(0, 1, 0) \rightarrow (1, 0, 0)$ and $(0, 0, 1) \rightarrow (0, 0, 1)$. The resulting matrix operator is:

$$\begin{pmatrix} 0 & 1 & 0 \\ -1 & 0 & 0 \\ 0 & 0 & 1 \end{pmatrix} \begin{pmatrix} 1 & 0 & 0 \\ 0 & -1 & 0 \\ 0 & 0 & 1 \end{pmatrix} = \begin{pmatrix} 0 & -1 & 0 \\ -1 & 0 & 0 \\ 0 & 0 & 1 \end{pmatrix}.$$

In the opposite order: $\begin{pmatrix} 1 & 0 & 0 \\ 0 & -1 & 0 \\ 0 & 0 & 1 \end{pmatrix} \begin{pmatrix} 0 & 1 & 0 \\ -1 & 0 & 0 \\ 0 & 0 & 1 \end{pmatrix} = \begin{pmatrix} 0 & 1 & 0 \\ 1 & 0 & 0 \\ 0 & 0 & 1 \end{pmatrix}.$

The operations are not equivalent.

6. Given: $A = \begin{pmatrix} 3 & 0 \\ -1 & 2 \\ 1 & 1 \end{pmatrix} B = \begin{pmatrix} 4 & -1 \\ 0 & 2 \end{pmatrix}$, complete $A + B$, $A \times B$, $2A$, B^2, A^2.

Solution: $A + B$ is not possible to compute;

$$A \times B = \begin{pmatrix} 3 & 0 \\ -1 & 2 \\ 1 & 1 \end{pmatrix} \begin{pmatrix} 4 & -1 \\ 0 & 2 \end{pmatrix} = \begin{pmatrix} 12 & -3 \\ -4 & 5 \\ 4 & 1 \end{pmatrix};$$

$$2A = 2 \begin{pmatrix} 3 & 0 \\ -1 & 2 \\ 1 & 1 \end{pmatrix} = \begin{pmatrix} 6 & 0 \\ -2 & 4 \\ 2 & 2 \end{pmatrix};$$

$$B^2 = \begin{pmatrix} 4 & -1 \\ 0 & 2 \end{pmatrix} \begin{pmatrix} 4 & -1 \\ 0 & 2 \end{pmatrix} = \begin{pmatrix} 16 & -6 \\ 0 & 4 \end{pmatrix}.$$

A^2 is not possible to compute (note that you can raise to a power only $n \times n$ matrices).

10.1 UNSOLVED PROBLEMS

1. Consider: $A = \begin{pmatrix} -1 & 0 \\ 2 & 3 \end{pmatrix}$ and $B = \begin{pmatrix} 1 & 2 \\ 3 & 0 \end{pmatrix}$.

    Find $A + B$, $A - B$, $3A$, $2B$, $A \times B$ and $B \times A$.

2. Rotate the vector $(0, 0, 1)$ around the y-axis $90°$ in the direction that takes it to $(0, 0, -1)$. Describe the resulting matrix operator.

3. Rotate the vector $(0, 0, -1)$ around the y-axis $90°$ in the direction that takes it into $(1, 0, 0)$. Describe the resulting matrix operation.

4. Scale about the origin by a factor of $a > 0$. Is any vector constant under this transformation?

5. Using the unit cube, describe geometrically the following transformation:
    $x' = a_1x + b_1y + c_1z$, $y' = a_2x + b_2y + c_2z$, $z' = a_3x + b_3y + c_3z$.

6. Consider the matrix $\begin{pmatrix} a_1 & b_1 & \lambda a_1 + \beta b_1 \\ a_2 & b_2 & \lambda a_2 + \beta b_2 \\ a_3 & b_3 & \lambda a_3 + \beta b_3 \end{pmatrix}$.

Describe geometrically what happens to the unit cube under this transformation.

7. Write the system of equations as a matrix product:

$$a_{11}x_1 + a_{12}x_2 + a_{13}x_3 + \ldots + a_{1n}x_n = b_1$$

$$a_{21}x_1 + a_{22}x_2 + a_{33}x_3 + \ldots + a_{2n}x_n = b_2$$

.

$$a_{n1}x_1 + a_{n2}x_2 + a_{n3}x_3 + \ldots + a_{nn}x_n = b_n$$

8. A matrix A such that $A = A^2$ is called indempotent. A diagonal matrix is a matrix that has zeros everywhere, except on its diagonal (top left to bottom right). Find the diagonal indempotent matrix of order 3.

9. If A is indempotent what can you conclude about $I - A$?

Identity matrix _I_	In two dimensions $I = \begin{pmatrix} 1 & 0 \\ 0 & 1 \end{pmatrix}$
	In three dimensions $I = \begin{pmatrix} 1 & 0 & 0 \\ 0 & 1 & 0 \\ 0 & 0 & 1 \end{pmatrix}$
Inverse _A_⁻¹ matrix (when it exists) for matrix _A_	$A \times A^{-1} = A^{-1} \times A = I$
Minor (M_{ij}) of a_{ij} in matrix _A_	The minor M_{ij} of a_{ij} is the submatrix that remains after the ith row and jth column are deleted from A
Cofactor (C_{ij}) of a_{ij} in the matrix _A_	$C_{ij} = (-1)^{i+j} M_{ij}$
Matrix of cofactors of _A_	The matrix formed from replacing the term a_{ij} in A by its cofactor
Adjoint of _A_	Adjoint A^{*} is the transpose of the matrix of cofactors of A

SECTION 10.2

MATRIX INVERSES

Notice that the 2×2 identity matrix is $I = \begin{pmatrix} 1 & 0 \\ 0 & 1 \end{pmatrix}$. To find the inverse of the matrix

$M = \begin{pmatrix} a & b \\ c & d \end{pmatrix}$, such that $\begin{pmatrix} a & b \\ c & d \end{pmatrix}^{-1} \begin{pmatrix} a & b \\ c & d \end{pmatrix} = \begin{pmatrix} 1 & 0 \\ 0 & 1 \end{pmatrix}$, consider $\begin{pmatrix} a & b \\ c & d \end{pmatrix}\begin{pmatrix} x \\ y \end{pmatrix} = \begin{pmatrix} x' \\ y' \end{pmatrix}$.

We have:

$x' = ax + by$ and $y' = cx + dy \Rightarrow (ad - bc)x = dx' - by'$ and $(ad - bc)y = -cx' + ay'$.

If we denote $\Delta = ad - bc$ as the determinant of the matrix $\begin{pmatrix} a & b \\ c & d \end{pmatrix}$, we have:

$$x = \frac{d}{\Delta}x' - \frac{b}{\Delta}y' \text{ and } y = -\frac{c}{\Delta}x' + \frac{a}{\Delta}y'.$$

The inverse of the 2 × 2 matrix $M = \begin{pmatrix} a & b \\ c & d \end{pmatrix}$ has the form $M^{-1} = \begin{pmatrix} d/\Delta & -b/\Delta \\ -c/\Delta & a/\Delta \end{pmatrix}$ where $\Delta = \det M = ad - bc$.

To check these calculations, notice that:

$$\begin{pmatrix} a & b \\ c & d \end{pmatrix} \begin{pmatrix} d/\Delta & -b/\Delta \\ -c/\Delta & a/\Delta \end{pmatrix} = \begin{pmatrix} \dfrac{ad-bc}{\Delta} & 0 \\ 0 & \dfrac{ad-bc}{\Delta} \end{pmatrix} = \begin{pmatrix} 1 & 0 \\ 0 & 1 \end{pmatrix},$$

$$\begin{pmatrix} d/\Delta & -b/\Delta \\ -c/\Delta & a/\Delta \end{pmatrix} \begin{pmatrix} a & b \\ c & d \end{pmatrix} = \begin{pmatrix} \dfrac{ad-bc}{\Delta} & 0 \\ 0 & \dfrac{ad-bc}{\Delta} \end{pmatrix} = \begin{pmatrix} 1 & 0 \\ 0 & 1 \end{pmatrix}.$$

A similar result for a three-dimensional matrix requires the definition of the adjoint matrix A^*.

Let $\begin{pmatrix} a_{11} & a_{12} & a_{13} \\ a_{21} & a_{22} & a_{23} \\ a_{31} & a_{32} & a_{33} \end{pmatrix}$ be a 3×3 matrix. Define the determinant of this matrix as

$$\begin{vmatrix} a_{11} & a_{12} & a_{13} \\ a_{21} & a_{22} & a_{23} \\ a_{31} & a_{32} & a_{33} \end{vmatrix} = a_{11}a_{22}a_{33} + a_{12}a_{23}a_{31} + a_{13}a_{21}a_{32} - a_{13}a_{22}a_{31} - a_{11}a_{23}a_{32} - a_{12}a_{21}a_{33}.$$

One way to compute the determinant is by recopying the first and second row. You then sum the products on the rightward arrows and subtract the products of the leftward arrows:

The determinant of the 3×3 matrix may also be expressed in terms of cofactors, a method that expresses the three-dimensional determinant in terms of two-dimensional cofactors. Notice:

$$\det A = a_{11}a_{22}a_{33} + a_{12}a_{23}a_{31} + a_{13}a_{21}a_{32} - a_{13}a_{22}a_{31} - a_{12}a_{21}a_{33} - a_{11}a_{23}a_{32}$$

$$= a_{11}(a_{22}a_{33} - a_{23}a_{32}) + a_{21}(a_{13}a_{32} - a_{12}a_{33}) + a_{31}(a_{12}a_{23} - a_{13}a_{22}).$$

We call $a_{22}a_{33} - a_{23}a_{32}$ the **cofactor** of a_{11}; $a_{13}a_{32} - a_{12}a_{33}$ the cofactor of a_{21}, and $a_{12}a_{23} - a_{13}a_{22}$ the cofactor of a_{31}. In general, the **minor** of entry a_{ij} (denoted by M_{ij}) is the (2×2) submatrix that remains after the ith row and the jth column are deleted from the matrix A.

For example, let $A = \begin{pmatrix} 3 & 1 & -4 \\ 2 & 5 & 6 \\ 1 & 4 & 8 \end{pmatrix}$. The minor of entry a_{11} is

$$M_{11} = \begin{vmatrix} 3 & 1 & -4 \\ 2 & 5 & 6 \\ 1 & 4 & 8 \end{vmatrix} = \begin{vmatrix} 5 & 6 \\ 4 & 8 \end{vmatrix} = 40 - 24 = 16$$

The cofactor of a_{11} is $C_{11} = (-1)^{1+1} M_{11} = (-1)^2 M_{11} = 16$.

Similarly, the minor of entry a_{32} is $M_{32} = \begin{vmatrix} 3 & 1 & -4 \\ 2 & 5 & 6 \\ 1 & 4 & 8 \end{vmatrix} = \begin{vmatrix} 3 & -4 \\ 2 & 6 \end{vmatrix} = 26$

The cofactor of a_{32} is $C_{32} = (-1)^{3+2} M_{32} = (-1)^5 M_{32} = -26$.

Notice that for the determinant A, the values of the terms in parenthesis for the expansion of the determinant, are just cofactors C_{11}, C_{21} and C_{31}.

We can write $\det A = a_{11}(a_{22}a_{33} - a_{23}a_{32}) + a_{21}(a_{13}a_{32} - a_{12}a_{33}) + a_{31}(a_{12}a_{23} - a_{13}a_{22})$

$$= a_{11}C_{11} + a_{21}C_{21} + a_{31}C_{33}.$$

By rearranging values for det A we also find that similar expressions are possible:

$$\det A = a_{11}C_{11} + a_{12}C_{12} + a_{13}C_{13} = a_{11}C_{11} + a_{21}C_{21} + a_{31}C_{31} = a_{21}C_{21} + a_{22}C_{22} + a_{23}C_{23}$$

$$= a_{12}C_{12} + a_{22}C_{22} + a_{32}C_{32} = a_{31}C_{31} + a_{32}C_{32} + a_{33}C_{33} = a_{13}C_{13} + a_{23}C_{23} + a_{33}C_{33}.$$

These expressions give cofactor expansions along the rows and columns of the matrix. For example, the cofactor expansion along the jth column is

$$\det A = a_{1j}C_{1j} + a_{2j}C_{2j} + a_{3j}C_{3j}. \text{ The matrix } \begin{pmatrix} C_{11} & C_{12} & C_{13} \\ C_{21} & C_{22} & C_{23} \\ C_{31} & C_{32} & C_{33} \end{pmatrix} \text{ is called the matrix of}$$

cofactors from A. The transpose of this matrix is called the **adjoint** of A,

$$A^* = \begin{pmatrix} C_{11} & C_{21} & C_{31} \\ C_{12} & C_{22} & C_{32} \\ C_{13} & C_{23} & C_{33} \end{pmatrix}.$$

We are now in the position to consider the relationship between the adjoint, determinant and **inverse** of a matrix (A^{-1}).

If A is a 3×3 matrix with a nonzero determinant: $A^{-1} = \dfrac{1}{\det A} \cdot adjA = \dfrac{A^*}{\det A}$

To show the result consider AA^* and $(\det A)I$. Notice that

$$AA^* = \begin{pmatrix} a_{11} & a_{12} & a_{13} \\ a_{21} & a_{22} & a_{23} \\ a_{31} & a_{32} & a_{33} \end{pmatrix} \begin{pmatrix} C_{11} & C_{21} & C_{31} \\ C_{12} & C_{22} & C_{32} \\ C_{13} & C_{23} & C_{33} \end{pmatrix},$$

where the entry in the ith row and jth column of AA^* is $a_{i1}C_{j1} + a_{i2}C_{j2} + a_{i3}C_{j3}$ (see the previous figure). If $i = j$, then this expression is the cofactor of $\det(A)$ along ith row of A^*. On the other hand, if $i \neq j$, then the a_{ij} terms and the cofactors come from different rows of A, so the value of this expression is zero. Therefore,

$$AA^* = \begin{pmatrix} \det A & 0 & 0 \\ 0 & \det A & 0 \\ 0 & 0 & \det A \end{pmatrix} = (\det A)I$$

By assumption: $\det A \neq 0$. It follows that:

$$\frac{1}{\det A}(AA^*) = I; \; A\left(\frac{A^*}{\det A}\right) = I; \; \left(\frac{A^*}{\det A}\right) = A^{-1}I \text{ or } A^{-1} = \frac{1}{\det A}A^*$$

10.2 SOLVED PROBLEMS

1. For the transformation $\begin{pmatrix} 1 & 2 \\ 3 & 4 \end{pmatrix}$ find the point that generates $\begin{pmatrix} 1 \\ 2 \end{pmatrix}$.

   Solution: We need to find (x, y) such that $\begin{pmatrix} 1 & 2 \\ 3 & 4 \end{pmatrix}\begin{pmatrix} x \\ y \end{pmatrix} = \begin{pmatrix} 1 \\ 2 \end{pmatrix}$.

   $$\begin{pmatrix} 1 & 2 \\ 3 & 4 \end{pmatrix}^{-1} = \frac{1}{4-6}\begin{pmatrix} 4 & -2 \\ -3 & 1 \end{pmatrix} = -\frac{1}{2}\begin{pmatrix} 4 & -2 \\ -3 & 1 \end{pmatrix}. \text{ Hence, } \begin{pmatrix} x \\ y \end{pmatrix} = \begin{pmatrix} -2 & 1 \\ \frac{3}{2} & -\frac{1}{2} \end{pmatrix}\begin{pmatrix} 1 \\ 2 \end{pmatrix} = \begin{pmatrix} 0 \\ \frac{1}{2} \end{pmatrix}.$$

2. Simplify I^{-1}, $(A^{-1})^{-1}$.

   Solution: By definition of inverses $I = I^{-1}I = II^{-1}$ while $I = A^{-1}(A^{-1})^{-1}$ or $A = (A^{-1})^{-1}$.

3. Show that the reflection of the plane in the x-axis is its own inverse.

   Solution: Reflection of the plane in the x-axis is given by $\begin{pmatrix} 1 & 0 \\ 0 & -1 \end{pmatrix}$, since

   $\begin{pmatrix} 1 & 0 \\ 0 & -1 \end{pmatrix}\begin{pmatrix} x \\ y \end{pmatrix} = \begin{pmatrix} x \\ -y \end{pmatrix}$. Notice that: $\begin{pmatrix} 1 & 0 \\ 0 & -1 \end{pmatrix}\begin{pmatrix} 1 & 0 \\ 0 & -1 \end{pmatrix} = \begin{pmatrix} 1 & 0 \\ 0 & 1 \end{pmatrix} = I$; so the reflection is its own inverse.

4. A matrix is called invertible if it has an inverse. If A and B are invertible matrices of the same size, show that $(AB)^{-1} = B^{-1}A^{-1}$.

   Solution: Notice that $(AB)(B^{-1}A^{-1}) = A(BB^{-1})A^{-1} = AIA^{-1} = AA^{-1} = I$.

   Similarly, $(B^{-1}A^{-1})(AB) = B^{-1}(A^{-1}A)B = B^{-1}IB = B^{-1}B = I$. Hence, $(AB)^{-1} = B^{-1}A^{-1}$.

5. Let E^k be an elementary row operation on an invertible matrix A (e.g., multiply a row by $c \neq 0$, interchange rows, and add c times row i to row j). Notice that such a row operation is equivalent to pre-multiplication by an elementary matrix. Furthermore, assume that one can perform such operations so that $E_k \cdot E_{k-1} \ldots E_2 E_1 A = I$, where I is the identity matrix. Show that $A^{-1} = E_k \ldots E_2 E_1 I$. (In this way one can find an inverse matrix using elementary row operations.)

   Solution: By assumption $E_k \ldots E_2 E_1 A = I$. Hence, $E_{k-1} \ldots E_1 \cdot A = E_k^{-1}I$. This means $A = E_1^{-1}E_2^{-1} \ldots E_n^{-1}I$. The results of problem 4 show that $A^{-1} = E_k \ldots E_1 E_n$.

6. To find the inverse of an invertible matrix, find a sequence of elementary row operations that reduces A to the identity matrix and then perform the same sequence of operations on I^n to obtain A^{-1}. Find the inverse for $A = \begin{pmatrix} 1 & 2 & 3 \\ 2 & 1 & 1 \\ 1 & 3 & 5 \end{pmatrix}$.

   Solution: We use an augmented matrix notation: $\tilde{A} = \begin{pmatrix} 1 & 2 & 3 & 1 & 0 & 0 \\ 2 & 1 & 1 & 0 & 1 & 0 \\ 1 & 3 & 5 & 0 & 0 & 1 \end{pmatrix}$

$\tilde{A} = \begin{pmatrix} 1 & 2 & 3 & 1 & 0 & 0 \\ 0 & -3 & -5 & -2 & 1 & 0 \\ 1 & 3 & 5 & 0 & 0 & 1 \end{pmatrix}$ Add -2 times the first row to the second

$\tilde{A} = \begin{pmatrix} 1 & 2 & 3 & 1 & 0 & 0 \\ 0 & -3 & -5 & -2 & 1 & 0 \\ 0 & 1 & 2 & -1 & 0 & 1 \end{pmatrix}$ Add -1 times the first row to the third

$\tilde{A} = \begin{pmatrix} 1 & 0 & -1 & 3 & 0 & -2 \\ 0 & -3 & -5 & -2 & 1 & 0 \\ 0 & 1 & 2 & -1 & 0 & 1 \end{pmatrix}$ Add -2 times third row, add to the first

$\tilde{A} = \begin{pmatrix} 1 & 0 & -1 & 3 & 0 & -2 \\ 0 & -3 & -5 & -2 & 1 & 0 \\ 0 & 0 & 1 & -5 & 1 & 3 \end{pmatrix}$ Add the second row to 3 times the third

$\tilde{A} = \begin{pmatrix} 1 & 0 & 0 & -2 & 1 & 1 \\ 0 & -3 & -5 & -2 & 1 & 0 \\ 0 & 0 & 1 & -5 & 1 & 3 \end{pmatrix}$ Add the third row to the first

$$\tilde{A} = \left(\begin{array}{ccc|ccc} 1 & 0 & 0 & -2 & 1 & 1 \\ 0 & -3 & 0 & -27 & 6 & 15 \\ 0 & 0 & 1 & 5 & 1 & 3 \end{array}\right)$$ Add 5 times the third row to the second

$$\tilde{A} = \left(\begin{array}{ccc|ccc} 1 & 0 & 0 & -2 & 1 & 1 \\ 0 & 1 & 0 & 9 & -2 & -5 \\ 0 & 0 & 1 & -5 & 1 & 3 \end{array}\right)$$ Multiply second row by $(-1/3)$

Hence, $A^{-1} = \begin{pmatrix} -2 & 1 & 1 \\ 9 & -2 & -5 \\ -5 & 1 & 3 \end{pmatrix}$.

7. Find the adjoint of the matrix $A = \begin{pmatrix} 1 & 0 & 0 \\ 0 & 0 & 2 \\ 0 & -1 & 0 \end{pmatrix}$.

Solution: Since $A = \begin{pmatrix} 1 & 0 & 0 \\ 0 & 0 & 2 \\ 0 & -1 & 0 \end{pmatrix}$ we see that the cofactors of A are $\begin{pmatrix} 2 & 0 & 0 \\ 0 & 0 & 1 \\ 0 & -2 & 0 \end{pmatrix}$.

Hence, the transposed matrix of cofactors A^* (adjoint of A), $A^* = \begin{pmatrix} 2 & 0 & 0 \\ 0 & 0 & -2 \\ 0 & 1 & 0 \end{pmatrix}$.

8. Given the matrix $A = \begin{pmatrix} 1 & 0 & 0 \\ 0 & 0 & 2 \\ 0 & -1 & 0 \end{pmatrix}$, show $AA^* = 2I$ and calculate A^{-1}.

Solution: As in problem 7, $A^* = \begin{pmatrix} 2 & 0 & 0 \\ 0 & 0 & -2 \\ 0 & 1 & 0 \end{pmatrix}$. This result implies:

$AA^* = \begin{pmatrix} 1 & 0 & 0 \\ 0 & 0 & 2 \\ 0 & -1 & 0 \end{pmatrix}\begin{pmatrix} 2 & 0 & 0 \\ 0 & 0 & -2 \\ 0 & 1 & 0 \end{pmatrix} = \begin{pmatrix} 2 & 0 & 0 \\ 0 & 2 & 0 \\ 0 & 0 & 2 \end{pmatrix} = 2I$. (Note that AA^* may not always

be equal to $2I$). Dividing by the scalar 2:

$AA^* = 2I$, $A\left(\dfrac{1}{2}A^*\right) = I$, which means $A^{-1} = \dfrac{1}{2}A^* = \begin{pmatrix} 1 & 0 & 0 \\ 0 & 0 & -1 \\ 0 & \dfrac{1}{2} & 0 \end{pmatrix}$.

10.2 UNSOLVED PROBLEMS

1. Find the inverse of the matrix $\begin{pmatrix} 1 & 1 & 1 \\ 1 & 2 & 2 \\ 1 & 2 & 3 \end{pmatrix}$ using elementary row operations.

2. Show that $\left[\left(A^{-1} \right)^{-1} \right]^{-1} = A^{-1}$.

3. Given the matrix $A = \begin{pmatrix} 1 & 2 & 3 \\ 3 & 1 & 2 \\ 2 & 3 & 1 \end{pmatrix}$, find its adjoint A^*.

4. Find the inverse of $A = \begin{pmatrix} 1 & 2 & 3 \\ 3 & 1 & 2 \\ 2 & 3 & 1 \end{pmatrix}$.

5. Use geometrical considerations to find the inverse of $\begin{pmatrix} -1 & 0 & 0 \\ 0 & 1 & 0 \\ 0 & 0 & 1 \end{pmatrix}$.

6. Given $A = \begin{pmatrix} 1 & 1 & 1 \\ 1 & 2 & 3 \\ 2 & 3 & 4 \end{pmatrix}$, find AA^*.

7. Find the inverse of $A = \begin{pmatrix} 1 & 1 & 1 \\ 1 & 2 & 3 \\ 2 & 3 & 4 \end{pmatrix}$.

8. Given the transformation $x' = x + 2y + 3z$; $y' = 2x + 3y + 2z$ and $z' = 3x + 3y + 4z$. Find its inverse transformation.

9. The point $(1, 2, 3)$ comes from what point under the transformation in problem 8?

OF TERMS

Determinant of A (two dimension)	$Det\ A = \begin{vmatrix} a & b \\ c & d \end{vmatrix} = ad - bc$

Determinant of A (three dimension)

$$Det\ A = \begin{vmatrix} a_{11} & a_{12} & a_{13} \\ b_{21} & b_{22} & b_{23} \\ c_{31} & c_{32} & c_{33} \end{vmatrix}$$

$$= a_{11}b_{22}c_{33} + a_{12}b_{23}c_{31} + a_{13}b_{21}c_{32} - a_{13}b_{22}c_{31} - a_{12}b_{21}c_{33} - a_{11}b_{23}c_{32}$$

Cramer's Rule for
$$a_1 x + b_1 y = c_1$$
$$a_2 x + b_2 y = c_2$$

Given $\begin{vmatrix} a_1 & b_1 \\ a_2 & b_2 \end{vmatrix} \neq 0$

$$x = \frac{\begin{vmatrix} c_1 & b_1 \\ c_2 & b_2 \end{vmatrix}}{\begin{vmatrix} a_1 & b_1 \\ a_2 & b_2 \end{vmatrix}} \qquad y = \frac{\begin{vmatrix} a_1 & c_1 \\ a_2 & c_2 \end{vmatrix}}{\begin{vmatrix} a_1 & b_1 \\ a_2 & b_2 \end{vmatrix}}$$

Cramer's Rule for
$$a_1 x + b_1 y + c_1 z = d_1$$
$$a_2 x + b_2 y + c_2 z = d_2$$
$$a_3 x + b_3 y + c_3 z = d_3$$

Given $\begin{vmatrix} a_1 & b_1 & c_1 \\ a_2 & b_2 & c_2 \\ a_3 & b_2 & c_3 \end{vmatrix} \neq 0$

$$x = \frac{\begin{vmatrix} d_1 & b_1 & c_1 \\ d_2 & b_2 & c_2 \\ d_3 & b_3 & c_3 \end{vmatrix}}{\begin{vmatrix} a_1 & b_1 & c_1 \\ a_2 & b_2 & c_2 \\ a_3 & b_3 & c_3 \end{vmatrix}} \qquad y = \frac{\begin{vmatrix} a_1 & d_1 & c_1 \\ a_2 & d_2 & c_2 \\ a_3 & d_3 & c_3 \end{vmatrix}}{\begin{vmatrix} a_1 & b_1 & c_1 \\ a_2 & b_2 & c_2 \\ a_3 & b_3 & c_3 \end{vmatrix}} \qquad z = \frac{\begin{vmatrix} a_1 & b_1 & d_1 \\ a_2 & b_2 & d_2 \\ a_3 & b_3 & d_3 \end{vmatrix}}{\begin{vmatrix} a_1 & b_1 & c_1 \\ a_2 & b_2 & c_2 \\ a_3 & b_3 & c_3 \end{vmatrix}}$$

SECTION 10.3

MATRIX SOLUTIONS OF SYSTEMS OF EQUATIONS

Two linear equations of two unknowns $a_1 x + b_1 y = c_1$ and $a_2 x + b_2 y = c_2$ may be written in the following matrix form: $\begin{pmatrix} a_1 & b_1 \\ a_2 & b_2 \end{pmatrix} \begin{pmatrix} x \\ y \end{pmatrix} = \begin{pmatrix} c_1 \\ c_2 \end{pmatrix}$.

Hence, the solution to this system may be written as a product involving the inverse matrix $\begin{pmatrix} a_1 & b_1 \\ a_2 & b_2 \end{pmatrix}^{-1}$ (if it exists) $\begin{pmatrix} x \\ y \end{pmatrix} = \begin{pmatrix} a_1 & b_1 \\ a_2 & b_2 \end{pmatrix}^{-1} \begin{pmatrix} c_1 \\ c_2 \end{pmatrix}$.

In a similar way, three linear equations may be written in matrix form:
$a_1x + b_1y + c_1z = d_1; a_2x + b_2y + c_2z = d_2; a_3x + b_3y + c_3z = d_3$

$$\begin{pmatrix} a_1 & b_1 & c_1 \\ a_2 & b_2 & c_2 \\ a_3 & b_3 & c_3 \end{pmatrix} \begin{pmatrix} x \\ y \\ z \end{pmatrix} = \begin{pmatrix} d_1 \\ d_2 \\ d_3 \end{pmatrix} \text{ or } \begin{pmatrix} x \\ y \\ z \end{pmatrix} = \begin{pmatrix} a_1 & b_1 & c_1 \\ a_2 & b_2 & c_2 \\ a_3 & b_3 & c_3 \end{pmatrix}^{-1} \begin{pmatrix} d_1 \\ d_2 \\ d_3 \end{pmatrix}.$$

Clearly, solutions of two systems of linear equations may be found if one can find inverse matrices. The method of a matrix solution complements that of linear elimination.

Cramer's Rule

In the two-dimensional case, Cramer's Rule can be used to solve two equations in two unknowns and to help find the inverse of a matrix using determinants. If $ax + by = c$ and

$dx + cy = f$, define $\begin{vmatrix} a & b \\ d & c \end{vmatrix} = ac - bd$. Then $x = \dfrac{\begin{vmatrix} c & b \\ f & c \end{vmatrix}}{\begin{vmatrix} a & b \\ d & c \end{vmatrix}}$, $y = \dfrac{\begin{vmatrix} a & c \\ d & f \end{vmatrix}}{\begin{vmatrix} a & b \\ d & c \end{vmatrix}}$. A similar result holds

for the three-dimensional case. For $M = \begin{pmatrix} a_1 & b_1 & c_1 \\ a_2 & b_2 & c_2 \\ a_3 & b_3 & c_3 \end{pmatrix}$ the inverse M^{-1} is $M^{-1} = \dfrac{M^*}{\det M}$

(provided $\det M \neq 0$). Using the concept of matrix inverse for 3×3 matrix (section 2) we can now state Cramer's Rule for three dimensions. Let $AX = B$ be a system of three linear equations in three unknowns (X_1, X_2, X_3) such that $\det A \neq 0$, then the system has a unique solution $X_1 = \dfrac{\det A_1}{\det A}, X_2 = \dfrac{\det A_2}{\det A}, X_3 = \dfrac{\det A_3}{\det A}$, where A_j is the matrix ob-

tained by replacing the entries of the columns of A by the entries in $B = \begin{pmatrix} b_1 \\ b_2 \\ b_3 \end{pmatrix}$. To prove this

result first notice that since $\det A \neq 0$, A^{-1} exists and $A^{-1} = \dfrac{1}{\det A} A^*$. Because $AX = B$,

$$X = A^{-1}B = \left(\dfrac{1}{\det A}\right) A^* B; \ X = \dfrac{1}{\det A} \begin{pmatrix} C_{11} & C_{21} & C_{31} \\ C_{12} & C_{22} & C_{32} \\ C_{13} & C_{23} & C_{33} \end{pmatrix} B = \dfrac{1}{\det A} \begin{pmatrix} b_1C_{11} + b_2C_{21} + b_3C_{31} \\ b_1C_{12} + b_2C_{22} + b_3C_{32} \\ b_1C_{13} + b_2C_{23} + b_3C_{33} \end{pmatrix}.$$

The entry in the jth row of X is $x_j = \dfrac{b_1 C_{1j} + b_2 C_{2j} + b_3 C_{3j}}{\det A}$. Let A_j be the matrix obtained

by replacing the entries of the jth column of A by the entries in $B = \begin{pmatrix} b_1 \\ b_2 \\ b_3 \end{pmatrix}$; for example,

$A_3 = \begin{pmatrix} a_{11} & a_{12} & b_1 \\ a_{21} & a_{22} & b_2 \\ a_{31} & a_{32} & b_3 \end{pmatrix}$. Since A_j differs only in the jth column, the cofactors of entries b_1,

b_2, b_3 in A_j are the same as the cofactors of the corresponding entries in the jth column of A. The cofactor expansion of $\det A_j$ along the jth column is $\det A_j = b_1 C_{1j} + b_2 C_{2j} + b_3 C_{3j}$.

Substituting for x_j gives $x_j = \dfrac{\det A_j}{\det A}$.

10.3 SOLVED PROBLEMS

1. Calculate the solution to the simultaneous equations $x - y = 6$ and $2x + 3y = 4$ using inverse matrices.

   Solution: $x - y = 6$; and $2x + 3y = 4$ may be written as $\begin{pmatrix} 1 & -1 \\ 2 & 3 \end{pmatrix}\begin{pmatrix} x \\ y \end{pmatrix} = \begin{pmatrix} 6 \\ 4 \end{pmatrix}$.

   Notice that: $\begin{pmatrix} 1 & -1 \\ 2 & 3 \end{pmatrix}^{-1} = \begin{pmatrix} 3 & 1 \\ -2 & 1 \end{pmatrix} \cdot \dfrac{1}{(1)(3) - (-1)(2)} = \begin{pmatrix} \dfrac{3}{5} & \dfrac{1}{5} \\ -\dfrac{2}{5} & \dfrac{1}{5} \end{pmatrix}$.

   Hence, $\begin{pmatrix} x \\ y \end{pmatrix} = \begin{pmatrix} \dfrac{3}{5} & \dfrac{1}{5} \\ -\dfrac{2}{5} & \dfrac{1}{5} \end{pmatrix}\begin{pmatrix} 6 \\ 4 \end{pmatrix} = \begin{pmatrix} \dfrac{22}{5} \\ -\dfrac{8}{5} \end{pmatrix}$; $x = \dfrac{22}{5}$ and $y = -\dfrac{8}{5}$.

2. Using determinants (Cramer's Rule) solve the simultaneous equations: $x - y = 6$ and $2x + 3y = 4$.

   Solution: $x = \dfrac{\begin{vmatrix} 6 & -1 \\ 4 & 3 \end{vmatrix}}{\begin{vmatrix} 1 & -1 \\ 2 & 3 \end{vmatrix}}$, and $y = \dfrac{\begin{vmatrix} 1 & 6 \\ 2 & 4 \end{vmatrix}}{\begin{vmatrix} 1 & -1 \\ 2 & 3 \end{vmatrix}}$; $x = \dfrac{18 + 4}{5} = \dfrac{22}{5}$, and $y = \dfrac{4 - 12}{5} = -\dfrac{8}{5}$.

3. Solve the following system of equations using augmented matrices:

$$x + y + z = 1$$
$$x + 2y + 2z = 2$$
$$x + 3y + z = 3$$

Solution: If $A = \begin{pmatrix} 1 & 1 & 1 \\ 1 & 2 & 2 \\ 1 & 3 & 1 \end{pmatrix}$ we can find A^{-1} by the augmented matrix method:

$$\tilde{A} = \begin{pmatrix} 1 & 1 & 1 & 1 & 0 & 0 \\ 1 & 2 & 2 & 0 & 1 & 0 \\ 1 & 3 & 1 & 0 & 0 & 1 \end{pmatrix}$$

$$= \begin{pmatrix} 1 & 1 & 1 & 1 & 0 & 0 \\ 0 & -1 & -1 & 1 & -1 & 0 \\ 0 & -2 & 0 & 0 & 0 & -1 \end{pmatrix} \quad r_2' = r_1 - r_2; r_3' = r_1 - r_3$$

$$= \begin{pmatrix} 1 & 0 & 0 & 2 & -1 & 0 \\ 1 & -1 & -1 & 1 & -1 & 0 \\ 0 & 0 & 2 & -1 & 2 & -1 \end{pmatrix} \quad r_1' = r_1 + r_2; r_3' = -2r_2 + r_3$$

$$= \begin{pmatrix} 1 & 0 & 0 & 2 & -1 & 0 \\ 0 & 1 & 1 & -1 & 1 & 0 \\ 0 & 0 & 1 & -\dfrac{1}{2} & 1 & -\dfrac{1}{2} \end{pmatrix} \quad r_3' = \dfrac{1}{2}r_3; r_2' = -r_2$$

$$= \begin{pmatrix} 1 & 0 & 0 & 2 & -1 & 0 \\ 0 & 1 & 0 & -\dfrac{1}{2} & 0 & \dfrac{1}{2} \\ 0 & 0 & 1 & -\dfrac{1}{2} & 1 & -\dfrac{1}{2} \end{pmatrix} \quad r_2' = -r_3 + r_2$$

In other words, $A^{-1} = \begin{pmatrix} 2 & -1 & 0 \\ -\dfrac{1}{2} & 0 & \dfrac{1}{2} \\ -\dfrac{1}{2} & 1 & -\dfrac{1}{2} \end{pmatrix}$. Let $A = \begin{pmatrix} 1 & 1 & 1 \\ 1 & 2 & 2 \\ 1 & 3 & 1 \end{pmatrix}$, $X = \begin{pmatrix} x \\ y \\ z \end{pmatrix}$, $B = \begin{pmatrix} 1 \\ 2 \\ 3 \end{pmatrix}$.

Then $X = A^{-1}B = \begin{pmatrix} 2 & -1 & 0 \\ -\dfrac{1}{2} & 0 & \dfrac{1}{2} \\ -\dfrac{1}{2} & 1 & -\dfrac{1}{2} \end{pmatrix} \begin{pmatrix} 1 \\ 2 \\ 3 \end{pmatrix} = \begin{pmatrix} 0 \\ 1 \\ 0 \end{pmatrix}$ and $x = 0, y = 1, z = 0$.

4. Evaluate the determinants $A = \begin{vmatrix} 1 & 3 \\ 2 & 4 \end{vmatrix}$ and $B = \begin{vmatrix} 1 & 2 & 3 \\ -4 & 5 & 6 \\ 7 & -8 & 9 \end{vmatrix}$.

Solution: $\begin{vmatrix} 1 & 3 \\ 2 & 4 \end{vmatrix} = (1)(4) - (3)(2) = 4 - 6 = -2$, while $\begin{vmatrix} 1 & 2 & 3 \\ -4 & 5 & 6 \\ 7 & -8 & 9 \end{vmatrix}$

$= 1 \cdot 5 \cdot 9 + 2 \cdot 6 \cdot 7 + 3(-4)(-8) - 7 \cdot 5 \cdot 3 - (-8)(6)(1) - (9)(-4)(2) = 45 + 84 + 96$
$- 105 - (-48) - (-72) = 240.$

5. Let $A = \begin{vmatrix} 3 & 1 & 0 \\ -2 & -4 & 3 \\ 5 & 4 & -2 \end{vmatrix}$. Evaluate A by cofactor expansion along first column.

Solution: $A = 3 \begin{vmatrix} -4 & 3 \\ 4 & -2 \end{vmatrix} - (-2) \begin{vmatrix} 1 & 0 \\ 4 & -2 \end{vmatrix} + 5 \begin{vmatrix} 1 & 0 \\ -4 & 3 \end{vmatrix} = 3(-4) - (-2)(-2) + 5(3) = -1.$

6. Evaluate $A = \begin{vmatrix} 3 & 1 & 0 \\ -2 & -4 & 3 \\ 5 & 4 & -2 \end{vmatrix}$ along the first row.

Solution: $A = 3 \begin{vmatrix} -4 & 3 \\ 4 & -2 \end{vmatrix} - (1) \begin{vmatrix} -2 & 3 \\ 5 & -2 \end{vmatrix} + 0 \begin{vmatrix} -2 & -4 \\ 5 & 4 \end{vmatrix} = 3(-4) - (1)(-11) = -1.$

7. What can you conclude from problem 5 and 6 in terms of cofactor expansions?

Solution: $\det A = a_{11}C_{11} + a_{12}C_{12} + a_{13}C_{13}$ while $\det A = a_{11}C_{11} + a_{21}C_{21} + a_{31}C_{31}$. In other words, the cofactor expansion along the first row equals the cofactor expansions along the first column.

8. Solve the following equations using Cramer's Rule:

$$x + y - z = 1$$
$$x - y + z = 2$$
$$2x - z = 4$$

Solution: $x = \dfrac{\begin{vmatrix} 1 & 1 & -1 \\ 2 & -1 & 1 \\ 4 & 0 & -1 \end{vmatrix}}{\begin{vmatrix} 1 & 1 & -1 \\ 1 & -1 & 1 \\ 2 & 0 & -1 \end{vmatrix}} = \dfrac{3}{2}, y = \dfrac{\begin{vmatrix} 1 & 1 & -1 \\ 1 & 2 & 1 \\ 2 & 4 & -1 \end{vmatrix}}{\begin{vmatrix} 1 & 1 & -1 \\ 1 & -1 & 1 \\ 2 & 0 & -1 \end{vmatrix}} = -\dfrac{3}{2}, z = \dfrac{\begin{vmatrix} 1 & 1 & 1 \\ 1 & -1 & 2 \\ 2 & 0 & 4 \end{vmatrix}}{\begin{vmatrix} 1 & 1 & -1 \\ 1 & -1 & 1 \\ 2 & 0 & -1 \end{vmatrix}} = \dfrac{-2}{2} = -1.$

10.3 UNSOLVED PROBLEMS

1. Using the concept of inverse matrices, solve the following simultaneous equations:

$$5x - 2y = 7$$
$$2x + 3y = -1$$

2. Use Cramer's Rule to solve the following simultaneous equations:

$$4x + 5y = 2$$
$$2x + 3y = 2$$

3. Solve the following simultaneous equations using the concept of inverse matrices:

$$x + y + 2z = 0$$
$$2x - y + z = 3$$
$$x - 2y + 3z = -5$$

4. Solve the following simultaneous equations using Cramer's Rule:

$$x_1 + 2x_2 + x_3 = -1$$
$$x_1 - x_2 + x_3 = 3$$
$$x_1 + x_2 = 4$$

5. Show that $\begin{vmatrix} 1 & a & a^3 \\ 1 & b & b^3 \\ 1 & c & c^3 \end{vmatrix} = 0$ if $b = c, c = a, b = a$.

6. Show that $\begin{vmatrix} 1 & a & a^3 \\ 1 & b & b^3 \\ 1 & c & c^3 \end{vmatrix} = (b-c)(c-a)(a-b)X$, where X must be linear expression.

Answers to Unsolved Problems

CHAPTER 1

Answers 1.1

1. $\dfrac{3}{8} \div 3 = \dfrac{1}{8}$

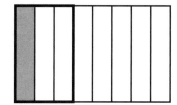

3. a) 1; no limit

   b) Some infinite series approach a finite sum, some do not

5. $\dfrac{13}{43}$

7. $3.54 - 3.5 = .04$

9. $\dfrac{40 - 16\sqrt{3} - 5\sqrt{5} + 2\sqrt{15}}{59}$

Answers 1.2

1. Yes
3. Yes
5. Notice a is the identity but no elements exists for c^{-1}.
7. d, e
9. The proof is similar to the one that shows that identity is unique.

Answers 1.3

1. $11 \cdot 3^2; 3 \cdot 7$
3. 2^n

Answers 1.4

1. $1 : 9$
3. $6\left(\sqrt[3]{\dfrac{v}{100,000}}\right)^2$
5. 22.5

CHAPTER 2

Answers 2.1

1. $a^2 + 2a + b^2 + 2b + ab(a+2)(b+2)$
3. $\dfrac{x^4 - 1}{x^2}$
5. $(x - 2a)^2$
7. $(-4x - 9)(3x - 2)$
9. 20003
11. $\dfrac{5}{6}$
13. $\dfrac{(m - 3n)(m + n)}{(m - 2n)^2}$
15. $a = -\dfrac{3}{2}, b = \dfrac{7}{2}$

Answers 2.2

1. $210

3. $\dfrac{1}{2}(\sqrt{5}-1)$

5. $\dfrac{2\pi \times 1.50 \times 10^8}{365 \times 24} km/hr$

7. one person takes $8\dfrac{1}{4}$, the other takes $16\dfrac{1}{2}$ hrs

Answers 2.3

1. $k = 1$

3. $\left(\dfrac{2(a+b+c)}{3}, \dfrac{5(a+b+c)}{3} \right)$

5. $(a + b, b + c, a + c)$

7. $S = \{2a, -6a\}$

9. $x > \dfrac{3}{2}$

11. $(6, 12)$

Answers 2.4

1. x is any number

3. $x > \dfrac{1}{2}$ or $x < -\dfrac{1}{2}$

7. All x in the closed interval $[a - \varepsilon, a + \varepsilon]$

9. $-5 < x < 8$

CHAPTER 3

Answers 3.1

1. $65\dfrac{5}{11}$ minutes

3. $m\angle A = 57.5°$, $m\angle B = 52.5°$, $m\angle C = 70°$

Answers 3.2

5. $30°, 60°$

Answers 3.3

1. $72°$
3. $85°$
5. 13

Answers 3.4

3. $0, 1, 2, 3, 4$
5. $60°$
7. $5, 5$

Answers 3.5

1. $\dfrac{25\pi}{2}$

3. 60

5. $57\dfrac{7}{24}\,ft^2$

7. $300 - 50\pi$

Answers 3.6

1. $r = \dfrac{3}{4}$

3. $(x^2)\dfrac{1}{12}\pi x^3$

5. $20(3^{-\frac{2}{3}})$

7. $(760\pi/3)\text{ cm}^3$

Answers 3.7

3. $y = 0$ and $x = 0$. The corresponding eigenvalues are -1 and 1

5. Eigenvectors $\begin{pmatrix} 1 \\ 0 \end{pmatrix}$ and $\begin{pmatrix} 0 \\ 1 \end{pmatrix}$; eigenvalues 3 and 1

7. $\begin{pmatrix} -\dfrac{1}{2} & -\dfrac{\sqrt{3}}{2} \\ \dfrac{\sqrt{3}}{2} & -\dfrac{1}{2} \end{pmatrix}$

9. The unit square collapses into the line $y = \dfrac{1}{2}x$; alternately $\begin{vmatrix} 6 & 2 \\ 3 & 1 \end{vmatrix} = 0$

Answers 3.8

7. a half circle

9. a cone

Answers 3.9

1. With given point P as center draw an arc that intersects the given line at A and B. With center at A draw an arc of radius r; with center at B draw an arc with radius r. Call P_2 the intersection point of these arcs. Connect $P\,P_2$

3. Draw a circle. Construct two perpendicular diameters. Bisect the angles formed by these diameters. Connect the eight points where these bisectors intersect the circle.

5. Draw a circle. Mark off the radius consecutively on the circumference (you get six points). Connect every other point with a line segment.

7. a half circle

9. a cone

CHAPTER 4

Answers 4.1

1. $\dfrac{5}{3}, \dfrac{4}{3}$

3. Any θ except $\theta = \dfrac{\pi}{2} + n\pi, n \in Z.$

9. $(y-1)^2 - \dfrac{(x-2)^2}{9} = 1$

11. The points $(n\pi, \dfrac{(2n+1)\pi}{2}) \, n \in Z.$

Answers 4.2

1. $\theta = 137°$

3.

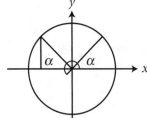

$$x = \alpha + 360°n$$
$$x = (180° - \alpha) + 360°n$$
$$n \in Z$$

5. $\{\ldots, -240°, -120°, 120°, 240°, \ldots\}$

   $\{x \mid x = \pm 120° + 360°n, n \in Z.\}$.

7. $b = 2.66, c = 5.24, C = 70°$

9.

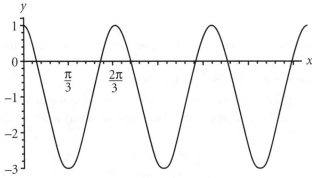

Answers 4.3

5. $\dfrac{\sqrt{6} - \sqrt{2}}{4}$ or $\dfrac{\sqrt{2 - \sqrt{3}}}{2}$

7. $\tan x$

9. $\sin^{-1} \dfrac{3}{5} = 36.9°, \dfrac{\pi}{2}$

Answers 4.4

1. Symmetric with respect to origin.

3. $\left(2, \dfrac{-\pi}{3}\right)$

5. Hint: The roots of the equation form a regular polygon with n vertices on the unit circle.

7. $\dfrac{1}{2}\sqrt{3} + \dfrac{1}{2}i, \ -\dfrac{1}{2}\sqrt{3} + \dfrac{1}{2}i, \ -i$

9. The points $z = \dfrac{1}{2} \pm \dfrac{\sqrt{3}}{2}i$

CHAPTER 5

Answers 5.1

1.

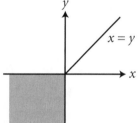

3.

5. Consider for that $x = 0$, the function is undefined; $f(x) = 1$ for $x > 0$; $f(x) = -1$ for $x < 0$.

7. $(-9)^{-2} = \dfrac{1}{81}$

9. The domain consists of all numbers except $x \neq 1$, $x \neq 2$; The range consists of all $y \leq -4$ and $y \geq 0$.

Answers 5.2

1.

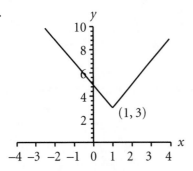

Graph of $y = 3|x|$ translated one unit to the right and three units up.

3. $y = |x^3|$.

5. The graph is a translation of the original graph three units to the left.

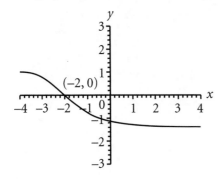

7. Notice the graph holds for $y = x^3$ or $y - x^2 = 0$.

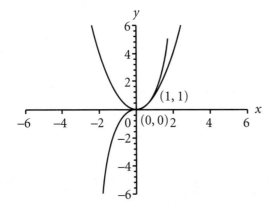

9. The slope of the secant connecting two points $(x, x^2$ and $(x + h, (x + h)^2)$ on the curve $y = x^2$ (see figure).

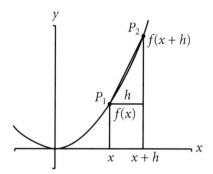

Slope $\overline{P_1P_2} = \dfrac{f(x+h) - f(x)}{h}$. If $f(x) = x^2$ then $\dfrac{f(x+h) - f(x)}{h} = \dfrac{(x+h)^2 - x^2}{h} =$

$\dfrac{x^2 + 2xh + h^2 - x^2}{h} = 2x + h.$

Answers 5.3

1. c

3. It does not have an inverse.

5. $f \circ g : x \to 2x + 1$

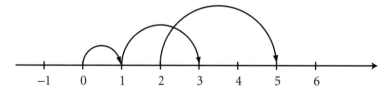

First double the x and then add 1. $g \circ f : x \to 2(x + 1)$.

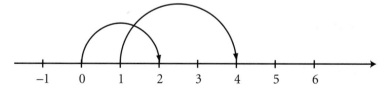

First add 1 and then double the result.

7. The relationship is self-reflective in the line $y = x$.

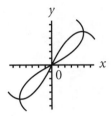

9. $x = 3$

CHAPTER 6

Answers 6.1

1. Histograms using relative frequencies show both methods are almost identical with respect to time taken.

3. Answers will vary. For example, the most frequently occurring score is 66; the scores look as if they "cluster around 67."

Answers 6.2

1. 2^8

3. both equal 5

5. $1 - 5x + 15x^2$

7. $n \cdot 2^{n-1}$

9. 257.026

Answers 6.3

1. $\dfrac{1}{6}, \dfrac{1}{6}, \dfrac{1}{36}$, independent

3. $\dfrac{1}{4}, \dfrac{1}{10}$, independent

5. $\dfrac{47}{48}$

7. $p = 0.0595$

Answers 6.4

1. 11, 19, 23, 14, 10, 3, 0.8

3. $\bar{x} \approx 63, s_x \approx 10$

5. $\dfrac{3}{8}$

7. Notice $V(X) = E(X^2) - [E(X)]^2$. But X only takes values of 0 and 1, so we have that $E(X^2) = E(X)$, or $V(X) = p - p^2$. Simplifying this expression one gets $V(X) = p(1 - p) = pq$.

Answers 6.5

1. a) $0.94 \cdot 10^{-4}$

   b) 0.885

   c) 0.107

3. a) 2

   b) $F(y) = \begin{cases} 0.5(y^2 + 2y + 1) & -1 \le y < 0 \\ 1 - 0.5e^{-2y} & 0 \le y < \infty \end{cases}$

   c) 0.125

   d) 0.932

   e) 0.0585

CHAPTER 7

Answers 7.1

3. $\dfrac{|x + y + 7|}{\sqrt{2}} = \dfrac{|3x + 2y - 5|}{\sqrt{13}}$

5. $\dfrac{\pi}{6}$

7. $37.43°$ where $0 < \theta < \dfrac{\pi}{2}$

9. $\sqrt{14} / 2$

Answers 7.2

1. Consider the slope of the tangent (in parametric form), then use the formula for $\tan 2x$.

3. $\dfrac{x^2}{a^2} + \dfrac{y^2}{b^2} = 1$ (an ellipse)

5. $y = k \pm \dfrac{b}{a}(x - h)$

7. A parabola.

9. $x = \cos s,\ y = \sin s$

CHAPTER 8

Answers 8.1

1. 1
3. No limit in real numbers
5. −1
7. 0
9. 0

11. Notice if $x \ge 0, \dfrac{x^5}{|x|} = x^4$ while if $x < 0$ then $\dfrac{x^5}{|x|} = -x^4$. Hence $\lim\limits_{x \to 0}\left|\dfrac{x^5}{|x|}\right| = 0 = \left|\lim\limits_{x \to 0}\dfrac{x^5}{|x|}\right|$.

Answers 8.2

1. $\dfrac{dy}{dx} = \dfrac{-2xy - y^2}{x^2 + 2xy + 2y}$

5. $y + 6 = -9(x - 1)$

7. 5

9. $\dfrac{dy}{dx} = 10^x \ln 10$

11. $\dfrac{dy}{dx} = x^{e^{x^e}} \cdot e^{x^e}\left(e x^{e-1} \ln x + \dfrac{1}{x}\right)$

13. $\dfrac{dy}{dx} = \left(\dfrac{1}{\tan e^x}\right)(\sec^2 e^x)(e^x)$

15. $\dfrac{dy}{dx} = \cos^x x(\ln(\cos x) - x \tan x)$

Answers 8.3

1. a) 3
   b) 0
   c) 0
   d) ∞
   e) 1
   f) e

3. $1.34\dfrac{ft}{min}$

5. $x = 4, y = 8$

7. The sequence $x_1, x_2, x_3 \ldots$ does not approach a root.

Answers 8.4

1. $\dfrac{\tan^6 x}{6} + C$

3. $-\dfrac{2}{\sin\sqrt{\theta}} + C$

5. $\tan x/2 + C$

7. $\dfrac{1}{-6(x^2+4)^3} + C$

9. $\dfrac{1}{2}\sec x^2 + C$

11. 4π

13. 10

15. $\dfrac{8}{3}$

17. a) $\dfrac{45}{8}$; b) 0

Answers 8.5

1. Convergent, $L = 2$

3. Convergent, $L = 2$

5. Convergent, $L = 0$

7. Converges conditionally

9. Converges conditionally

11. $-3 < x < 5; \dfrac{4}{5-x}$

13. a) $\ln(1+x) \approx x - \dfrac{x^2}{2} + \dfrac{x^3}{3}$

b) $P_3(x) = \dfrac{1}{\sqrt{2}} - \dfrac{1}{\sqrt{2}}\left(x - \dfrac{\pi}{4}\right) - \dfrac{1}{2\sqrt{2}}\left(x - \dfrac{\pi}{4}\right)^2 + \dfrac{1}{6\sqrt{2}}\left(x - \dfrac{\pi}{4}\right)^3$

CHAPTER 9

Answers 9.1

1. Truth table that has all true entries (such a truth table is called a tautology).
3. The truth table has all false entries.
5. a) T; b) T; c) F; d) T
7. Always true

Answers 9.2

7. Notice $x + y = y + x$ for all real numbers, since the real numbers are commutative under addition. The proposition $\forall x \forall y P(x, y)$ is true.

Answers 9.3

3. let $a_1 = 1$; define $a_{n+1} = (n+1)a_n$
5. $f(n) = n!$

Answers 9.4

1. $M = \begin{bmatrix} 1 & 1 & 0 \\ 0 & 1 & 0 \\ 0 & 0 & 0 \end{bmatrix}$

3.

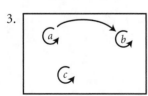

Notice $m_{ij} = 1$ if and only if $i = j$. In other words either $m_{ij} = 0$ or $m_{ji} = 0$ if $i \neq j$.

5. $M_{s_1} \wedge M_{s_2} = \begin{vmatrix} 0 & 0 & 1 \\ 1 & 0 & 1 \\ 0 & 0 & 1 \end{vmatrix}$, $M_{s_1} \vee M_{s_2} = \begin{vmatrix} 0 & 1 & 1 \\ 1 & 0 & 1 \\ 1 & 1 & 1 \end{vmatrix}$

CHAPTER 10

Answers 10.1

1. $A + B = \begin{pmatrix} 0 & 2 \\ 5 & 3 \end{pmatrix}$, $A - B = \begin{pmatrix} -2 & -2 \\ -1 & 3 \end{pmatrix}$, $3A = \begin{pmatrix} -3 & 0 \\ 6 & 9 \end{pmatrix}$, $2B = \begin{pmatrix} 2 & 4 \\ 6 & 0 \end{pmatrix}$,

$A \times B = \begin{pmatrix} -1 & -2 \\ 11 & 4 \end{pmatrix}$, $B \times A = \begin{pmatrix} 3 & 6 \\ -3 & 0 \end{pmatrix}$.

3. $\begin{pmatrix} 0 & 0 & 1 \\ 0 & 1 & 0 \\ -1 & 0 & 0 \end{pmatrix}$

5. The geometrical effect transforms the three-dimensional lattice of cubes into a lattice of parallelepipeds with $(1, 0, 0) \rightarrow (a_1, a_2, a_3)$, $(0, 1, 0) \rightarrow (b_1, b_2, b_3)$ and $(0, 0, 1) \rightarrow (c_1, c_2, c_3)$.

7. $\begin{pmatrix} a_{11} & a_{12} & . & . & a_{1n} \\ . & . & . & . & . \\ . & . & . & . & . \\ . & . & . & . & . \\ a_{n1} & a_{n2} & . & . & a_{nn} \end{pmatrix} \begin{pmatrix} x_1 \\ x_2 \\ . \\ . \\ x_n \end{pmatrix} = \begin{pmatrix} b_1 \\ b_2 \\ . \\ . \\ b_n \end{pmatrix}$

9. I-A is also indempotent

Answers 10.2

1. $A^{-1} = \begin{pmatrix} 2 & -1 & 0 \\ -1 & 2 & -1 \\ 0 & -1 & 1 \end{pmatrix}$

3. $A^* = \begin{pmatrix} -5 & 7 & 1 \\ 1 & -5 & 7 \\ 7 & 1 & -5 \end{pmatrix}$

5. $A^{-1} = \begin{pmatrix} -1 & 0 & 0 \\ 0 & 1 & 0 \\ 0 & 0 & 1 \end{pmatrix}$

7. The inverse doesn't exist.

9. $(1, 0, 0)$

Answers 10.3

1. $x = 1, y = -1$

3. $x = 3, y = 1$ and $z = -2$.

5. Hint: If $(x - a)$ divides a polynomial $P(x)$ then $P(a) = 0$. In other words if $b = c$ that implies that $P(x) = 0$, then $b - c$ is a factor of $P(x)$.

Index

About the Authors

Allen Cook

Allen Cook received his B.A. from Harpur College, his M.A. from Columbia University (Mathematics) and his Ph.D. from Stanford University (Education). He has taught mathematics to middle and high school students, undergraduates and graduates in the United States, Germany, Spain, Tanzania, Israel and Lesotho. He has held a post-doctoral research position at University of California Berkeley, and was Director of Research at the National Council of Teachers of Mathematics. He is presently on the faculties of Education and Mathematics and serves as the Associate Dean of the School of Education at the University of Bridgeport.

Allen's interest centers on improving secondary teacher content knowledge in mathematics, and translating classical mathematics texts from other languages into English.

Natalia B. Romalis

Natalia B. Romalis received her B.S. and the Candidate of Science in the Physical-Mathematical Sciences degrees from the Voronezh State University, in Russia. She did her post graduate research at the Latvian Academy of Sciences, where she received the degree Doctor of Physical and Mathematical Sciences. She then taught, supervised graduate students and did research at Voronezh State University. From 1991 to 1994 she taught undergraduate and graduate courses in Mathematics and Applied Mathematics at Illinois Institute of Technology, in Chicago. She also conducted her post-doctoral research at Northwestern University in Evanston, IL.

In the Fall of 1994 Dr. Natalia B. Romalis joined the faculty of the University of Bridgeport, Connecticut. Presently she is the Head of the Mathematics Department. Her area of research is applications of singular integral equations to the problems of fracture of inhomogeneous materials. She has published more than 100 papers and two books on the topic. Her present area of interest is Mathematical Education and preparation of highly qualified teachers

About the Authors